Eighth Edition

Real Estate Finance

JOHN P. WIEDEMER

University of Houston

Prentice
Hall

Upper Saddle River, New Jersey 07458

Library of Congress Cataloging-in-Publication Data

Wiedemer, John P.
 Real estate finance / John P. Wiedemer.—8th ed.
  p. cm.
 Includes index.
 ISBN 0-13-020453-6
  1. Mortgage loans—United States. 2. Real property—United States—Finance.
 3. Housing—United States—Finance. I. Title.
 HG2040.5.U5 W54 2000
 332.7'2'0973—dc21

                                                        99-086820

Acquisitions Editor: Elizabeth Sugg
Managing Editor: Mary Carnis
Director of Production and Manufacturing: Bruce Johnson
Editorial Assistant: Delia Uherec
Editorial and Production Services: WordCrafters Editorial Services, Inc.
Prepress Manufacturing Buyer: Ed O'Dougherty
Marketing Manager: Shannon Simonsen
Cover Director: Jayne Conte
Cover Designer: Bruce Kenselaar
Composition: Publishers' Design and Production Services, Inc.
Printer/Binder: Banta, Harrisonburg, VA

Prentice-Hall International (UK), Limited, *London*
Prentice-Hall of Australia Pty., Limited, *Sydney*
Prentice-Hall Canada, Inc., *Toronto*
Prentice-Hall Hispanoamericana, S.A., *Mexico*
Prentice-Hall of India Private Limited, *New Delhi*
Prentice-Hall of Japan, *Tokyo*
Pearson Education Asia, *Singapore*
Editora Prentice-Hall do Brasil, Ltda., *Rio de Janeiro*

10 9 8 7 6 5 4 3 2
ISBN 0-13-020453-6

Contents

Chapter 4   OTHER PRIMARY MARKET LENDERS   38

Chapter 5   MORTGAGE MONEY: THE SECONDARY MARKET   54

Chapter 6   THE MORTGAGE DOCUMENTS   75

Chapter 10   PROPERTY ANALYSIS   179

Chapter 11   COMMERCIAL LOANS: CONSTRUCTION AND LAND LOANS   204

Chapter 12   COMMERCIAL BUILDING AND FARM LOANS   219

Chapter 13   OTHER FINANCING PRACTICES   236
. . . .

Chapter 14   TECHNOLOGY ADVANCES
. . . .   IN MORTGAGE LENDING   256

Chapter 15   ENVIRONMENTAL ISSUES   265
. . . .

Preface

....

Real estate, in its broadest definition, is land and that which is attached to it. The subject of financing real estate could include the activities of farming, mining, drilling, the supporting services for each of these, plus surface development. This text focuses on surface development: the building of houses, shopping centers, office buildings, warehouse space, factories, and recreational facilities. Primary emphasis is given to residential financing because it comprises three-fourths of total mortgage lending and has developed some uniform practices not yet found in commercial loans. The financing of surface development was the largest single demand on this country's credit markets until 1992, when it was surpassed by needs of the federal government. Even so, at the end of 1998, mortgage debt outstanding exceeded $5.7 trillion while the government reported a surplus that is reducing its demand for credit.

The present-day practices and procedures that make the mortgage loan system function have resulted from long-term experience in meeting constantly changing needs. Still, a few of the basic credit restraints go back to lessons learned and regulations created during the Depression years of the 1930s. Since then, many improvements have been made, reflecting the efforts of men and women working through private industry and government agencies to achieve a more stable and equitable system.

Any person interested in real estate—as an investor or a sales agent—should have a sound understanding of the specialized financing procedures that are used today. A major change has occurred in the shift of sources for mortgage money. The former dependence for funding on a limited pool of savings accounts held primarily by savings associations has shifted to the huge financial markets through the sale of mortgage-backed securities. This has opened the door to many new primary market lenders. Further, in 1998 the Federal Home Loan Bank system began to encourage the banking system to originate more mortgage loans by offering its Mortgage Partnership Finance program to all of its members.

An important new factor in mortgage lending has resulted from the use of Internet facilities. Today, thousands of Web sites offer considerable information on the mortgage loan market. It is possible for a consumer to arrange for a mortgage loan via the Internet. Unfortunately, sound advice by a knowledgeable loan officer is not always available on the Internet. Nevertheless, the availability of competitive information on many Web sites and the freedom for an individual to act will change the mortgage market of the future.

The variety of mortgage repayment plans that proliferated for a while has settled down to a few more commonly used methods. Loan qualification standards, never fully uniform, continue to reflect lenders' concern for full repayment of their loans. Government assistance programs, as offered by both the FHA and VA, continue to support the goal of providing suitable housing for all qualified persons.

However, overtaking government-assisted loans has been a series of conventional mortgage loan programs instigated by the Community Reinvestment Act and its amendments, under the umbrella term of "affordable housing loans." These programs offer different standards for credit qualification and add some prepurchase home buyer education requirements for low- and moderate-income families to qualify. Other conventional loans now offer up to 97 percent loan-to-value ratio with more flexibility in meeting down payment requirements.

The real estate market has a cyclical nature: it will flourish at times, then languish for a while. Such ups and downs are the normal workings of the free market system. There is no central government planning authority empowered to set limits on the number of housing units that can be built in any given market area. So market demand is controlling. Overbuilding does occur and provides the necessary check rein. Nevertheless, other things than market influences can drive supply. An example of this occurred in the early 1980s when tax incentives substantially distorted true market needs and created substantial overbuilding. Even so, an overall reading of market needs presents some problems. As one wag recently commented: "We had a need for 5,000 new units here and ten developers jumped in, each building 5,000 units!" Some are hurt financially, but in the long run, we all benefit from the freedom on which the system is based. It could be said that the mortgage lending industry attempts to match dreams with reality and make them come true.

John P. Wiedemer

Acknowledgments

The author gratefully acknowledges the expert advice, assistance, and encouragement of the following individuals who have contributed to making this book possible.

PADDY D. AMYETT, McLennan Community College, Waco, Texas

JO ANN CAMPBELL, Summit Mortgage Company, Houston, Texas

RICHARD L. CHUMBLEY, Richland College, Dallas, Texas

LEE E. DILLENBECK, Elgin Community College, Elgin, Illinois

JOE GOETERS, Houston Community College, Houston, Texas

CHARLES J. JACOBUS, Attorney at Law, Bellaire, Texas

DOROTHY A. LEWIS, Houston Community College, Houston, TX

DONALD McGREGOR, JR., Real estate investor, Houston, Texas

GEORGE YOUNG, In memoriam and grateful remembrance, University of Houston, Houston, Texas.

And a special acknowledgment to my wife, Margaret Ivy Wiedemer, for organization and editing assistance plus her kind patience.

History and Background

INTRODUCTION

The history of real estate financing presents a fascinating record of civilization's learning to live with, and enjoying the benefits of, the land it lives on. While private ownership of land can be traced back to civilizations existing over 2,500 years ago, only in the last several hundred years has it become possible for the average person to own land. Nevertheless, many of the practices used in modern real estate financing trace their origins to earlier civilizations.

The underlying concept of real estate finance has changed very little over centuries and remains rather simple. It involves the pledging of land as collateral to secure a loan. The rights to land that can be pledged have undergone some changes. And the availability of money that can be borrowed reflects an earlier record of restricted practices and very limited pools of money. A brief background follows.

LANDOWNERSHIP

Pledging of land as collateral has long been a normal protection for the lender. How land is pledged involves how it is owned and this concept has developed along two paths, one called the **allodial** concept of ownership; the other, the **feudal** right of ownership.

In Roman times, the allodial system applied. Ownership of land by individuals was absolute. The landowner had few limitations or restrictions on the right to use or dispose of it.

The feudal system came into existence as continental Europe developed. In medieval times, Roman authority disintegrated and marauding tribes became more common. In return for protection, small groups of people would grant a form of landownership to a leader. Occupants of the land also held rights to their parcels as tenants with fees consisting of produce from the land and personal services due to the "landlord." Thus the feudal system primarily granted the right to occupy and use the land owned by a superior. English land law developed as a modified feudal system dating from the Norman conquest in 1066.

While both systems shaped the ownership of property in the United States, the allodial concept dominates because ownership of real property is free and absolute, subject only to governmental and voluntary restrictions. As the country grew, states developed variations of land ownership and how rights could be conveyed. The initial colonies on the East Coast carried much of the English law and its concept of male dominance in marriage into its property rights laws. The southwestern states were more influenced by Spanish law and its concept of family protection, which is the source of community property laws in marriage and homestead protection. Louisiana is unique in its adherence to following French laws and customs. The result has been a mix of real property laws that require different mortgage documents for each state.

BACKGROUND OF FINANCING

In earlier civilizations, landownership was restricted and the availability of borrowed money was limited. There were no insurance companies or depository institutions with cash to loan. In Roman society, landowners were joined in the *curia* with tax gatherers who made funds available for loans. In medieval Europe and later, only a few wealthy individuals were capable of loaning money. Access to this money was limited to an elite class which, by definition at that time, were the landowners. Thus, land became a fairly standard form of collateral.

Historically, the growth of widespread landownership parallels the increase in pools of money available for long-term loans. With the advent of the Industrial Revolution in the eighteenth century, more individuals became capable of producing wealth with their ideas and their machinery. People began to find that another option was open to them; the life of a serf grubbing an existence from land owned by the nobility was no longer the only way to sustain a living. With more widespread wealth came the demand for ways to make better use of accumulated money, and the seeds of our publicly owned savings institutions began to grow.

FINANCING REAL PROPERTY LOANS

Real property financing is the pledging of land as collateral to borrow money. **Collateral,** meaning something of value, is conveyed by a limited pledge as protection for a lender to assure repayment of a loan. The pledge as protection for a lender is called **hypothecation.** This means the borrower remains in possession of the property while it also offers security for the loan. It is only by defaulting on the loan agreement that a borrower can forfeit possession and title to the property. **Default** is nonperformance of an obligation that is part of a contract. Failure to repay the loan is the most common act in default and can activate rights that allow a lender to claim title to the property.

The loan itself is evidenced by a **promissory note** which is an unconditional written promise of a person (or persons) to pay a certain sum to another person. The "loan agreement" is commonly identified as a **mortgage.** A mortgage pledges property (collateral) as security for the note. If the note is not paid, or other default occurs, the terms of the mortgage instrument can trigger action allowing the lender to take title to the property. Such action is called **foreclosure,** which means the property offered as collateral for the loan is sold to satisfy the debt.

The instruments and steps just discussed have variations that are more fully explained in later chapters. Nevertheless, the underlying procedure remains clear: Land is pledged as security for a loan by a conveyance that limits the lender to claiming title only if a default occurs.

Compensation for Borrowed Money

Even in earlier societies, pledging rights to landownership as security for a loan meant some kind of compensation was due the lender. This created a problem: Charging interest for the use of one's money was considered a sin by many societies, including Christians, until the Middle Ages. Acceptable income was essentially that earned by one's labor. Even today, in many parts of the world some societies do not permit interest to be paid for the use of another's money. To bypass the religious constraint, a common practice developed: Simply charge for the use of money "up front," that is, deduct the cost of the borrowed money from the amount loaned and call it something other than interest. Just call it a discount!

A **discount** is a portion of the loan amount taken by a lender as a cost for borrowed money. It is measured today in **points;** one point is 1 percent of the loan amount. In financial markets today, some borrowed money is paid for with interest only, some with discount only, and some by a combination of the two. Real property loans are most often paid for by a combination of both interest and discount.

THE MORTGAGE LOAN MARKET

The mortgage loan market functions at two different levels, identified as the **primary market,** which is loan origination, and the **secondary market,** which consists of investors who purchase loans made by others.

A person or company seeking a mortgage loan contacts a **loan originator.** This may be a bank, an insurance company, a mortgage company, or other source. The negotiation involves the loan amount, interest rate and discount to be charged, the collateral, qualification of the borrower, and the terms for repayment of the loan. Each of these important items is discussed in later chapters.

Once a loan has been finalized, the promissory note and its security instrument become salable to others. Almost all mortgage notes are written as **negotiable instruments,** which means the holder of the note has the right to sell it. Even so, the originator may opt to retain the loan in its own investment portfolio to earn the interest and discount it produces. If the decision is to sell the loan, a secondary-market investor is contacted who will purchase the loan. The purchaser is most interested in two aspects of the loan: (1) its quality, meaning its level of risk, and (2) its yield.

Secondary-market purchasers consider interest relatively unimportant; it is the yield that matters as that is the return that will be received. **Yield** is a combination of the interest plus the discount. If the interest is too low, the discount must be increased to make up any difference necessary to meet the secondary-market yield requirement.

Financial Market Instruments

An increasing portion of the money flowing into residential loans comes from the sale of various kinds of securities in the financial markets, rather than from savings deposits. The sale of securities is the business of investment bankers and stock brokers. It is the method by which corporations raise equity money and one way they borrow money. Because of the importance of this market, the student of real estate finance should understand some of the terminology that applies to securities and the purpose for which they are issued.

Corporations can be financed through the sale of securities, which are paper certificates that represent some kind of an investment in the corporate structure. There are two major classes: (1) stock certificates, representing an ownership, or equity, interest in the corporation, and (2) bonds, representing a loan to the corporation. Stock evidences ownership; bonds evidence indebtedness.

Stock Certificates

Shares of stock representing an ownership interest in a corporation are not relevant to the subject of real estate finance and will not be considered further in this text. The category is mentioned here only to distinguish it from bonds, which are debt instruments.

Bonds

A corporation can borrow money through the sale of bonds to investors. Thus, the corporation has an additional source of funds not generally available to an individual or even to small, lesser known corporations. To those unfamiliar with financial markets, the idea of "selling" a bond does not relate to "borrowing" money. But it is just that: A **bond** is a debt instrument representing borrowed money that must be repaid with interest. A share of stock carries no obligation for the corporation to repay. Bonds are offered in several categories:

Debenture bonds. An unsecured promise to repay; in effect a corporate IOU. The sale of debenture bonds is widely used by the Federal National Mortgage Association (Fannie Mae) to raise most of the money it needs to buy mortgages for its own portfolio.

Mortgage bonds. Secured by a pledge of real estate.

Equipment bonds. Secured by a pledge of equipment such as railroad cars or airplanes.

Utility bonds. May be secured by a pledge of certain assets of a state-regulated utility company.

Government bonds. Federal government promises to pay (no specific assets pledged) with maturity over 10 years.

Municipal bonds. Can be state or municipal issue, may or may not pledge tax or improvement revenue, and offer interest that is exempt from federal income tax with certain limitations. This category of bond may be used for the private purpose of financing home and apartment loans.

Mortgage-backed bonds. Secured by the pledge of a large pool of mortgage loans. The loans are normally held by a trustee or a pooler that issues the mortgage-backed security. A **pooler** is a corporation, such as investment banker Salomon Smith Barney, Inc., that buys loans to create these pools.

The Securities Market

To qualify for sale to the general public, securities must have prior approval by the federal Securities and Exchange Commission (SEC). Each state adds its own security requirements for protection of consumers. Regulatory approval is based primarily on the disclosure of relevant financial information, not on an issue's potential value. Approved securities are bought and sold daily on major exchanges throughout the world, but are dominated by the New York markets. Stock exchanges deal in securities that trade in fairly large volume and offer near continuous price quotes.

Mortgage-backed bonds, more commonly called **mortgage-backed securities,** may bypass federal and state regulatory approval if underwritten by certain federal agencies, such as Fannie Mae or Freddie Mac. However, a growing category of privately issued mortgage-backed securities must comply with SEC regulations.

These securities are bought and sold every day in the financial markets and trade at fluctuating prices. Since almost all of them offer holders a fixed return on the investment, value in a resale is sensitive to the fluctuation of interest rates. The fixed interest rate on such a security (the face rate or nominal rate) controls the price for which it may be sold. If market interest rates go up, the price falls. The reason is that a security purchased at the lower price still receives the fixed interest on the initial face amount, resulting in an increased return to match the higher interest rates. Thus, there is an inverse movement in the bond market; if bond prices rise, it means that interest rates are falling, and if bond prices fall, it means that interest rates are rising.

Bonds and mortgage-backed securities are normally offered in $1,000 denominations or multiples of $1,000, and the price can be quoted in a dollar amount or a percentage figure.

••

EXAMPLE

A $1,000 bond offers an interest rate of 10 percent, paying $100 each year to the holder of the bond. Say, for some valid reason, the bond is sold at a discount for $925. (Or the "price" could be quoted as a percentage at 92.5 percent.) The party paying $925 still receives an interest payment of $100 each year, which amounts to a return of 10.81 percent on the $925 invested. At maturity, the issuer of the bond is required to redeem the paper at its face amount of $1,000. Thus, the bond holder would pick up an additional $75, which is the difference between the $925 paid and the face amount of $1,000 at which the bond is redeemed. So the total return, or yield, on the investment includes both the annual interest and the price differential when the bond is redeemed. However, if the bond is sold prior to maturity, the holder could sustain a loss if the market is down, meaning, in this instance, that interest rates have risen and a greater discount must be given to match the yield.

••

Commercial Paper. One other type of corporate borrowing should be mentioned, as it is being used to finance construction by a few large builders. This is the sale of **commercial paper.** Commercial paper is a simple promise to pay that is unsecured (a corporate IOU). The term is generally short, possibly 30 days to 270 days. The largest issuer of commercial paper, General Motors Acceptance Corporation, uses it to finance its car loans. Yields offered on commercial paper are generally competitive with short-term money market rates, running about one-half to 1 percent higher than 90-day Treasury bill yields.

Competitive Market. There is a considerable variety of investments offered in the securities market. Whatever security is offered, it must compete with other kinds of securities based on its return or yield. Both the price at which the security is offered and the interest to be paid affect yield. The yield demanded by an investor varies with both risk and the length of time of the investment: The higher the risk, the higher the yield must be; and the longer the term, the higher the yield required. This means that interest rates on mortgage loans must be competitive with other available security investments.

Investment Risk. For a mortgage-backed security, the risk is low. After all, each loan held in a pool usually carries some kind of default insurance (private mortgage insurance, FHA, or VA). And, in today's market, about half of the mortgage-backed securities are guaranteed by a federal agency, and thus, are doubly insured. Federal agency underwriting is a form of credit enhancement that reduces the risk allowing a lower yield requirement. This is reflected in lower interest rates for the borrower.

The function of a mortgage-backed security is to convert a mortgage loan into a financial instrument that can be more easily sold to investors. By opening the financial markets as a source of money to fund mortgage loans, adequate money at a competitive cost for sound loans has been made more available.

The fuel that has expanded this market is federal agency underwriting, accounting for more than half the funding of all residential loans. Four federal agencies are involved: Fannie Mae and Freddie Mac are the largest and fall under oversight authority of the Department of Housing and Urban Development (HUD). Ginnie Mae is limited to underwriting FHA and VA loans and is a part of HUD. When the fourth agency, Farmer Mac, was created in 1987 it had too many restraints and was not very active; then in 1996 Congress gave Farmer Mac similar powers to Fannie Mae and Freddie Mac. It is limited to underwriting agricultural loans and rural home loans outside incorporated areas.

Constraints are increasing on the underwriter's loan purchase policies and pressure has been applied by HUD to direct activities into more diverse areas of lending. Two results are probable: (1) an increase in home loans available to minority groups, immigrants, and underserved urban areas; and (2) a growth in the issuance of private mortgage-backed securities that are not subject to federal restraints and can provide an increase in the securitization of commercial loans.

Home-Buyer Education Programs

A corollary to the need to expand mortgage lending to new markets as just described is a recognition that many people are simply not familiar with normal real estate acquisition and lending procedures. Such questions as how to acquire a home, how to assure proper title, how the acquisition might be financed, and how to care for a home become most important. Home ownership to some is just an unobtainable dream, which may not be true. By adding prepurchase home-buyer education programs to the requirements for loan qualification, many can benefit. Benefits include finding more people who are eligible for home ownership. Education makes borrowers more aware of responsibilities to lenders, resulting in sound loans with fewer defaults. Initial implementation of these programs has already proven their value to home buyers and lenders. One further gain is the fact that increasing the market for homes creates many new jobs.

Questions for Discussion

1. From whom and under what conditions did people borrow money prior to the Industrial Revolution?
2. What is meant by *collateral? Hypothecation?*

3. What is the purpose of a promissory note? A mortgage?

4. Describe the origin of a loan discount.

5. How does federal agency underwriting function and what does it do for the mortgage market and the ultimate borrower?

6. Describe a mortgage-backed security and its collateral.

7. Distinguish between the functions of the primary and secondary mortgage markets.

8. What is a bond? Identify at least two categories of bonds.

9. Discuss the effects of risk and term of a bond on the interest rate paid.

10. How can prepurchase home-buyer education programs affect the mortgage market?

Chapter 2
Money and Interest Rates

KEY WORDS AND PHRASES

Money • Monetary system • Federal Reserve Bank • Money supply • Open market operations • Discount rate of interest • Prime rate • Federal funds rate • Credit market • Interest rate indicators • Treasury bill rate • Prime rate • Usury laws

INTRODUCTION

No commodity is more widely used and less understood than **money.** In a limited sense we know very well what money can do; its value lies primarily in our confidence that other people will accept money in exchange for their goods and services. A brief reference to history shows that money has been with us in all known civilizations as a means to improve the barter system of trading goods and services among people. Commodities of high intrinsic value have long been used to facilitate trade, including precious metals, gemstones, furs, and even salt and other spices. In fact, many areas of the world still use such standards today. Our modern business, however, floats on an intangible: the trust and confidence that individuals and nations place in currency and credit lines extended for bonds or other promissory certificates issued under a recognized government's authority. Certainly, the confidence placed in a government and its international trading power is indicated by the relative value placed on a nation's money in the realm of international trade.

The **monetary system** used in the United States was molded over many years of practical experience generated from trial-and-error methods. There are no provisions in the U.S. Constitution to control its development. Monetary policy has been shaped by political debates extending through the Civil War during the 1860s, the Great Depression years of the 1930s, on up to the present. In the early years of this country's growth, lacking constitutional guidance, the control of money was considered a right of each state. The political battles between state's rightists and Federalists were clearly reflected in how the monetary system developed. Two early efforts to create a central national bank

9

failed, and it was not until the Civil War that the federal government actually took over the issuance and control of currency. Prior to that time, individual states authorized their state-chartered banks to do this.

FEDERAL RESERVE BANK SYSTEM

The step that firmly established federal control over the nation's money supply was the creation of the **Federal Reserve Bank** in 1913. The Fed became the nation's bank and was given responsibility for handling the country's monetary policies. Its seven-member board of governors is appointed by the president of the United States, and the members hold tenure for terms of 14 years, thus shielding them from politics—at least, in theory.

The chairman of the Federal Reserve Bank Board, also named from its members by the president, serves a four-year term, but not concurrent with the presidency. While the chairman has only one vote on the board, the authority to influence the selection of the 12 Federal Reserve District presidents adds to the power of that office. And the chairman's influence is also felt in the selection of which 5 of the 12 district presidents sit on the powerful Open Market Committee.

The board is responsible for many other functions, such as overseeing the Truth-in-Lending Act, monitoring the Equal Credit Opportunity Act, and implementing other national credit policies. But it is the Fed's monetary policies that most influence the cost and availability of mortgage money.

Monetary Policies

What is it that the Fed controls when charged with deciding on monetary policies? The underlying mission in setting its policies is to help create a stable and prosperous economy that can provide jobs and better living conditions. However, the nation's monetary policies now affect a global economy, and the monetary policies of other nations directly affect the United States. So the Fed must function within global constraints.

The Fed uses four basic tools to influence the economy through the country's monetary system:

1. Controlling the amount of money in circulation in the country, called the **money supply.**
2. Adjusting funds available within the commercial banking network, which is manipulated by the Fed's "open market operations."
3. Signaling interest rate movements through changes in the Fed's discount rate of interest, or in the federal funds rate which is a short-term (sometimes just overnight) rate that banks charge each other for loans.
4. Setting cash reserve requirements for depository institutions.

Each of the four tools will be further explained, beginning with the most important: money supply decisions.

Money Supply

The difficult task faced by the Fed is to create a balance so that growth in the nation's money supply is commensurate with growth in the country's population and productivity. Too much money in circulation can cause destructive inflation, and too little growth in the available money supply can create damaging recessions. Even so, true measures of the amount of money in this country are not clearly defined, which makes sound decisions difficult.

The size of our total **money supply** and of the enormous economy it serves makes the problem appear almost beyond comprehension. For clarification, let's use a simplified example. First, remember that the value of money used today is represented by the amount of goods and services that it can buy (or be traded for).

....

EXAMPLE

If we have an economy with exactly 10,000 units of goods and services and an amount of money available to purchase these products totaling $1 million, each unit of goods and services would be worth $100. By increasing productivity over several years, say the economy now has 20,000 units of goods and services for sale. But assume that no increase has been made in the available money. With twice as much to buy for the same amount of money, the price of each unit of goods and services would drop to $50. Or stated another way, the value of the dollar would double; it would take only 50 cents to buy what a dollar did before.

If a different policy were used so that over the same period of time that our increased productivity supplied 20,000 units of goods and services, the money supply was increased to $3 million, then each unit would be worth $150. With so much more money available the dollar becomes less valuable. It would take $1.50 to buy what formerly cost $1.00, which amounts to a debasement of the value of the currency, a major component of inflation.

To support a stable pricing structure, a careful balance must be maintained between the money supply and the increase in productivity. Failure to do so can result in inflation or recession.

....

Definition of Money. To better understand how decisions are made on whether or not to increase the available money, it is first necessary to define what money is. The broad definition used by the Fed is that money consists of those assets that have immediate purchasing power. In this definition, bank deposits are a key factor. A problem arises in that recent banking laws and regulations have altered the way bank accounts can be used. The line between "time deposits" and "demand deposits" is no longer so clear-cut: Some banks allow a savings account to be automatically drawn on to replenish an overdrafted checking account. In a "zero balance" checking account offered to businesses, the checking account is automatically fed daily from the savings account by the amount of checks cleared. The savings account pays interest to the depositor.

Another problem with the Fed's handling of money supply in this country is the declining role of commercial banks as the keepers of monetary assets. Today, the assets of all mutual funds have increased to where they exceed the total time and savings accounts in the banking system. The measure of money that the Fed uses in making its decisions excludes some money market funds, all individual retirement balances in IRA and Keough accounts, deposits with non-bank institutions, and some dollar deposits held overseas. Nonbank companies, such as Merrill Lynch, hold customer's deposits and have checking accounts that are not subject to banking regulations. Nor are the deposits insured.

Thus, decisions on money supply must be made using only a partial measure of the total market. Nevertheless, the Fed considers "money supply" to be currency in circulation plus both demand and time deposits within the banking system. To distinguish between some of the differences in the nature of money and to provide a base for its measurement, the Fed identifies four categories of money, using the letter "M" for money as follows:

M1　Currency in circulation, nonbank travelers' checks, demand deposits in commercial banks and mutual savings banks, negotiable orders of withdrawal (NOW) accounts and automatic transfer service (ATS) at both banks and thrift institutions, and credit union share draft accounts. As of February 1998, M1 totaled $1,076 billion, a decrease from $1,151 billion at the end of 1994.

M2　The total of M1 plus savings and small-denomination time deposits at all depository institutions, overnight repurchase agreements, and general-purpose money market mutual funds. As of February 1998, M2 totaled $4,096 billion, an increase from $3,503 billion at the end of 1994.

M3　The total of M2 plus large-denomination ($100,000 and over) time deposits at all depository institutions, term Eurodollars held by U.S. residents at foreign and U.S. banks, term repurchase agreements at commercial banks and savings associations, and balances of institutional money market mutual funds. As of February 1998, M3 totaled $5,462 billion, an increase from $4,334 billion at the end of 1994.

L　The total of M3 plus other liquid assets such as nonbank holdings of U.S. savings bonds, short-term Treasury securities, commercial paper, and bankers' acceptances. As of January 1998, L totaled $6,694 billion, an increase from $5,316 billion at the end of 1994.

A cursory analysis of the growth in money supply between 1994 and 1998, as indicated in the preceding figures, shows a modest 7 percent decline in M1 but a 26 percent increase in L. Overall, the Fed has maintained a fairly stable rein on the money supply that has been reflected in a slow but steady growth in the economy.

Management of the Money Supply. The amount of money available in the United States is controlled by the Federal Reserve Bank Board. It operates through a system of 12 districts, each with some branch Federal Reserve Banks to facilitate local operations. The system works with the approximately 4,500 commercial banks that handle most of the cash transfers in the country. The Fed's Open Market Committee, comprising the 7 Governors and 5 of the 12 Federal Reserve District presidents, meets each month. At these meetings, the committee reviews monetary aggregates, examines the influence of current interest rates, and considers the state of the economy. Then it makes a decision on whether or not an increase in the available money supply is justified.

To increase the supply of money, the Fed simply creates additional money and uses it to purchase U.S. Treasury securities on the open market. In a sense, the Fed writes "hot checks" to buy government securities! Of course, the checks are not hot because the Fed clears them through its own bank. In practice, no checks are written; the Fed grants a credit to the U.S. Treasury bank account in exchange for Treasury securities. This authority to create money, backed only by government promises, gives the Fed tremendous influence in financial markets. Obviously, an influx of new money creates an increase in the supply and is expected to lower interest rates and thus give the economy a lift. It works that way some of the time!

Open Market Operations

Another tool that the Fed can use to influence the economy is identified as **open market operations.** With a large supply of both government bonds and cash in its hands, the Fed can move these two assets in and out of the banking system at any time it deems desirable. If the Fed decides the economy needs slowing down, it can issue an order through a limited group of approved investment bankers, who must be qualified and capable, to sell some of the Fed's supply of government bonds.

As these bonds are purchased by investors throughout the country, the money to buy them is withdrawn from various banks, sent to the Fed in payment for the bonds, and locked away in the Federal Reserve. This means the cash is no longer available for banks to use in making further loans. In the alternative, if the decision is to speed up the economy a bit, then the Fed can buy government bonds, thus increasing the cash in the hands of banks. The increased cash should enhance the banks' ability to make more loans, thus improving business activity.

Open market operations can be used to influence interest rates for the short term. For example, it takes about $1 billion in bond purchases in the New York market to lower effective interest rates about one-quarter percent. However, many other factors influence interest rates over the long term such as supply and demand for money, foreign money markets, government taxing and spending policies, and investors' perceptions of the general economy.

Discount Rate of Interest

A third tool that the Fed might use from time to time is to change its **discount rate of interest.** The discount rate is that rate charged by the Fed to those depository institutions eligible to borrow from it. This is probably the most widely publicized influence because it is the easiest to recognize. Yet, in practice, it is the least effective tool because a change in the discount rate is not a critical factor in the banking industry as it does not represent a cost of funds. Even though an institution is eligible to borrow from the Fed, this money cannot be used as a source of capital. The purpose of such loans to depository institutions is to provide a cushion when unanticipated needs for cash arise. Thus, the Fed's discount rate of interest is more a signal to the banking community than a true cost of funds.

By increasing the discount rate, the Fed signals all lenders that an increase in rates is in order. The immediate effect of an increase is almost always an increase in most institution's **prime rate** of interest—the rate on which a bank bases its charges to borrowers. Conversely, a reduction in rates signals a lowering of all interest rates. In practice, the "signal" may or may not be heeded by lenders who remain free to adjust their rates as they see fit.

As indicated earlier in this chapter, what the Fed has been acting on more recently is to change the **federal funds rate** rather than the discount rate of interest. While any such change is widely reported in the media as an increase, or decrease, in interest rates, it is not a mandatory change. The federal funds rate is a constantly changing rate, different in all parts of the country, as it is what banks charge each other for short-term loans that enable a bank to meet its liquidity requirements under federal rules. Thus, it has picked up the name of "federal funds rate." Between banks, it is a negotiated rate. The rate that the Fed targets is the one involving the big New York banks. The Fed moves this rate by injecting or withdrawing cash from its large deposits with New York banks.

Eligibility to borrow at the Fed's "discount window" was broadened by the 1980 Depository Institutions Deregulation Act to include all institutions holding transaction accounts (primarily checking accounts). A further requirement of this eligibility was an extension of reserve rules to these depository institutions, as explained next.

Reserve Requirements

The fourth tool held by the Fed to influence the economy through the banking system is control of the reserves that must be set aside (unavailable for loans) by all federally insured depository institutions. These institutions must maintain certain cash reserves on deposit with the Fed that pay no interest. In effect, this allows the banking system to borrow its own non-interest-bearing deposits from the Fed at the discount rate of interest. The Federal Reserve is a very profitable operation for the government! The reserve held by the Fed represents a cushion, a back-up for the banking system to use on short-term loans that allows an eligible institution greater flexibility in meeting unexpected demands for funding. All such loans must be fully collateralized by the borrowing institutions.

The 1980 Depository Institutions Deregulation Act set a new reserve requirement of 3 percent of the first $25 million in demand deposits and 12 percent for all over that amount. The reserve requirement on savings deposits is 3 percent. The Fed made no change in this requirement for 12 years, then on April 2, 1992, it lowered the rate on over-$25 million demand deposits from 12 percent to 10 percent. The decrease in the reserve requirement brought a release of $8 to $9 billion in additional cash into the banking system with the expectation that it would spur the economy with minimal effect on inflation.

THE UNITED STATES TREASURY

While the Federal Reserve Bank Board holds responsibility for the amount of money circulating in the country, the United States Treasury is responsible for raising the cash to pay the government's bills. How the Treasury decides to handle this requirement can easily upset the Fed's best laid plans.

In its simplest terms, the money to pay the government's obligations comes from three sources: tax revenues, borrowed funds, and printing money. If the government lives within its income, tax revenues would be sufficient to pay all obligations. When it spends more than it raises in taxes, the additional money must either be borrowed or printed. This crucial decision (whether or not to borrow rather than print more money) rests primarily with the Treasury. However, to pay for overspending by printing additional money is a choice that requires the consent of the Federal Reserve's Board of Governors. The reason is that the Fed, with its "open-ended checking account," is the only entity with the power to create money by purchasing government securities issued by the Treasury. It is this authority to create money based solely on Treasury securities that gives the Fed its tremendous aura of power.

As an alternative, if Treasury opts to borrow money rather than printing it to pay for deficit spending, it can do so without the Fed's approval. Treasury borrowing is accomplished through periodic sales of government bonds, notes and bills to the general public at open auctions. Since both procedures, printing or borrowing money, require the issuance of government bonds, the only limit is the national debt ceiling established by Congress. In practice, this is little hindrance, as the ceiling is raised periodically to accommodate such overspending as Congress deems necessary.

The politically less obvious method of covering deficit spending is for the Fed to agree to an increase in the money supply. By printing more money to cover the deficit (known as *monetizing* the debt), the need to borrow money from the general public is reduced. When government securities are sold to the Fed for the purpose of increasing the money supply, the securities are held off the market in reserve by the Fed. The down side to this practice is that an increase in the money supply in excess of the country's growth rate is certain to cause an increase in the rate of inflation. The reason is that excessive increases in the amount of money debase the value of the currency. But such a result—an increase in inflation—is not an immediate one and is much less obvious to the average citizen.

Thus, politicians generally prefer that the Fed be more accommodating with its approval of money aggregate increases, particularly in election years. The popular political call to the Fed for "lower interest rates" (translation: create more money) is really a call for an increase in the money supply with little mention that it can debase the nation's currency. In the economy of the late 1990s, the government seemed to be running a surplus, which substantially reduces the amount of borrowing that is necessary.

From the viewpoint of the real estate industry, borrowing by the government to pay its obligations competes directly with the demand for mortgage money. Any increase in demand can easily increase the cost of money. In this sense, increasing the money supply rather than borrowing the money may hold interest costs lower for mortgages, but it is always at the risk of a growing rate of inflation and higher rates later on. It is not an easy trade-off. Some industries have found short-term benefits can be derived from an inflationary trend, real estate being one.

INTEREST RATES

How are interest rates determined? While the Fed has substantial influence on short-term rates, long-term rates follow additional influences.

First, interest is the cost of using another's money, and that cost reflects supply and demand factors somewhat similar to a commodity. However, the effect of the cost of money differs from that of a commodity in that its demand does not always respond to a change in its price. If, for instance, sugar, oil, or copper decline in price, the tendency is for demand to increase. Housing follows a similar pattern primarily because borrowed money has become an integral and major part of the housing cost. If borrowing costs decrease, the cost of housing is reduced with an obvious increase in the potential market. However, if money goes down in price, many other kinds of demand may not respond at all. This is because additional factors influence money.

The reason for borrowing money is for a purpose other than acquiring the money itself. For instance, money is borrowed to build a building, buy a car, or expand a business, but if the economy is in a decline, there may be no need for that building, or car, or even the business expansion. So what determines interest rates? It has to be a complex mix of influences, not the least of which is that generated by the government's needs, which are clearly colored by its unique power to create money. To further explain, there are four major influences on interest rates, which can be summed up as follows:

Supply of Money. Prior to the 1980s, dependence on savings accounts as a source of mortgage money caused periodic shortages in the availability of funds. This was caused by occasions when savings were withdrawn from depository institutions to invest in higher yielding investments, such as money market funds. As financing real estate shifted to the use of mortgage-backed securities, the capability of tapping huge financial markets for funds accelerated. This has brought ample cash into the mortgage market. Shortage of mortgage money has become a thing of the past. Now, the supply of money derives from a much broader base of sources including pension funds, money market funds, and mutual funds, all in addition to savings deposits in the banking system.

Demand for Money. The demand for credit comes from four different categories of borrowers:

1. *Government*—includes net debt increase for federal, state, and local governments.
2. *Corporate*—business borrowing for inventory requirements, capital needs, and longer term investment.
3. *Mortgage loans*—includes housing, construction, industrial, and other investment purposes.
4. *Consumer*—personal loans for such things as automobiles, furniture, appliances, or other personal needs.

A normal balance between the four categories of credit demand would be that each take about one-quarter of the available supply of funds each year. However, the demand for borrowed money by business and consumers is generally less in an economy with slow to modest growth as has been the situation in the 1990s.

While mortgage money competes with all other demands for credit seeking essentially the same pool of funds, that pool has been large enough in recent years to supply all requirements even at declining interest rates.

Table 2–1 compares credit demand in 1993 with that in 1997.

The Table 2–1 shows an increase in total demand for credit from 1993 to 1997 with corporate and government taking a lesser share. Mortgage lending increased because of a growing economy and lower interest rates. It should be noted that the federal government borrows substantially more than the publicized amounts in order to pay for off-budget items. In 1997 mortgage loans took $426 billion in net credit, which means new money. The $800 billion loan origination market that year was about half a rollover of existing cash from refinancing and loan payoffs.

TABLE 2–1   Funds Raised in U.S. Credit Markets* (in billions of dollars)

	1993		1997	
	Amount	*Percent*	*Amount*	*Percent*
Total Net Borrowing	$953	100%	$1,945	100%
Government (Fed, local)	496	52	457	24
Corporate	280	29	387	20
Mortgage loans	129	14	426	22
Consumer	61	06	32	02
Other	267	28	1,030	53

*Figures interpolated from *Federal Reserve Bulletin,* May 1998, Table 1.57, "Funds Raised in U.S. Credit Markets."

An interesting point on **credit markets** is the position of federal borrowing. Since there are no legal limits on what the government can pay for its money, it is capable of driving all other demands for credit out of the market. Of course, such action is an extreme scenario and not likely to happen again. But it did happen in 1944 at the peak of World War II when the government took 99 percent of available credit.

Monetary Policies of the Federal Reserve. A substantial influence on interest rates is the ability of the Fed to increase the money available in this country at any time as described earlier in this chapter. In addition, the other "tools" available to the Fed can be used to effectively change short-term interest rates.

Fiscal Policies of the United States Government. The way in which the federal government handles its tax and spending policies is called *fiscal policies,* and is a key factor in the competitive markets that control interest rates. If Congress and the president decide to spend more than the income (tax revenues) available, the difference must be made up by either borrowing or printing money, thus forcing Treasury and the Fed to act almost regardless of the effect on interest rates.

Interest Rate Indicators

There are a number of different interest rates published daily in leading business magazines and newspapers and all give good clues as to the direction in which money costs are moving. Following are four rates that represent important **interest rate indicators** for the real estate mortgage business.

Treasury Bill Rate. The cost of short-term borrowing by the federal government is clearly determined each week at the auctions of three-month and six-month Treasury bills. The T-bills are sold by the Federal Reserve banks every Monday in minimum denominations of $10,000 and can be purchased from banks or through authorized security dealers. The return on this type of investment is expressed, not as an interest rate, but as a yield because it is determined by the difference between the purchase price and face value of the bill. The auctions provide an accurate indication of current short-term rates and the trend, up or down, gives a clue to the future.

••

EXAMPLE

In a Treasury bill auction on June 22, 1998, bills dated June 25, maturing June 24, 1999, were bought for an average price of 94.813. This means that a T-bill receipt in the face amount of $10,000.00 was purchased for $9,481.30. At maturity the T-bill is redeemed for $10,000.00. Thus, the investor earns the difference between the purchase price of $9,481.30 and the redemption price of $10,000.00, or $518.70 in one year. The return (not an interest rate but expressed as a yield) on an annual basis amounts to 5.12 percent based on a $10,000.00 investment using a 360-day year. However, since the investment was $9,481.30 rather than $10,000.00, the effective return amounts to 5.41 percent based on a 365-day year. Effective return is called the *coupon equivalent.*

••

Prime Rate. The **prime rate** has been defined as the interest rate charged by a commercial bank to its most creditworthy customers. Each bank may set its prime rate by any method it chooses as it is not regulated. Some use complicated formulas and others depend on the wisdom of their boards of directors. In practice, most banks simply follow the lead of one of the major money center commercial banks.

Today, the prime rate is used more as a base upon which to float an interest rate for many kinds of loans rather than an actual lending rate. A good example is a construction loan that may be quoted at two points over prime: if the prime rate is 8 percent, the construction loan will be 10 percent. If the prime rate moves up to 9 percent, the construction loan automatically will be increased to 11 percent and is calculated from the date the prime rate change is announced. Another direct effect of the prime rate on the mortgage field is that warehouse lines of credit held by mortgage companies with commercial banks are usually quoted at prime or a point over prime.

Fannie Mae/Freddie Mac-Administered Yield Requirements. During the early 1980s, both the Federal National Mortgage Association and the Federal Home Loan Mortgage Corporation phased out their frequent auctions for loan commitments to their sellers/servicers. The auctions have been replaced by daily access to these secondary-market purchasers by its seller/servicers through what Fannie Mae calls its "open window" commitment method. Both use an administered or "negotiated" rate in telephone contacts to their Washington, D.C. offices. While these rates can fluctuate during any one working day, Fannie Mae does issue a weekly news release reporting its posted yield requirements.[1] The yield requirements of both Fannie Mae and Freddie Mac are quoted in what might be called the "wholesale" market rate for mortgage loans at that time. Within the industry, this wholesale rate is called a *net basis yield,* that is, the yield that must be delivered to the loan purchaser. Loan originators add 0.25 to 0.375 percent for servicing the loan, and the cost of private mortgage insurance is often combined as a part of the gross rate quoted to a borrower.

U.S. Treasury Security Rates. Shorter term (one- to five-year) Treasury rates have become more important as an indicator of mortgage rates. Not only do they accurately reflect the shorter term money market rates that affect mortgage money, but they are also being used as a major index for setting adjustable rate mortgage (ARM) loan interest rates. Because the market for Treasuries is

---

[1]For copies of releases, contact Federal National Mortgage Association, 3900 Wisconsin Avenue, N.W., Washington, DC 20016.

constantly changing to reflect the money markets, the rates reported are usually averages of daily rates for weekly or monthly time periods. All financial publications carry information on U.S. Treasury yields, and the Federal Reserve Board now offers a weekly release covering selected interest rates.[2]

USURY

Usury laws are state laws, not federal statutes, that limit the amount of interest that may be charged on different kinds of loans and to various categories of borrowers. Until the late 1970s, market interest rates remained generally below the various state limits, and there was little concern for this particular restriction. But as interest rates continued to climb in the late 1970s, usury limits began to surface and restricted mortgage lending in some states. The rising cost of money made it more and more difficult to make loans at interest rates within the statutory limits and retain a safe operating margin. Further, states with higher interest limits were able to attract the big secondary market investors that can purchase mortgages anywhere. Many states were simply excluded from the national market by restrictive usury laws. To help resolve the dilemma, Congress preempted state usury limits for first-mortgage residential loans as of March 31, 1980.

The concept supporting usury laws is that the individual borrower should have some protection from the substantial power represented by a lender. In earlier times, and perhaps in some smaller communities today, the protection may be appropriate. But where mortgage loans are concerned, the growth of lending across state lines, coupled with the big national markets for loans, have made restrictive usury laws somewhat counterproductive.

Questions for Discussion

1. Describe the monetary system used in this country.
2. How does the Federal Reserve increase the money supply?
3. How does the Treasury raise money when it has to borrow?
4. Explain the major factors that influence interest rates.
5. Explain what is meant by fiscal policies and by monetary policies.
6. Define the *discount rate of interest*. The *prime rate*.
7. Identify the four major areas of demand for money.
8. How does a change in interest rates affect business borrowing?
9. How do the rates charged by savings associations compare with mortgage company rates in your community?
10. Suggest ways to improve our banking system.

[2]For further information, contact Publications Services, Mail Stop 138, Board of Governors of the Federal Reserve System, Washington, DC 20551, and ask for "Selected Interest Rates and Bond Prices (Weekly)."

Chapter 3

Mortgage Money: Regulated Lenders

KEY WORDS AND PHRASES

Mortgage debt outstanding • *Mortgage pools* • *Primary market* •
Secondary market • *Regulated lenders* • *Time deposit* • *Financial
Institutions Reform, Recovery and Enforcement Act (FIRREA)* • *Office of Thrift
Supervision (OTS)* • *Federal Deposit Insurance Corp. (FDIC)* • *Resolution
Trust Corporation (RTC)* • *Savings banks* • *Comptroller of the Currency* •
Warehouse line of credit • *Credit unions* • *Community Reinvestment Act* •
Life insurance companies

INTRODUCTION

While the money that funds mortgage loans comes from a number of sources, most of it originates from private sources. This includes individual and company savings such as passbook savings accounts, money market accounts, or certificates of deposit. It includes premium reserves for policyholders held by life insurance companies, retirement programs such as IRA and Keough accounts, various mutual funds, plus the huge and growing pool of pension funds—all money that belongs to people.

A common misconception is that governments supply much of the mortgage money. The federal government does have a number of direct-loan programs directed toward farmers, but this is only a very small percentage of the total loan market. Most states and some cities have housing agencies that offer direct loans and subsidy assistance, primarily for low-income home buyers. Various federal government agencies do offer underwriting programs that encourage private sources to fund loans, but these are in the form of guarantees rather then government money. To the contrary, the federal underwriting agencies charge fees for their guarantees with the expectation of making a profit and not burdening taxpayers.

THE MORTGAGE CREDIT MARKET

The demand for mortgage money shares the credit market with all other demands for borrowed funds. While the mortgage share of this market fluctuates, it normally commands 20 to 25 percent of the total credit available each year. Total **mortgage debt outstanding** at the end of 1998 totaled over $5,782 billion, the second largest single class of debt in this country. Only the federal debt exceeds this demand for credit.

Analysis of Mortgage Debt

The term *mortgage debt* includes all kinds of loans secured by mortgages and all types of lenders handling these loans. Mortgage debt includes long-term residential loans, short-term construction loans, and warehouse lines of credit as used by mortgage companies. To better understand how this debt is distributed, Table 3–1 identifies the four major categories of mortgage debt by type of loan. Clearly, residential loans dominate the market with more than three-fourths of the total debt outstanding. Farm loans continue to decline in both dollar amount and as a percentage of the total debt.

Analysis of Loan Sources

The mortgage loan analyst must distinguish between those making mortgage loans and those holding mortgage loans. They are not necessarily the same. Loan originators make the loans. Some originators hold these loans in portfolio, meaning as their own investment in an income-producing asset. But today most originators sell their loans within a few months to secondary market investors.

Table 3–2 gives the percentage of mortgage loans held by the principal lender sources. The percentages held in 1994 are compared with those at the end of 1998 to illustrate how the market has shifted. The migration of mort-

TABLE 3–1   Major Categories of Mortgage Debt
1998 (in billions of dollars)

	Amount	Percent
Total Mortgage Debt	$5,782	100%
Residential (1- to 4-family)	4,376	76
Apartments (multifamily)	362	06
Commercial	949	16
Farm	95	02

Table 3-2 Mortgage Debt as Held by Class of Lender
A Comparison from 1994 to 1998 (in billions of dollars)

Lender Source	1994		1998	
	Amount	Percent	Amount	Percent
ALL HOLDERS	$4,392	100%	$5,782	100%
Commercial banks	1,013	23	1,338	23
Savings institutions	596	13	644	11
Life insurance cos.	289	6	212	4
Federal & related	316	7	292	5
Mortgage pools	1,732	39	2,632	46
Individuals	524	12	665	11

gage lending away from savings associations began in the late 1970s. Since then, the major source for residential loans has been through **mortgage pools** which serve as collateral for the issuance of mortgage-backed securities.

THE MORTGAGE MONEY MARKET

The market for mortgage money functions at two separate levels: one is the loan origination market called the **primary market;** the other is the **secondary market** consisting of investors who buy mortgage loans. For the borrower, the source of funds is the primary market where many lending companies compete for business. These include regulated lending institutions, mortgage companies, commercial credit companies such as General Electric Capital Mortgage, investment bankers such as Merrill Lynch, finance houses such as Household Intercontinental, large home builders, and consumer credit companies such as GMAC.

The secondary market is where loan originators sell their loans, thus recovering cash to originate more loans. Many companies, trust funds, some pension funds, and others are the purchasers of these loans. The federal underwriting agencies, such as Fannie Mae and Freddie Mac, are popularly believed to be the entire secondary market. While they are big participants and buy or underwrite about half of the residential loans each year, their major contribution to the secondary market is to guarantee loan pools as a means of providing credit enhancement for mortgage-backed securities. Again, it is not government money at risk in mortgage loans; it is private money in the form of savings deposits, insurance reserves, and pension fund cash that provides most of the money to fund mortgage loans. The secondary market will be further examined in Chapter 5.

THE PRIMARY MARKET

The loan origination market is one of borrowers and lenders. The negotiation for a loan at this level is a discussion of the interest rate and discount. How the requirements for loan qualification are determined depends on who the lender is and whether or not the loan will be sold to secondary-market investors. Regulated lenders must adhere to the rules set by their regulatory authority. Nonregulated lenders are not so restricted. If a loan is intended for sale rather than to be held by the lender as its own investment (held "in portfolio"), then the loan must meet the secondary-market purchaser's requirements.

First, let's examine the nature of the lenders who deal one-on-one with borrowers; the loan originators. In this chapter we will examine regulated lenders and the constraints on their lending practices. In the next chapter, Chapter 4, other loan originators will be explained including mortgage companies, the loan programs that bring government agencies into making direct mortgage loans, and other primary-market lenders.

Since 1995, loan origination has become more involved with automated loan analysis, which involves a computer program using artificial intelligence to help analyze a loan application. This actually began in the secondary market with the large purchasers of loans as a method of expediting their own loan analysis. As will be discussed in the next chapter, it is even possible for an individual to negotiate a mortgage loan through the Internet. Even so, regulated lenders still handle about 40 percent of the mortgage loans today and will continue to assist people to arrange for the money needed to purchase or refinance real estate.

Regulated Lenders

Regulated lenders are those depository institutions and life insurance companies that are subject to various government regulatory agencies. This class of lender is limited in many ways: in the kind of loans it can make, the percentage of its total assets that can be held in certain types of loans, the kind of mortgage repayment plans it can offer, and the qualifications that can be accepted for borrowers and for property that is pledged as collateral. Because there are a number of different regulatory authorities involved, including separate state and federal chartering systems, there is an overlap of authority and no countrywide uniform standards that can be clearly defined.

Until the late 1970s, regulated lenders dominated the mortgage market, particularly that for home loans. This was true since about 75 percent of the money for residential mortgage lending at that time came from savings accounts held by institutional, or regulated, lenders. This source of money began to disappear as an escalation of interest rates beginning in the late 1970s siphoned cash out of lower-interest-bearing savings association deposits. With their depositors' money invested in long-term mortgage loans, depository institutions were caught in a serious cash shortage dilemma. The late 1980s saw the collapse of many savings associations. As a consequence, this particular source began withdrawing from the mortgage loan market.

Even though regulated lenders have reduced their investment in the mortgage market (that is, holding loans in portfolio), they are still major players in the primary market. Some still hold loans as sound portfolio investments, while others originate loans that are sold to investors. Most regulated lenders retain the loan servicing function on their loan originations (meaning collection of the monthly payments and proper disposition of the money). However, some now sell even this function to specialized servicing companies.

Following is a discussion of the four major classes of regulated lenders: (1) savings institutions, (2) commercial banks, (3) credit unions, and (4) life insurance companies.

Savings Institutions

As now defined, *savings institutions* describes both savings associations and mutual savings banks (now called savings banks). Because both of these institutions were initially limited to holding only time deposits (savings accounts), they also acquired the combined name of *thrift institutions,* or *thrifts.*

A **time deposit** is one that does not permit withdrawal on demand, usually requiring a waiting period of 14 to 30 days depending on which regulatory authority controls. In addition to the obvious time factor in savings certificates and certificates of deposit that give a withdrawal date or time period on their face, all passbook savings accounts are classed as time deposits. Even though the withdrawal limit on time deposits exists, few institutions attempt to use it under normal conditions. To delay a withdrawal would most likely discourage further deposits by their customers. Nevertheless, it is this access to the more stable time deposits that has provided the justification for savings institutions to make long-term mortgage loans.

Savings Associations

The origin of savings associations was to provide a source of money for home loans. In earlier years, some were called *building societies* because of this purpose. When Congress established the Federal Home Loan Bank Board in 1934, with authority to charter new federal savings associations, it required all federal charters to keep at least 80 percent of their deposit assets in residential loans (*residential loans* by this definition includes multifamily housing loans).

As interest rates began to climb in the late 1970s, savings associations found it difficult to retain their savings deposits because they were limited by law to paying an interest rate of 5.50 percent on passbook savings accounts (Federal Reserve Regulation Q), which was well below market rates at that time. To help overcome this problem, new savings certificates were introduced that allowed payment of higher rates for longer term deposits. The result of this and other factors was a rapid increase in the cost of funds. Indeed, the national average cost of funds for FSLIC-insured savings associations rose from 7.87 percent at the end of 1979 to 11.58 percent at the end of 1981. At that time, savings associations held most of their mortgage loans in portfolio, and the fixed income generated by low interest, long-term mortgage loans failed to keep pace with the rising cost of funds.

In 1980, Congress passed the Depository Institutions Deregulation and Monetary Control Act. The act substantially altered many rules that had formerly distinguished the various kinds of depository institutions from each other. No longer were savings associations firmly committed to making mostly residential loans. New rules allowed them to expand their investment portfolios to many new kinds of loans, including higher risk investments. In addition, they could now offer their customers checking account services, credit card accounts, and the advice of trust departments—services formerly restricted to only commercial banks. While the intention of Congress was to help savings associations recover from the dilemma created by escalating interest rates, they overlooked the role played by federal deposit insurance.

To cope with massive losses on insured deposits, Congress enacted legislation, signed by President Bush on August 9, 1989. This was the **Financial Institutions Reform, Recovery and Enforcement Act** (FIRREA) which created an overhaul of banking practices with a primary target of restructuring the savings and loan association system. The 900-plus-page act touched many aspects of mortgage lending including federal/state licensing of appraisers, setting minimum capital requirements, and providing more stringent enforcement of banking regulations.

In 1996, Congress passed legislation that sets the stage for eventual elimination of savings institutions which will be rechartered as banks. The two separate deposit insurance funds (SAIF for savings associations and BIF for commercial banks and savings banks) were merged into one fund under FDIC management. To facilitate this merger, savings associations and a few banks agreed to pay $4.7 billion into the SAIF fund, which had been the weaker of the two funds. Two reasons for the weakness of the savings association fund were the declining number of S & Ls, (below 1,900) plus the annual $780 million paid by this fund on government bonds issued to help bail out troubled associations.

Because the deposit insurance funds, with the additional cash added mostly by savings associations, had reached the legal protection requirement ($1.25 for each $100 of insured deposits), most insured institutions were no longer required to pay an assessment to the fund except for the $2,000 per year membership fee.

Savings Association Regulatory Authorities

Office of Thrift Supervision (OTS). Until the rechartering of savings associations as banks, the federal regulatory authority for them remains the Office of Thrift Supervision. The OTS is an arm of the Treasury Department, replacing the FHLBB as regulator for the associations. Its authority extends to both federal- and state-chartered institutions that carry federal deposit insurance.

Federal Housing Finance Board (FHFB). OTS was not given all the authority formerly held by the FHLBB. The new Federal Housing Finance Board was assigned as overseer of mortgage lending for the 12 regional Federal Home Loan Banks. In addition, the FHFB is responsible for handling statistical data for the housing industry.

Federal Deposit Insurance Corporation (FDIC). As before, FDIC remains under the Treasury Department and was given increased authority to manage both the bank deposit insurance fund and the savings association insurance fund. Before FIRREA in 1989, the savings associations' insurance fund was under the management of the Federal Savings and Loan Insurance Corporation (FSLIC). It was this fund that became insolvent, not the bank's FDIC fund, necessitating a taxpayer bailout of the system. The FSLIC was dissolved by FIRREA.

Resolution Trust Corporation (RTC). The remaining problems of this agency were transferred to the FDIC in July 1995, and the RTC was dissolved. Nevertheless, it had an important role in handling the liquidation of failed savings associations and needs to be recognized. The RTC was created by FIRREA in 1989 and was given authority to take the necessary steps to sell or liquidate failing thrifts.

RTC was a receiver, not a regulator, and was responsible for those assets assigned to it by either the OTS or the FDIC. RTC could close and liquidate a failed institution or it could take over its management under a conservatorship. Funding was under the supervision of the RTC Oversight Board, a high-level agency charged with selling the authorized government bonds to raise the money required for liquidation. It met most of its goals, albeit with much criticism along the way. RTC inherited some overvalued loan collateral and quite a bit of inadequate loan documentation in its takeover of insolvent associations. This made fast resolution difficult. Since the core of its personnel initially consisted of FDIC employees, its remaining functions and personnel were transferred back to the FDIC.

Savings Banks

Savings banks originated in the early years of this country when most individuals traded in cash and needed a place to deposit their surplus for safekeeping. The "check society" was still a long way off, and there was little need for checking accounts.

For many years thereafter, savings banks (formerly called "mutual savings banks" as most were owned by their depositors), operated with good success in the northeastern part of the country, particularly in New York and Massachusetts, with a few in the far Northwest. In the past they were all state chartered.

Because of the emphasis on savings account deposits over demand deposits, savings banks have looked with favor on longer term mortgage loans. With their location in generally cash-rich areas of the country, plus the conservative nature of their investment policies, many savings banks favored FHA and VA loans. There was no restraint on making this kind of loan out of state, and savings banks purchased these loans from originators all over the country. In recent years, however, lending policies shifted away from individual mortgage loans to investing in federally underwritten mortgage-backed securities.

In the late 1970s, the Federal Home Loan Bank Board began experimenting with federally chartered, stockholder-owned savings banks. The idea was accelerated when the FSLIC, faced with major problems disposing of failed savings associations in the mid- to late-1980s, undertook a new policy. Instead of dissolving troubled savings associations, it would selectively merge four or five such institutions into one and recharter the operation as a "federal savings bank" or FSB. There were some advantages to this procedure. It postponed the need for bailout cash in the hope that the reorganized entity might resolve its own problems. And it took direct regulation away from state banking commissions that may have been in some conflict with federal deposit insurance policies. Further, the cost of deposit insurance was much less at that time for a savings bank than a savings association, which gave the newly reorganized groups a lower operating cost. (In the late 1980s, commercial banks and savings banks, both insured by the FDIC, were paying an 8.33 cent premium per hundred dollars of insured deposit while savings associations were paying nearly double that amount with further increases expected.)

As mentioned earlier in this chapter, the 1980 Depository Institutions Deregulation Act altered the way the banking system could serve the public. One of the changes was formal approval for savings associations and savings banks to offer checking accounts. In addition, the door was opened for these institutions to make other kinds of loans. The result of these changes allowed savings banks and savings associations to offer services very similar to those of a commercial bank.

Commercial Banks

The original purpose of commercial banks in this country was to serve the business community and the governments. As such, they were expected to provide the services of checking accounts, including the transfer of money, and the protection available in a depository institution.

Initially, states chartered their own banks and, prior to the Civil War, granted commercial banks authority to issue their own currency. It was not until passage of the National Bank Act in 1863 that issuance of currency was placed under control of the federal government. The act also authorized federally chartered banks to be organized under the regulatory authority of the **Comptroller of the Currency.** Interestingly, later amendments to this law prohibited national banks from making real estate loans, which, of course, was rescinded in 1913.

The creation of the Federal Reserve Bank in 1913 brought nationally chartered banks under credit regulations of the Fed and established lines of cooperation between them. The act establishing the Fed also allowed national banks to make real estate loans within certain specified limits. The regulatory authority over commercial banks is a separate system from that regulating savings associations and is also a dual system with both federal and state governments issuing charters and regulations. In an effort to reduce conflicts between overlapping authorities, FIRREA placed all depository institutions that carry federal deposit insurance under federal regulation.

Limits on Real Estate Loans. In 1991, Congress passed the Federal Deposit Insurance Corporation Improvement Act which, among other things, requires the four federal banking regulators (Federal Reserve Bank System, FDIC, Office of the Comptroller of the Currency, and the Office of Thrift Supervision) to establish limits for various categories of real estate loans. It should be noted that in 1980 the Bank Deregulation Act had eliminated loan-to-value limits for real estate loans that had been in place since the 1930s Depression years. The limits that became effective in March 1993 are as follows:

- No ceiling on one- to four-family property loans except that loans over 90 percent must have private mortgage insurance.
- Certain loans are exempt from limits such as those guaranteed by the federal government; problem loans that must be renewed, refinanced, or restructured; and loans to facilitate the sale of foreclosed properties.
- Other limits are:

Loan Category	Loan-to-Value
Improved property	85%
1- to 4-family construction	85
Nonresidential construction	80
Land development	75
Raw land	65

The National Credit Union Administration, which administers the National Credit Union Insurance Fund, has joined in requiring the same loan-to-value limits for its credit unions.

Investment Policies. Because of the business orientation of commercial banks, their lending policies have favored the short-term loan for specific business purposes. They have not been very active in the long-term home loan market. Some only make mortgage loans through subsidiary mortgage companies. One basic reason is that a substantial share of a commercial bank's deposits are demand-type (checking accounts) and they are limited in allowing such money to fund long-term loans. What is changing this policy is the growth of secondary mortgage market funding through the sale of mortgage-backed securities. The ability of large commercial banks to originate long-term residential loans then fund them through the sale of securities is opening a new market that does not commit their own deposit assets. Loan origination expands the use of a bank's credit expertise and provides additional income from origination charges and servicing fees.

Certain kinds of shorter term mortgage loans (less than the older 30-year standard term) are more suited to commercial banks, including lines of credit for mortgage companies and construction loans. In addition, commercial banks handle some medium-term mortgage loans as may be needed by their business customers. The four kinds of lending activity that can be found in a commercial bank's mortgage operations are described as follows:

Direct loans. Mortgage loans made for medium terms, such as 10 to 15 years, for good commercial customers.

Construction loans. The shorter term, two- to three-year construction loans are attractive to banks due to higher returns. Larger banks are better able to employ the specialized talent necessary to monitor the disbursement of funds as construction progresses.

Warehouse lines of credit. Short-term, 6- to 12-month loans made to mortgage companies for interim funding of their loans until they can be sold. It is a line of credit for the mortgage company and is listed as a mortgage loan for the bank.

Loan origination. Origination of home loans is a growing activity for commercial banks. Banks can initially fund these loans with their own deposit assets then sell them to secondary-market investors. Another path open to the larger banks is to create their own loan pools that serve as collateral for private issuance (meaning not federally underwritten) of mortgage-backed securities.

Regulation of Commercial Banks. Commercial banks can be either state or nationally chartered. National charters (not called "federal charters" when commercial banks are involved) are issued by the Comptroller of the Currency, part of the U.S. Treasury Department. National charters must belong to the Federal Deposit Insurance Corporation (FDIC) and carry deposit insurance to protect depositors. State-chartered banks may join the FDIC system if they meet the qualifications and become subject to such federal regulations as may apply.

Commercial banks are responsible to an additional regulatory body. Besides the chartering agency and the deposit insuring agency that normally provides regulation and periodic examination, commercial banks come under the jurisdiction of the Federal Reserve Bank Board as regards their credit policies. The Fed also is responsible for setting reserve requirements for all depository institutions and monitors compliance with the Truth-in-Lending Act through its Regulation Z.

Credit Unions

Credit unions may be chartered by any group of people who can show a *common bond*. The bond has generally been that of a labor union, a company's employees, or a trade association. However, a recent interpretation of this rule allowed the American Association of Retired Persons (AARP) to form a credit union. With some 28 million members, the common bond would be their age.

There are now over 18,000 credit unions operating in this country. Credit unions offer a special attraction as a depository institution because they pay no income taxes. (They are classed as nonprofit organizations.) Most credit unions are relatively small and often managed by nonprofessional personnel. Their primary lending is to their members on small loans for such purposes as buying a car or furniture. However, as savings associations met with highly publicized reverses in the mid-1980s, many individuals transferred their savings to credit unions, which now have over 70 million members.

It was not until 1978 that federally chartered credit unions were authorized to make 30-year mortgage loans; prior to that the limit was 12 years. Also in that year, they were authorized to sell loans to secondary-market investors while retaining the loan servicing function. Even then, there was little growth in this particular activity for the smaller unions because of the specialized nature of mortgage lending. The larger unions with professional staff are capable of, and do engage in, the business of making long-term mortgage loans.

The 1980 Depository Institutions Deregulation Act increased credit unions' authority to make all types of loans and to accept all kinds of deposits. In 1982, the National Credit Union Administration expanded the definition of *common bond* to allow small businesses, which alone lacked enough workers to form viable credit unions, to join existing credit unions. As a result, some credit unions expanded membership to anyone living in their area of trade. Further, there has been an expansion in the services offered, including some formerly available only through their competitors. These include safe deposit boxes, credit cards, and money market accounts. Also, credit unions are not prohibited from paying interest on checking accounts as are other financial institutions. These extra services plus the tax-exempt status of credit unions may not be their only advantages; many identify the intangible item of a closer personal touch to their membership than can be found in other institutions.

Because of the tax-exempt status and other advantages found in a credit union, bankers have tried to limit their expansion through a lawsuit contesting what is meant by a *common bond* required of credit union members. After some years wending its way through lower courts, the U.S. Supreme Court ruled on February 25, 1998, that federally chartered credit unions are limited to membership as originally defined by law.

While the banks were the victors in this lawsuit, Congress then passed legislation to restore credit union membership guidelines to employees of companies with 3,000 or less personnel. The act adds a requirement that credit unions must adhere to the Community Reinvestment Act (not previously required) but does not change their nonprofit status.

Regulation of Credit Unions. Credit unions can be either state or federally chartered. An independent agency of the federal government, the National Credit Union Administration (NCUA), charters, regulates, and supervises activities of federal credit unions. State charters adhere to their own state rules and laws.

Deposits in credit unions can be protected by the same kind of insurance as other regulated depository institutions. The federally chartered National Credit Union Share Insurance Fund, administered by the NCUA, covers deposits up to $100,000. Federal charters must offer this coverage and state charters that qualify are eligible to join.

RESERVE REQUIREMENTS FOR DEPOSITORY INSTITUTIONS

Institutions handling deposits are required to hold a certain percentage of their deposit assets in a reserve account, not available for lending purposes. The reason is to provide a back-up, a source of emergency money should it be needed.

Prior to 1980, state-chartered institutions operated under their respective state laws governing reserve requirements, while national charters adhered to federal requirements. They often differed as to the amount of reserves required and whether or not the reserves could earn interest. Further, the Federal Reserve Bank Board had authority to alter reserve requirements for its own member banks, but not nonmember state charters. Changing reserve requirements gave the Fed one more tool in its efforts to stabilize the national economy. But it also created some inequities within the banking system as application of reserve requirements was not uniform.

In 1980, Congress passed the Depository Institutions Deregulation and Monetary Control Act which established uniform reserve requirements for all depository institutions offering transaction accounts. A *transaction account* is essentially a checking account that allows withdrawals payable to a third party. Examples include checks, drafts, negotiable orders of withdrawal (NOW accounts), and share drafts. The reserve rules apply to commercial banks, savings associations, savings banks, and credit unions whether they are state or federal charters.

The uniform reserve requirements were phased in over an eight-year time period—from November 13, 1980 to September 2, 1987—to minimize the impact on lending institutions. The requirements call for 3 percent of the first $25 million plus 12 percent on all transaction balances over $25 million to be placed on deposit with the Federal Reserve Bank without interest. In addition, there is a reserve requirement for time deposits in the amount of 3 percent. A *time deposit* by this definition is one allowing the institution at least 14 days' notice prior to withdrawal.

The reserve requirement is under the control of the Federal Reserve Bank Board but no change was made in it for 12 years. Then in April 1992 the Fed announced a reduction from 12 percent to 10 percent for transaction balances over $25 million. The change put about $9 billion back into the hands of banks which allowed them to make more loans and earn interest.

Note that reserves held by the Fed do not pay interest to the institutions that own the reserves, but do provide a cushion for the industry to draw upon to meet unusual money demands. Thus, any institution holding reserves on deposit with the Fed has the right to borrow from the Fed at the discount rate of interest—a very profitable operation for the Fed! The Fed's "discount window" is open for emergency use but the money cannot be used as additional capital for ordinary lending purposes.

DEPOSIT INSURANCE

Savings associations, savings banks, commercial banks, and credit unions are all classed as depository institutions. This means they are specifically authorized by their charters to hold deposits for their customers. Governments treat this activity as a special kind of trust. When the Great Depression of the 1930s caused the collapse of about one-half of these institutions, savings were lost and depositor confidence was destroyed. To help restore this trust, the federal government created a deposit insurance system.

In 1934, Congress established the **Federal Deposit Insurance Corporation (FDIC)** to insure deposits in commercial banks and savings banks. At the same time, the Federal Savings and Loan Insurance Corporation (FSLIC) was created to insure deposits in savings associations. Later, the National Credit Union Share Insurance Fund was set up for credit union depositors. Life insurance companies are not considered depository institutions and are not federally insured. A few states opted to establish their own deposit insurance funds for their state-chartered institutions, and a few permitted private insurance companies to underwrite the risk. Due to several failures of state insurance funds in the early 1980s, the federal protection has proved to be more effective.

Reorganization of Deposit Insurance Funds

The 1989 Financial Institutions Reform, Recovery and Enforcement Act dissolved the FSLIC and reorganized the deposit insurance system. A new Deposit Insurance Fund (DIF) was created, administered by the FDIC. Under DIF, there are two separate insurance funds. One is the Savings Association Insurance Fund (SAIF) which replaced the insolvent FSLIC. The other is the Bank Insurance Fund which is simply the old FDIC fund under a new name. Effective in 1994, Congress prohibited the FDIC from reimbursing depositors for accounts in excess of the $100,000 limit that had become an option in previous years to avoid further collapsing an already weakened banking system.

In 1996, Congress passed legislation that will phase in the merging of the separate insurance funds (the BIF and the SAIF), retaining the FDIC as administrator. In addition, the legislation calls for rechartering savings associations as banks. This should simplify somewhat the regulatory confusion and overlap that presently exist within the banking system.

COMMUNITY REINVESTMENT ACT (CRA)

The **Community Reinvestment Act,** which took effect in November 1978, expands the concept that regulated depository institutions must serve the needs of their communities. The purpose of the act is to require regulated institutions to publicize their lending services in their own community and to encourage participation in local lending assistance programs. Enforcement of the requirements is handled by the federal supervisory agency regulating the institution. There are four: Comptroller of the Currency, Federal Reserve Bank, FDIC, and the Office of Thrift Supervision. This means the act covers most of the nation's financial institutions. The penalty for failure to comply is a limitation on any approval that may be required from federal authorities by the offending institution.

Research as of our local Banks!

The act requires that each institution undertake four procedures:

1. *Define the lender's community.* Each lender must prepare a map of the area it serves, which is the neighborhood from which it draws its deposits and into which it makes loans.

2. *List types of credit offered.* A list of credit services available from the institution must be submitted to the regulators and made available to the public. The act is directed toward publicizing methods of borrowing rather than saving money.

3. *Post public notice and public comments.* Each institution covered by this act must post a notice in its place of business stating that the institution's credit performance is being evaluated by federal regulators. Further, the notice should state that the public has the right to comment on the institution's performance and to appear at open hearings on any request for expansion.

4. *Report on efforts to meet community needs.* A periodic report must be made available to the public on the efforts of the institution to ascertain the credit needs of its community and how it is attempting to meet those needs.

CRA Amended by FIRREA

The 1989 FIRREA amended the Community Reinvestment Act, which sharpened the performance ratings for regulated institutions and required public disclosure of what each is doing to meet local needs. FIRREA also amended the 1975 Home Mortgage Disclosure Act by expanding its reporting requirements to include all mortgage lenders, both regulated, and for the first time, nonregulated lenders. The purpose is to encourage greater participation in home buyer assistance programs through increased publicity of the lender's actual performance.

CRA Grading of Regulated Lenders. FIRREA requires that CRA ratings be made public for each institution on how well it performs the following:

1. Knows the credit needs of its community
2. Involves its board of directors in setting up and monitoring CRA programs
3. Informs the community about its credit services
4. Offers a range of residential mortgages, housing rehabilitation, and small business loans
5. Participates in government-insured, -guaranteed, or -subsidized loans
6. Distributes credit applications, approvals, and rejections across geographic areas
7. Does not discriminate in its lending practices

The grading is made in four categories: outstanding, satisfactory, needs to improve, and substandard compliance. Each institution's grade level is publicized periodically and that has proven to be a substantial incentive to comply with the CRA requirements. Further, a satisfactory or better CRA rating is necessary to obtain regulatory approval of an institution's request for such activities as mergers, acquisitions, expansions, and siting new branches. Previously, third parties could petition regulatory agencies to deny approval of these activities for an institution with a poor CRA record. However, in January 1997, the Office of the Comptroller of the Currency issued a rule change that cuts out such community groups, announcing that the OCC would send in its own team to review a bank's lending record and render a verdict.

The incentive generated by the recent CRA requirements has spawned a new loan qualification pattern that will be examined under the umbrella term *affordable housing* in Chapter 9 as another kind of borrower qualification standard.

LIFE INSURANCE COMPANIES

While **life insurance companies** are not considered depository institutions, they are fully regulated by the various states that charter them. There are no federally chartered insurance companies, although Congress has explored the need for such from time to time. As new insurance companies have entered the health insurance and accident insurance business, an increase in some abuses of consumers has occurred. Further legislation is being examined at this time. However, in general, life insurance companies respond to older regulatory standards that have continued to offer sound protection for insured parties.

The cash that life insurance companies hold for investment comes from premium reserves and accumulated earnings. Because these reserves are not necessarily subject to demand withdrawal, life insurance companies have long favored the longer term nature of mortgage loans as investments. At one time, life insurance companies and savings associations held equal total investments in mortgage loans. But life insurance companies were not chartered for the purpose of providing mortgage money as were savings associations. Their primary interest in using their substantial investment funds has been to provide the highest yield possible commensurate with the safety of their policyholder's money. And this has dictated some flexibility in the movement of their investment funds from time to time to achieve better returns.

When a life insurance company sells an ordinary life policy or certain other kinds of life insurance, regulations normally require that a portion of the premium paid be set aside as a reserve to protect future obligations to the policyholder. The insurance company pays interest to the policyholder on the reserve amount (depending on the terms of the policy) and invests the money as it wishes so long as it adheres to the state's regulatory limitations on investments. Over the years, this reserve pool has produced substantial returns for the companies while protecting the future payment of death benefits.

Casualty insurance companies—those that handle fire coverage, automobile insurance, and a host of other types of hazard insurance—have tremendous premium incomes but are not required to maintain the larger permanent reserves demanded for life insurance companies. Therefore, casualty companies hold their reserves in short-term investments due to the need for liquidity to pay claims. They negotiate practically no mortgage loans and are not a source for our consideration.

In the United States there are over 1,900 life insurance companies, and a few from Canada, selling policy contracts. They range in size from a very few million dollars in assets to the multibillion-dollar giants that have become household words, such as Prudential, Equitable, and Metropolitan Life.

Investment Policies

While insurance companies invest most of their reserves in high-grade securities, they also make mortgage loans. The larger companies have generally confined their real estate activity to making loans for large commercial ventures in which they can also acquire a participating interest. Smaller companies follow a different path and often look upon individual home loans in their local communities as good business and a way to make contacts for the sale of life insurance. This kind of loan is intended for holding in the insurance company's own portfolio.

Regulation of Life Insurance Companies

All insurance companies are chartered and operate under the control of state regulatory authorities. Since there are no federal charters for life insurance companies, they adhere to policies that vary from state to state, but the regulations are generally directed toward protecting the policyholders. State regulations also apply to out-of-state charters doing business within the state.

The state regulations usually set limits on the types of investment that are permissible; the percentage of total portfolio that may be kept in stock, bonds, or mortgage loans; or the amount of liquidity that must be maintained for each policy dollar outstanding. And most states establish limits on the maximum amount of any one loan or for any one property. Some states have limited their own chartered insurance companies to investments within their own states, and others have placed limits on out-of-state companies selling insurance within their state unless proportional investments are made within the state.

ADDITIONAL FEDERAL REGULATION OF HOME MORTGAGE LENDING

Federal legislation passed in 1975 that was initially directed toward only regulated lenders has since been expanded to include independent mortgage companies. This is the Home Mortgage Disclosure Act (HMDA) which requires most financial institutions to disclose the number of mortgage loans and the dollar amount of these loans by geographical area. The intent was to generate a statistical basis for judging if and where discrimination was prevalent in lending practices.

In 1989, FIRREA expanded the reporting requirements to include all home loan originators and to report information relating to income level, racial characteristics, and gender of mortgagors and mortgage applicants. This includes loans originated as well as applications rejected. In addition, disclosure is required as to whom the loans are sold. The intent is to determine what loan originators are doing with the loans they make. For this purpose, each of the federal underwriters of mortgage pools (Ginnie Mae, Fannie Mae, Freddie Mac and Farmer Mac) are classed separately.

Information generated through HMDA is enabling Congress to take steps toward further structuring of the home loan market. In the 1992 Federal Housing Enterprises, Financial Safety and Soundness Act, a goal was set for federal secondary-market agencies to purchase at least 30 percent of their mortgages on housing units located in central city areas. Further discussion of this effort can be found in Chapter 5 in the discussion of the secondary markets.

Questions for Discussion

1. How would you define the *primary mortgage market?*
2. Identify the classes of regulated lenders.
3. How does the government intend to simplify the banking system?
4. What is the present status of federal deposit insurance?
5. Explain the reserve requirement placed on depository institutions by the Federal Reserve Bank.
6. In what way has the Community Reinvestment Act affected the operation of regulated institutions?
7. What is the general policy of life insurance companies toward mortgage lending?
8. Identify the basic responsibility of each of the following four banking regulators: Federal Reserve Bank Board, Office of Thrift Supervision; Comptroller of the Currency, and the Federal Deposit Insurance Corporation.
9. What advantages do credit unions hold that banks consider unfair?
10. Identify at least two kinds of shorter term mortgage loans that are made by commercial banks.

Chapter 4

Other Primary Market Lenders

....

KEY WORDS AND PHRASES

Mortgage broker • *Mortgage banker* • *Loan servicing* • *Warehouse line of credit* • *Forward commitment* • *Immediate commitment* • *Application fee* • *Origination fee* • *Servicing fee* • *Farm Credit Administration (FCA)* • *Federal Land Bank* • *Rural Development Services Agency* • *Pension funds* • *Real Estate Investment Trust (REIT)*

....

INTRODUCTION In the last chapter, we studied regulated lenders' sources of mortgage money and the regulatory systems under which they must function. Historically, they have dominated the mortgage industry because savings deposits were necessary to be able to make a long-term loan—and federal laws encouraged such use of deposit assets. As financial institutions suffered through changes in the 1980s, another source of mortgage money expanded. This was the growth of secondary-market funding of mortgage loans by creating loan pools and selling securities backed by these pools. Mortgage-backed securities are more easily sold to investors than mortgages. It opened the door to many newcomers entering the loan origination business.

This chapter will examine first the substantial field of mortgage companies that serve as intermediaries between lenders and borrowers. The term *mortgage companies* covers a mix of mortgage bankers and mortgage brokers, some operating in the wholesale market, some in retail brokerage. Altogether they handle close to half of all loan originations each year. A far smaller segment of the loan market involves direct loans by federal and state government agencies, which will be reviewed later. Another portion of the loan origination market involves individuals and others who, for various reasons, participate in making mortgage loans.

MORTGAGE COMPANIES

From its origin as a brokerage-type service that arranged loans, the mortgage banking industry has grown to a major business, handling over half of the conventional loans and three-fourths of HUD/FHA and VA loans in this country.

In the early years of this century, mortgage companies arranged for the sale of their own bonds and used these funds to make small home and farm loans. Because of the thrift-conscious nature of farmers and homeowners, mortgage loans were amazingly free of defaults and provided a steady return for the holders of mortgage bonds. Mortgage companies achieved such a good record of repayments that the small-denomination bonds they sold to the general public for mortgage financing became known as *gold bonds!*

The 1920s brought further expansion of mortgage company financing beyond home loans and into income properties such as office buildings, apartments, and hotels. With little regulation and a "buyer beware" attitude, some projects were overfinanced as speculators moved into the lucrative markets. The Depression years beginning in 1929 showed many basic weaknesses in the mortgage loan system as the nation's economy foundered. Most of the mortgage companies that had issued bonds as well as those that guaranteed bonds for other development companies were faced with massive foreclosures. Unable to meet their obligations, many were forced into bankruptcy.

Unlike regulated depository institutions, mortgage companies without depositors were not a concern of the government. The money that mortgage companies used to make their loans had come from the sale of bonds, which was considered a business transaction, not a savings account deposit procedure. Hence, mortgage companies were granted no help in recovery from the Depression years. One avenue mortgage companies used to reestablish their business was to promote FHA and, later, VA loans which had been widely rejected by regulated lenders. This is one good reason that mortgage companies are still the major source for origination of FHA and VA loans.

Mortgage companies as a group share the mortgage market with regulated lenders; each has a market share of about half of loan originations. A major difference between mortgage companies and regulated lenders is that mortgage companies do not hold depositors' cash that can be used to fund their loans. Nor do they normally have investment cash with which to hold loans. To fund loans at closing, most mortgage companies rely on commercial banks that grant "warehouse" lines of credit to them. The loans are short term, collateralized by the mortgage notes they fund, and are normally repaid through sale of these notes to secondary-market investors.

Even within the industry, mortgage companies have substantial differences in how they operate. Some, including the mortgage bankers, offer a full-service facility including loan origination, funding, and servicing. Others, including the mortgage brokers, specialize in serving as agents for large lenders.

In between, a number of individuals and companies serve as correspondents or agents representing specific investors. First, a review of mortgage brokers.

Mortgage Brokers

Mortgage brokers are one of the growth areas in loan origination today. The complex nature of mortgage lending has increased the need for special expertise to advise borrowers and open doors to the most effective lenders. The historic role of mortgage brokers as primarily handling commercial loans has changed. Today, home loans are being offered by many knowledgeable individuals working in the capacity of mortgage brokers, structuring loans and placing them with the best source.

Mortgage brokers have formed their own association, the National Association of Mortgage Brokers (NAMB), and are expanding their influence within the industry. NAMB offers its members a series of designations defining levels of expertise based on experience and education. The association works in cooperation with mortgage bankers and others to explain the needs of the industry and of the borrowing public to state legislatures and to Congress. It is helping to change regulatory practices into more effective channels.

A mortgage broker specializes in serving as an intermediary between the customer-borrower and the client-lender. While brokers are capable of handling all arrangements for the processing, or packaging, of the loan, they normally do no funding, nor do they service the loan once it has been closed. Some brokers serve as "retail" offices for large mortgage bankers or big institutional lenders, providing a lower cost outlet than a branch office. Or they may serve as a correspondent in the local area for a major lender that specializes in a particular category of loans, such as hotels or shopping centers. The broker earns a portion of the normal origination fee plus an application fee.

Large commercial loans are normally funded directly by the lending institution, say, an insurance company, and the monthly payments on debt service go directly to the lender. This procedure works very well for mortgage brokers. On the other hand, residential loans require an intermediary who will assemble the smaller loans into larger blocks for easier selling to the big investors. Further, residential loans produce relatively small monthly payments and require substantial servicing capacity that can be found with a mortgage banker. However, the differences between commercial and residential loans have diminished in the present market as many mortgage brokers operate in the so-called "retail" market for residential loans and pass them on to various "wholesale" mortgage banking companies.

Other types of mortgage brokers are companies operating on a national scale that primarily arrange purchases and sales of mortgage loans between originators and investors, or between investor and investor. In so doing, they greatly aid the free flow of mortgages across state lines in the private mortgage market. These brokers seldom originate a loan and do not service them. However, they are part of the secondary market in some of their operations.

Occasionally, a commercial banker, or a savings association, will broker a loan for a customer with another lender. Money may not be readily available through regular channels, or the loan request may be for something the local banker cannot handle with its own funds. The banker may then turn to other sources and earn a brokerage fee for handling the loan. This type of extra service is more commonly found in smaller communities.

Mortgage Bankers

As mentioned in the previous section on mortgage brokers, the former distinction between "bankers" and "brokers" has diminished. Nevertheless, an essential criterion remains, and that is the full-service facility offered by **mortgage bankers.** *Full service* in this instance means (1) originating a mortgage loan, (2) funding the loan at closing, and (3) servicing the loan as it is paid off. Even this distinction between a mortgage banker and a broker is blurring as brokers are dividing themselves into those who close loans in their own names and those who close in another lender's name.

Looking back, the need for a full-service facility developed from both the desire for a new approach to mortgage lending after the economic collapse of the 1930s and implementation of the Federal Housing Administration (FHA) programs handled in conjunction with private industry. Economic pressures of the early 1930s dried up lendable funds, construction had been halted, and many banks had closed their doors. The shortage of available funds made the mortgage banker an intermediary for the only remaining sources of cash: insurance companies, a few large savings banks, and the Federal National Mortgage Association.

In the 1930s, Federal Housing Administration programs were rejected by regulated depository institutions as a government intrusion into the field of banking. Within the industry, extension of credit was then considered a banker's prerogative. The FHA's desire to work in cooperation with private industry was met by mortgage bankers. They offered the full-service facilities and market contacts that enabled the FHA to fulfill its purposes in meeting the needs of homebuyers.

As early as 1914, mortgage bankers formed a trade association known as the Farm Mortgage Bankers Association, indicating the original emphasis placed on farm loans. The name was changed to its present title of Mortgage Bankers Association (MBA) in 1923. MBA is a major communications and information center for the industry. It sponsors educational programs to keep the many persons employed by mortgage bankers up to date in an ever-changing business. MBA actively promotes legislation favorable to the industry and its borrowers.

With a better understanding of the variations among the businesses and individuals who serve those seeking mortgage loans, let's examine the question, What does it take to become a mortgage company?

Qualifications of a Mortgage Lender

At present, there are no federal requirements regarding the qualifications or licensing of an individual or company handling conventional mortgage loans. But most states have established some requirements, mostly registration and the posting of a bond. Many states are now exploring the possible need for further regulation, including licensing. In the past, any individual meriting the confidence of a lending institution could assist in arranging a loan, thereby earning a fee for his or her services.

In practice, qualifications for a mortgage company are set mostly within the industry. If a mortgage company elects to deal with a government agency involved with mortgage lending, that agency's standards must be met. This includes HUD/FHA, VA, Fannie Mae, Freddie Mac, Ginnie Mae, and Farmer Mac. The requirements are similar: a reasonable net worth, experienced personnel, and adequate office facilities available to the general public. Even so, approval must be obtained from each agency with which a mortgage company wants to do business. And the same is true of any other client-lender of a mortgage company. Approval by either HUD/FHA or VA in itself is often accepted by conventional lenders as adequate qualification.

Licensing of Mortgage Loan Officers. The complexity of residential mortgage lending with its many guidelines and requirements has increased the number of cases wherein consumers are misinformed, either from a loan officer's lack of knowledge or deliberately. Problems such as correct loan documentation, several hundred variations in repayment plans, proper handling of escrow account money, accurate advice on loan prepayments, compliance with the Equal Credit Opportunity Act, and the increasing concern with possible discriminatory lending have expanded the need for persons with full knowledge of the mortgage lending industry. More states are following a trend to create licensing commissions for proper qualification of those who handle mortgage loans for consumers.

Mortgage Company Operations

Although mortgage companies vary widely in their methods, the business organization common to most operates with three basic divisions:

1. Administration
2. Loan servicing
3. Loan acquisition

The administrative group supervises and directs all operations and seeks out and maintains contact with its sources of money: the lending institutions and, more recently, the poolers of mortgages for issuance of mortgage-backed securities. The development of stable, continuing relations with a group of investors is a source of pride for the mortgage companies. And there is always more than one investor, since it is not considered good business for either the mortgage company or the lender to maintain an exclusive arrangement. Lenders are in and out of the market as their particular investment needs fluctuate, while the mortgage company must maintain a steady supply of funds. Mortgage company officers must know which sources are available for loans and what particular type of loan each lender prefers.

Loan servicing includes the record-keeping section that maintains customers' or borrowers' accounts. Larger companies have converted much of this accounting to computerized methods for more efficient handling. One part of the records involves the escrow section, which holds the required insurance and tax deposits. Escrow account personnel must maintain a continuous analysis of taxes and insurance costs for each property to assure the company that sufficient money will be available when needed for payment. Another responsibility of the servicing section is to ensure prompt collection of borrower's monthly payments and to send out notifications if delinquencies occur. All lenders insist on knowing the borrowers' account status and depend on the mortgage company to use diligence in keeping its accounts current. Laxity in this area could jeopardize a lender's rights in a foreclosure action.

The loan acquisition group, the division best known to outsiders, consists of loan representatives or supervisors who make the contacts with potential borrowers. These are made through real estate agents, banks, accountants, and others to seek out the best loans and to handle the actual application for a loan. A loan processor normally works with one of these representatives to maintain the files and to help collect information required on both the property and the borrower. Complete documentation of the loan must be included in the loan package.

How a Mortgage Company Funds Loans

As discussed earlier in this chapter, mortgage companies do not hold deposit assets that can be loaned as do the regulated depository institutions. Therefore, they must use somewhat different procedures to obtain an assurance of funds with which to make loans. When dealing with residential loans, mortgage bankers generally borrow money from a commercial banker on a **warehouse** **line of credit** to fund a loan at closing. The loan is pledged at the bank as collateral and held, or "warehoused," by the bank until it can be sold.

Other methods are used by mortgage companies dealing with the larger commercial loans. These are more likely to be placed on a "case-by-case" basis with the most suitable lender at that time. Mortgage bankers, and some brokers, use several methods to assure themselves of adequate funding at known costs, as described next.

Sale of Loans to Secondary-Market Investors. A procedure long used by mortgage companies is to purchase a **forward commitment** in advance of mak- ing any loans. This commitment is a promise by a lender (meaning a purchaser of loans or an investor) to have certain funds available for qualifying loans submitted to them over a limited period of time, such as 30 days to 6 months. With a forward commitment in hand, the mortgage company can give assurance to a commercial banker that loans pledged on a warehouse line of credit do have a ready market. A forward commitment generally includes an agreement for the mortgage company to service the loans delivered to the loan purchaser. The agreement between originator and purchaser is known as a *sales and servicing contract.* Savings associations, insurance companies, some commercial banks, plus Fannie Mae, Freddie Mac, and other loan poolers buy loans from originators. Mortgage companies maintain contact with various loan purchasers who are in and out of the market.

Both Fannie Mae and Freddie Mac are continuously in the market for the purchase of loans that conform to their requirements. This assurance gives their "conforming loan" parameters special importance for lenders seeking liquidity in loan portfolios. Like other secondary-market loan purchasers, Fannie and Freddie buy loans through the sale of forward commitments to make such purchases.

Large mortgage companies with substantial assets may make loans without a forward loan commitment. They can hold loans temporarily in their own portfolio or, more likely, pledge them with a commercial bank on a warehouse line of credit. When a suitable buyer is found, the mortgage company can sell loans that have already been made on an **immediate commitment** basis. "Immediate" means the loans do exist and can be delivered now. However, industry practice allows up to 60 days for delivery on this basis. The advantage of an immediate type of sale is that the purchaser's yield requirements will be slightly less (the purchaser's money is put to work now) than for a forward commitment, which allows the mortgage company a little better margin of return.

Representative or Correspondent Basis. Insurance companies and other loan purchasers sometimes specialize in handling certain kinds of property loans, such as those for hotels or shopping centers. Rather than deal with a variety of loan originators, these companies often work through selected representatives throughout the country. The representatives, sometimes identified as agents and sometimes as correspondents, are commercial loan companies that understand the special requirements of each loan purchaser or investor. If a mortgage company customer is seeking a hotel loan, for example, the mortgage company will handle the contact with a secondary-market investor most interested in that particular kind of loan. In a situation such as this, the mortgage company serves as a loan broker, negotiating the loan for an investor. The investor then funds the loan at closing and usually handles the servicing.

Selling Mortgage-Backed Securities. Converting mortgage loans into mortgage-backed securities that enjoy a broader market is not practical for smaller mortgage companies. Most loan originators sell their loans to large loan poolers, such as investment banker Salomon Smith Barney or Fannie Mae, which are more capable of dealing with financial market needs. However, a few of the larger mortgage companies have been successful in tapping financial markets for this purpose.

One method used is to place a multimillion-dollar block of mortgage loans in the care of a trustee, such as an authorized bank. Then the mortgage company issues a series of certificates backed by the block of loans, which is the collateral for the securities. The certificates are sold to investors, and the money reimburses the mortgage company. The procedure is often identified as *securitizing mortgages*. As the mortgage company that originally made the loans services them, the principal and interest payments are sent each month to the trustee. The trustee then passes these payments on to holders of the securities. Thus, the expression *passthrough securities* has developed. When privately issued, such as described here, mortgage-backed securities may or may not be guaranteed. Investment bankers have entered the field of mortgage securities with a number of variations that are discussed more fully in the next chapter.

Mortgage Company Income

For the handling of mortgage loans, the profit margin is rather narrow. Mortgage companies make little, if any, money from the discount since that passes to the loan purchaser as part of the cost of money. While the borrower measures the discount in a specific number of points, in practice, the mortgage company originator does not receive that precise amount. What the mortgage company is really doing is buying a piece of paper—the mortgage note—when it funds the loan at closing. Then the note is sold to a secondary-market purchaser. The difference between what is funded at closing and what the mortgage company sells the note for is what it makes, measured in dollars. If the mortgage company has handled its commitments carefully, the margin covers its origination fee and maybe a small cushion. And if it makes a mistake, or misjudges the secondary market yield requirements, losses can be incurred.

The dependable income for loan originators comes from various fees: application fees, origination fees, and servicing fees. These are more fully explained next.

Application Fee. Loan originators normally charge a nonrefundable **application fee** at the time an application is taken. In the jargon of the industry, lenders will "entertain an application" for a loan if it is in general conformance with the kind of loan they make. The application fee covers certain costs involved in screening an application, such as a credit report, a property appraisal, and the time it takes a loan officer to review the information. The fee is not regulated (except for HUD/FHA and VA) and is charged by almost all originators, not just mortgage companies. For residential loans, the fee is in the $200 to $600 range, while commercial loans are often based on the size of the loan rather than on the work involved.

Origination Fee. An **origination fee** is sometimes combined with an application fee. However, in most cases, it is a separate charge amounting to 1 to 2 percent of the loan amount payable if and when the loan closes. It is a charge incurred for assembling a loan package and making the decision to accept or reject the loan. The charge is for services rendered but is tax deductible for the borrower if certain rules are followed. It is a separate charge from the discount, which is also tax deductible, but the two are not always differentiated when loan costs are quoted. The distinction should be disclosed to the borrower for more accurate comparison of charges between lenders.

Mortgage companies usually split the origination fee with about half going to the loan representative who contacts the borrower and takes the loan application. It is considered the "commission" earned by the representative and is not paid if the loan fails to close. In contrast, most savings associations and banks pay their loan officers on a salary basis rather than on by commission.

Servicing Fee. In mortgage lending, a **servicing fee** is that charge made for handling the loan after it has been funded. The services involve collecting and accounting for periodic loan payments, handling the escrow portion of the payments, and following up on delinquent accounts. The fee amounts to 0.25 to 0.50 percent of the loan balance and is collected by all loan servicers: mortgage companies, savings associations, banks, and others. The servicing charge is normally added to the interest rate for the loan and is not distinguishable to the average borrower. In the terminology of secondary-market investors, a yield requirement quoted as "net basis" means one that does not include a servicing fee; the loan originator must add that to the rate. Net basis rates are sometimes identified as the "wholesale rate." To illustrate, the rate delivered to a loan purchaser might be 8.5 percent, while the charge to the borrower would be 8.75 percent; the 0.25 percent difference is the service fee.

Because the servicing of large blocks of mortgage loans can be a lucrative business by itself, specialized companies have developed in recent years to do just this. Sometimes a loan originator accumulates several billion dollars in loans to service and will sell a portion of the block to acquire cash. For example, if a $100 million block of loans is paying 0.25 percent in servicing fees, that amounts to $250,000 per year. The profit potential in this kind of cash flow could make the servicing alone worth $750,000 to $1.5 million in a sale.

Loan Servicing Disclosure Notice

As the residential mortgage market has expanded and changed, an older practice of making monthly payments to the loan originator has given way to a new trend. The servicing function may be transferred to a distant collection company that specializes in computer management of the cash flows. The ease with which a lender can now ask a borrower to send monthly checks to a new servicing agent created an opportunity for some abuse. Scam artists using unauthorized, or stolen, lists of borrowers could direct payments to a post office box, skim the collections for perhaps a month or two, and disappear with the money.

To help give borrower/consumers some protection from this possibility, Congress amended the Real Estate Settlement Procedures Act (RESPA) as of April 20, 1991, requiring loan originators to provide borrowers with a servicing disclosure notice. The notice must include an explanation of two points: (1) the possibility that loan servicing may be transferred to another company, and (2) the rights of a borrower should that occur. The loan originator must provide a borrower with an estimate, expressed as a percentage, of the possibility of transfer. Further, a notice of transfer must be sent to the borrower not less than 15 days prior to any transfer, and the new servicing company must confirm the change within 15 days after the date of transfer. A toll-free or collect telephone number must be provided for the borrower to contact the servicing company. Borrowers may collect damages and costs from companies that violate the requirements.

AUTOMATED LOAN UNDERWRITING

An explosive growth since 1995 has brought the use of computer programs using artificial intelligence into the analysis, and even the final approval, of residential loans. While they did not originate the idea, HUD has encouraged the greater use of computerized loan underwriting as it can lower costs and give a more unbiased analysis. The method has brought an increase in the use of credit scoring and offers ways to expedite appraisals. Because of the many advances in technology, it is now possible for an individual to negotiate a mortgage loan on the Internet. A later chapter will discuss these advances.

GOVERNMENT LOAN PROGRAMS

While most government programs involved with mortgage financing are designed to encourage private lenders to make such loans (further discussed in Chapter 5, "Mortgage Money: The Secondary Market"), there are some programs that handle direct loans to borrowers; that is, the agencies work in the primary market. However, to avoid the appearance of direct competition with private business, many such programs require that the loan applicant first attempt to borrow the money from private sources. This is true of the Small Business Administration (not covered in this text) and the Rural Development Service, which has taken over most of the loan programs formerly offered by the Farmers Home Administration (FmHA).

Direct mortgage loan programs offered by the federal government are almost all farm related. State- and municipal-sponsored loan programs are mostly housing related and are usually handled by one or more local housing authorities. Because of its earlier importance in the mortgage credit structure of the country, let's first consider the federal Farm Credit System.

Farm Credit System

The Farm Credit System dates back to 1916 with the passage of the federal Farm Loan Act. Over the years since then, other federal agencies became involved with farm credit and have now been brought under the supervision of one agency. Today, the Farm Credit System (FCS) is an elaborate cooperative, borrower-owned network of farm lending banks. They are under the supervision, examination, and coordination of the **Farm Credit Administration (FCA),** an independent federal agency. Administratively, the FCS is composed of 12 regional farm credit districts owned by nearly a million American farmers and 4,000 of their marketing and business services cooperatives. The system makes long-term mortgage loans and short-term production, or crop, loans through different organizations.

Prior to 1979, individual components of the Farm Credit System raised funds independently through the sale of various agency bonds. Since then, the FCS has funded its loans and other assets primarily through the sale of systemwide consolidated securities. Most of the financing is handled through the sale of 6- to 9-month securities, and some with 2- to 5-year coupon notes. The interest rates charged to borrowers are determined periodically based on the FCS average cost of the system's funds.

Three different FCS organizations make direct loans to the farming community: Federal Land Banks, Federal Intermediate Credit Banks, and Banks for Cooperatives. Each is examined next.

Federal Land Banks. There are 12 **Federal Land Banks** (one in each district) that account for about 68 percent of the total loans within the system. The Land Banks make long-term mortgage loans and machinery and livestock loans through more than 400 Federal Land Bank Associations. The associations are cooperative credit organizations owned by local member/borrowers.

The local Associations assist member/farmers in need of a loan, screen and approve acceptable loan applications, and forward the applications to the district Federal Land Bank for funding. Approved loans are guaranteed by the local associations which makes all members liable and encourages peer pressure and assistance in loan repayments.

Generally, loans are limited to 85 percent of the appraised value of the property, with a maximum term of not less than 5 years or more than 40 years. Interest rates for most loans apply a variable-rate plan allowing interest to be adjusted periodically. Rates are based on the FCS cost of funds.

Federal Intermediate Credit Banks. There are also 12 Intermediate Credit Banks accounting for about 22 percent of the system's loans. They are wholly owned by, and the main source of, funds for 370 member/borrower-owned Production Credit Associations that make short-term production loans to their members. The FICB also serves as a secondary market for farm loans, dealing with national and state banks and agricultural credit corporations in addition to serving the Production Credit Associations.

Banks for Cooperatives. One central bank in Denver, Colorado, plus 12 district banks handle credit for co-ops. Each district bank serves marketing, supply, and business service cooperatives for farmers in its own territory while the central bank participates in making larger loans. They are an important source of funds for agricultural and aquatic cooperatives.

Rural Development Services Agency

To give perspective, the Farm Credit System just described holds about one-third of the nation's $200 billion in farm debt. The **Rural Development Services Agency** holds another $30 billion of the debt owed by farmers. In 1995 the Farmers Home Administration (FmHA) was eliminated and its essential programs were transferred to the Rural Development Service, also under the

Department of Agriculture. FmHA was established in 1946 as part of the Department of Agriculture for the purpose of making and insuring loans to farmers and ranchers. The scope of FmHA activities extended well beyond farm and home loans into financing for parks, camping facilities, hunting preserves, access roads, and waste disposal systems and to making loans in designated disaster areas. Many of these programs are now under the administration of the Rural Development Service.

Rural Development provides loan guarantees to help local lenders provide credit that is needed for expansion and preservation of jobs. It has expanded its traditional lending base to include cities of up to 50,000 population but gives priority to towns of less than 25,000 population. Suburbs and urbanizing areas that surround cities of over 50,000 are not eligible. Eligibility for loan assistance involves saving existing jobs, expanding existing business, and new plant location or business start-up. There is no minimum loan size and the maximum considered is up to $10 million.

Home Ownership Loans

The Rural Development Service's home loan program is limited to rural areas and to low- and moderate-income families who are unable to qualify for home financing in the private market. Loans can be made up to 100 percent of the appraised value of a house for a maximum term of 33 years. Eligibility is limited to those with an adjusted family income (AFI) of not more than approximately $27,500 per year for a family of four. The Rural Development county supervisor determines applicants' eligibility.

The AFI limits vary in different sections of the country, recognizing the difference in costs. A typical limit for a single person might be $19,250. For a family of four, it could be $27,500, with higher limits for larger families. Calculation of the qualifying income follows HUD standards generally, with certain additional limitations. The method used to determine income eligibility is to add the family income, then deduct $480 from the total for each dependent child under 18 living in the home. If the result is less than the AFI limit for that area, the family is eligible to make application.

Evaluation of the loan application is handled in a manner similar to other lending agencies and requires a complete financial statement, a history of family income, and a credit report. Each loan is reviewed periodically to determine if the borrower's financial condition has improved to the extent that the loan could be handled by a private lending institution.

For single-family housing, Rural Development will make loans on new or existing structures. However, the living area cannot exceed 1,200 square feet. The maximum amount of a loan permitted for this size house is determined by the applicant's ability to repay the loan.

State and Local Government Programs

Because of the opportunity for assisting home buyers, and perhaps some political advantage for the officials involved, many state and local housing agencies have developed since the mid-1970s. Some offer direct loans to qualified buyers. Many offer secondary-market assistance to established mortgage lenders. Almost all programs are funded with lower cost, tax-exempt bonds, which will be considered more fully in the next chapter.

OTHER PRIMARY MARKET LENDERS

The opening of the secondary market and the wide acceptance of mortgage-backed securities as sound investments have encouraged many newcomers to enter the loan origination market. The major players, not subject to banking regulations, are discussed next.

Nonbank Lenders. Companies with long experience in handling loan qualification and funding for other kinds of consumer-type loans have entered the mortgage market. These include such major operators as General Motors Acceptance Corporation, General Electric Capital Mortgage Corporation, and AT&T Capital.

Investment Bankers. As many investment bankers expand into handling various money market accounts, retirement funds, and even checking accounts, some have entered mortgage loan origination. Salomon Smith Barney, Dean Witter Reynolds, and Merrill Lynch are examples of this kind of lender.

Finance Companies. Many small loan companies, such as Household International, that formerly made mostly unsecured personal loans, have expanded into mortgage lending as a better method of securing their loans.

Home Builders. Several large home builders, such as Kaufman and Broad, Pulte Homes, and others, have entered the origination market through subsidiaries that process the loans and sell them into mortgage pools. By exercising some control over the mortgage money, home builders are able to structure loans that better suit their buyers' needs, thus enhancing sales potentials.

Real Estate Brokerage Firms. Companies that have developed national real estate brokerage operations, through direct acquisitions or franchise networks, have entered the loan origination business. Such companies as Century 21 and Prudential are able to offer mortgage loan services in their own offices.

Internet. The newest method of negotiating a mortgage loan is by contacting a mortgage loan site on the Internet. An individual who may have a tarnished credit record and wants to remain anonymous, or a person living in a rural area who wants to avoid traveling a long distance, or maybe even someone with an excellent credit record who feels more comfortable with an impersonal interview are lured to the Internet. There are some down sides, of course. Waiting periods are still necessary for certain verifications, fees and interest rates are about the same, and there is no real person to give much-needed advice on financial needs. Also, the Internet has its share of shady operators who may be harder to distinguish in cyberspace.

Computerized Loan Origination (CLO). As a forerunner to computerized loan analysis, computers were first used as a means of transmitting loan information to a human underwriter who did the analysis work and, after proper verifications, approved or disallowed the loan application. It involves computer network tie-ins between independent agents and major money sources. Today, CLO is one method used by real estate brokers to assist buyers in negotiating a loan to purchase a property. Current HUD rules allow a person or company who initiates the loan and assists in helping a borrower furnish the necessary information to earn a fee that is reasonably commensurate with the work performed. The procedure is further discussed in Chapter 14.

Pension Funds. In the past decade, **pension funds** have become large investors in mortgage loans. By far the most common method is through the purchase of mortgage-backed securities. In this way they avoid the management problems associated with individual mortgage loans and are able to treat such investments as just another kind of security.

However, a few pension groups, particularly those operated by state agencies and by labor unions, offer home loan programs as primary lenders. Some funds restrict participation to their own members, and some offer such loans to the general public if qualifying standards are met. Most of these direct loans are available to middle- and low-income families and offer attractive interest rates.

Real Estate Investment Trusts (REIT). In 1960, when mortgage money was derived mostly from savings accounts, Congress passed the Real Estate Investment Trust Act. The intent of the act was to make it more profitable for the small investor to enter the real estate market, thus increasing available capital. To achieve this purpose, a **Real Estate Investment Trust (REIT)** must derive most of its income from real estate investments and distribute at least 90 percent of its profit to its certificate holders. If these requirements are met, the REIT is not subject to federal income taxes at the corporate level. However, the dividends paid to interest holders are treated as taxable income to the recipients.

Two kinds of REITs developed. One made equity investments in real estate and derived its income from operation of properties. The other arranged for mortgage loans, a lucrative business when interest rates were reaching peak levels. Both kinds of activity declined in the 1980s as the real estate market lost much of its lustre. The 1990s have seen a return of equity-type REITs as a sound method of raising investment capital.

In the mid-1990s, REITs began a large scale operation of selling stock on the public markets. The stock was of interest to investors because of its tax advantages and the required distribution of any profit. REITs backed by the public markets were stronger than earlier REITs. Many showed equity of around 70 percent of capital, while earlier ones operated on about 30 percent equity with the rest borrowed.

With cash raised in the public markets, REITs began buying real estate, ranging from prisons to apartment buildings. In 1997, REITs made several big hotel deals; the purchase of ITT (Sheraton Hotels) and LaQuinta Inns were two of them. Because of an overload of stock on the market, the price stalled and in 1998 the Federal Reserve warned its banks to raise its credit standards on loans to REITs as such loans were dependent on real property which could fluctuate downward.

Individuals. Individuals do not come under the legal restrictions and reporting requirements of institutional lenders. Therefore, good statistics on individual participation in the mortgage market are not readily available. However, many individuals make mortgage loans, albeit sometimes with considerable reluctance!

As a general rule, the individual lender has motives other than profiting from the loan itself. Most common is when a second mortgage (or a first mortgage) is accepted for the primary purpose of consummating a house sale. In some cases the motivation is to help a member of the family, or perhaps to assist a valued employee acquire suitable housing.

Another area that individuals sometimes participate in is the second- and third-mortgage market for investment. The attraction is that junior mortgages offer higher yields than do first mortgages. The high yields are often obtained through substantial discounts. There is, of course, a greater risk in junior mortgages, as prior lienholders must be satisfied first in the event of foreclosure.

MISCELLANEOUS OTHER SOURCES

In different parts of the country, various types of companies and institutions have established themselves as sources of mortgage funds, usually limiting the geographic area in which they will loan money. As a general rule, this type of lender does no advertising as lending money is not its primary business. In the following paragraphs, the most important of these sources are identified.

Title Companies. Because title companies have a close association with, and considerable knowledge of, the mortgage industry, a few have developed direct loan departments or subsidiary companies to handle loans. These affiliated companies may act as primary sources in lending their own funds; they may raise money from the sale of mortgage bonds; or they may serve as correspondents or agents for other major lenders.

Endowment Funds Managed by Universities, Colleges, and Hospitals. As a group, endowment funds prefer to maintain their assets in high-grade stocks and bonds that have a good record for security, are considered more liquid and, most importantly, require less administrative attention than a portfolio of mortgage loans. However, many endowments are passed on in the form of land and other real property, and these have required more expertise in the mortgage loan field. The endowment funds can, and do, assist in the development of their own land by experienced developers, and they are increasing their activities in mortgage lending with investments such as the GNMA mortgage-backed security.

Foundations. Foundations are established primarily by corporations or wealthy families as a means of continuing charitable or other activities through the use of income earned from the foundation's investments. Like endowment funds, foundations are primarily interested in high-grade stocks and bonds as investments but are not adverse to mortgage loans, particularly if a purpose of special interest to the foundation can be served.

Fraternal, Benevolent, and Religious Associations. Over the years some fraternal, benevolent, and religious organizations have accumulated substantial pools of investment money from earnings, bequests, and other donations. These funds are generally little known and very seldom advertised. Administration is usually handled on a careful, conservative basis with security of the loan of greater importance than the yield. Some of these organizations limit lending to their own members and will provide low-cost loans to qualified members in good standing.

Questions for Discussion

1. Distinguish between the operations of a mortgage banker and a mortgage broker.
2. What qualifications are necessary to become a mortgage banker? Are there any special requirements for mortgage lenders in your state?
3. What is meant by *loan servicing?*
4. Identify the principal sources of mortgage company income.
5. How does the Federal Land Bank handle its mortgage lending function?
6. Describe qualification for the Rural Development Service's home loan program.
7. Explain the origin and purpose of Real Estate Investment Trusts.
8. Name three primary market lenders that are not subject to banking regulations.
9. Describe a warehouse line of credit and who may use it.
10. Are there any good sources of mortgage money available in your locality outside of mortgage companies and regulated lending institutions?

Chapter 5

Mortgage Money: The Secondary Market

INTRODUCTION

In the last two chapters the focus was on the primary market—the loan origination market. Prior to the mid-1970s, the loan origination market was dominated by regulated depository institutions. This group of lenders held the major source of deposit assets that could be used to fund long-term loans. Unless a lender had money on deposit to fund loans, there was little opportunity to enter the business except in a loan brokerage capacity. Mortgage companies handled the brokerage function.

Using deposits to fund mortgage loans worked fairly well for about four decades following the Depression of the 1930s. There was a federal limit on interest rates that never exceeded 5 1/2 percent paid to depositors (Federal Reserve's Regulation Q). This allowed long-term mortgage loans to be made at not more than 7 to 8 percent with reasonable protection for the lender of a stable cost of funds. Access by home buyers to this huge, low-cost source of funds started to unravel as interest rates began to escalate in the late 1970s.

While the real growth of the secondary market began in the early 1970s, its participants throughout that decade were generally limited to loan purchasers who normally invested in mortgage loans. These included large savings associations and savings banks, plus Fannie Mae and Freddie Mac. This was because the purchase of a mortgage loan by a secondary-market investor generally included certain responsibilities for managing the loan itself. It was not until the development of the mortgage-backed security concept, which converted mortgage loans into a more acceptable type of security, that the secondary market was opened to investors throughout the international financial markets.

EXPANSION OF THE SECONDARY MARKET

Besides the earlier constraints of interest rates, there were other problems limiting the mortgage market prior to the 1970s. It was difficult to sell mortgage loans for two important reasons: First, the documents used for conventional loans were not uniform; and second, there was no acceptable insurance protection against loan default. Only the FHA and VA had been able to overcome these problems. Both of these agencies offered uniform documentation that enabled an investor anywhere in the country to know in advance exactly how a note and mortgage instrument would be worded, and both offered a very acceptable underwriting guarantee (the VA terminology) or an insured commitment (the FHA term).

It was not until 1972 that steps were taken to create a class of conventional loans offering similar advantages to the FHA/VA loans. The move was undertaken by the Federal National Mortgage Association (FNMA, or better known as Fannie Mae) in an effort to increase its market. Prior to that time, only FHA and VA loans could be purchased by Fannie Mae, and they amounted to only about 20 percent of the total residential mortgage market.

Introduction of Uniform Documentation

In 1968, Fannie Mae was partitioned by Congress; one part became the Government National Mortgage Association (Ginnie Mae) and the other remained as Fannie Mae but converted to a federally chartered private corporation, no longer a government-owned entity. Obviously, conventional loans with 80 percent of the market offered a big opportunity for expansion for a private corporation. Thus, Fannie Mae, joined by Freddie Mac (the Federal Home Loan Mortgage Corporation that was created in 1970), began a several-year process of devising uniform documents acceptable for conventional loans. The result was the *conforming loan*, a loan written with uniform documents and loan qualification parameters that is readily marketable throughout the country.

Private Mortgage Insurance

The other problem of needing some form of default insurance was solved at about the same time (1972). At that time, the Federal Home Loan Bank Board approved the writing of 95 percent loans (formerly the limit was 90 percent loan to value) by federally chartered savings associations. The requirement for writing the higher ratio (95 percent) loan was that anything over 90 percent must be insured against default. Prior to that time, there had been no default insurance requirement. Thus, within a matter of a few months, the private mortgage insurance industry that had been rather dormant suddenly came alive. Within two years of the FHLB approval, one insurance company, Mortgage Guaranty Insurance Co. (MGIC) of Milwaukee, was writing more default insurance than the entire FHA!

In essence, with conforming loans providing uniform documentation and private mortgage insurance offering protection for the lender, the secondary market was able to expand beyond the limited market of trading in FHA and VA loans.

SELLING MORTGAGE LOANS

So what is the **secondary market?** The foregoing information described its expansion as a market for buying and selling mortgage loans. Basically, it is the market wherein loan originators are able to sell loans, thus recovering their cash for originating more loans. But the secondary-market uses a different terminology as its function differs from loan origination. The secondary market investors do not "lend" money, they "purchase" mortgage notes as investments to earn a return. The return is also called *yield* and it represents the money earned on an investment. In the mortgage market, yield is the combination of interest earned over the life of the loan, plus the discount taken at loan origination. Both are combined and expressed as an **annual return.** This is more fully explained next.

Procedures Used in Secondary Markets

Now note the difference in terminology at this point. The originator of a loan speaks to customers, who are borrowers, in terms of loaning money and expresses the cost of the borrowed money as interest plus points of discount and fees. Once the originator closes the loan to the borrower, the note and mortgage instrument become marketable paper that can be assigned—and the terminology changes. The mortgage note is now a salable commodity and is negotiated as such. The originator of the loan becomes a seller, and the large investing institutions that deal in the secondary market for mortgage loans are called purchasers. When a mortgage loan is thus offered for sale, the potential purchaser is interested in only one factor for loans of similar type, size, and quality, and that is the **net yield.**

Pricing Loans to Adjust Yields

Since the interest rate on the loan or loans held by the originator has already been established, the only way a seller can change the yield to a purchaser is to adjust the **price** of the loan. For example, if the mortgage note is for $10,000 at 7 percent interest, the yield would be 7 percent. If the seller must offer a higher yield than 7 percent to attract a purchaser, the loan must be sold for less than $10,000; that is, the face value is discounted to increase the yield. By selling the $10,000 loan for, say, $9,500, the purchaser is putting up less cash but still collects the originally agreed interest and principal payment applicable to the $10,000 loan at 7 percent. Hence, a greater return, or yield, for the $9,500.

The principal balance due on an existing mortgage loan normally changes each month as installments are paid, making it difficult to quote a price in dollars as is commonly done in the bond market. (Unlike the mortgage note, for a bond with a fixed denomination of, say, $1,000, the principal is normally not paid until the bond matures.) For this reason, the price on a mortgage note is quoted as a percentage figure. The price is that percentage of the loan balance for which the loan is sold. One hundred is, of course, par. If we were quoting the $10,000 loan just mentioned to sell for $9,500, the price would simply be "95." This indicates a 5 percent reduction in whatever the principal balance due on the mortgage note may be, or a five-point discount. (One point is 1 percent of the loan amount.)

In times of falling interest rates, a loan calling for a higher than current market interest can sell for a premium[1]—at, say, 102 percent or even 104 percent of its face value. Examples of prices and yields are shown in Table 5–1 to illustrate their relationship.

A simple reading of the table shows that the length of time a loan is outstanding has a direct effect on the yield for that loan. Since loans vary considerably in the time for payoff, it is necessary to use some standard payoff time in order to compare yields when a loan is originated. The reason is that the discount is a lump-sum amount paid at closing and must be spread over the life of the loan to calculate an expected annual yield.

TABLE 5–1 Price/Yield Table Calculated at 7% Interest for Term of 30 Years

Price	Discount	Yield if Prepaid 8 Years	Yield if Prepaid 10 Years	Yield if Prepaid 12 Years	To Maturity
102	+2 (premium)	6.66	6.71	6.74	6.81
100	0	7.00	7.00	7.00	7.00
96	4	7.70	7.61	7.54	7.41
92	8	8.44	8.24	8.12	7.85

[1]Paying a premium for higher than market interest rate debt instruments is a common practice in the bond market. However, many investors in mortgage loans refuse to pay any premium because of the ease with which mortgage loans can be refinanced at lower rates when the market declines.

Yield and Discount

For this purpose, **yield** can be defined as the return to the investor expressed in percentage of the price paid for the note. **Discount** is the difference between the face value of the note and the price the investor paid for the note. Yield includes both the interest earned and the discount taken. So to express the discount as a part of the yield, it must be converted to an annual percentage rate. The discount is a one-time charge, a lump sum taken at the time the loan is funded. To determine how much this adds to each year's earnings, or yield, the discount must be converted to an annual amount spread over the life of the loan. But what is the life of the mortgage loan? While most residential loans, including FHA- and VA-supported loans, are granted for a term of 30 years, the realistic life of a loan is approximately 10 to 12 years; that is, within 10 to 12 years the average loan is paid off, usually by resale or refinancing. So Fannie Mae and Freddie Mac use a time span of 12 years to determine the yield value of a discount. In round figures this means that one-twelfth of the discount amount would be considered as earned each year.

The purchase requirements for Fannie Mae to buy a loan are expressed in terms of a yield, usually carried to two decimal places. The accepted yield can be converted to a discount mathematically, or more easily by means of a standard conversion table. Table 5–2 shows several typical yield figures. The sequence of steps in the table shows the fixed interest rate for the note, the price that is used to achieve the yield, and the discount needed to achieve the price.

The mortgage banking industry is able to use both Fannie Mae and Freddie Mac's daily posting of required yields as solid criteria from which to base its own handling of individual mortgage loans. For example, say a mortgage company is making mortgage loans at 9.5 percent, which is competitive in its current market, and must meet a yield of 9.80 percent to sell the loans. Using Table 5–2, we determine that the price must be 97.45, which requires a discount of 2.55 points to achieve. The mortgage lender would probably ask a discount of 2.75 points as a rounded-out figure if the market is strong. Added to the quoted discount is the origination fee of about 1 percent for a total of 3.75 points taken at closing.

Consider the 9.5 percent interest rate just quoted as a *net basis rate*—the rate applied to dealing with a secondary-market purchaser. The *gross rate*—that applied to the borrower—must include two additional charges. One is the servicing fee of about 0.25 percent and the other is for private mortgage insur-

TABLE 5–2   Example: Conversion of Yield to Price

For a Yield Amount	At Interest Rate	Price Must Be	Points to Achieve
9.500	9.500	100	0
9.800	9.500	97.45	2.55
10.600	9.500	91.12	8.88

ance, if applicable, say another 0.25 percent. Thus, the market rate paid by a borrower in this transaction would amount to 10 percent interest plus 3.75 points.

Loan originators using Fannie Mae/Freddie Mac yields as a guide to trends would be watching for an upward or downward movement to further influence decisions as to what interest rate and discount might be needed to make loans that could be profitably sold.

POINTS

A **point** is one percent of the loan amount. In the jargon of mortgage lending, discounts are sometimes identified as "points." It is accurate insofar as a discount is usually measured in points. But the two words, point and discount, are *not* synonymous. A point as a unit of measure is frequently used to identify other costs such as mortgage insurance premiums, an origination fee, a finance charge, and various other charges. Yet it is not uncommon to lump all the costs of financing, even attorney's fees and title insurance, into one lump sum and call it "points." This practice can be confusing to the borrower-consumer.

From a practical standpoint, the borrower should demand that each cost be identified. It may help to uncover an error or possibly an overcharge. Former tax law distinguished between points taken as discount, considered a deductible cost of borrowed money the same as interest, and fees charged, which were considered nondeductible expenses. However, the difference in the make-up of points taken at closing is no longer a tax question. Recent rulings by the IRS (several revisions involved) allow a home buyer to take a tax deduction on all points paid in the tax year, regardless of the purpose involved, whether paid by buyer or seller. (Commercial loans and refinanced home loans must amortize point deductions over the life of the loan.)

Basis Points. To identify fractions of a point, the financial markets use a finer measure. A **basis point** is one one-hundredth of 1 percent (not of the loan amount as is a point). This unit of measure has long been used to report the small daily fluctuations in Treasury bill rates and is now moving into the mortgage language. For example, to identify a servicing fee of, say, 0.25 percent, it can also be called "25 basis points."

LOAN PURCHASERS

As defined earlier in this chapter, the secondary market is where loan originators can sell their loans, where they can convert their loans back into cash in order to originate more loans. Loan purchasers operate in two different ways:

1. **Purchase for portfolio.** Purchasers of loans may acquire them as a sound investment for the purpose of earning interest. This would include some savings institutions, insurance companies, pension funds, housing agencies, Fannie Mae, and, to a lesser degree, Freddie Mac.

2. **Acquisition for underwriting.** Some loan purchasers do so with the intention of creating mortgage pools that can be used as collateral for issuance of mortgage-backed securities. These purchasers, as well as some loan originators, use their own funds to create the mortgage pools, then recover their cash through the sale of securities. Among those active in this field are large investment bankers such as Salomon Smith Barney, large commercial banks such as Citicorp and Chase, plus Fannie Mae and Freddie Mac.

Purchase for Portfolio

The secondary market originated with the idea of purchasing mortgage loans to be held in portfolio. It began when Congress created the Federal National Mortgage Association (Fannie Mae) as part of the act that also created the Federal Housing Administration in 1934. The original purpose was a simple one: provide a market for FHA loans. As an agency of the federal government, Fannie Mae was able to sell debenture bonds (unsecured promises to pay) that paid a fairly low rate of interest, such as 4 to 5 percent. The money derived from the sale of bonds was then used to buy FHA mortgage loans that paid 6 to 6 1/2 percent interest. That gave Fannie Mae a margin of 1 to 2 percent over its cost of funds. In 1968 Fannie Mae held $7 billion of such loans.

The risk to Fannie Mae was to maintain that margin. If its cost of funds increased, there was no way it could increase the interest earned on its investment in fixed-interest, long-term loans. To finance its mortgage loan purchases, Fannie Mae sold short-term debenture bonds (3- to 5-year maturities) because the interest paid to short-term investors is customarily lower than that for long-term money. For many years the system worked very well. In industry jargon, Fannie Mae was borrowing money on the short term and lending on the long term. It was not until market interest rates began to escalate between 1979 and 1981 that cost of funds exceeded the interest earned. Losses ensued for all holders of mortgage loans, not just Fannie Mae.

During this same time period, the largest group of loan purchasers holding mortgage loans was savings institutions. Their cost of funds had been protected by the federal limitation on interest rates paid to their savings account depositors. While the federal limit was not removed until March of 1986, it was substantially undermined in the late 1970s by the introduction of a variety of savings certificates that paid higher interest rates. To hold deposits, savings associations had to pay higher rates to their depositors as they could not call in their long-term mortgage loans. The result was devastating losses for savings institutions and a general dissatisfaction with the "portfolio approach" to mortgage loans.

Nevertheless, there remains a substantial market for mortgage loans purchased by those who hold them as investments. Some of the risk of fluctuating interest rates has been reduced by the introduction of adjustable rate mortgage designs. Also, mortgage rates that were once held low by an artificial restraint on lenders' cost of funds are now free to fluctuate in a competitive market that has produced a near steady decline from earlier peaks. Indeed, in 1982 home loan rates reached 15 percent! In 1998 mortgage rates hovered just below 7 percent.

Purchase for Underwriting

"Purchase for underwriting" is an overly abbreviated title for this section. It is meant to explain the process through which loans are purchased, or otherwise acquired, for the express purpose of creating **mortgage loan pools.** A mortgage pool is a collection of loans, a block of loans. The pool can be made up of a particular kind of mortgage loan distinguished by its collateral, such as all-condominium loans. It can be a geographically diversified block of residential loans as is most commonly found in the Freddie Mac offerings. It can be exclusively FHA/VA as is required for a Ginnie Mae-type pool. Or it can be a block of commercial loans.

Participants in this type of secondary-market activity are mostly investment bankers, commercial banks, Fannie Mae, and Freddie Mac. These companies have the cash to acquire huge blocks of loans and establish the specific mortgage pools with identification of the individual mortgages assigned to them, then issue a series of securities that are backed by the mortgage pool. The securities are then sold to various investors.

All pools are organized in a manner that collects and accounts for the payments received on the individual loans, then passes this "cash flow" on through to the investors who have bought the securities. The intricacies involved with proper handling of these huge cash flows could not be managed without recent advancements in computer technology. Just how the cash flow is handled as it passes through to the security holders differs in a number of ways. It is these differences that distinguish one kind of mortgage-backed security from another, as will be explained later in this chapter.

How do the participants in the creation of mortgage pools make money? It is easier to understand if you think of the process as selling the cash flows rather than the mortgages. In fact, the mortgages remain locked up in the care of a trustee. The trustee may be a bank's trust department, or it could be the creator of a pool if properly authorized to hold the mortgages in trust. (The pooler is the company that issues the securities backed by the mortgages.)

The point is that the mortgages themselves are not "delivered" to the purchaser of a mortgage-backed security; just the cash flows generated by those mortgages are passed through to the purchaser/investors.

There has to be a margin between what the mortgages deliver in cash flows to the pool and what is passed on to the holders of the securities, or there would be no benefit to loan poolers. That margin is generated by three factors:

1. Investors in high-grade securities accept lower interest rates than produced by the mortgages because of lower risk for the investments. In spite of some adverse publicity about foreclosures, home loans are classed as a low-risk investment, and when converted to a security, they can command lower interest rates than more risky investments.

2. Larger investments are usually made for lesser rates than are small ones, so long as the risk justifies it. Mortgage-backed securities are generally offered in large denominations.

3. By segmenting the cash flows to the security holders, issuers can attract even lower cost money from the short-term money market. This is the purpose of the "collateralized mortgage obligation," which is explained later.

While the handling of cash flows differs, and the margins between what mortgages pay and what is delivered to the security holders vary slightly with almost every issue, the following example illustrates a hypothetical profit margin for an issuer of a mortgage-backed security.

....

EXAMPLE

Assume a residential mortgage pool of $1 million with each of the mortgages in the pool paying 10 percent interest. This amounts to a cash flow of $100,000 in interest plus whatever is repaid on principal each year. Say the issuer of the security backed by this block of mortgages offers to pay 9 percent interest to the security holder. A logical purchaser of such a security could be a pension fund. Say the pension fund pays $1 million for the security and accepts $90,000 a year in interest. The $10,000 difference between what is paid into the pool by home buyers in interest and what is paid to the security holder/pension fund must be shared: the loan servicer (usually the loan originator) will earn between one-quarter and three-eighths of that 1 percent differential; if a trustee is involved, it would earn maybe 20 basis points (one-fifth of 1 percent), and the rest, perhaps 45 to 55 basis points, belongs to the security issuer.

....

This example is deliberately reduced in size to $1 million for easier understanding. In practice, it would be much too small to attract any issuer of securities. Loan pools range from $100 million up to more than $800 million. With those kinds of numbers, the margins are far more interesting! To attract investors, interests in the huge pools are sold through a series of securities in smaller denominations such as $100,000 units. Mutual funds may offer much smaller denominations for individual investors.

A key point in this kind of transaction is that the risk of interest rate fluctuation passes to the holder of the mortgage-backed security. In the past, those who held mortgages in portfolio were exposed to the risk of rising interest rates. This meant their cost of funds might increase to an amount greater than the earnings on their portfolio of loans. While this fact has not changed—those who hold mortgage loans in portfolio are still exposed—there is now another option. By converting mortgage loans to securities, the risk is passed on to the security holder.

To explain the meaning of this "passing of the risk," let's take another look at the example of the $1 million block of loans and say it is converted to a single $1 million denomination security. Say that security was sold to a pension fund. What the pension fund now holds as an asset is a $1 million security (call it a mortgage-backed bond) that pays 9 percent each year on the principal balance. What happens if the market interest rate now moves from 9 to 11 percent? This would reduce the pension fund's $1 million asset value by about a 12-point discount, to an asset value of approximately $880,000. If the pension fund has to sell that mortgage-backed bond for some reason, it would take a $120,000 loss. However, pension funds, and other investors of their kind, do not face depositors who can withdraw their cash whenever they want, so it is very unlikely that such an investor would be forced to accept such a loss. If held to maturity, the underlying mortgage pool would eventually repay the full $1 million in principal plus interest, and all parties would recover precisely what they expected when the investment was made.

In fact, the attraction of mortgage-backed securities has encouraged savings institutions to exchange their portfolios of mortgages for securities. This was the cause of the massive "swaps" that boosted pool underwriting between 1982 and 1984. A swap occurs when an institution exchanges its own portfolio of mortgages to, say, Freddie Mac, in return for a series of mortgage-backed securities. This may appear to be an unrealistic exchange. After all, doesn't the savings institution still carry the risk of interest rate fluctuation if it holds a security tied to the mortgages? And the answer has to be "yes," in that the principal value of a mortgage-backed security may rise or fall depending on the fluctuation of market interest rates as described in the previous paragraph.

But there are two differences that account for the attraction of mortgage-backed securities over holding mortgages themselves. First, a security is more easily sold than a mortgage loan, thus providing greater liquidity should cash be needed. Second, the security can carry an additional protection against loss that was not available for the individual mortgage loan. The additional protection is an underwriting guarantee of the mortgage-backed security by a federal agency. About half of the mortgage-backed securities backed by residential mortgage loans have this protection. This kind of underwriting is the subject of the next section.

FEDERAL UNDERWRITING OF MORTGAGE POOLS

The concept of a block of loans serving as collateral for the issuance of a security is not new. And it is not limited only to mortgage loans. It is used in other areas of supplying credit, such as with car loans, student loans, and even for credit cards. In market jargon, it is called an "asset-backed" security. Those who issue securities backed by blocks of loans can range from banks to home builders, from investment bankers to finance companies, and from retail merchants to real estate brokers.

But what has substantially enhanced the wide acceptance of **mortgage-backed securities** has been the rapid growth of federal agency underwriting.

To expand upon the idea presented in the previous section: Remember that the issuers of mortgage-backed securities earn a margin between what the individual mortgages pay each month and what the issuers have to pay the holders of the securities. The larger the margin, the greater the profit. Add to that, the lower the risk, the lower the rate that has to be paid security investors. What federal underwriting has added is an element of reduction in the risk for holders of mortgage-backed securities.

Since reducing the risk for the investor encourages lower interest rates, the long-range results are not only slightly higher margins for the issuers, but also lower interest rates for home buyers. In fact, the reduction in risk was quantified by the Federal Reserve Bank Board with a ruling effective in 1989. That rule increased banks' capital requirements from 6 to 8 percent tied to the risk level of their assets (meaning loans outstanding). For most kinds of commercial loans held in portfolio by a bank, capital required is 100 percent of the 8 percent requirement, or $8.00 for every $100.00 of loans outstanding. For approved residential mortgage loans, the risk-based capital requirement is reduced to 50 percent or $4.00 for every $100.00 of such loans. If the investment is made in mortgage-backed securities that are federal agency insured, the risk drops to 20 percent or $1.60 for every $100, and to zero for federal government guaranteed loans (the last category includes government bonds and Ginnie Mae mortgage-backed securities).

So who are the federal underwriters offering these benefits? There are four involved with mortgage loans: Ginnie Mae; Freddie Mac; Fannie Mae; and the newest entrant in the field in July of 1989, Farmer Mac. None of the agencies is limited in its activities to only underwriting mortgage loan pools. Each will be described next as to origin, ownership, underwriting requirements, and other functions.

Government National Mortgage Association (Ginnie Mae)

Ginnie Mae was created by partitioning the Federal National Mortgage Association in 1968. As a result, Fannie Mae became a federally chartered public corporation (listed on the New York Stock Exchange) and Ginnie Mae was assigned to the Department of Housing and Urban Development (HUD). Of the four federal underwriting agencies, Ginnie Mae is the only one that belongs to the government and thus carries unique powers.

Ginnie Mae was assigned two of the three functions formerly handled by Fannie Mae: (1) to implement special assistance for housing as may be required by Congress or the president, and (2) to manage the portfolio of loans assigned to it by the partition from Fannie Mae. (The third function—stabilizing the mortgage market through the purchase of loans—was not assigned to Ginnie Mae.) To minimize duplication of facilities, some of Ginnie Mae's operations are handled by agreement through the offices of Fannie Mae.

What has overwhelmed the original intent for creating Ginnie Mae is the success it has had with "managing" its loan portfolio. To liquidate some of the loans acquired in its partition from Fannie Mae, Ginnie Mae created pools of these loans and issued a guarantee certificate backed by the pools as a type of security. The pool guaranty concept became the mechanism by which mortgage loans are converted into more salable securities. Ginnie Mae pools today are limited to FHA, VA, and certain Rural Services Agency loans. (This was formerly the Farmers Home Administration [FmHA] which was eliminated in 1996 and the name changed to Rural Development Services, remaining under the administration of the Department of Agriculture.)

However, Ginnie Mae does not purchase mortgage loans to create its pools. It approves "loan poolers," usually investment bankers such as Salomon Smith Barney, who purchase mortgage loans from loan originators across the country. These loans must comply with Ginnie Mae requirements. Then, Ginnie Mae issues its guaranty certificates, which are backed by specific loan pools. The loan poolers then sell the Ginnie Mae certificates. As the individual mortgage loans produce monthly payments, the cash passes through the servicing agent, to the loan pooler, and on to the holders of the Ginnie Mae certificates. Ginnie Mae guarantees the payment to holders of the certificates but not the individual mortgage loans.

Of the four underwriting agencies, Ginnie Mae is the only one authorized to issue a "government guarantee," a commitment backed by the full faith and credit of the United States. For this commitment, Ginnie Mae charges a fee amounting to 6 basis points (six one hundredths of 1 percent of the commitment amount). A pooler is limited to a fee of 44 basis points.

A Ginnie Mae certificate, called a "Ginnie Mae" in financial markets, offers a powerful incentive for an investor. It carries the zero-risk equivalent of a government bond and offers up to 1 percentage point higher return than the bonds! While the smallest denomination of a Ginnie Mae is $25,000, a number of mutual funds offer participations in much smaller denominations.

In the last quarter, 1998, Ginnie Maes outstanding amounted to $537 billion, or 12 percent of the $4,376 billion of residential mortgage debt in this country. Ginnie Mae held a little less than $7 billion in its own portfolio, which is the only government money actually invested at this time in mortgage loans among the four agencies.

Federal Home Loan Mortgage Corporation (Freddie Mac)

With a bit of imagination added, the acronym applied to FHLMC becomes "Freddie Mac." It is a federally chartered corporation owned primarily by the savings association industry. It functions in a similar manner to Fannie Mae with an 18-member board of directors and is subject to an oversight committee under HUD. HUD sets target goals for both Freddie and Fannie, including loan purchase requirements in central city areas and for low- and moderate-income families, which both agencies report meeting.

Freddie Mac holds ties to the federal government with five of its directors appointed by the president of the United States and a $2.25 billion line of credit with the U.S. Treasury. Congress sets limits from time to time on the maximum loan amount that all federal agencies may purchase.

From its creation as a part of the savings association system in 1970 for the purpose of purchasing mortgage loans, Freddie Mac has favored securitizing loans. Rather than purchasing loans for its portfolio, a practice initially followed by Fannie Mae, Freddie Mac elected to raise its money through the sale of mortgage participation certificates. These certificates, called "PCs" in the financial market, are backed by multimillion dollar blocks of geographically diversified single-family (one- to four-family) loans that serve as collateral. The certificates are unconditionally guaranteed by Freddie Mac. While this is an "agency" guarantee, it falls short of a federal government guarantee. What is meant by an agency guarantee is that, while the agency is not legally a part of the government, its ties are close enough that investors assume the government will not allow it to default on an obligation. But there is no legal obligation to do so.

Freddie Mac acquires its loans through purchases from its approved sellers/servicers. While these have been mostly savings associations, the right to do business with Freddie Mac is open to any loan originator meeting its qualifications. However, as a part of the savings association system, its policies are more suitable for loan originators who hold deposit assets. Most of its purchases are conventional loans that must carry private mortgage insurance unless there is a 20 percent or more down payment. Freddie Mac may also acquire FHA and VA loans but almost all of these loans are now handled through Ginnie Mae.

Even though Freddie Mac earns most of its money from fees charged for underwriting blocks of mortgage loans, it still holds a relatively small amount of mortgage loans in its own portfolio earning interest. In the last quarter, 1998, its loan portfolio amounted to a little over $57 billion, while its mortgage-backed securities programs amounted to $646 billion, totaling a market share of 16 percent of all residential mortgage loans. This is an increase from a 12 percent market share in 1989.

Federal National Mortgage Association (Fannie Mae)

The oldest participant in the secondary mortgage loan market is Fannie Mae. Fannie Mae began its life in 1938 as a government agency responsible for purchasing only FHA loans. At that time, Congress correctly anticipated a rejection of the newly formed FHA-insured loan program by regulated lenders. The solution was to create another method of funding loans through their sale to secondary market investors. Since this market was close to nonexistent in those days, Fannie Mae was established as a part of the original act creating the FHA for the purpose of purchasing FHA loans. Later, Fannie Mae was authorized to buy VA loans.

In those early days, the loan originators willing to work with FHA loans were mostly mortgage companies. They were able to fund these loans through sale to Fannie Mae, thus bypassing depository institutions. Ever since, Fannie Mae has worked closely with mortgage companies by providing forward loan commitments that give good assurance of funding.

In 1968, Fannie Mae was converted from a government agency to a federally chartered private corporation with its stock publicly listed on the New

York Stock Exchange. However, by its federal charter, it retains close ties to the United States government. For example, five of its 18 directors are appointed by the president of the United States, and it can borrow up to $2.25 billion from the U.S. Treasury. Fannie Mae is subject to an oversight committee under HUD, the same as Freddie Mac, and its policies must conform to government requirements. After becoming a private corporation in 1968, Fannie Mae expanded its loan purchases from only FHA and VA loans to include the much larger market for conventional loans.

Fannie Mae has long followed the policy of selling short-term securities, mostly debenture bonds, and using the proceeds to buy loans for its own portfolio. Its profits have been the difference between what it paid its bond holders and what it could earn on its mortgage loan portfolio. When this margin began to dry up in the early 1980s, Fannie Mae shifted to selling services for fees. In 1982, one service it undertook was to guarantee mortgage-backed securities for its sellers/servicers. The guarantee is by Fannie Mae, an "agency" guarantee, the same as Freddie Macs's. In addition, Fannie Mae began assembling its own blocks of mortgage loans to use as collateral for other mortgage-backed securities (called "MBS" in financial markets).

In a very few years, Fannie Mae's MBS programs exceeded its portfolio of loans! In the last quarter, 1998, Fannie Mae held $158 billion in portfolio while its mortgage-backed securities exceeded $834 billion. Fannie Mae's combined activities, amounting to $992 billion, represent 23 percent of total residential mortgage debt, an increase from 14 percent in 1989.

Federal Agricultural Mortgage Corporation (Farmer Mac)

To expand the source of funds for farm lenders, Congress passed the Agricultural Credit Act of 1987 creating the Federal Agricultural Mortgage Corporation under the supervision of the Farm Credit Administration. Its initial capitalization was through a $20 million subscription sale of common stock sold primarily to financial institutions that deal in agricultural loans. Farmer Mac, as it has become known, was originally patterned after Ginnie Mae as an underwriting agency for pools of farm loans. Farmer Mac could not purchase loans, rather it granted approval for loan poolers and the loans that were permitted in its pools.

Farmer Mac originally had other restrictions. For instance, it could provide only a 90 percent guarantee for the timely repayment of its mortgage-backed securities. The other agencies could guarantee 100 percent. Further, its securities had to pass requirements of the Securities and Exchange Commission, which the other agencies did not, and poolers were required to establish a 10 percent reserve for each pool. These restrictions impeded the credit enhancement for agricultural loans. Another factor that hampered its growth was a substantially improving farm economy in the late 1980s which did not need as much help with credit.

This was changed by Public Law 104-105, signed by President Clinton on February 10, 1996. Farmer Mac was granted about the same powers as Fannie

Mae and Freddie Mac. It can now purchase agricultural loans directly from originators and can issue its own 100 percent guaranteed mortgage-backed securities based on its loan pools.

A *qualified agricultural real estate loan* is defined as one secured by land or structures that are used for the production of one or more agricultural commodities. In general, individual loans may not exceed $2.5 million, a measure intended to preserve the concept of the smaller, family-run farm. Loan pools may also consist of *rural housing loans*. Such loans are defined as those made to finance single-family residential dwellings in rural areas and communities with not more than a 2,500 population.

Farmer Mac did not issue its first guaranty certificates until 1992. This was a $233 million package of securities collateralized by agricultural loans originated by Travelers Insurance Company. Not much has been done since then and at this writing, the 1996 law giving Farmer Mac greater powers had not had sufficient time to become more effective in the credit markets.

LOAN POOLS

Assembling a block of loans into a loan pool can be arranged by a number of different types of companies: investment bankers, commercial banks, finance companies, large real estate brokerages, Fannie Mae, Freddie Mac, and even home builders. Loan pools serve as the collateral for a class of securities generally identified as mortgage-backed securities. Three of the federal underwriters, Fannie Mae, Freddie Mac, and Farmer Mac, serve a dual function: They may form their own pools and issue guarantee certificates for themselves or they may approve pools assembled by others and issue guarantees covering other pools. Either way, the guarantee enables those who pool loans to sell the securities more readily and at slightly lower interest rates. The guarantee, of course, provides credit enhancement that reduces the risk of the security.

However, not all loan pools are guaranteed by a federal agency, nor are all mortgage loans assigned to pools. Many mortgage loans are held by individual investors and by institutions as part of their portfolio. Some pools that are not federally underwritten are assembled by large financial institutions that issue their own mortgage-backed securities collateralized by their pools. This is particularly true of jumbo residential loans (those that exceed conforming loan limits) and some limited types of commercial loans. Such securities are sold on the strength of the issuing institution and are generally not guaranteed. They are called **private mortgage conduits** and in the last quarter, 1998, with $613 billion in loan pools, they comprised 23 percent of total loan pools.

Assembling a Loan Pool

A pool can be assembled by two different methods. One is to acquire the loans first; the other is to first sell the securities that provide cash for the purchase of loans. If the method is to acquire the loans first, this may be accomplished through either outright purchase or by internal origination of the loans. For example, purchasing of loans from loan originators throughout the country may be handled by an investment banker, such as Merrill Lynch. Or, a commercial bank, such as Citicorp or Chemical Bank, may generate its own block of loans through its retail branch offices.

The other method of assembling a loan pool is to first sell the securities, then use the proceeds of the sale to purchase those mortgage loans that meet the requirements of the issuer of the securities. This method is most commonly implemented through the sale of tax-exempt bonds. It is often used by states and municipalities to fund various housing agency programs for low- and moderate-income families.

If the origin of the pool is not by one of the federal underwriters but is to be so underwritten, the assembled loans must comply with that underwriter's requirements. Once underwriting approval is obtained, a fee is then paid to the federal agency underwriter for the guarantee certificate. With the underwritten loan pool serving as collateral, a series of securities can be issued and sold to investors throughout the world, thus recovering the initial investment to acquire the loans.

Following is a more detailed explanation of the two methods. First, we cover the tax-exempt bond procedure that raises money before the loans are acquired. This is followed by a more detailed explanation of the alternative method which consists of assembling a pool of loans first, then issuing mortgage-backed securities. Some of the variations in mortgage-backed securities are then explained.

TAX-EXEMPT BONDS

The most effective way of bringing lower cost money into the mortgage market has been through the sale of **tax-exempt bonds.** A tax-exempt bond is a type of security sold by states and municipalities paying interest that is not subject to federal income taxes. The federal government does not tax states or municipalities. Whether or not this freedom from taxation should extend to funds used to assist an individual purchasing a house, or for entrepreneurial industrial development, has been a debatable question for many years. However, the procedure has proven beneficial to home buyers and other community development projects. So it carries substantial political support.

Approval by Congress to allow the tax exemption for private use of municipal bonds was made permanent on August 10, 1993. However, since any claim of tax exemption falls under the scrutiny of the U.S. Treasury and its IRS arm, some qualifying requirements have been issued. For instance, properties financed with tax-exempt bond money may be subject to a recapture tax if sold during the early years of ownership. Almost every year, changes have been made in what states and municipalities may do in qualifying tax-exempt issues when the proceeds are used to make mortgage loans. Generally, the total of such issues is limited by an allocation of dollar amounts to each state.

The reason "bond money" is lower cost for a consumer is that the tax savings are generally passed on to the borrower. The attraction to invest in tax-exempt bonds comes from people in upper tax brackets: They can benefit from a lower interest rate not subject to income taxes. For example, a corporate bond paying a 10 percent rate subject to tax would yield only about a 6.1 percent return to a taxpayer if he or she is in the 39.6 percent tax bracket.[2] Thus, a tax-exempt bond yielding an investor 6.1 percent would be roughly an equivalent return to the investor and of substantial benefit to the home buyer.

Almost all states and many municipalities have entered this market to raise the lower cost money through the sale of various kinds of securities. In some cases, the money raised from the sale is used to buy mortgage loans from approved lenders within the state or community. Thus, tax-exempt bond money becomes another source of secondary-market funding. In some cases, however, housing authorities use this money to make direct loans to qualified borrowers. Almost always, there is an upper-income limitation for home buyers so as to direct the money primarily to lower- and middle-income families.

Another use of tax-exempt bonds is to finance industrial development projects. Sometimes a single developer may be the beneficiary of the low-cost money, or it can be used to finance a project open to any qualified commercial development. The basic purpose of these bond issues is to attract business to a community or state, and thus increase available jobs and increase the tax base.

MORTGAGE-BACKED SECURITIES (MBS)

The growth of the secondary market indicates the success lenders and investors have had with developing practical procedures and uniform instruments for mortgage loans. Yet mortgage loans carry certain problems as investments, such as a need for long-term supervision of each individual loan and an uncertain return caused by unpredictable prepayments. Further, most major investors are more comfortable dealing in securities—a type of investment that can be bought and sold with greater ease than mortgage loans. By packaging a block of mortgage loans to be held as collateral for an issue of securities, mortgage loans are in effect converted to securities and become more acceptable to investors.

While both Freddie Mac and Ginnie Mae have offered mortgage-backed securities since the early 1970s, it has only been since the early 1980s that other institutions and companies began entering this field. One reason for the surge of activity in mortgage-backed securities was losses sustained by traditional mortgage lenders, beginning in the late 1970s as interest rates escalated. Holding long-term, fixed-rate investments inevitably lost some of its appeal. Another reason was the climb in mortgage interest rates to levels at, or above, other long-term investments, particularly government bonds. The higher rates proved attractive to investors and allowed those packaging the blocks of mortgages a profitable margin for their work. Securities are a far more attractive investment vehicle than mortgage loans in the big financial markets.

[2]A simple formula to determine comparative yields for investors: Divide the municipal bond rate offered by the result of 100 percent less the taxpayer's tax bracket. The result is the yield equivalent for an investment subject to tax. Example: A municipal bond offering 7 percent for a taxpayer in the 39.6 percent tax bracket: 7 divided by .6040 equals 11.59 percent, the equivalent taxable yield.

So the shift to the securities market to raise mortgage money proved to be a more than adequate replacement for the loss of passbook savings money, but initially at a somewhat higher cost. As the market expanded, competition reduced the interest rates charged so that it is now a cost-saving method for home buyers. In the growth of securities as a source of funding, a number of variations have developed. Two of the most popular types are mortgage pass-throughs and collateralized mortgage obligations (CMOs) as described next.

Mortgage Pass-Throughs

The original concept of a mortgage-backed security was to assemble a diversified block of mortgage loans, generally identified as a "pool" of loans, then issue a series of securities collateralized by that block of loans. The issuer of the securities may or may not guarantee them. If the securities are issued by a private institution or company, they are seldom guaranteed, and they are more difficult to sell. As the popularity of a government agency underwriter dominated the market, the guarantee certificate became the security that is sold.

At first, the purpose was to simply pass on the risk of a fluctuating interest rate to other investors more familiar with the risks involved. And the way payments were handled was to simply pass the income derived from the underlying block of loans in pro rata shares on to the security holders. If a loan was paid off prematurely, the additional principal was passed through to the security holder, thus repaying a portion of the principal itself. If interest rates increased, the payments on the underlying block of loans remained unaffected. In such an instance, the security holders would suffer a loss of value in the security, but that was a risk they understood.

The **pass-through** type of payment created some uncertainty in its cash flows and thus in the true yield on the investment itself. To overcome this inherent problem, the financial market issuers of these securities developed an alternative method of handling cash flows to investors. This is the collateralized mortgage obligation more fully described next.

Collateralized Mortgage Obligations

Another method of offering a variation on the mortgage-backed security is the **collateralized mortgage obligation (CMO).** The first CMO was issued by the Federal Home Loan Mortgage Corporation in June 1983. It has several advantages over the mortgage pass-throughs that are attractive to traditional investors in corporate-type bonds. By early 1986, securities dealers (investment bankers), home builders, mortgage bankers, thrift institutions, commercial banks, and insurance companies had also issued CMOs.

Differences Between CMOs and Mortgage Pass-Throughs

The innovation of the CMO structure is in the segmentation of the mortgage cash flows. The older pass-through-type of mortgage-backed security offers its holders an irregular cash flow since it includes the repayment of principal whenever a home buyer prepays a loan or refinances to achieve a lower interest rate. This happens because holders of mortgage pass-throughs own undivided interest in a pool of mortgages. Whatever the particular pool of mortgages produces in principal payments and interest is then passed directly through to the security holders. In contrast to this procedure, the CMO investor owns bonds that are collateralized by a pool of mortgages or by a portfolio of mortgage-backed securities. The variability and unpredictability of the underlying cash flows remain, but since the CMO substitutes a sequential distribution process instead of the pass-through's pro rata distribution of these cash flows, the stream of payments received by the CMO bond holder differs dramatically from that of the holder of a pass-through security.

Structure of a CMO

The CMO structure creates a series of bonds with varying maturities that appeal to a wider range of investors than do mortgage pass-throughs. While all CMOs follow the same basic structure, wide variations have developed in how the segmentation is set up. Following is the basic pattern:

1. Several classes of bonds are issued against a pool of mortgage collateral. The most common CMO structure contains four classes of bonds: the first three pay interest at their stated rates from date of issue; the final one is usually an accrual-class bond.

2. The cash flows from the underlying mortgages are applied first to pay interest and then to retire bonds.

3. The classes of bonds are retired sequentially. All principal payments are directed first to the shortest maturity class A bonds. When these bonds are completely retired, all principal payments are then directed to the next shortest maturity bonds—the B class. This process continues until all the classes of bonds have been paid off.

One of the attractions of CMOs for investors is that some of the bonds offer shorter maturities. Many investors prefer to make short-term investments. For the issuers of the securities, tapping the short-term money market means they can pay a lower interest rate for the money used to buy mortgage loans. This enlarges the margin that can be earned in such a transaction. Short-term money almost always receives lower interest rates than long-term money.

The first-priority class A bonds may offer maturities as short as 2 years. Class B and C bonds may offer maturities from 4 to 10 years. The interest rate offered on these bonds is usually measured against U.S. Treasury securities of similar maturities, only at a slightly higher rate to attract investors. Following is a general description of the basic bond classes:[3]

---

[3]In the financial community, these bond classes are also identified as "tranches," such as first tranche, second tranche, and so on. *Tranche* is the French world for "slice."

Class A Bonds. The shortest maturity class of bonds receives all principal payments and any prepayments from the entire pool of mortgage collateral until the entire Class A issue is paid off. Holders of A bonds begin to receive significant principal payments from the first payment date.

Class B and C Bonds. The intermediate classes receive only interest payments until each of the prior bond classes has been retired. The interest payment is a known, fixed amount, but the principal repayment will depend on how quickly the mortgage collateral pays down.

Class Z Bonds. Class Z bond holders receive no principal or interest payments until all earlier classes have been retired. However, the interest earned by the Z bond is added to the principal balance (compounded), accruing additional interest. During this accrual period, the cash that would otherwise be used to pay interest on the Z bonds is used to accelerate the retirement of the shorter maturity classes. When all the earlier classes are retired, the accrual period ends, and principal and interest payments to Z bond holders commence.

The purpose of CMOs is to broaden the market for mortgage-backed securities and thus assure a sufficient flow of capital into the mortgage market. They attract investors by offering higher returns than Treasury securities of similar maturities, albeit with a slightly greater risk. This kind of financing—that is, a variety of mortgage-backed securities deriving income from huge, multimillion dollar pools of loans—became practical with the help of high-grade computer technology. The process simply would not be possible without recent advances in computer capabilities.

REAL ESTATE MORTGAGE INVESTMENT CONDUITS (REMIC)

Tax liabilities of the various handlers and holders of mortgage-backed securities created some confusion. For instance, does the issuer of a mortgage-backed security owe income taxes on the interest income that is passed through to a security holder? To clarify the situation and avoid double taxation that might diminish the availability of mortgage money, Congress approved the **Real Estate Mortgage Investment Conduit** concept in 1986. A REMIC is a tax device that allows cash flows from an underlying block of mortgages to be passed through to security holders without being subject to income taxes at that level. Thus the interest income is taxed only to the security holder, not to the trustee or agent handling the pass-through of cash. Various requirements must be met to establish a REMIC and reports on its activities, which are handled by the issuer of the security involved, must be made to the IRS.

MORTGAGE PARTNERSHIP FINANCE PROGRAM (MPF)

In 1997 the Federal Home Loan Bank System started the Mortgage Partnership Finance program to fund mortgage loans through the Chicago FHLBank to its member institutions in Illinois and Wisconsin. The program was well received and in 1999 the Federal Housing Finance Board, which oversees the

FHLBanks, authorized an expansion of the program to all 12 FHLBanks and raised the funding limit from $750 million to $9 billion systemwide.

While $9 billion represents only about 1 percent of the annual mortgage market in this country, the initial expansion comes from a huge financial resource. The FHLB System was created by Congress in the Depression years to help banks finance housing as one effort to restore the nation's economy. In the 1930s, banks were not too interested in making more mortgage loans as they had experienced substantial defaults. The FHLBanks found other kinds of investments and grew manyfold over the years of operation. Today, in net assets the FHLB System ranks second only to Fannie Mae.

The MPF represents an important incentive to regulated lenders to expand their efforts in the mortgage loan origination market. For a number of years, mortgage companies have expanded their market share of the residential mortgage market to well past 50 percent, dealing primarily through nonbank lenders and the sale of mortgages to federal agencies and private lenders to be securitized.

The MPF program allows the FHLBank to purchase mortgages from, or fund them through, its participating member institutions. The program is limited to fixed-rate mortgages on one- to four-family residences originated by such members. The size of eligible loans is limited to conforming loan limits.

The program is an alternative to selling these loans to a secondary-market agency and paying a guarantee fee. The FHLBank manages the funding, interest rate, liquidity, and prepayment risks associated with the loans. Participating lenders eliminate the interest rate risk of their fixed-rate loans while fully maintaining their customer relationships.

Questions for Discussion

1. Without a national mortgage exchange, how are mortgages traded in the United States?
2. Explain the relationship between the price and the yield on a mortgage loan.
3. Define the word *point,* how it is used, and list the different charges that can be quoted in points.
4. What market does Freddie Mac serve and how does it raise money for the purchase of mortgage loans?
5. How can tax-exempt bonds offer lower cost mortgage money and how is the money generally used?
6. Explain the two basic kinds of mortgage pools used to back securities and the two different methods used to generate the securities.
7. Explain the differences between a CMO and a mortgage pass-through-type of security.
8. Define a mortgage purchase "for portfolio."
9. Discuss the purpose and operation of Ginnie Mae.
10. What would be the price of a $100,000 loan if discounted by three points?

Chapter 6

The Mortgage Documents

KEY WORDS AND PHRASES

Redemption • *Lien theory* • *Principal* • *Mortgage* • *Promissory note* • *Prepayment* • *Acceleration* • *Assumption* • *Alienation clause* • *Due on sale* • *Hazard insurance* • *Ad valorem taxes* • *Deed of trust* • *Open-end mortgage* • *Construction loan* • *Junior mortgage* • *Purchase money mortgage* • *Package mortgage* • *Blanket mortgage* • *Contract for deed* • *Equitable title* • *Recording* • *Subordination*

INTRODUCTION

Loans made with real estate as the collateral security can be traced back as far as the ancient Pharaohs of Egypt and the Romans of the pre-Christian era. Even then, some form of pledge or assignment of the property was used to ensure repayment of an obligation to the lender. The development over many centuries of this type of property assignment illustrates the interplay of individual rights, more specifically, the rights of a borrower as against the rights of a lender.

HISTORY AND DEVELOPMENT

In its earliest concept, the mortgage instrument as security for a loan actually granted title to the collateral property to the lender to assure repayment. As time passed, and the means to borrow became more prevalent, the rights of borrowers became a concern and some modifications were made. Another form of mortgage pledge was introduced that granted the lender a lien on property pledged as collateral. This meant primarily that foreclosure would be subject to a court's determination. Both basic forms of mortgage pledges are in use today and are discussed next.

The Mortgage as a Grant of Title

Initially, a loan secured by real estate involved granting legal title to the lender. During the term of the loan, the lender might even have the physical use of that land and was entitled to any rents or other revenues derived therefrom. The borrower held equitable rights to the property which meant that title must be returned upon satisfactory repayment of the loan. However, due to the primitive conditions of communication and transportation then in existence, the practice of granting title to property for a loan tended to foster some abuses by lenders. For example, a slight delay in payments, which might even be encouraged by the lender, could easily create a default and forfeit the borrower's rights for any recovery of the land. Dispossession could be made without notice, and there was no return of money already paid to the lender.

Sometimes borrowers who felt they had been unjustly deprived of their property appealed to the king, or perhaps to an appointed minister, to seek a hearing for their grievances and to petition for just redress. And if it was subsequently determined that a wrong had been committed, the borrower might be given a chance to redeem the land with a late payment of the obligation. Thus the right of **redemption** came into being.

However, lenders were not happy with this redemption privilege and initiated a countermove by inserting a clause in future loan agreements that specifically waived the right of redemption. The borrower had to accept this clause or be denied the loan. As civilization progressed from the unchallenged rule of an absolute monarch into written codes of law, the granting or refusal of redemption became a matter of law called *statutory redemption*. This right to redemption of property after foreclosure action has passed from medieval times and is now incorporated in the laws of about half the states. Redemption periods vary among the states from three months to two years.

The Mortgage as a Lien

As modern law has developed, rights of borrowers became a greater concern and most states have adopted the **lien theory** for a mortgage pledge. With this method, the borrower retains legal title to the property and grants a lien to the lender as security for repayment of a loan. In law, to *hypothecate* property is to pledge it as security for an obligation without surrendering possession of it,

A *lien* constitutes an encumbrance on property. It is a declaration of a claim to a parcel of land for some purpose and is recorded in the public record. In states where the lien form of mortgage is prevalent, a defaulted borrower retains possession and legal title until the lien is perfected through court action by the lender.

The mortgage as a lien shifts considerable power from the lender to the borrower and can cause problems. It is possible for defaulted borrowers to remain in possession of the property for substantial periods of time without making loan payments. Coupled with statutory redemption periods, the result has been numerous problems for lenders trying to recover their losses within a reasonable period of time. Some states have modified borrower's rights under the lien theory and allow lenders to take possession of collateral property in the event of a loan default without waiting for the conclusion of foreclosure proceedings.

While there is obvious variation in the precise usage of the lien as a form of pledge, and the limited assignment of title as another form of pledge, mortgages can be classified into either of the two. The advantages and disadvantages can be weighed as legal arguments, but for purposes of finance, it is important mainly to be aware of the existing differences and to know under what laws a particular property can be mortgaged. Lenders have learned to live with various requirements and can obtain adequate security for their loans by adapting mortgage pledges to the state specific laws. Recognizing these differences, the conforming loan documentation required by Fannie Mae and Freddie Mac varies the mortgage instrument for each state.

STATE LAWS CONTROL PROPERTY RIGHTS

Property rights in the United States are spelled out primarily under state laws, not by the federal government. Each state has written into its code of law specific rights and procedures that must be adhered to with regard to land ownership and its conveyance. The local variations and shadings in these laws reflect the background and origins of the particular region. In the East, for example, the great body of English parliamentary law and common law guided the New England and mid-Atlantic states in setting up their constitutions and subsequent statutes. In the South, on the other hand, the French legal codes were reflected in the Louisiana Territory and were especially evident in the growing city of New Orleans. In still another section of the country, the Southwest, Spanish heritage colored the laws recognizing Catholic religious ties in marriage as well as patriarchal protection of wife, children, and family relationships. One result was community property statutes that give special protection for both parties to a marriage.

The Mortgage Instrument

While the broad field of real property law exceeds the scope of this text, it should be pointed out that a mortgage is a conveyance instrument as it transfers certain property rights. The transfer of property rights should be handled by qualified attorneys, skilled in interpreting these rights according to the laws of each state. Most states limit any conveyance of property rights solely to written agreements, and all states require certain procedures to record conveyances of land in the public records. One result has been an increasingly accurate record of land titles, with a corresponding increase of protection for property owners' rights and those of other interested parties.

Some basic instruments used in real estate loans have essentially the same purpose throughout the country. One of these, the **mortgage,** is the pledge of collateral that has given its name to the entire field of real estate finance. A mortgage is simply a pledge of property to secure a loan. It is not a promise to pay anything. As a matter of fact, without a debt to secure, the mortgage itself becomes null and void by its own terms, or, as the French derivative of the word *mortgage* indicates, a "dead pledge." Due to the differences in state laws, the precise definition varies somewhat, but for our purposes a mortgage can best be defined as a conditional conveyance of property as security for the debt recited therein, which can only be activated by failure to comply with its terms.

The Promissory Note

The **promissory note** is a debt instrument. It creates the obligation to repay a loan. Both promissory notes and mortgage instruments must contain certain standard words and phrases to assure the accomplishment of their purposes. Nevertheless, the balance of the terms and conditions can be worded however the individual attorney preparing the documents deems proper. Obviously, the variations could be substantial and, in years past, this made the selling of conventional mortgage loans very difficult. HUD/FHA and VA have always required their standardized forms to be used if the loan is underwritten by these agencies. But there was no such requirement for conventional loans, meaning those not underwritten by government agencies such as FHA and VA. Conventional loans underwritten by federal agencies, such as Fannie Mae, are known as conforming loans as they must meet, or conform, to the requirements set by the underwriting agencies.

CONFORMING LOANS

In 1970, Fannie Mae was authorized to purchase residential conventional loans. Prior to that time, it was limited to purchasing only HUD/FHA and VA loans. To buy conventional loans from lenders across the country, standards were needed. To develop standards, Fannie Mae worked in cooperation with Freddie Mac to create a series of uniform conventional mortgage documents. Since both entities are quasi-government, public hearings were required before formal approval could be given. Consumer advocates participated in the hearings to help decide what should and should not be included in these important documents.

No single mortgage form could be used throughout the country because of variations in state property laws. So the result of this work has been a series of standardized mortgage instruments designed specifically to meet each state's requirements. Conforming mortgage instruments contain a section that covers universal standards and another section that covers state-specific requirements.

However, promissory notes are unilateral promises to pay and convey no property rights, so there are fewer differences between the states' laws. This has allowed greater standardization of promissory note instruments with one note serving a number of states as a "multistate" document. Examples of a note and a mortgage instrument are reproduced in the Appendix of this text.

The work begun in 1970 to create uniform mortgage documents for residential loans has formed the basis for a standardized conventional loan known as a *conforming loan*. Besides uniform documents, a conforming loan must meet Fannie Mae/Freddie Mac standards for qualification of borrowers, preparation of an appraisal, and limits on the dollar amount of a loan. As a standardized conventional loan, the conforming loan has achieved wide acceptance. Since both agencies are always in the market to purchase loans, albeit at their own yield requirements, many primary-market lenders adhere to conforming loan standards to make sure their loans can be sold when money is needed.

While the preparation of mortgage instruments is certainly a legal matter, real estate agents are involved with them in negotiations. So there are a number of important points for the layman to understand. For this purpose, the following discussion is generalized.

Promissory Note

As stated earlier, the promissory note is a debt instrument. It is a written promise by a person, or persons, to pay a sum of money to another. It is almost always a separate instrument but is sometimes included as a part of the mortgage document. The Uniform Commercial Code sets standards for drafting an enforceable and negotiable promissory note.

If in foreclosure, the collateral securing the note (as pledged by the mortgage instrument) proves insufficient to cover the indebtedness, the holder of the note may obtain a deficiency judgment against the debtor for the balance due (state laws vary as to borrower's and lender's rights in a claim for deficiency judgment). If the note is labeled "nonrecourse," the borrower cannot be held personally liable on the note.

Use of the wording "or order" or "or bearer" in defining the payee is important as it is these words that make it possible for the note to be endorsed and transferred, thus becoming negotiable. Most mortgage promissory notes are negotiable to allow transfer to secondary-market investors. If the note is negotiable, only one copy should be executed. If other copies are made, the note maker may initial them, but should not sign them.

Mortgage Instrument

A conforming loan mortgage instrument is divided into two major sections: (1) uniform covenants that are standard across the country and (2) nonuniform covenants that cover special requirements of state law. While some of the details vary, the underlying purposes of mortgage covenants are very similar and are discussed next.

Parties Involved

The mortgage instrument must identify the names of all parties involved with an ownership interest in the property being mortgaged. They may not be the same as those obligated on the promissory note. Since the mortgage is a conveyance-type instrument, it is necessary to have all of the owners indicate agreement by signature. The rules of contract law apply to mortgages, so they must be in writing, and the parties must be legally competent to contract. Whether or not the marital status of the parties involved needs to be stated depends upon state law. If the parties are married, both signatures may be required, as marital rights, homestead rights, and/or community property rights may be involved.

Identification of Property

Identification of the property offered as collateral to secure the promissory note must be accurately described so as to distinguish it from any other property in the world. A street address is never acceptable as it can be changed over the years. Nor are boundary lines based on physical features, such as the "big live oak by the river bend," acceptable as long-term identification. Several methods are used to legally define real property. One is by "metes and bounds" which uses a surveyor's description of boundary lines from a fixed starting point, thence proceeding in specific compass directions and distances around the property back to the starting point. In urban areas, the most common method is by a "lot and block" description taken from a subdivision plat which must be registered and approved by a local government authority. A third method, found mostly in western states, is by geodetic survey. By this method, large tracts of land were surveyed, marked by stakes in the ground, and designated by townships of 36 square miles which can be used to identify land. Legal description of real property is more fully explained in Chapter 10, "Property Analysis."

An erroneous description of the property, even a typographical error, can render the mortgage instrument void but does not necessarily invalidate the promissory note. If a loan has been funded and the promissory note properly signed, there is an obligation to repay whether or not the mortgage is valid. If the mortgage is not valid, a properly signed and funded note becomes an unsecured obligation.

Principal Amount Due

Most mortgage notes are paid on an installment plan, wherein each payment includes all the interest due to that payment date, plus a portion of the principal due. Thus, with each payment, the total amount owed is reduced. When mortgage notes are transferred, only the principal balance then due can be conveyed. Business practice places confidence in the seller of a note to deliver accurate information on the precise balance due at the time of transfer. However, when a large commercial loan is transferred, some kind of legal assurance of the amount conveyed is usually required.

Estoppel. The term *estoppel* is sometimes applied to a mortgagee's information letter. This letter is a statement from the mortgage lender to the borrower giving information on the current status of that loan, including the amount of principal balance then due. Such information is normally obtained as part of the property listing process. An older practice, and one still used sometimes with large commercial loans, is to require an estoppel agreement when a note is transferred. The purpose of the agreement is an acknowledgment by both borrower and lender of the loan amount due at that time. In effect, it "stops" a subsequent purchaser of the note from claiming any greater amount. The legal doctrine of estoppel has a broader application in that it prevents a person from asserting rights that are inconsistent with a previous position.

Prepayment Penalty

If all or part of the principal balance of a loan is paid before it becomes due, there is a possible additional charge involved. The purpose of the **prepayment** penalty (some lenders call it a prepayment premium) is to allow the lender to recoup a portion of the interest that the lender had expected to earn when the loan was made. The following example serves to explain the lender's viewpoint.

....

EXAMPLE

A loan of $100,000 for 30 years at 9 percent interest is expected to earn the lender $189,670.40 in interest over the life of the loan. (Monthly payment $804.64 times 360 payments equals $289,670.40. The principal is $100,000; the balance is interest.)

....

Lenders do not loan money for the purpose of recovering the principal. There is a contractual right to the interest and some claim to compensation for a forfeiture of this right.

On the other hand, the borrower views the repayment as placing cash in the hands of the lender that can easily be loaned to another and continue to earn interest plus additional origination fees. So there is no compensable loss to the lender.

In mortgage instruments today, there are a variety of compromises on these conflicting views. First, no prepayment charges are permitted on HUD/ FHA, VA, or conforming loans. On other residential loans the prepayment penalty might range from 1 to 3 percent of the loan amount that is prepaid. For instance, if the charge is 3 percent and the amount prepaid is $20,000, the borrower would owe an additional $600 at time of prepayment. Another fairly common solution to the prepayment question, sometimes found in commercial loans, is to allow up to 20 percent of the original loan amount to be prepaid in any one year with no additional charge. Under this option, the borrower could repay the loan in full within five years at no extra cost. Prepayment requirements must be clearly specified in the loan documents.

Lock-in Provisions. Another kind of prepayment requirement found in some commercial loans is the "lock-in." Commercial loans do not fall under the same kind of regulatory protection for borrowers that can be found in residential loans, making it easier for lenders to set harsher terms. A lock-in is one example. What it does is lock in the interest charge for a certain minimum number of years. For example, a loan for an apartment project might require all interest to be paid for the first eight years of the loan term. Prepayment at any time during the first eight years would cost all interest otherwise due for that time period and most likely would make any prepayment too costly.

Acceleration Clause

The **acceleration** clause in a mortgage instrument, or promissory note, gives a lender the right to call the entire balance due, in full, in advance of due date upon the occurrence of a default. This is most likely to be a failure to make timely payments. But there are other kinds of defaults that could trigger an acceleration clause, including destruction of the premises, placing an encumbrance on the property, or its unauthorized sale or assignment. It is a very important clause in an installment obligation, as without it the alternative could be to foreclose each month as the payments actually come due.

Right to Sell–Due-On-Sale Clause—Assumption

As a general rule, mortgaged property can be freely sold by the owner, or mortgagor, either with an assumption of the existing debt by the new buyer or, if that is not permitted, by paying off the balance due on the existing mortgage. The popularity of loan **assumptions** follows the rise or fall of interest rates; in a period of increasing rates, an older, lower interest loan is attractive to a potential buyer. Looking back, in 1982 the contract rate on mortgage loans as reported by regulated savings associations reached 15.01 percent. In the following 15 years, contract rates slowly declined to nearly 7 percent and have remained fairly stable since then. Obviously, assumption of older, higher interest loans has not been so attractive.

Nevertheless, it is a subject worth examining as rates could move upwards once again, and an assumption might be practical for reasons other than a saving on interest cost. Prior to about 1980, mortgage instruments did not always include specific language as to the right-to-sell and assumptions. When interest rates began to escalate in the late 1970s and assumptions became very popular, lenders took the position that any change in collateral ownership gave them the right to allow assumptions only at higher interest rates. Borrowers countered that an increase in interest rates restricted their right to sell. The contention was that this amounted to an unreasonable restraint on the owner's right to sell. In legal terminology, this restraint on a sale is called a *restraint on alienation* (meaning the right to transfer an interest in real estate to another). Thus, a right-to-sell clause in a mortgage is sometimes referred to as the **alienation clause.**

Most states prohibit any unreasonable restraint on alienation—a limitation that has been mostly concerned with discrimination. For example, a restrictive covenant in a property deed that forbids any sale to a female would be classed as an unreasonable restraint on the owner's right to sell. The question of whether or not a lender's right to increase an interest rate on an assumption, or otherwise deny the right to sell, amounts to an unreasonable restraint was the subject of much controversy and court battles during the early 1980s.

In 1982 the U.S. Supreme Court[1] decided that a federally chartered institution does have the right to enforce a **due-on-sale** provision rather than accept a loan assumption. Since then the practice has been for assumption of a conventional loan to be cleared with the lender before any title is conveyed.

Mortgage instruments now carry more specific language regarding the lender's right to change an interest rate, or call the loan due, in the event of an assumption effort. The uniform mortgage for Fannie Mae/Freddie Mac-conforming loans uses broad terminology to apply its "due-on-sale" provision. Covenant 17 is entitled "Transfer of the Property or a Beneficial Interest in Borrower" and simply prohibits any such transfer of interest without prior written consent of the lender. Failure to comply can result in a call for immediate payment of the entire loan balance. Both FHA and VA have limitations on assumptions that vary by date of loan origination as more fully described in Chapter 8.

One further point: Even though there have been some rational arguments on both sides of the assumption/due-on-sale issues, there is no obligation on the part of any lender to allow a loan assumption today. However, there is a need to disclose this fact in the loan agreement. This is particularly important when a home seller helps finance the sale of a house. Home sellers are not normally in the business of making loans and can include a more stringent clause simply forbidding any loan assumption; that is, if the buyer subsequently resells the house, the existing loan must be paid in full.

Property Insurance

If a building is included in the mortgage pledge, rather than only raw land, the mortgage will require property insurance coverage for both the lender's and borrower's protection. This is also termed **hazard insurance.** Principally, it includes fire and extended coverage and is required by the lender in an amount at least equal to that of the loan (even though the loan amount usually includes the value of the land). To make certain that collateral property is insured, the lender generally requires a full year's paid-up insurance policy before releasing loan proceeds. To assure future payment of premiums, the lender requires two months of the annual premium paid into an escrow account as a cushion at closing. (The Real Estate Settlement Procedures Act, RESPA, limits this escrow cushion to not more than two month's premium.) Then, added to each monthly payment, one-twelfth of the annual premium must be paid. The original policy is held by the lender, and it is part of the lender's servicing responsibility to maintain the coverage with timely payments from the borrower's escrow account.

---

[1] *Fidelity Federal Savings and Loan Association v. de la Cuesta*, June 28, 1982.

Minimum Requirement for Hazard Insurance. Insurance companies in most states must comply with another requirement controlling the minimum amount of coverage that can be carried to establish full repayment in case of a partial loss. Since most fire losses are partial in extent, it is not unusual for a property owner to want to carry only partial coverage, hoping that any fire would be brought under control before the damage exceeds the amount of insurance coverage. To distribute the cost of insurance more equitably over all policyholders, insurance company regulators set some minimum standards for coverage. So insurance companies generally include a required minimum coverage if the policyholder expects full recovery for a partial loss.

Such a clause will require an amount of insurance coverage not less than a given percentage of the actual cash value of the building at the time of loss. These clauses are known variously as *coinsurance clauses, average clauses,* or *reduced rate contribution clauses.* A common minimum amount of insurance to assure full payment of partial losses is 80 percent of the actual cash value of the building at the time of loss. By carrying less than the minimum percentage of insurance, the property owner cannot collect in full for a loss but will have to bear a part of the loss personally.

If coverage is below the required minimum, the insurance company's liability is limited to the same percentage of the loss as the amount of insurance carried bears to 80 percent of the actual cash value. The insurance company's liability may be expressed by the formula:

$$\frac{C}{R} \times L = A$$

where

C = the amount of insurance carried
R = the amount of insurance required
L = the amount of the loss
A = the amount for which the insurance company is liable

Example:

$$\frac{65,000}{90,000} \times 40,000 = 28,800$$

In areas of the country where property values undergo substantial increases, any failure to maintain proper insurance coverage can expose the lender as well as the property owner to uninsured losses.

Disbursement of Hazard Insurance Proceeds. Another insurance problem to be considered with mortgaged property involves determining just how the proceeds should be paid in case of an actual loss. Earlier mortgages required payment of the insurance money to the lender, who in turn decided how to apply the funds; that is, whether to permit the funds to be used for restoration of the property, the usual procedure for smaller losses, or to apply the proceeds to payoff of the loan. Today, most residential mortgage instruments give the borrower a stronger position in the distribution of insurance proceeds, as is apparent in the Fannie Mae/Freddie Mac conforming mortgage covenants. This instrument, in Covenant 5, states: "Insurance proceeds shall be applied to restoration or repair of the Property damaged, if the restoration or repair is economically feasible and Lender's security is not lessened."

Flood Insurance

Property located in a flood-prone area serving as collateral for a loan handled by a federal-related institution or agency must carry flood insurance. The requirement stems from the 1994 National Flood Insurance Reform Act which became effective as of September 23, 1995. This act places responsibility on the *lender* to force-place the necessary insurance if it is required and the borrower fails to buy the coverage. The borrower is allowed 45 days to purchase the required insurance when notified by the lender. The lender may rely on information provided by the Director of the Federal Emergency Management Agency (FEMA) stating whether or not the building is in a special flood hazard area.

This is not the first effort of the government to require flood insurance. The Flood Insurance Act of 1968 provided federal subsidies to make flood insurance available on a national basis through private insurance companies. In addition, subsidies were established to encourage state and local governments to adopt and enforce land use control measures that limit development in flood-prone areas.

The Flood Disaster Protection Act of 1973 imposed stricter rules. It required communities to participate in the insurance program as a condition for receiving federal financial assistance. And it required property owners in flood hazard areas to purchase flood insurance as a condition for obtaining financing through a federally regulated, supervised, or insured financial institution. Even though the requirements included carrying flood insurance in an equal amount to the outstanding loan balance for the full term of the loan, compliance was not good. Many borrowers simply stopped paying premiums during the term of the loan.

The 1994 act makes nonpayment more difficult. Lenders and servicers must escrow flood insurance premiums for covered loans along with taxes and other insurance premiums. This places both a responsibility and a liability on lenders to make sure loan collateral in flood-prone areas is insured for at least the loan amount.

Property Taxes

Property tax, also known as **ad valorem tax** (according to value tax), becomes a specific lien on real property on the date the tax is assessed by an authorized taxing authority. Release of lien is automatic upon payment of the tax. Tax records are normally filed in each county as a separate section of information. Property subject to tax (some land is exempt) must stand good for its payment. If the tax is not paid, the property is subject to foreclosure by the state. In some states an assessment by a properly authorized neighborhood maintenance association carries the same status as a property tax. A tax assessment is a high priority claim in a foreclosure action, preceded only by the administrative costs of the sale. Thus, property taxes hold a higher priority than other secured claimants regardless of the date their claims are recorded.

This means property taxes take precedence over a first mortgage lien even though the mortgage may be filed of record earlier. For this reason lenders normally require the protection of handling tax payments as a part of the escrow requirements. To accomplish this, a cushion of one-sixth of the annual tax is usually deposited with the lender at loan closing. In addition, the tax escrow at closing includes that amount of taxes that have accrued to that date (payable by the buyer or seller as may be owed by each). Then, one month (one-twelfth of the annual amount due) of taxes is added to each monthly payment of the mortgage loan. Once the money is in escrow, the lender is responsible for making tax payments directly to the tax authority as part of its loan servicing function.

Federal Tax Claims. A tax claim by the federal government is considered a general lien,[2] but only when it is filed of record. While a taxpayer may be delinquent in payment of taxes, such debt is not a lien until a claim is recorded. Such a lien may be assessed against any taxpayer's property, real or personal and, under the federal claim of supremacy, would carry a higher priority than a property tax or a mortgage lien in a foreclosure proceeding. However, the property tax would not necessarily be satisfied in such a foreclosure action; it simply rides with the land as a continuing claim unless title actually passes to the federal government.

Another problem has surfaced regarding federal tax liens: If a buyer has a federal lien against him or her, it would become a prior claim on any property acquired. As a result, title companies are now checking tax records for any such liens on the buyer and the seller.

MORTGAGE VARIATIONS

The underlying purpose of the mortgage instrument is to provide a pledge of property as collateral to secure a promissory note. To properly serve the needs of lenders and borrowers, there are variations in how loans are used that create differences in the wording of mortgage instruments. This is not the same as the special differences that derive from how a mortgage is repaid, which is considered in the next chapter. The principal kinds of mortgages are identified next to distinguish their purposes and unique features.

Regular Mortgage

A regular mortgage is a two-party legal document used to secure performance of an obligation. The borrower is the "mortgagor" who grants certain rights to

[2]A *general lien* is a claim against all assets of the target of the lien; a *specific lien* is a claim against one specific asset, such as a tract of land.

the lender (the "mortgagee") that pledges property as collateral. The rights granted may be in the nature of a lien or a conditional grant of title. Foreclosure with a regular mortgage is usually handled through court action. The mortgage is a conveyance instrument and creates rights in real property. It should be recorded.

Deed of Trust

A **deed of trust,** sometimes called a *trust deed,* is a mortgage in which title to property is conditionally conveyed to a third-party *trustee* as security for an obligation owed to the lender, who is called the *beneficiary.* The trustee can be an individual (usually an attorney), a trust company, or a title insurance company as selected by the lender. The trustee in this instrument is normally granted the right to undertake foreclosure through its "power of sale" clause. The procedure can be implemented without benefit of court action. In the event of a default, the lender notifies the trustee to request that action be taken to protect the lender's interest. The trustee then notifies the debtor in accordance with the state law that foreclosure is pending. On the date of foreclosure, the trustee offers the property to the highest bidder and has the authority to deliver title to the property in a nonjudicial action. In those states that allow it, the procedure is much faster and at lower cost than a judicial procedure, which requires court action to convey title in a foreclosure action.

Open-End Mortgage

The **open-end mortgage** sets a limit to the amount that may be borrowed and allows incremental advances up to that amount secured by the same mortgage. It reduces closing costs and appraisal costs. Nevertheless, new money advanced under an open-end mortgage may be at a different, current rate of interest. This type of mortgage is often used in farm loans to meet seasonal needs, much like a line of credit. By maintaining some balance due on the mortgage obligation, the priority of the mortgage lien can be retained. Even so, it is a good idea for the lender to require a title search when an incremental advance is made, as certain claims, such as property taxes, can create a higher priority claim than the mortgage.

Construction Loan

A **construction loan** is short-term to cover the costs of building. It is sometimes called an "interim" loan although that term describes a broader range of loans. A construction loan differs from other mortgage loans in that it is funded through periodic advances as construction progresses. The loan may be funded by either of two different methods: (1) after certain stages of construction are completed or (2) after certain time periods, such as each month, for work completed up to that point. It takes a construction-wise loan officer to ensure that funds are released as the building progresses. In this way, the value of the building as collateral increases at approximately the same rate as the amount of the loan. Nevertheless, the risk of a construction loan lies in the ability of the borrower/builder to complete the project within the budget—the total amount of money available to do so. Failure to complete the building precludes release of the permanent loan from which the construction loan most likely expected repayment. (For additional information, see Chapter 11.)

Interim Loan

The term *interim* is often used synonymously with the term *construction loan*. While jargon varies somewhat, an interim loan has a broader meaning. It is any loan that is expected to be repaid from the proceeds of another loan. To better illustrate the meaning, compare this with other kinds of loans. For instance, a home loan is expected to be repaid from the borrower's personal income; an income property loan is expected to be repaid from income derived from the property itself. So an interim loan is expected to be repaid from other borrowed money. An interim loan is sometimes used for short-term financing until regular financing has been completed. When used for this purpose, the financing is also called a *gap loan* or a *bridge loan*. Since most construction loans are made with the expectation of repayment from a permanent loan when the building is completed, they easily qualify as an interim type of financing.

Mortgage with Release Clauses

When money is borrowed for the purpose of land development, it is necessary to have specific release procedures to enable the developer to sell lots, or a portion of the land, and deliver good title to that portion. This is the purpose of a release clause. The conditions are structured so that a developer can repay a portion of the loan and obtain a release of a portion of the collateral from the original mortgage. In a subdivision of building lots, loan repayment would be based on a percentage of the sales price of the lot or a minimum dollar amount for each lot released. The lender normally calculates partial payoffs so that the loan would be fully repaid when around 60 to 80 percent of the lots are sold.

With regular mortgages, partial sale of the collateral is normally not an option. So a development loan requires considerable negotiation to work out all the details necessary for success. The lender will want some control over the direction of development; that is, lots must be completed and sold in an orderly manner that will not undermine the value of any remaining land. A time pattern must be negotiated to allow realistic limits on how fast lots must be sold. The clause that permits release of a portion of the mortgaged land is also called a *partial release clause,* since the remainder of the land continues to be held as security for the remaining balance on the loan.

Junior Mortgage

The term **junior mortgage** applies to those mortgages that carry a lower priority than the prime or first mortgage. These can be second, third, or even fourth mortgages. The lower priority carries higher risk and requires corresponding higher interest rates. No mortgage instrument carries a designation in its title or text describing its lien position. The order of lien priority, which determines the exact order of claims against a piece of property, is established by the time of its recording. This becomes of extreme importance in a foreclosure proceeding.

••

EXAMPLE

Say a property valued at $50,000 carries a first mortgage for $30,000 and a second mortgage for $8,000. If this property is forced into a foreclosure sale that results in a recovery of $35,000 in cash after payment of court costs and legal fees, how should the money be distributed? The priority of liens controls and, assuming that no other liens, taxes, or otherwise have shown priority, then the first-mortgage holder is in a position to recover the full $30,000 from the $35,000 proceeds. The remaining $5,000 is awarded to the second-mortgage holder, leaving that payment $3,000 short of recovering the $8,000 loan. Due to the promissory note, the second-mortgage holder may have a right to seek a deficiency judgment against the borrower to recover that $3,000. However, the land serving as collateral has been wiped out by the foreclosure.

••

Later in this chapter, the subject of recording, as related to the question of establishing priority of mortgage liens, will be discussed in more detail.

Purchase Money Mortgage

A **purchase money mortgage** is one taken by the seller of property as all or part of the consideration. Such a mortgage carries certain priorities over other claims. This is possible because the delivery of a deed occurs simultaneously with the taking back of the purchase money mortgage, allowing no time for any other lien to intervene. A purchase money mortgage of this kind carries the special status of a vendor's lien. A *vendor's lien* may be defined as an equitable lien of the grantor upon the land conveyed. It is an implied right held by a seller until all purchase money due the seller is repaid. Also, depending on state law, a defaulting buyer may or may not be subject to a deficiency judgment upon default of a purchase money mortgage.

A second definition of a *purchase money mortgage* is one where the loan proceeds are used exclusively to buy the property secured by that mortgage.

Chattel Mortgage

Chattel is tangible personal property and it can be mortgaged to secure a debt; thus, *chattel mortgage*. This procedure is more likely to be used when additional security is needed for a loan. Or it could be used as part of a loan on real property when it is important to identify certain personal property assets. In the acquisition of personal property, chattel mortgages have been replaced by the *bill of sale* as a security agreement that is regulated by the Uniform Commercial Code.

Package Mortgage

A **package mortgage** pledges both real and personal property to secure a loan. It is often found in the acquisition of a new house. The buyer/borrower includes in the collateral package a number of essential furnishings and appliances needed for the house, and is thus able to pay for them over an extended period of time. Most package mortgages also require the borrower to sign and file a financing statement in accordance with the provisions of the Uniform Commercial Code. A package mortgage normally calls for simple interest rather than add-on interest as found in many installment-type loans.

Blanket Mortgage

A mortgage is not limited to pledging a single parcel of land as collateral. Sometimes the security pledged for a loan may include several tracts of land. When more than one tract is pledged, the security instrument is called a **blanket mortgage.**

"Subject to" Mortgage

In the conveyance of property, it is possible for title to be delivered *subject to* an existing mortgage. The phrase has a legal intent and means that the buyer is not accepting personal liability to the lender for payment of that mortgage note. It in no way changes the claim of a lender holding the mortgage; it simply means that the new buyer does not accept the liability. It also means that the new buyer's rights to the property could be wiped out if the grantor of the property fails to make mortgage payments. In the event of a default, the lender holds whatever rights were granted by the mortgage but has no additional right to pursue the new buyer for any deficiency. Such liability remains with the original debtor.

The "subject to" procedure may be used for a number of different transactions, such as when property is acquired for the purpose of rehabilitation and resale. Such a transaction does not create a contingent liability and would not be shown on a financial statement. However, "subject to" clauses are most commonly found when a wraparound mortgage is used (see next section).

It should be pointed out that transferring property with a "subject to" procedure is definitely a transfer of interest and could trigger a due-on-sale clause. This is true even though the loan itself is not assumed.

Wraparound Mortgage

A *wraparound mortgage* is a new mortgage that encompasses, or "wraps around," one or more existing mortgages and is subordinate to them. The purpose is to acquire additional funding from a loan while retaining the priority of lien of existing mortgages. In periods of escalating interest rates, this design has the additional benefit of retaining an older, lower interest rate loan which could benefit both buyer and seller.

The wrap procedure can be used when an owner borrows additional money with the wrap as a junior mortgage, or it can be used in financing the sale of property. While declining interest rates limit usage of this procedure, it carries some attraction for seller-financed transactions. Since seller financing entails a transfer of interest, the existing mortgage must be assumable in order to consummate a wrap procedure. This is true even though the property is transferred "subject to" an existing mortgage. Following is a hypothetical example of how a wrap might fit into a seller-financed transaction advantageous for both parties.

••

EXAMPLE

A property worth $150,000 has a mortgage with a $40,000 balance at 8 percent interest. In today's market, say new financing costs 10 percent.

To acquire the property, the buyer is willing to pay $20,000 down and is seeking $130,000 in financing. The buyer has three possibilities:

1. All new financing of a $130,000 first-mortgage loan at an interest rate of 10 percent.
2. Assume the existing loan of $40,000 and borrow the additional $90,000 (difference between 40,000 and 130,000) from a regular lender needed on a second-mortgage loan that would carry a higher interest rate of, say, 12 percent.
3. Arrange a wraparound loan with the seller for $130,000 at, say, 9 percent, that includes the existing $40,000 loan—net new cash is $90,000.

••

Further examination of the wrap procedure illustrated in the preceding example shows that it could be advantageous for both the buyer and seller. The advantage to the buyer, obviously, is lower cost (9 percent) financing than otherwise would be possible. For the seller accepting a wraparound mortgage, the advantage is 9 percent on the new funding of $90,000 plus 1 percent additional earned interest on the existing $40,000 loan that requires no new cash. The net yield to the seller would thus be greater than 9 percent. In effect, the buyer makes payment to the seller on a $130,000 loan at 9 percent interest, while the seller passes on payments to the existing mortgage holder on $40,000 at 8 percent interest.

Contract for Deed

A **contract for deed** is a sale and financing agreement that allows the purchase price of property to be paid in installments. It is not a mortgage although it is often misunderstood as one. Under a contract for deed, the buyer receives only the rights of possession and enjoyment, much the same as in a lease with option to buy. However, it is distinguished from a lease by the fact that a contract for deed grants the buyer an **equitable title** to the property during the payment period. This means that after a part, or all, of the payments have been made as agreed, the seller is obligated to deliver legal title to the property.

State law varies as to how it treats the buyer/borrower under a contract for deed. Some states grant the buyer certain rights to the property as payments are made. Others recognize only the ownership rights retained by the seller to the extent that such contracts may not even be recordable. So there are some pitfalls.

These are the risks that most concern a buyer:

1. The greatest risk for the buyer is that title is not delivered until after payment has been made. During the payment period, it is possible that the seller will become unable to perform. While legal title remains in the seller's name, it is subject to any adverse claim that may accrue against the seller. The seller may suffer a legal disability, file bankruptcy, or die. Or the seller may be a corporation with only limited liability for the directors and shareholders. Holding an executed deed in escrow pending final payment does not remove this risk because the deed would not be recorded.

2. If there is an underlying mortgage on the property, a payment escrow account should be used to assure the buyer that payments are properly made to the mortgage holder.

Next, the risks that concern a seller:

1. If a buyer defaults or becomes bankrupt there could be a problem of clearing title, which might be costly.

2. A contract for deed is subject to contract law that offers differing interpretations.

Although there are special problems with a contract for deed transaction, the procedure serves some valid purposes. One use is to allow someone who has difficulty qualifying for a mortgage loan to possess a home. A problem might arise if a person is laid off, then finds a new job but is unable to meet a lender's length of time on the job requirement. While the time requirement is met and a proper mortgage loan can be achieved, the buyer has possession of the home. Another possibility is when a property has a known title defect that is curable but will take time. The present condition of its title disqualifies the property as collateral. A contract for deed could convey possession, while allowing time for the title to be cleared. Once good title is achieved, a mortgage loan could then be obtained to pay off the seller.

Contracts for deed are often used in the sale of lots in resort areas. And they can be found when the purpose is to achieve a fast sale under high-pressure tactics. With legal title to the property held by the seller, there is less need to fully qualify a buyer. It is easier to push for a quick closing. And because title is not conveyed at closing, there appears to be less need to assure good title with a search of the abstract or require title insurance. This can be dangerous for an unwary buyer as title defects can just as easily interfere with a later delivery of title as with an immediate delivery.

Contracts for deed can be found under an assortment of names that cause some confusion for buyers. Among names that may be used are land contract, installment contract, agreement of sale, conditional sales contract, or even just real estate contract. Properly handled and in the right circumstances, a contract for deed is a practical procedure for transferring property. But legal counsel is urged before entering into such an agreement regardless of its name.

MORTGAGE PROCEDURES

Several important procedures are associated with mortgage instruments that merit further discussion. While legal practices do differ between the states, the purpose or reason for certain procedures is generally the same, as considered next.

Recording

Modern society protects land ownership with the help of its public records, which are open to anyone with an acceptable instrument to file. **Recording** is the act of entering into the public record a written instrument that affects title to property. There are other sets of public records separate from that for real estate that have a bearing on the quality of title to real estate. These include records regarding taxes, probate, marriage, and judgments.

State laws define what is necessary for an instrument to be recorded; generally, it must be in writing and properly acknowledged. The instrument must be recorded in the county in which the land is located. Recording a document gives constructive notice to the world of the existence of the document and its contents.

Failure to record a document does not invalidate the agreement between the parties thereto. Nor does such failure to record invalidate the agreement for any other parties who have notice of its existence. What recording laws state is that if a document is not recorded it generally is void as against any subsequent purchaser, lessee, or mortgagee acting in good faith who does not have knowledge of the unrecorded document. What this means, for one example, is that if a deed transferring property ownership is not recorded, the record title remains with the seller insofar as innocent third parties are concerned. In such an instance, a subsequent judgment against the seller could result in a valid claim against the property that has already been sold. Where does that leave the purchaser who did not bother to record the deed? Most likely with a difficult lawsuit and possible loss of the property to the judgment claimant.

One more point on the nature of recording: If a recorded document is, for some reason, void, recording does not make it valid.

Priority. From a practical point of view, recording gives priority to documents based on the time they are recorded; thus, a mortgage filed before another has a higher priority. However, there is a separate class of liens whose priority is not based on time of filing. This includes tax liens, mechanics liens, and special assessment liens that are a matter of public record. Property taxes become liens when assessed. This is not true of federal income and payroll taxes which must have claims filed of record to take a priority position as liens. One other way to alter the priority of a claim is a subordination agreement, which will be discussed in a later section.

Releases. Recording is so often thought of in terms of conveying property, or asserting a claim, that the reverse procedure is sometimes overlooked. It is also important to record a release when a claim has been satisfied. If a claim is based on a written document, so should the release be a written document.

Recording a release is most important when dealing with a mortgage. While it is true that payoff of a mortgage note voids the mortgage pledge, the document remains a matter of record and a cloud on the title unless released. Depending on state law, two releases may be needed. If there is a vendor's lien (a claim that derives from a purchase-money debt), a release is needed when that is paid off. And if there is another mortgage claim against the property it, too, requires a release.

Releases must be in a recordable form. Sometimes return of original lien instruments to the grantor, or the note marked "paid in full," are thought to satisfy release requirements. That kind of release is valid between the parties involved, but it takes recorded documents to actually clear title to property.

Subordination

Subordination is a method of altering the priority of claims to property by a written agreement. It is a method commonly used in development projects when the land is seller-financed, or even when the land is leased. In a typical transaction, the land seller would hold a purchase-money mortgage on the land sold. Then, to facilitate development, the land seller would agree to subordinate that mortgage in favor of a construction lender. This allows the developer/purchaser to obtain a first-mortgage loan to build the intended improvement. Thus, the subordination agreement alters the normal rule of giving priority to the mortgage that is recorded first.

If land is leased to a developer for a development project, rather than sold, the landowner could subordinate the fee in favor of a construction loan (or other mortgage claim). Technically, the fee cannot be subordinated to a leasehold mortgage; the procedure is more properly called *encumbering* the fee. But the end result is the same: The construction lender holds a prior claim on the property for repayment of the loan.

A subordination clause can be included in a mortgage instrument permitting a subsequent mortgage to take a higher priority. This is a fairly standard type of clause found in a junior mortgage when an existing prior mortgage is recognized in the junior instrument.

STANDARDIZING LOAN DOCUMENTATION

Documentation for residential loans has become more uniform throughout the country. Both regulators and the industry have worked to promote standard procedures. Uniform methods make it easier for consumers to better understand the process and it enables them to make more accurate comparisons between lenders. Standardization has become a necessity for loan pools where individual loans are assigned as collateral for securities and the cash flow from each must be accounted for. However, this is not true of commercial loans which are still mostly one of a kind types of transactions and are not subject to the regulations imposed on residential loans.

Three standardized instruments are now required for residential loan transactions. All three are mentioned here and examined in later chapters. The forms are reproduced in the Appendix of this text.

Uniform Residential Loan Application. The Equal Credit Opportunity Act imposed certain nondiscriminatory requirements that must be incorporated in all residential loan applications. The form used to implement the requirements is a modified version of Fannie Mae's Form 1003 and Freddie Mac's Form 65. It has undergone several revisions, with the most recent one made mandatory for use as of January 1, 1992.

Uniform Residential Appraisal Report (URAR). FIRREA established standards for appraisals that apply to federally regulated lenders. The requirements resulted in a revision of the URAR form made mandatory for use with certain loans after January 1, 1994. The form is required for all loans involving Fannie Mae, Freddie Mac, VA, and HUD/FHA. Also, the "Statement of Limiting Conditions and Appraiser's Certification" (Form 1004B) must be filed with each URAR appraisal after January 1, 1994. While all residential loans are not included in this mandate, it is a widely used document and another step toward standardization.

HUD-1 Settlement Statement. RESPA sets standards for closing all residential loans and a part of the requirements is the use of a HUD-1 Settlement Statement. The purpose is proper disclosure of information to a consumer/borrower.

It is an itemized listing of the consideration tendered in closing a transaction and how the money is distributed to the various parties to the transaction. HUD-1 is detailed in Chapter 16.

Conforming Loan

A conforming loan is one that can be purchased by Fannie Mae and Freddie Mac as it meets all of their requirements. It was introduced in 1972 and has become a widely used procedure for conventional loans. While neither Fannie Mae nor Freddie Mac are limited to purchasing only conforming loans, use of the procedures by loan originators avoids time-consuming examinations necessary for nonconforming or nonuniform documented loans.

Conforming loans require more than uniform documentation. To be acceptable a loan must also meet not-to-exceed loan limits which are set annually, plus property standards, and borrower qualification guidelines. In addition to use of the three standardized documents listed in the preceding section, Fannie Mae and Freddie Mac require use of their own forms for conforming loans as follows:

Verification of Employment

Verification of Deposit

A uniform state-specific mortgage instrument

A uniform promissory note that complies with state requirements

It is not uncommon to find conforming loan standards explained to a borrower as "government limits." And, in a general sense, they are, as both Fannie Mae and Freddie Mac are quasi-government agencies. But the limitations are not in the same class as a government regulation. The standards apply only if the loan originator sells the loan to either Fannie Mae or Freddie Mac.

Loan Document Mandate. In practice, loan originators retain considerable freedom in loan documentation as there are many secondary-market purchasers who do not require conforming loan standards. Basically, residential loans need only two mandated forms: (1) Uniform Residential Loan Application and (2) the HUD-1 Settlement Statement. Standardized documents become important when a loan originator wants to sell a loan; then it becomes necessary to meet the requirements of whomever purchases the loan.

Questions for Discussion

1. What procedure is used in your state to handle a pledge of collateral for a mortgage loan?
2. What is the purpose of a promissory note? Of a mortgage instrument?
3. In a foreclosure, how are priorities determined among lien claimants on the collateral property?

4. What is the underlying purpose of requiring a borrower to escrow money each month for payment of property taxes?

5. Identify the rights of borrowers and lenders in regard to assumptions.

6. Explain the differences between a regular mortgage and a deed of trust.

7. What is the principal risk for the buyer-borrower in a contract for deed?

8. Describe a conforming loan.

9. What is meant by the legal phrase "subject to"?

10. What is the purpose of recording documents?

Chapter 7

Mortgage Repayment Plans

KEY WORDS AND PHRASES

Amortization • Adjustable rate mortgage • Rate index • Caps • Margin • Graduated payment mortgage • Pledged-account mortgage • Buy-down mortgage • Balloon payment • Straight note • Shorter term loans • Biweekly payment • Growing equity mortgage • Home equity revolving loan • Shared appreciation mortgage • Shared equity mortgage • Reverse annuity mortgage • Home Equity Conversion Mortgage (HECM)

INTRODUCTION

Prior to the 1970s, the fixed-interest-rate, constant-level, fully amortized payment plan dominated mortgage lending. This orderly system began to change in the 1970s when the economy became unsettled with high inflation and interest rates, encouraging alternative methods of repaying mortgage loans. Today, with more stable conditions, fixed-interest-rate loans again dominate the market. But this could change again if interest rates rise. Alternative repayment plans are sometimes quite useful in helping a borrower qualify for a larger loan than fixed rates may allow or keep interest rates and payment amounts low for a short term. Alternative plans may make sales happen that otherwise wouldn't be.

Repayment plans can be classed as follows: (1) fixed-interest, constant-level plans, (2) adjustable rate mortgages, (3) graduated payment mortgages that allow lower early monthly payments, (4) mortgages that can reduce total interest cost, and (5) other alternative procedures. A discussion of each follows.

FIXED-INTEREST, CONSTANT-LEVEL PLAN

The repayment schedule for a fixed-rate loan involves a constant payment for the life of the loan. Each payment is calculated so that all interest due to payment date is included, plus a portion of the principal. The periodic reduction of the principal balance is called **amortization.** This mortgage design gives assurance to home buyers that the loan payment will not increase during the life of the loan. As mentioned earlier, by the 1970s it became obvious that more flexible repayment plans were needed to meet changing market requirements.

Nevertheless, the fixed-rate loan has remained a very popular design, holding well over half the new loan-origination market. This is true even though it is normally offered at interest rates about 2 percentage points higher than adjustable-rate mortgages. There are several reasons for its continuing popularity:

1. In periods of relatively low interest rates, borrowers are reluctant to commit to an adjustable-rate mortgage that might start increasing in cost. So the fixed rate offers a sense of protection.

2. The growing use of mortgage pools to raise lendable funds in the financial markets tends to encourage fixed-rate loans. One of the problems for an investor in a mortgage-backed security is the uncertainty of cash flows: How frequently will borrowers prepay the principal? When you add to that the uncertainty of an adjustable-rate pool of mortgages, the projection of an accurate return to the investor becomes even more difficult.

ADJUSTABLE RATE MORTGAGE (ARM)

An adjustable rate design allows a lender to make a change in the rate of interest at periodic intervals without altering other conditions of the loan agreement. The term **adjustable rate mortgage,** or ARM, is not always used in a precise manner. In media reports, the term has been used to indicate any mortgage wherein the payment amount can change. Another repayment plan, the graduated payment mortgage, offers changes in payment amounts but it is calculated on a very different basis and should not be confused with an ARM. With an adjustable mortgage, the interest rate can be changed; with a graduated design, the interest rate is fixed.

Adjustable rate mortgages are not new. Other free-world countries have wondered how the United States has been able to stick with fixed rates for so long. British mortgage lenders, called Building Societies, have offered only variable rate mortgages since 1932. Canada developed a pattern of short-term mortgage loans, such as five years, that allow a lender to renew the note when it comes due and to make an adjustment in the interest rate. This renewal type of note has become known as the *Canadian Rollover.*

When banking regulators first considered adjustable-rate mortgages they were concerned with the potential impact on home buyers of possible increases in payment amounts. So approval to write this kind of mortgage included constraints on how an interest rate could be adjusted. A change in the rate must be justified by tying the adjustment to change with a regulator-approved **rate index**—one not under control by the lender. The frequency of adjustment was limited to fixed time periods such as once a year. The interest rate change was limited at each time period and a ceiling was placed on the total amount of increase over the life of the loan. (In that time period interest rates were moving only one way—up.)

The first such design approved by the FHLBB in 1979 for federally chartered savings associations was called a *variable rate mortgage (VRM)*. The initial VRM design limited interest rate changes to a maximum of 0.5 percent per year and not more than 2.5 percent over the life of the loan. Even though the intent was to assist lenders, it was not widely accepted primarily because limitations on how much interest rates could be adjusted were too restrictive in an escalating market. Remember, no lender is required to make any kind of a loan. An "approved" mortgage plan only means that it is legal for a regulated lender to offer such a mortgage; the lender does not have to offer the plan.

Borrower Protection

The right to change an interest rate during the term of a mortgage loan can cause hardship for a borrower. Also, borrowers have been easily confused with indexes and how an adjustment might be calculated. Because both lenders and regulators are concerned over these problems, a number of protective measures have been added to residential ARM requirements. These go beyond simply limiting how interest rates can be changed. To better meet this need, the Federal Reserve Bank Board amended its Regulation Z (the Truth-in-Lending regulation), effective as of October 1, 1988. It requires lenders to provide more extensive information to consumers/borrowers on the characteristics of adjustable-rate mortgages. The rules have been adopted by federal agencies and other lending authorities and provide more uniform requirements. More specifically, the requirements fall into two categories: (1) up-front information and (2) subsequent disclosures, as explained next.

Up-Front Information Required

Certain information must be provided to the consumer at the time an application form is provided, or before a nonrefundable fee is paid, whichever comes first. The following information is required:

1. An educational brochure about ARMs must be given to the applicant. This can be either the *Consumer Handbook on Adjustable Rate Mortgages* published jointly by the Federal Reserve Bank Board and the Office of Thrift Supervision, or a suitable substitute.

2. The applicant must be shown by historical example how payments on a $10,000 loan would have changed in response to actual historical data on the index to be applied.

3. A statement must be given to the applicant showing the payment amount on a $10,000 loan at the initial interest rate (the most recent rate shown on the historical example), and the maximum possible interest rate that could apply to the loan during its term.

Subsequent Disclosure Requirements

Notices must be given to the borrower during the term of the loan showing any adjusted payment amount, interest rate applied, index rate, and the loan balance at the time of adjustment. This notification must be made once each year during which there is a rate adjustment whether or not there is a payment change. The notice must be mailed not less than 25 days, nor more than 120 days, before the new payment is due. Further, the disclosure must indicate the extent to which any increase in the interest rate has not been fully implemented (meaning how much the index rate plus margin would exceed the rate **cap**). The notice must also state the payment required to fully amortize the loan if that payment is different.

Following is a more detailed explanation of the meaning of these requirements.

Use of an Index

One of the major protections offered to borrowers who accept an ARM loan is that any change in the rate of interest must be tied to the change in an index. An index is a published rate or yield approved by the lender's regulatory authority. The rule applies to regulated lenders making residential loans. Unlike the well-known banker's prime rate of interest which is determined by each lender, an ARM index cannot be controlled by the lender. While a number of indexes have been approved by authorities across the country, four have achieved greater popularity. These are:

1. **Cost of funds.** The national median cost of funds is derived each month from reports of SAIF-insured savings associations as reported by the Office of Thrift Supervision. This figure is the average cost of all interest paid to depositors on passbook savings accounts, savings certificates, and certificates of deposit.

2. **Contract rate.** The national average contract interest rate for major lenders as reported by the Federal Housing Finance Board. Each month, insured savings institutions report the interest rate charged for mortgage loans made the previous month. The rate reported covers new and existing home loans.

3. **11th district cost of funds.** The cost of funds for the 11th district as released by the Office of Thrift Supervision in San Francisco. California is the largest single market for residential loans in the country.

4. **One-year Treasury securities.** The one-year constant maturity yield on U.S. Treasury securities as reported by the Federal Reserve Bank Board.

While it is a more volatile rate than the others, it is the one most used by Fannie Mae and Freddie Mac.

Historical Record of Indexes

To illustrate the differences that can be found in the most popular indexes, Table 7–1 gives a comparison.

Application of an Index

Indexes are applied differently. Of the four indexes described in the previous section, only the "contract rate" would normally be applied directly as the rate charged to the borrower. That is, if the contract rate indicated 7.26 percent in December 1994 (as shown in Table 7–1) at the time of loan origination, that would become the rate charged to the borrower. Assuming a one-year adjustment period, the rate shown in the index for December 1995 as 7.65 percent would apply for the second year. Then, for the third year, the rate would become 7.56 percent as shown in the table for December 1996. Lenders normally adjust these rates to the nearest quarter percent; thus, the 7.56 percent rate would become 7.50 percent for the new period.

TABLE 7–1   Historical Record of Indexes

Year*	Cost of Funds	Contract Rate	11th Dist. COF	1-yr. Treas. Securities
1983	9.90	11.94	10.192	10.11
1984	9.92	12.26	10.520	9.33
1985	8.48	10.70	8.867	7.67
1986	7.28	9.29	7.509	5.87
1987	7.11	8.86	7.645	7.17
1988	7.44	9.61	8.022	8.05
1989	7.73	9.69	8.476	7.72
1990	7.54	9.58	7.963	7.05
1991	6.25	8.25	6.245	4.38
1992	4.51	7.53	4.432	3.71
1993	4.44	7.41	4.305	3.43
1994	4.31	7.26	4.218	5.32
1995	4.38	7.65	4.329	5.94
1996	4.34	7.56	4.291	5.52
1997	4.39	7.26	4.314	5.63
1998	4.12	6.76	4.223	4.63

*Figures are as of December of each year.

Source: Mortgage Bankers Association, Economics Department.

Rate Based on Index Plus Margin. Indexes other than the contract rate as illustrated in the previous section require the addition of a **margin.** The margin is determined by the lender and it is not a regulated amount. Normally it amounts to 2 to 2 1/2 percentage points and is added to the index amount. The margin remains fixed for the life of the loan; it is the index that changes. The most widely used index today is the one-year Treasury security rate and its application is illustrated in the following example.

EXAMPLE

Using a one-year Treasury security rate as shown in Table 7–1 plus a 2 1/2 percent margin, applying it to a $100,000, 30-year loan, we show:

Loan Year	Index Rate	+	Margin	=	Rounded Rate	Remaining Term	Monthly Payment $100,000 Loan
1994 First	5.32		2.5%		7.75%	30 yrs.	$716.42
1995 Second	5.94		2.5		8.5	29 yrs.	768.92
1996 Third	5.52		2.5		8.0	28 yrs.	733.77

Rate Based on Index Movement. Another way to apply an index is to originate the loan with an agreed rate, then add or deduct the *movement* of an index.

Note: The initial rate charged is not a regulated or controlled rate. This allows the lender greater flexibility in setting an initial interest rate while still complying with the requirement to tie any change to a regulator-approved index. The following example applies the same index as used in the previous example. The difference is that an origination rate of 9 percent is applied rather than the 7.75 percent rate in the previous example. Then the change in the index each year is added or deducted from the previous year's rate.

EXAMPLE

Using the one-year Treasury security rate as shown in Table 7–1 and applying the movement of that index to a $100,000, 30-year loan that is originated at a 9 percent rate, the following higher monthly payments result.

			Movement of Index			
Year	Rate Last Year	Previous Rate	Present Rate	Percent Change	Rate Next Year	Monthly Payment
1994						
First					9.0%	$804.63
1995						
Second	9.0%	5.32%	5.94%	+.62%	9.5	840.86
1996						
Third	9.5	5.94	5.52	−.42	9.0	804.63

Obviously, there can be a difference in the rate and amount paid by a borrower even though the identical index is applied. The repayment clause in a mortgage document must be read very carefully. While disclosure of the key provisions is mandatory, the terminology can be confusing.

Regulations require that a rate be reduced if the index declines. However, an increase to match an index is optional for a lender. The fairly steady decline of index rates over the past decade has meant that homeowners with adjustable rate mortgages made lower payments almost every year. More recently, the expectation that interest rates may fluctuate upwards has discouraged many from undertaking adjustable rate loans.

Limitations on Changes (Caps)

Since the introduction of adjustable rate mortgages in the 1970s, there has been a shift in who sets limits on how much an interest rate might be changed during the life of a home loan. Initially, regulatory authorities were concerned with the potential of catastrophic increases in mortgage payments hurting both home buyers and lenders alike. Limitations were tight in the introductory years and happened to span the 1979–1981 time period when mortgage interest rates jumped about 2 percent each year during the three-year period. The result was little encouragement for lenders to offer the new designs. In the next year or two, regulators backed off the tight limitations in an effort to encourage the use of adjustable plans. Some caps were eliminated, others increased.

Since the design is basically a lender-benefit plan, lenders began to show more support for ARMs and recognized the inherent advantage of being able to adjust the rate on a long-term loan. Lenders realized that some of the risk of fluctuating rates was passed on to the borrower, and ARMs became competitive. Initial interest rates on ARMs were lowered to 1 1/2 to 3 percent less than rates on fixed-interest loans.

Burgeoning foreclosures in 1984 and 1985 brought renewed interest in limitations on rate changes, this time by lenders hurt from foreclosures. At the same time, secondary-market purchasers began to set limits on the kinds of ARM loans they would buy. While regulations vary, and lenders' self-imposed limitations vary, the caps center on the following four aspects of adjustable-rate plans:

1. **Periodic interest rate change.** Almost all ARM loans limit the amount of change that can be made at each adjustment period. A 1 percent cap is commonly used, but some plans permit 2 percent. If a 1 percent cap is applied it means that even though an increase in the index rate would allow, say, a 1 3/4 percent increase, the new rate can only be increased by 1 percent.

2. **Interest rate change over the life of loan.** Sometimes called a limit on "rate swings," a common cap is 5 percent but some use a 6 percent cap. This means that over the life of the loan, regardless of index fluctuation, the payment cannot be increased, and in some loans decreased, more than 5 percent (or 6 percent).

3. **Frequency of rate change.** This is a limit on how often a rate can be changed. It is a distinguishing feature of residential mortgage lending that does not permit a rate change every time the lender may want to do so. Federal regulations permit a change at least once a year, and up to once every five years. Some states permit changes as often as every six months. By far the most popular adjustment period is once a year.

4. **Mortgage payment amount.** A more recent popular limitation has to do with the payment amount itself. This kind of cap limits any increase in the payment amount to a percentage of the payment. The most common limit has become 7.5 percent. Thus, a $1,000 per month payment could not be increased to more than $1,075 in the second year, regardless of what the index might show on the interest rate.

Caveat. A very important point in regard to all limitations: The cap may apply to the amount the borrower pays during the year, but may not limit the amount owed. There is no real standard on how the limits may be applied. Thus, even though a rate change, or a payment amount, may show a specific limit on what the borrower pays, if the index shows a greater amount is actually due, the lender may add the unpaid amount to the principal balance. The procedure is another method of creating negative amortization. Fannie Mae, for one, will not buy this kind of loan. Like all other repayment conditions, this, too, must be disclosed and agreed to in the mortgage terms. Careful reading of these clauses becomes most important!

Another condition, of perhaps lesser concern, is the fact that some limitations apply to both increases and decreases in the application of an index. Thus, a 5 percent life-of-loan limit could stop a 13 percent loan from ever falling to less than 8 percent. This is not a big problem when market rates are in the 6 to 7 percent range!

GRADUATED PAYMENT MORTGAGE (GPM)

The **graduated payment mortgage** concept was first tested by the FHA as a method of allowing home buyers to pay lower initial monthly payments in the earlier years of a mortgage term, with payments rising in successive years to a level sufficient to amortize the loan within a 30-year term. With a lower initial monthly payment, the buyer with a lower income might qualify for a loan, or conversely, be able to buy a larger house with the same income.

An added requirement for qualification is that the borrower must show reasonable expectation of an increase in annual income so as to meet the annual increase in monthly payments. It was this near-impossible prediction of continuing income increases that helped undermine the viability of the GPM design. Nevertheless, it is a type of loan that might make a deal possible that otherwise would be lost.

An inherent problem with the GPM is that even a constant-level payment, long-term mortgage loan allows very little money to be paid on principal in the early years. So, with only a modest reduction in the payment amount, any allocation to principal may easily be eliminated along with a portion of the interest payment due.

EXAMPLE

The constant-level payment on a $50,000 loan at 10 percent with a term of 30 years amounts to $438.79. The amount of this monthly payment allocated to pay off principal is about $25.00 during the first year. Thus, a reduction of the monthly payment below $413.00 per month would not allow for any reduction of principal and would result in a probable accumulation of unpaid interest. When the graduated payment plan allows for payments so low that not all the interest is paid, each year's unpaid interest is added to the principal balance for repayment in later years.

For most of the plans currently in use, there is an accumulation of unpaid interest, called *accrued interest*, in the early years of the mortgage term; thus, the borrower ends the year with larger principal balances owing than when the loan was first undertaken. As mentioned previously, this is called *negative amortization*—the loan balance increases with each payment, rather than decreases. To avoid the possibility that the increasing amount of the loan balance could exceed the initial value of the property serving as collateral, GPMs generally call for higher down payments than are necessary for constant-level payment plans. Down payments for this type of loan are calculated so the loan balance will not exceed the limits permitted, which is 95 percent of the initial property value for conventional loans and 97 percent of the initial value for FHA-type loans.

A legal qualification is necessary in some states for this type of loan. The act authorizing the FHA program specifically preempts any state law that prohibits the addition of interest to the principal of a mortgage loan as it pertains to the manner in which the loan is repaid. This preemption is also claimed by federally chartered institutions that come under federal banking rules, not state rules.

The popularity of the FHA Section 245 GPM program has made the term "graduated payment mortgage" almost synonymous with FHA. (See Chapter 8 for more details on the FHA program.) However, a graduated-payment design was approved by federal regulators in 1979 as a *conventional* loan. Essentially, the procedures adopted are the same as those developed by the FHA but have seldom been used for conventional loans. Under different market conditions, there could be greater interest in this mortgage design as it fulfills a need. Young families buying their first home do not have the benefit of a growing equity interest in an existing house to trade with. So, permitting lower initial monthly payments enables more family incomes to qualify for loans.

PLEDGED-ACCOUNT MORTGAGE

Instead of the graduated payment mortgage, some conventional lenders have been offering a variation that provides similar benefits for a borrower. It is the **pledged-account mortgage,** which was another of the designs approved by federal regulators in 1979. With this plan, a part of the down payment is placed in an escrow (pledged) account with the lender rather than paid to the seller. Then the lender makes a loan of sufficient size to cover the purchase. The lender considers the escrow deposit as additional collateral which allows a larger loan amount.

The borrower makes monthly payments in the early years of less than the full amortization payment amount. Then, each month the lender withdraws sufficient cash from the pledged account, adds the interest earned on that pledged account, and supplements the mortgage payments so that it equals a fully amortizing amount. The purpose of the procedure is the same as that of the GPM: to establish a lower initial monthly payment that can be used to qualify a lesser income for a larger house. It has the advantage of not creating negative amortization and provides the lender with a new savings account.

BUY-DOWN MORTGAGE

An older repayment plan that has been used successfully to sell houses is the **buy-down mortgage**. It has greater appeal when interest rates are high but can still be a useful procedure with lower rates. The attraction is the same as for other graduated payment designs: the borrower may obtain qualification of income based on a lower initial monthly payment. The normal procedure is for the seller, usually a home builder, to "buy down" the initial payment amounts. This is simply a variation on the normal discount procedure. The major difference is that a buy-down is a prepayment of interest costs for only a few years, whereas the discount is normally considered a prepayment of interest costs over the life of a loan.

Buy-downs can span any period, but generally are offered for periods of one to five years. The average buy-down, and the one generally acceptable for purchase by Fannie Mae, is for three years amounting to a 3 percent less-than-market rate in the first year, 2 percent for the second, and 1 percent the third. The procedure is sometimes called "3-2-1." By encouraging easier loan qualification, the seller opens a larger market of qualified buyers.

What the seller is actually doing is paying a portion of the interest cost in the early years. The following example illustrates the cost reduction of interest on a $50,000 loan at a nominal interest rate of 9 percent with a three-year buy-down. The *nominal rate* is the one named on the note and is the only interest rate shown.

• •

EXAMPLE

First, consider the round-figure cost of a buy-down: To reduce the interest cost from 9 percent to 6 percent for the first year, the seller must pay 3 percent of the cost:

$$.03 \times \$50,000 = \qquad \$1,500$$

For the second year, the cost is 2 percent:

$$.02 \times \$50,000 = \qquad 1,000$$

For the third year, the cost is 1 percent:

$$.01 \times \$50,000 = \qquad \underline{500}$$

Total cost of buy-down $3,000

With a portion of the interest paid in advance, the buyer makes reduced monthly payments on a 30-year loan in the following amounts:

Year 1: $50,000 @ 6% = $299.78
Year 2: $50,000 @ 7% = $332.66
Year 3: $50,000 @ 8% = $366.89
Year 4 and on $50,000 @ 9% = $402.32

These figures do not consider the time value of money paid in advance nor the declining balance of the loan amount, both of which are considerations. Because of this, the cost of a buy-down is not always uniform as lenders vary somewhat in how the calculation is made; it is not a regulated procedure.

• •

While buy-down mortgages are an attractive inducement for buyers, they have lost favor with secondary-market purchasers. Buy-downs have caused more than their share of home foreclosures and some limitations have been added. One is to qualify the buyer at the note rate, not the first year's payment amount. Another similar limit is to require borrower income qualification to be based on the payment amount that will amortize the loan within its term.

BALLOON PAYMENT NOTE

The word *balloon* now has two meanings as used in the mortgage business. An older use of the term indicated payments less than necessary to amortize the loan within its term, resulting in a substantial balance still due at maturity. A more recent application of the wording means a loan with a lower initial interest rate that allows renewal at a market rate after five or seven years. The distinction is more fully explained next.

Balloon Due to Amortization

An installment note that is only partially amortized over its term reaches maturity with a balance due. (The periodic installments are insufficient to fully repay the loan during its term.) This means that a final payment larger than the previous installment payments comes due. The final payment is called a **balloon payment** because of its greater size.

The purpose of a balloon note is to keep the periodic installment payment smaller than would otherwise be required. One fairly common way of handling this kind of note is to set a term of, say, 10 years, for repayment. Then the periodic payments are calculated as if the term were 30 years.

••

EXAMPLE

A $100,000 loan is made at an interest rate of 10 percent for a term of 10 years. To fully amortize the loan over 10 years requires a monthly payment of $1,321.57. To allow a lesser payment, the amount is calculated as if the term is 30 years, thus offering a monthly payment of $877.58. At the end of 10 years, the balance due amounts to a balloon payment of $90,900.

••

If the federal Truth-in-Lending provisions apply to the loan, the amount of the balloon payment must be clearly stated in the contract.

Balloon Allowing an Adjusted Rate

As a compromise between low interest rates and payment predictability over a relatively long term, a new mortgage repayment design was introduced in 1990. To attract borrowers, a "five-year balloon" is offered with payments based on a 30-year amortization schedule at an initial rate 1 1/2 percentage points below the current 30-year market rate. On a $100,000 mortgage at this rate, savings can reach $3,000 per year. At the end of five years, the mortgage is refinanced at current market rate which remains fixed for the remaining term of the loan. This plan is also called a "two-step" mortgage.

The refinancing is not automatic as there are some requirements that differ a bit among lenders. One example is Freddie Mac's requirements for loans it purchases, which are:

- The borrower must still be the owner/occupant.
- No payment for the preceding 12 months can be more than 30 days late.
- No other liens may exist on the property except taxes and special assessments not yet due.
- The new interest rate cannot be more than five percentage points above the original note rate.

STRAIGHT NOTE

A **straight note** is one that calls for payment of the interest only at periodic intervals and the principal balance due in full at maturity. It is also known as an *interest-only note* and as a *term loan*. A straight note is a nonamortized note usually made for a short term, such as three to five years. It may allow renewal at the end of the term. If this kind of note is secured by a mortgage, it is called a *term mortgage*.

Prior to the 1930s, straight loans were very common in residential mortgage lending but have generally been replaced with fully amortized notes. Today this repayment plan is common in certain business loans and in personal bank loans.

SHORTER TERM LOANS

The 30-year loan became so deeply imbedded in mortgage lending that many thought it to be the best of all terms. Indeed, during the escalation of interest rates in the 1980s, HUD encouraged even longer term 40-year loans as a method of reducing monthly payments. The longer terms do achieve smaller monthly payments but at a dramatic increase in the interest cost. It is difficult to believe today, but an older theory of home ownership was to maintain a low equity in the property so that it could be more easily sold. Certainly one good way to keep a low equity is to make payments on a 30-year loan!

For many years little thought was given to the cost of long-term loans. After all, didn't housing prices enjoy a fairly steady increase in value that more than offset loan costs? But the 1980s produced a shocker as housing prices flattened and actually began to decline in some areas of the country. As the value of equity lost part of its allure, home buyers began looking for other ways to reduce housing costs. What had been overlooked is the beneficial effect of reducing, rather than increasing, the loan term. Cost-conscious borrowers looked favorably on **shorter term loans.**

Another factor that increased concern for shorter term loans was the wave of refinancing that occurred in the early 1990s. To capture even lower interest rates, many homeowners shifted from 30-year loans to refinance with 15- and 20-year loans. Rather than take advantage of lower monthly payments, many opted to pay about the same amount as before and take shorter term loans.

The substantial cost of a long-term loan derives from the very small reduction of principal in the early years of repayment, not interest compounding. Interest for almost all mortgage loans is calculated as simple interest. Table 7–2 indicates the interest cost for mortgage loans of differing terms. As buyers have become more aware of the true cost of long-term loans, attention has focused on the savings that can be achieved with shorter term loans.

A brief examination of Table 7–2 indicates that a reduction in the term of the loan from 30-year to 20-year increases the payment amount by $98.91 or by 13 percent. The savings in interest amounts to $68,532 or 39 percent. In today's market, a 15- or 20-year loan offers an interest rate of at least 0.5 percent less than a 30-year loan making an even larger savings for the home buyer.

Biweekly Payment Plan

Another method of accelerating the payment of principal to reduce total interest costs is the **biweekly payment.** For borrowers who are paid every other week, this method might be easier to budget. The calculation for such a payment amount is normally just one-half of a monthly payment, paid biweekly. For example, if the monthly payment for a 30-year loan amounts to $1,000, the borrower would pay $500 every other week. This amounts to 26 biweekly payments over the span of one year, amounting to $13,000. Compare this to the 12 monthly payments, which would total $12,000. The additional payments applied to principal reduction in the biweekly plan will pay off the loan in about 20 years, depending, of course, on the rate of interest.

An important encouragement for this type of loan is that it is an approved loan for purchase by Fannie Mae. Loan originators can offer this kind of loan and be assured of funding.

TABLE 7–2   Cost Comparison by Term for a
$100,000 Mortgage Loan at 8 1/2 Percent Interest

Term	Monthly Payment	Months Paid	Total Cost	Interest Cost
40-year	$ 733.10	480	$351,888	$251,888
30-year	768.92	360	276,811	176,811
20-year	867.83	240	208,279	108,279
15-year	984.74	180	177,253	77,253
10-year	1,239.86	120	148,783	48,783

Growing Equity Mortgage

Still another method that can be used to shorten a loan term, and thus reduce interest costs, is called a **growing equity mortgage**, or a graduated equity mortgage, both having the acronym of GEM. Many variations may be found, but the basic pattern is to make certain increases in the payment amount each year. Then, the entire amount of the increase is applied to repayment of the principal. Depending on the interest rate, an increase of, say, 4 percent in the payment amount (not the interest rate) each year can reduce the term of a 30-year loan to 18 or 20 years. And the impressive reduction in total interest costs is similar to that described for the 15-year loan.

Both the FHA and VA have approved this concept for early payment of a loan. For the FHA, acceptance comes under its Section 245 program (the graduated payment program) because it authorizes insurance on mortgages with varying rates of amortization.

Opportunity Cost

Critics of the 15- or 20-year loan, the biweekly loan plan, and GEM mortgages contend that any increase in the payment amount creates a loss for the borrower from the amount that might be gained had the payment increase been invested in order to earn interest. From a mathematical point of view, there is no question that making a larger mortgage payment than may be necessary to pay off a loan does reduce the opportunity to invest that money elsewhere. In Table 7–1, the difference between a monthly payment on a 30-year loan and that for a 15-year loan amounts to $215.82 (987.74 minus 768.92 equals 215.82). If that sum is deposited monthly in an interest-bearing account earning compound interest, in 15 years, depending on the interest rate, it could easily total a sum sufficient to pay off the balance due on that loan. Whether or not a net savings would result varies with each borrower as the analysis must include any gain or loss of savings resulting from the tax-deductible nature of home loan interest. It would take a self-discipline greater than this author possesses to make such an investment work!

HOME EQUITY REVOLVING LOANS

Pledging the equity in a home, or other property, to borrow money on a second mortgage has been a common procedure for many years. What is new is pledging the property to secure a revolving line of credit. Unlike a traditional second mortgage, which provides a single lump-sum payment, a home equity credit line stays in place for years. It gives the borrower more flexibility to finance everything from a child's education to a trip around the world. Interest is paid only on the portion of the credit that is used, just like a credit card account. Generally, the interest rate on the loan is adjusted periodically and floats without a maximum ceiling other than usury limits.

Equity credit lines have grown since the concept was first tried in California in the 1970s. Today, **home equity revolving loans** are a major component of total outstanding second mortgages. What increases interest in this type of credit is the tax consequence. Since the collateral is a home, it is eligible for the same tax treatment for interest deductions as a home loan, but with certain limitations.

Not all financial institutions offer home equity revolving credit lines. The concept presents some risks in that collateral may be adequate, but the borrower's income may become too easily overextended. It is this kind of credit line that gives some justification to the comment: "I bought the house on my credit card!"

OTHER ALTERNATIVE PLANS

Several other basic concepts need to be considered in the many variations now available in mortgage repayment plans. Two are shared financing methods and the other is borrowing against home equity with a reverse annuity mortgage that allows payments to the borrower.

Shared Appreciation Mortgage (SAM)

The **shared appreciation mortgage** became practical when interest rates reached all-time highs in the early 1980s. While it is not much used at this time, the concept is another alternative mortgage method and may have a resurgence in the future. A brief review of the procedure will explain how it functions. A portion of the collateral's appreciation is accepted as "contingent interest."

When home values showed a prolonged appreciation in value and interest rates were in the 12 to 15 percent range, some lenders found it profitable to take a portion of the expected return of their money from the appreciation. For example, if market rates are at a 15 percent level, the lender could offer to make a loan at 10 percent and take one-third of any appreciation in property value over, say, the next 10 years. If the property is sold sooner, the lender is entitled to one-third of the appreciation at the time of sale. If the owner does not sell, the loan agreement could call for an appraisal at the end of 10 years. Based on the appraised value, the lender could then claim one-third of any net increase (additions to property not included). Payment to the lender could be made in a lump-sum cash payment, or it could be added to the loan balance and a new note written.

Shared Equity Mortgage

Shared equity is sometimes confused with shared appreciation, but they are quite different. In the shared appreciation mortgage, the lender holds a claim, a lien, on that portion of property value representing an increase from the time of loan origination. But it falls short of title to the property. With a **shared equity mortgage,** two or more parties hold an ownership interest in the property.

The shared equity might be used in a family wherein a parent wants to help a son or daughter purchase a house. Or the concept is sometimes used by an employer, such as Stanford University, wishing to attract a new employee. Starting salaries may be insufficient to purchase houses in a high-cost area. In such a case, the employer shares ownership and mortgage liability with the employee. Or shared equity might be used as an added inducement to encourage an employee to move to a remote or less desirable area. Normally, the employee in such cases is given an option to buy out the employer's share within a limited number of years. Or, in case of a transfer, the employer would be obligated to purchase the entire property at a fair price.

REVERSE ANNUITY MORTGAGE (RAM)

The **reverse annuity mortgage** is another of the mortgage forms approved by the Federal Home Loan Bank Board as of January 1, 1979. It does not finance the acquisition of real estate as is inherent with other mortgages. Rather, the reverse annuity utilizes the collateral value of a home as a means of financing living expenses for the owner. The basic purpose is to assist older homeowners who are pressed to meet rising living costs on fixed retirement or pension income. With the use of a reverse annuity, the equity value of a home may be utilized without the owner being forced to sell the property.

Where state laws permit (an owner's homestead rights may preclude this form of mortgage), a lender can advance monthly installment payments to the homeowner (instead of a lump sum), using a mortgage on the home as collateral. Federal agency rules governing the writing of RAMs require extensive disclosures to reduce the possibility of misunderstandings by the homeowner. Among the requirements is that a seven-day rescission period be allowed the borrower should a change of mind occur. Another is that a statement must be signed by the borrower acknowledging all contractual contingencies that might force a sale of the home. Repayment of the loan must be allowed without penalties and, if the mortgage has a fixed term, refinancing must be arranged at market rates if requested at maturity of the loan.

Interest on this type of loan is added to the principal amount along with each monthly payment made to the borrower. For a savings institution, the monthly payout of loan proceeds with interest added to the principal presents an altogether different cash flow problem.

Reverse annuity mortgages present the lender with a concern for repayment. If the borrower needs more money for living expenses now, what would enable repayment in later years? The early result was a not very extensive offering of this type of loan. In 1989, HUD/FHA introduced an experimental program to insure a limited number of "reverse mortgages," and both Fannie Mae and Freddie Mac agreed to purchase them for their own portfolio investments. The amount of the loan is based on the equity value of the home but, for HUD/FHA approval, it cannot exceed the maximum loan permitted for that geographic area. The monthly advances, plus accrued interest added each month, are designed to reach the maximum loan amount in terms of 3 to 12 years. Several different repayment plans are offered, including a sale of the house at time of death. To qualify, borrowers must be 62 years or older and living in the house, with little or no mortgage debt. A loan origination fee of one point may be charged, plus an up-front HUD/FHA mortgage insurance premium of two points. The annual insurance premium for the loan is one-half of 1 percent of the loan balance each year.

With an FHA policy insuring loan repayment, an obvious problem was alleviated. Further, in 1997 Fannie Mae introduced its own Home Keeper for Home Purchase Mortgage which is similar to FHA's reverse annuity mortgage called the **Home Equity Conversion Mortgage (HECM).** The market for this type of loan has been expanding as more seniors take advantage of the possibilities.

Fannie Mae's Home Keeper for Home Purchase Mortgage

In 1997 Fannie Mae introduced another type of mortgage aimed at the senior citizen market that activates a reverse annuity type of mortgage at the time a house is purchased. It allows senior citizens (62 or older) to obtain a mortgage against the equity in a house if a substantial down payment is made.

••

EXAMPLE 1

A senior citizen sells an existing home for $100,000 with the intention of buying another $100,000 home nearer his or her children or in a milder climate. Under this mortgage plan, the buyer would immediately qualify for $52,000 in equity financing. These available funds constitute the new reverse mortgage, requiring $48,000 from cash reserves as a down payment. There are no monthly mortgage payments.

••

EXAMPLE 2

A senior sells a home and retains $75,000 in profit. A retirement home is to be purchased costing $115,000. Typically, to avoid further mortgage payments, the entire $75,000 must be used plus $40,000 to come from savings. However, using the Home Keeper for Home Purchase plan, the senior would qualify immediately for $60,000 in equity funding (the reverse mortgage) and could add $55,000 from the sale proceeds, retaining $20,000. No additional funds are needed from savings and no mortgage payments are required.

••

Repayment of this mortgage is deferred until the borrower no longer occupies the principal residence. The borrower cannot be forced to sell or vacate the property to pay off the loan even if the balance due on the mortgage exceeds the value of the house. If the loan balance does exceed the value of the property, the borrower, or the estate, will owe no more than the value of the property. The mortgage is an adjustable-rate plan and standard origination and closing fees are applicable but most can be included in the loan balance.

Questions for Discussion

1. How does a graduated payment mortgage help a home buyer?
2. What is the major constraint on lenders in setting new interest rates for an adjustable rate mortgage?
3. Discuss the quality of the major indexes cited in the text.
4. Identify the limits or caps placed on changes in the interest rate on an adjustable rate mortgage.
5. Define *negative amortization.*
6. Distinguish between the two types of balloon mortgages.
7. Describe a buy-down mortgage.
8. Discuss the advantages and disadvantages found in shorter term mortgage loans.
9. What is a *home equity revolving loan?*
10. Describe Fannie Mae's Home Keeper for Home Purchase Mortgage plan.

Chapter 8

Federal Government Underwriting Programs

KEY WORDS AND PHRASES

Federal Housing Administration (HUD/FHA) • *Acquisition cost* • *Closing costs* • *Prepaid items* • *Upfront mortgage insurance premium (UFMIP)* • *Annual premium* • *Simple assumption* • *Formal assumption* • *Section 203(b) home mortgage insurance* • *203(k) Purchase and Rehab* • *Section 234(c) Condominium* • *Section 245 Graduated Payment Mortgage* • *Title 1 Home Improvement* • *Department of Veterans Affairs (VA)* • *Eligibility* • *Entitlement* • *Certificate of Reasonable Value (CRV)* • *Release of liability*

INTRODUCTION

There are many federal agencies with programs that provide assistance to people buying homes, rehabilitating homes, renting apartments, needing farm loans, or needing housing following a natural disaster. All involve government help in the form of a loan, a grant, or an underwriting guarantee that insures private lenders against loss. Several of the government agencies that make direct loans to borrowers were discussed in Chapter 3 as a part of the primary-market lenders. However, this chapter is limited to two major agencies with home loan underwriting programs that have helped many people to buy and/or rehabilitate their homes. Neither is in the business of making direct loans although they do offer financial assistance when disposing of repossessed properties. One is the Federal Housing Administration (FHA), an agency that is under the Department of Housing and Urban Development (HUD), and the other is the Department of Veterans Affairs (still called "VA").

The oldest, and probably best known, of all government housing agencies is the FHA. Its most popular mortgage insurance programs will be outlined in this chapter. The VA was granted authority during World War II to offer housing assistance to qualified veterans in the form of a partial guaranty of a home loan.

Both agencies have one feature in common: Their underwriting activities are not expected to be paid for from tax revenues. They are supposed to be paid for by fees charged to those who use the programs. The FHA has always charged an insurance premium for its underwriting commitment. The VA loan program was initially a veteran's benefit at no charge but today a funding fee is required. The increased cost of both agency programs plus the higher loan-to-value programs offered by conventional lenders has made them less competitive with conventional loans and they have declined in market share. Occasionally, Congress approves housing subsidy programs that may be handled through HUD/FHA, but these are a separate category from the underwriting programs discussed in this chapter.

FEDERAL HOUSING ADMINISTRATION (HUD/FHA)

The **Federal Housing Administration** was one of several score of agencies spawned during the Depression of the 1930s to help resolve the economic problems that plagued the nation. It is one of the very few that survived, and it has proven its value over nearly seven decades of operation.

The reasons why the FHA was formed in 1934 are still valid today, although the area of operations has expanded substantially from the initial assistance program for home buyers. The purposes of the FHA are (1) to encourage wider homeownership, (2) to improve housing standards, and (3) to create a better method of financing mortgage loans. All these aims have been realized, even beyond original hopes. This was accomplished without making a single loan, simply by sound use of government credit to insure mortgage loans. From its initial widespread rejection by many private lenders, a government-insured commitment now is readily salable to a large number of investors. Even in the tightest money markets, there has always been funding available for a government-insured loan.

Early History

When the FHA stepped into the housing picture in 1934, houses had been financed for 50 to 60 percent of their sales price on a first mortgage of three to five years, with a small second and even a third mortgage at increasingly higher interest rates. The FHA introduced a better way. By offering to insure a single large loan up to 80 percent of value (an extremely high ratio in those days), the FHA was able to insist that the down payment be made in cash, permit no secondary financing, and command a moderate interest rate. The loans were for long terms—up to 20 years at first—and fully amortized over the life of the loan. Equal monthly payments covered principal and interest. Escrow accounts were established for hazard insurance and property taxes, requiring payment of one-twelfth of the yearly cost each month. Each monthly payment also included a premium to cover the cost of FHA's mortgage default insurance.

Most of these features were later incorporated into the loan guarantee program of the Veterans Administration and have now become normal procedure for conventional loans as well. While none of these ideas actually originated with the FHA, this agency gave them wide usage for the first time and brought about a sweeping reform in the field of residential financing.

As the FHA gained strength in its housing assistance, more titles and sections were added to its operations. While the FHA has over 50 different programs in its portfolio of assistance to borrowers for home loans, improvement loans, nursing home loans, mobile home park loans, multifamily project loans, and land development loans, our concern in this chapter is primarily with loans for single-family residences. Under the assistance programs for home loans, the FHA has special help for members of the armed services, civilian employees of the armed services, and disaster victims, as well as programs in experimental housing, urban renewal, and condominium housing.

In 1993, HUD Secretary Henry Cisneros undertook a major overhaul of all multifamily housing programs which had suffered accumulated losses in excess of $6 billion. By then, single-family programs had recovered from a period of substantial foreclosures, and the Mutual Mortgage Insurance fund that sustains the programs was again operating in the black.

HUD/FHA Terminology and Basic Procedures

All underwriting programs are implemented by the issuance of a Certificate of Insurance that protects the lender against default. The differences between the programs are based on the kind of property and qualifications of the individual who needs the help. There may be lower cash requirements for some and, in certain programs, an actual subsidy of interest costs. Also, the property must meet certain standards to qualify as collateral for an insured commitment.

To handle qualification of borrowers and the property offered as collateral, HUD/FHA follows certain procedures as detailed in its *Underwriter's Guide*. There are some words and phrases with special meaning in the world of HUD/FHA loan qualification. For example, a conventional lender measures the loan amount against the property value almost regardless of its value. With an FHA loan, a distinction is made between loans of $50,000 or less and those exceeding $50,000. The conventional lender focuses its cash requirement on a down payment; the FHA requires 3 percent in cash at closing which may come from the down payment plus closing costs. Regardless of the details, the basic qualification procedures are the same, whether FHA, VA, or conventional, and their purpose is to distinguish a creditworthy borrower and evaluate the property to make sure it serves as adequate collateral for a loan. Nevertheless, to understand FHA procedures, it is necessary to understand the basic requirements as detailed in the following sections.

Acquisition Cost

The amount of mortgage insurance available under any HUD/FHA program is limited to a percentage of the acquisition cost. **Acquisition cost** is the *lesser* of the purchase price or the appraised value.

Simplified Calculation of Down Payment

As of October 21, 1998, federal legislation was implemented to simplify the formerly rather complex calculation of the insured commitment for an FHA loan. For this purpose, there are only two categories of loans: (1) those $50,000 and less and (2) those more than $50,000. For loans of $50,000 and less, the FHA insures 98.75 percent. For loans over $50,000, the FHA insured commitment is 97.75 percent.

Cash required to close is now 3 percent, which can be met with the down payment plus closing costs. Previous rules allowed closing costs to be included in the insured commitment; new rules do not allow this but the buyer can add closing costs to the down payment to achieve the 3 percent cash requirement to close.

Closing Costs

Permissible **closing costs** are defined by regional FHA insuring offices, in accord with local practices, and thus are not always uniform. These costs include the HUD/FHA application fee, a lender's origination fee, costs of the title search, legal fees to prepare necessary closing instruments, and miscellaneous costs such as notary fees, recording costs, and a credit report charge. New rules were released in 1992 that gave more flexibility in determining acceptable closing costs. A limitation on maximum amount was established that includes a one point origination fee. However, the limit can be exceeded if costs are documented and adequate protection is provided for the borrower.

Prepaid Items

HUD/FHA distinguishes between closing costs and prepaid items. Closing costs are described more fully in the above paragraph. **Prepaid items** are property taxes, insurance premiums including the FHA mortgage insurance premium, and possibly subdivision maintenance fees, most of which must be placed in an escrow account with the lender.

Property Taxes. The borrower must pay whatever pro rata share of property taxes may fall due for the first year plus one month in escrow at closing. (HUD/FHA requires one month of all annual prepays to be held by the lender but allows two months to be held at lender's option as a cushion.)

Subdivision Maintenance Fees. In some areas, maintenance fees are considered to be in about the same category as taxes. That is, nonpayment can result in foreclosure of the property. To protect the lender, such charges may be required to be paid into escrow.

Hazard Insurance Premium. A full year's premium for property insurance must be paid in advance of closing plus one month of premium placed in escrow. The same requirement applies to flood insurance if applicable.

Mortgage Insurance Premium. Two premiums are now required for FHA coverage. One is an "upfront" premium payable at closing or added to the loan amount and, since July 1, 1991, an annual premium is required. The annual premium only is included under "prepaid" costs. It amounts to one-half percent of the loan amount (payable at one-twelfth of the annual amount each month). FHA premium requirements are more fully explained next.

Mortgage Insurance Premium (MIP)

As of July 1, 1991, Congress increased the cost of an FHA loan by requiring the payment of two premiums for its default insurance: an upfront charge plus an annual premium.

Upfront Mortgage Insurance Premium (UFMIP). In 1983, the older annual premium was replaced with a "one-time MIP" in the amount of 3.8 percent of the loan amount to be paid at closing. Then, in 1991 a new law established a phased-in reduction of the rate to a permanent 2.25 percent and changed the name to UFMIP. The permanent rate became effective October 1, 1994. The premium is the same regardless of the term of the mortgage or whether it is financed or paid in cash. The UFMIP can be added to the loan amount.

In certain cases, when UFMIP is added to the loan it can result in an amount in excess of the property value. This is acceptable to the FHA inasmuch as the MIP payment is earned over the life of the loan and, under certain circumstances, would be subject to a partial refund to the borrower.

In 1996, a special category of home buyers was given a reduced upfront premium rate of 2.00 percent. This rate was further reduced in 1997 to 1.75 percent. The rate is limited to first-home buyers living in inner city areas and requires completion of a home buyer education course. All other borrowers must still pay the 2.25 percent upfront premium.

Premium Refund. The UFMIP is subject to partial refund when a loan is paid off prematurely. The refund is also a consideration when a loan is assumed or refinancing is undertaken. To calculate a refund of unearned premium, the FHA uses factors that are scaled on the number of years the loan is outstanding. It behooves an owner or sales agent to contact the local HUD/FHA office for current information on possible refund when a transaction involves property with an existing FHA loan.

Annual Premium. In its earlier years, the FHA charged only an annual premium of one-half percent of the loan amount. This charge was dropped in 1983 and replaced by a one-time premium charge that amounted to 3.8 percent of the loan amount, later reduced to 2.25 percent. The annual premium of one-half percent was reinstated in 1991 as an additional premium charge. The one-half percent premium is charged on the loan balance each anniversary date of the loan but does not include the UFMIP in the loan balance. One-twelfth of the annual premium is added to the monthly loan payment amount and must be included as part of the housing expense for qualification of an applicant's income.

The length of time over which the annual premium must be paid depends on the amount of down payment. Since October 1, 1994, if the downpayment exceeds 10 percent, the term for premium payment is 11 years. For 10 percent or less in down payment, the term for payment is 30 years. For calculating this down payment amount (or loan to value ratio), the base loan amount without UFMIP is divided by the value of the property excluding closing costs. The annual premium is nonrefundable and must be prorated to date of closing.

ASSUMPTION OF AN FHA LOAN

From its beginning in 1934 up to 1986, an FHA loan was classed as "freely assumable." This meant that a borrower holding an FHA mortgage loan had the right to sell the property, deliver title, and assign repayment of the loan to a new buyer without FHA or the mortgagee's approval. While this right did exist, what was overlooked was the fact that an assignment by the mortgagor resulted in no release of liability for the mortgagor/seller. Thus, the seller remained fully liable for repayment for the remaining life of the loan. So long as house prices escalated, as they did in the 1970s through the early 1980s, there was not a big problem. The few foreclosures that occurred generally resulted in repossession of a house of greater value than the mortgage obligation.

This situation began to change in the mid-1980s when repossessions increased as house values declined in some depressed areas of the country. What the FHA encountered when defaults occurred was houses occupied by persons unknown to them. The effort to notify an original obligor who remained liable was difficult since he or she most likely had moved away. Further trouble resulted when original obligors contended that they had not been notified of any default. They felt no further responsibility since the house had been conveyed along with the mortgage in accordance with what they believed to be an acceptable procedure.

To correct the situation, HUD/FHA changed the assumption rules. What has made it more difficult for mortgagors to understand is that the rules were changed twice between 1986 and 1989 with the result that there are now three separate sets of requirements. The differing requirements are distinguished by date of loan origination (which is the date of the FHA insured commitment) and are not retroactive. To better understand the changes, examine first the two methods that have always applied to FHA loan assumptions: one is called a simple assumption and the other a formal assumption, as explained next.

Simple Assumption

With a **simple assumption,** property may be sold and the loan assumed without notification to the FHA or its agent (the mortgage lender). However, with this method the seller remains fully liable to the FHA and the lender for repayment of the loan regardless of the buyer's assumed obligation.

With a **formal assumption,** the property is not conveyed to a new buyer until that person's creditworthiness has been approved by the FHA or its agent. With a creditworthy buyer assuming the loan, the seller may obtain a full release of liability from the FHA. This is the method that has always been recommended by the FHA, but it was not required until 1989.

The three separate categories of FHA loans for assumption purposes distinguished by date of origination are as follows.

1. **For loans originated prior to December 1, 1986.** The original rules still apply: The borrower has an option to sell the mortgaged property by simple or formal assumption rules. It should be noted that in this category, using a formal assumption, a release of liability from the FHA is available but is not automatic. The release should be obtained as one of the documents delivered when the transaction is closed and should also be filed of record.

2. **For loans originated between December 1, 1986 and December 15, 1989.** For loans in this category, there is a restriction on early assumptions, after which time the loan can be freely assumed by simple assumption. Specifically, an owner-occupant cannot sell the property with an assumption during the first 12 months after execution of the mortgage except to an approved buyer, meaning by formal assumption. If the seller is an investor (rental property), a simple assumption sale cannot be made during the first 24 months after execution of the mortgage. Failure to comply with this restriction can result in acceleration of the loan balance.

   After the one- or two-year period, this category of loans may be assumed without prior approval of the buyer. However, should a simple assumption be undertaken, both the seller and buyer remain fully liable for five years after the new mortgage is executed. If the loan is not in default after five years, the seller is automatically released from further liability.

3. **For loans originated on or after December 15, 1989.** Creditworthiness approval of the new buyer must be obtained prior to conveyance of title for all assumptions. Failure to comply can result in acceleration of the note. If an acceptable borrower assumes the mortgage loan, the lender cannot refuse to release the original borrower from further liability.

In addition to regular mortgage loans, the rules on assumptions apply to subsequent sale transactions consummated with a contract for deed, a lease purchase agreement, or a wraparound note. An exception applies if properties are transferred by operation of law such as devise or descent.

The additional time necessary to meet qualification standards for a new buyer can be irritating to both buyer and seller, but it is a safer course to follow. This is particularly true now that the FHA policy is to pursue collection of defaulted loans to the original obligors if they remain liable.

INVESTOR MORTGAGORS ELIMINATED

A primary purpose of HUD/FHA since its origin has been to provide suitable housing to qualified people. To promote this goal, rental housing has been encouraged as a means of increasing available dwelling units in this country. Unfortunately, in the late 1980s, investor loans experienced a much higher rate of default than owner-occupied housing loans and it became necessary to limit the FHA's risk exposure. As a result, insured loans for investors were eliminated as of December 15, 1989.

While new loans to investors were eliminated, loans made prior to December 15, 1989 may still be assumed by investors but some restrictions apply. Essentially, additional cash could be required so that the balance due on a loan assumed by an investor does not exceed 75 percent of the value of the property.

A procedure that is considered an attempt to circumvent the restriction on investor financing is sometimes referred to as a *friendly foreclosure*. In this process, an investor "lends" a portion of an FHA mortgagor's equity to the owner and places a second lien on the property. This step in itself does not violate HUD requirements. The next step is a preplanned default by the owner on the second mortgage and a foreclosure transferring title to the investor. This step does violate the provision barring investors from acquiring HUD-financed properties. This provision provides for acceleration of the note if all or part of the property is transferred (other than by devise or descent) to a purchaser who does not occupy the property.

Exceptions to Restrictions on Investor Financing

There are two important exceptions that allow investors to acquire property with an FHA-insured commitment:

1. **HUD foreclosures.** Investors may still purchase HUD foreclosed properties with a 25 percent down payment and the balance financed with an FHA-insured commitment.
2. **Section 203(k) Rehabs.** Section 203(k) Rehabilitation Home Mortgage Insurance is available to investors. This program combines a purchase money mortgage with a construction loan. It targets the restoration of run-down houses as a practical means of adding to the country's housing stock. More details on the 203(k) program are provided in a later section of this chapter.

LOAN DEFAULT AND FORECLOSURE

The insured commitment on a HUD/FHA loan covers 100 percent of the loan amount since lenders normally loan exactly the insured amount. In the event of a default and foreclosure action, previous practice has been for the

FHA to pay off the loan balance with interest in exchange for an assignment of the mortgagee's claim to the foreclosed property. The property becomes federally owned and subject to rehabilitation and resale as permitted under FHA rules.

With the substantial escalation of foreclosures beginning in the mid-1980s, HUD/FHA undertook a new policy in an effort to stem depletion of its Mutual Mortgage Insurance Fund (the back-up fund for single-family insurance programs). The new policy calls for a case by case review of each foreclosure prior to taking action. When a foreclosure becomes necessary, HUD/FHA appraises the property to determine its fair market value. If this value proves to be less than the amount due on the loan, the FHA will pay the difference between the fair market value of the property and the balance due on the loan to the lender. The lender is then asked to make its claim for that difference without a conveyance of the property. The practice is known within the industry as a *claim without conveyance.*

Its purpose, of course, is to limit both the cash pay-out on claims and the number of properties returned for the FHA to manage, rehabilitate, and resell. So long as the determination of fair market value by HUD/FHA is accurate, losses to the lender could be minimized. Nevertheless, lenders have been skeptical of the practice as it allows the FHA to set its own value on the amount of an insured commitment. Further, lenders feel much better served if they never have to undertake repossession of a foreclosed property. Claim without conveyance is one of the changes that has increased the risk of an FHA loan for a mortgage lender.

Reporting Defaults and Foreclosures

Another change in practices since late 1986 is that the FHA, having been faced with massive foreclosure problems, requires mortgagees to notify credit bureaus of defaults and foreclosures. This report must include the names of original obligors who allowed loans to be assumed without obtaining a release of liability.

In 1987, HUD introduced the Credit Alert Interactive Voice Response System (CAIVRS) to collect and furnish credit data from its own files for lenders' and borrowers' use. By maintaining a file of information on those who default on its loans, HUD is able to minimize the problem of borrowers obtaining a second or third HUD loan after defaulting on an earlier obligation. In 1992, the system was expanded to include default information on guaranteed loans made by the Rural Development Services (formerly the Farmers Home Administration program), Small Business Administration, Department of Veterans Affairs, and the Department of Education.

For any federal-guaranteed loan, as evidence that screening was performed, the lender must enter a CAIVRS response code on the loan analysis sheet. If a claim was caused by unavoidable circumstances, or if a satisfactory repayment plan has been arranged, the applicant may still be approved.

INTEREST RATE

In August 1982, HUD/FHA offered the Negotiated Interest Rate Program, which abandoned the long-standing mandatory limit on permissible interest rates. For the first time a borrower was permitted to pay a discount under certain popular FHA programs. The change was slow to be recognized within the industry partly because a similar change was not made by the VA at that time. (VA changed in 1992.)

The purpose for limiting interest rates to begin with was to protect a government underwritten loan from being abused by private lenders. Clearly, the borrower should not be forced to pay extra fees to a private lender for a benefit from government assistance. In practice, however, the marketplace has long matched the yield on a lower fixed interest rate with current market requirements through an adjustment upward of the discount. Prior rules prohibited a borrower from paying a discount that passed the expense to the seller and was often added to the price of a house. As the market for mortgage loans shifted from local savings associations to national financial markets, the true purpose of a discount became more obvious: It was not a charge for government assistance but an effort to meet a market yield requirement.

No lender is interested in earning less money simply to accommodate a government program. They can easily invest funds in other kinds of loans. So in recognition of this market practice, HUD/FHA now permits the acceptable interest rate to float with current market conditions. Or in FHA terminology, loans will be underwritten at whatever interest rate is agreed to between lender and borrower.

LIMITATIONS ON LOAN AMOUNTS

HUD/FHA-insured commitments are restricted by two kinds of dollar limitations. One is determined by geographic location—whether or not the property is located in a high-cost area as defined by HUD. The other dollar limit is based on the value of the property to be pledged as collateral. The insured commitment cannot exceed certain specified percentages of the property value (meaning loan-to-value ratio). The lesser of the two limits applies and both are explained more fully next.

Loan Limits Based on Geographic Location

As of September 28, 1994, FHA increased its limits on home loans to a percentage of the Fannie Mae/Freddie Mac conforming loan limits which are adjusted in January each year. For non-high-cost areas, which cover about 2,300 counties across the country, the limit is 48 percent of the Fannie Mae/Freddie Mac limit. In 1999 this amounted to $115,200 (48 percent of $240,000) for single-family houses.

In high-cost areas, about 130 counties, the FHA limit is calculated at 95 percent of the median single-family house price in the designated local area but cannot exceed 87 percent of the Fannie Mae/Freddie Mac loan limits. In 1999, 87 percent of the conforming loan limit amounted to $208,800 for single-family houses. Selective increases for high-cost areas that do not reach the 87 percent limit (held down by the 95 percent of median single-family house price) are approved by FHA regional offices from time to time as changing conditions may require.

Loan Limits Based on Value of Collateral Property

The other dollar limitation on the amount of an FHA-insured commitment is set by calculating a percentage of the value of the property. This calculation was substantially simplified by Congress in 1998 by creating only two classes of property applicable to major progams: (1) $50,000 and less on which FHA will issue a 98.75 percent insured commitment, and (2) over $50,000 on which the insured commitment is 97.75 percent.

Value of Property, Down Payment, and Closing Costs

The FHA values the property itself as the lesser of the appraised value or the purchase price. The 1998 change requires the borrower to pay 3 percent of the acquisition cost in cash to close. The cash requirement can be met with the down payment plus closing costs. The older rules allowed closing costs to be added to the property value, thus increasing the amount that could be borrowed. New rules do not allow this. Closing costs are those listed in the Good Faith Estimate (same GFE as required by RESPA to be furnished to a loan applicant) but cannot exceed certain FHA limitations as determined in the local area. Acceptable closing costs include attorney's fees, credit report, appraisal costs, origination fee, title insurance, and other costs.

••

EXAMPLE

For houses priced higher than $50,000.

Acquisition cost	$100,000
Loan amount (97.75%)	97,750
Down payment	2,250

••

To meet the $3,000 (3 percent of acquisition cost in preceding example) cash required to close, the borrower may add the money paid for closing costs to the down payment.

In addition, to meet the 3 percent requirement the borrower may also use proper gift money if supported by a gift letter. A seller may pay up to 6 percent in costs but anything over that amount is considered a reduction in selling price. The 3 percent cash requirement cannot consist of discount points, prepaid expenses or any portion of such charges.

The 1998 revised mortgage amount calculation applies to the following programs: 203(b) Home Mortgages; 203(i) Outlying Areas; 203(n) Cooperative Units; 203(k) Rehabilitation Home Mortgage Insurance; 223(e) Home Mortgages in older, declining urban areas; and 234(c) Condominiums. The new calculation does NOT apply to 203(h) Housing for Disaster Victims and 221(d)(2) Low Cost and Moderate Income.

SECONDARY FINANCING WITH HUD/FHA-INSURED COMMITMENTS

If the mortgagor uses any funds that require a lien to be placed on the property, it is considered secondary financing and must be taken into account when determining the maximum insurable amount. This is true whether or not the note may be forgiven at some future date depending on the borrower's continued employment. HUD/FHA will insure first mortgages on property with secondary financing under the following conditions:

1. The sum of the first and second mortgages cannot exceed the applicable loan-to-value ratio or maximum mortgage limit for that area.
2. The payments under the insured first mortgage and the second mortgage do not exceed the mortgagor's reasonable ability to pay.
3. Any periodic payments on the second mortgage are collected monthly and are substantially in the same amount.
4. The repayment terms of the second mortgage (a) do not provide for a balloon payment before 10 years or such other terms not acceptable to HUD/FHA, and (b) permit prepayment by the mortgagor without penalty.

HUD/FHA PROGRAM DETAILS

There are now over 50 different programs offered by HUD/FHA. They include multifamily housing, manufactured home parks, nursing homes, planned unit developments (PUDs), as well as the better-known single-family housing programs. Their utilization varies somewhat across the country according to local situations. Some programs have become inactive due to loan limitations or qualification standards that no longer fit the changing housing market.

This section examines the qualifications needed and the restrictions placed on several of the more popular programs.

1. Section 203(b)—Home Mortgage Insurance (including the special assistance offered veterans).
2. Section 203(k)—Rehabilitation Home Mortgage Insurance.
3. Section 234(c)—Mortgage Insurance for Condominiums.

4. Section 245—Graduated Payment Mortgage.

5. Title 1—Home Improvement Loan Insurance.

Section 203(b)—Home Mortgage Insurance

The basic 203(b) program authorized in the initial act of 1934 is still the most widely used home mortgage insurance program. Experience gained from this program has been used extensively in the development of many succeeding plans. It is used as a standard with some of the other housing assistance programs which refer to qualification requirements simply as "same as 203(b)."

As with all HUD/FHA programs, the property to be acquired and used as collateral for the loan must meet applicable standards. While there are no special requirements for the individual borrower under 203(b), he or she must have an acceptable credit rating and demonstrate an ability to make the required investment as well as handle the monthly mortgage payments.

Section 203(b) offers the simplified calculation of the down payment (FHA loan commitment of 97.75 percent of acquisition value for houses over $50,000 and 98.75 percent for houses $50,000 and less) with 3 percent cash required to close.

Section 203(b)(Veteran)

Under 203(b), HUD/FHA has a special concession for qualified veterans: It allows an insured commitment of 100 percent of the first $25,000. Regular 203(b) limits apply to all over that amount.

The FHA veterans' program has additional value as it offers broader eligibility measures than those available under the VA program. The basic differences are:

1. The FHA qualification requires 90 days of active duty and a discharge other than dishonorable. The VA has longer time spans of required service at different periods of time such as hot war, cold war distinctions. (See VA requirements later in this chapter.)

2. The FHA does not take into consideration any prior commitment of the veteran's entitlement, while the VA must deduct any previous usage of the entitlement if the loan has not been paid off or assumed by another qualified veteran.

Section 203(k)—Rehabilitation Home Mortgage Insurance

To help restore and preserve the nation's existing housing stock, the 203(k) program has been revised and expanded. In June 1993, this kind of loan was made eligible for "direct endorsement," which means lenders can underwrite them without prior HUD field office approval. Further stimulus for the program was given by allowing the loans to be sold to secondary-market investors when the loan is originated and before rehabilitation is completed.

Unlike any other HUD-insured program, 203(k) combines a purchase money mortgage with a construction loan. The new revision offers an insured commitment {same limits as 203[b]) that allows the purchase of an existing house over one year old, plus sufficient additional money to rehabilitate the property. The program is limited to one- to four-family dwellings and can be utilized as follows:

1. To purchase and rehabilitate a dwelling and the real property on which it is located.
2. To refinance existing indebtedness and rehabilitate such a dwelling.

While the program does not specifically list it, Section 203(k) can also be used to convert existing single-family homes into multiple-unit dwellings for up to four families.

A single insurance commitment combines the funds needed to purchase the property or refinance existing indebtedness, the costs incidental to closing, and the money needed to complete the proposed rehabilitation. The money allocated to rehabilitation must be escrowed at closing in a rehabilitation escrow account. This fund includes any money allocated to the contingency reserve as determined by the HUD construction analyst, but the contingency cannot exceed 10 percent of the cost of rehabilitation. This account must be kept separate and cannot be used to pay taxes or insurance. The account must pay interest each month to the borrower at not less than 5 percent per annum.

If the 203(k)-insured commitment involves insurance of advances, which would be normal when rehabilitation is required, then a Rehabilitation Loan Agreement must be executed by the lender and the borrower. As a part of this agreement, there must be an inspection and release schedule that details the amount of escrowed money that can be released at each stage of completion.

Before any release of funds can be made by the lender holding the escrow account, an inspection must be made to determine satisfactory completion of the work to that stage. Inspection is made by HUD-approved fee inspectors from a list provided by the HUD field office. The number of inspections required will vary with the complexity of the rehabilitation but cannot exceed four plus the final one.

Because this program is fairly complex and requires additional supervision by the mortgage lender, higher charges are permitted. Lenders may add one percentage point to the normal 1 percent origination fee for a purchase money mortgage and 1 1/2 percent more than normal for the rehabilitation loan.

Section 234(c)—Mortgage Insurance for Condominium Housing

HUD/FHA insures mortgages for the purchase of individual family units in multifamily housing projects under Section 234(c). It also insures loans for the construction or rehabilitation of housing projects intended for sale as individual condominium units under Section 234(d).

A *condominium* is defined as joint ownership of common areas and facilities by the separate owners of single-family dwelling units in the project. To be acceptable for FHA insurance, the project must include at least four dwelling units. At least one other unit in each project must be acquired under a government-underwritten program.

Before a loan can be insured for a single condominium, the entire project must meet HUD/FHA minimum standards just as a new subdivision must meet compliance standards. The agreement under which a homeowners' association may function comes under scrutiny, as do the rights of the developer. A question such as "When does the developer vacate the premises?" becomes more important with a condominium as it affects control of the common areas. Under FHA requirements, the developer may not claim a right of first refusal to offer condominiums for resale.

Mortgage Limits and the Insured Commitment. Both the maximum amount of mortgage loan permitted and the calculation of the maximum insured commitment are determined on the same basis as that for the 203(b) program described earlier in this section.

Section 245—Graduated Payment Mortgage (GPM)

Several years of experimental testing provided the groundwork for HUD/FHA to offer an insurance program for graduated payment mortgages approved nationally in November 1976. The purpose of the program is to reduce monthly payments in the early years of the mortgage term so that families with lower income and reasonable expectation of future increases can qualify for suitable housing in a higher cost market.

The program was well received through the early 1980s as it enabled many young families to purchase their first home. Initially, the program was targeted for first-home buyers but was not so limited. The key benefit for the applicant is that income qualification is based on the monthly payment required for the first year which is normally much less than necessary to fully amortize the loan. The repayment plan worked well in times when housing prices escalated and inflation was an accepted fact of life. However, the GPM and its borrowers faced difficulties when the economy reversed into a downslide in the late 1980s. To avoid further problems, qualification guidelines were tightened a bit.

Section 245 is limited to owner-occupant applicants; there are no other special qualifications, such as income limitations. As in other programs, the applicant must have an acceptable credit record, demonstrate ability to make the required down payment, and be able to handle the monthly mortgage payments. There is one additional requirement: The applicant must have reasonable expectation of an increased annual income in future years.

The lower monthly payments in the early years under most of the HUD/FHA Section 245 plans are insufficient to pay anything on principal and do not cover all of the interest due each month. Consequently, each year the unpaid interest is added to the principal balance due. Since the loan balance is increased, rather than reduced or "amortized," the result is called *negative amortization*. To prevent an increase in the loan balance from exceeding the value of the property, higher down payments may be required.

Mortgage Limits. The maximum amount of the insured commitment for Section 245 is derived as the lesser of two calculations as more fully described later. Section 245 plans make it possible for the loan amount (that is, the principal balance due on the loan) to increase due to the negative amortization feature (adding unpaid interest to the principal balance each year). Thus, the loan balance can increase to an amount greater than the initial authorized loan amount. This possibility is recognized and does not constitute a violation of the National Housing Act, so long as the down payment computations are made in accordance with Section 245 instructions.

Section 245—Repayment Plans

HUD/FHA insures graduated-payment mortgages with five different repayment plans. These are differentiated by the rate of payment increases each year and the duration of the escalation period. Three plans offer 2 1/2, 5, and 7 1/2 percent annual increases for the first 5 years; two plans offer 2 percent and 3 percent increases for the first 10 years. Stated another way, the initial monthly payment amount is calculated so that it can be increased each year at a fixed, or predetermined, rate until it reaches a constant-level payment amount by the 6th year for the 5-year plans and by the 11th year for the 10-year plans. The amount of monthly payment, the mortgage insurance premium, and the down payment required depend on the interest rate and the term of the loan. To simplify the calculation of these amounts, the FHA has published a series of tables that give factors to be used in the calculation of payment requirements.

Calculating the 245 Insured Commitment

To comply with the requirements, it is necessary to make two separate calculations to establish the correct maximum insured commitment. Since the insured commitment almost always becomes the amount of the loan, the dif-

TABLE 8–1   HUD/FHA Section 245 GPM Factors

	Principal Balance Factor	Monthly Principal and Interest (P & I) Factors (per $1,000 of original loan balance)					
		Year 1	Year 2	Year 3	Year 4	Year 5	Year 6+
INTEREST RATE: 8.00%							
Plan I	1000.0195	6.6651	6.8317	7.0025	7.1775	7.3570	7.5409
Plan II	1012.8612	6.0579	6.3608	6.6789	7.0128	7.3634	7.7316
Plan III	1030.9550	5.5101	5.9233	6.3676	6.8452	7.3585	7.9104
INTEREST RATE: 9.00%							
Plan I	1002.3085	7.3244	7.5075	7.6952	7.8876	8.0848	8.2869
Plan II	1021.0154	6.6706	7.0042	7.3544	7.7221	8.1082	8.5136
Plan III	1043.5617	6.0788	6.5347	7.0248	7.5517	8.1181	8.7269

ference between the commitment and the contract price is the required down payment. The first calculation that determines the insured commitment, called Criterion I in the example that follows, is the same as that required for Section 203(b) qualification. The second calculation, Criterion II, is in accordance with the Section 245 formulas. The lesser of the two results is the amount of the insured commitment.

Under Criterion II for the nonveteran applicant, the procedure is to take 97 percent of the property value (including closing costs) and divide the result by the highest outstanding balance factor for the applicable plan and interest rate. Different procedures apply for veterans and for property constructed without prior FHA approval that is less than one year old.

....

EXAMPLE

To calculate the down payment amount and the monthly mortgage payments applicable to a HUD 245 loan the applicant must refer to a HUD/FHA Graduated Payment Factor Table available at any HUD/FHA office. The table provides factors listed in accordance with differing interest rates and the HUD payment plan that applies. An example of the factors is shown in Table 8–1 on a very limited basis as applied to only three plans and two different interest rates.

For this example, assume a property value of $90,000 and closing costs of $1,900, for a total value for mortgage insurance purposes of $91,900. Say the loan requested is for a 30-year term, at an interest rate of 8 percent, using Plan III. (Plan III offers payment amounts increasing at 7 1/2 percent each year for the first five years.) Remember, the calculation must be made by two separate criteria to determine which offers the lesser loan amount.

Criterion I [same as 203(b)]
Value of property   90,000
(Acquisition cost)
Insured commitment (97.75%)   87,975

Criterion II (245 Calculation)
Value of property $91,900 \times 0.97 = 89,143$
                                 $89,143/1030.9550 = 86.4664$
                                 $86.4664 \times 1,000 = 86,466.40$

By the calculations, Criterion II offers the lesser loan amount of $86,466.40, and, therefore, is the applicable number, rounded down to $86,450. The difference between the loan amount and the purchase cost is the down payment; thus, $91,900 minus $86,450 equals $5,450.

Now the cost of the mortgage insurance premium must be added as a one-time charge at closing. For this example, consider that 100 percent of the

2.25% UFMIP will be financed (added to the loan amount at closing). To calculate:

86,450 × .0225 =	$ 1,945
Add: Property loan	$86,450
Total insured commitment	$88,395

The next step is to figure the monthly payment amounts. Again, refer to the abbreviated Table 8–1. At an 8 percent interest rate for Plan III, the table shows a monthly P & I factor of 5.5101 for the first year's payments. To calculate, first change the loan amount to $1,000 units and multiply as follows:

For the first year:
$$88.395 \times 5.5101 = 487.06 \text{ (first year's P \& I payments)}$$

And for the second year:
$$88.395 \times 5.9233 = 523.59 \text{ (second year's P \& I payments)}$$

Then continue the calculation for each successive year, always applying the P & I factor to the initial loan amount. The amount of the sixth-year payment in this example remains constant for the balance of the life of the loan.

··

Title 1—Home Improvement Loan Insurance

One of the popular programs offered by HUD/FHA is insurance on loans to finance home improvements. The money may be used for major or minor improvements, alterations, or repairs of individual homes and nonresidential structures, whether owned or rented. Lenders determine eligibility for these loans and handle the processing themselves. The smaller loans in this category are usually handled as unsecured personal loans (recording of a mortgage instrument is not required).

Any creditworthy property owner is eligible for a Title I loan. Loans may also be made to tenants for improvement of leased apartment units, providing the lease term is at least six months longer than the term of the loan. In addition, Title I covers the insurance of loans on mobile homes (manufactured housing) that do not qualify as real estate. Whether or not a mobile home qualifies as real estate depends on state laws, the nature of its title, and how it is taxed. States generally claim an ad valorem property tax if the unit is permanently attached to the ground.

HUD/FHA QUALIFICATION PROCEDURES

Since its beginning, HUD/FHA has trained its own valuation and mortgage credit staff to handle the qualification of loan applicants so as to assure compliance with the special requirements of the various programs. Guidelines are furnished in a comprehensive *Underwriter's Guide,* supplemented with an almost continuous flow of updated information to stay abreast of changing needs and new laws.

While the process has been difficult to fit into a computerized analysis program, in 1996 the FHA approved the use of Freddie Mac's Loan Prospector as a system to analyze loan applications. The purpose is to expedite loan processing, reduce its cost, and possibly to qualify some applicants who might otherwise be rejected. As pointed out earlier, the computer does not reject an applicant but asks the lender's underwritng department for further information to help process the loan application.

No two applications are alike, and judgment calls sometimes become necessary to determine proper approval or disapproval. The system has always permitted sufficient flexibility to allow a review of the decision if the applicant feels an error has been made.

In 1983, HUD established the Direct Endorsement Program in an effort to both reduce costs and simplify the process for mortgagees (mortgage lenders) to secure insurance endorsements. Under this program, the mortgagee underwrites and closes a mortgage loan without prior HUD review or approval. The authority to participate in this program is a privilege granted to mortgagees on the basis of demonstrated qualifications, experience, and expertise.

In this procedure, the mortgagee is given sufficient certainty of HUD approval to justify undertaking the responsibility. Essentially, HUD requires compliance with its rules and does not "second-guess" the underwriters' qualifications decisions. HUD does make a postendorsement review, and if underwriting deficiencies are discovered in the loan documents an underwriting report is sent to the mortgagee. However, the insurance contract is incontestable except in cases of fraud and misrepresentation. If the mortgagee continues to submit marginal-type loans under this program, its authority under Direct Endorsement may be withdrawn.

ANALYZING THE LOAN APPLICATION

In the past decade, the various government agencies involved with underwriting home loans have made a concerted effort to simplify procedures, including the use of standard forms by all agencies plus the acceptance of each others' appraisals and general procedures. The present form used by lenders to apply for government underwriting is a uniform version that combines HUD Form 92900, VA Form 26-1802a, and the Rural Development Services (formerly FMHA) Home Loan Guaranty form. This is the form that a mortgage company submits to HUD/FHA to apply for mortgage insurance. It is based on information obtained from the borrower's loan application and subsequent verifications. The borrower's application to the lender for a loan is also a standard form that has been made mandatory for all residential loans as will be explained more fully in the next chapter.

One of the standardization chores that the industry is working on is to make the various computerized loan analysis systems compatible. As they were originated, each system was designed to operate with different software making it more difficult for lenders to work with more than one system. It is the intention of major lenders to offer systems that can be used by others with similar software.

When computerized analysis of loan applications was introduced in 1995 by several major lenders, FHA did not approve any one system. Its procedure at first was to approve an FHA lender's use of an automated system, but not the system itself. Then in 1996, FHA gave approval for a joint pilot project for its lenders to use Freddie Mac's Loan Prospector system for loan analysis. The agency hoped to reduce processing time and to qualify some borrowers who would not have qualified through ordinary lender underwriting.

Analysis of Property and the Borrower

The property and the borrower are processed separately in determining qualification. Procedures that are followed for approval of the property are outlined in the sections that follow. Qualifying the borrower is explained in Chapter 9, "Borrower Qualification," which compares FHA methods with both VA and conventional methods to better illustrate the similarities and differences.

Qualifying the Property

The FHA requires an appraisal to be made of property offered as collateral by one of its staff appraisers or by an FHA-approved fee appraiser. Following are the distinctions made for four basic categories of property:

1. **Proposed construction.** To qualify, plans and specifications are submitted to HUD/FHA prior to the start of construction. If found acceptable, the approved plans and specifications are certified and returned to the mortgagee.

2. **Low-ratio properties.** For loans of 90 percent of the value, not approved by HUD or VA prior to construction, not covered by an acceptable warranty plan, and the property is less than one year old at date of application, HUD requires an appraisal by its own staff or a HUD-assigned fee appraiser to determine the value.

3. **Existing construction.** Property completed at least one year prior to date of application must be appraised by a staff appraiser or a fee appraiser assigned by HUD/FHA.

4. **Warranty plan.** If a property is covered by a warranty plan approved by HUD, a conditional commitment by HUD/FHA or a VA CRV (Certificate of Reasonable Value) may be used to qualify the property.

Property Value. HUD/FHA defines *property value*—that is, the value of the house and land—as the lesser of the FHA-appraised value or the purchase price. Since it is possible for an earnest money contract to be signed prior to making an appraisal, the value in an appraisal can be different from the agreed-upon price. Should the appraised value be *less* than the agreed price, FHA rules permit a buyer to withdraw from the earnest money contract (unilaterally rescind it) and recover the earnest money in full. Or, should the buyer prefer, the purchase can be consummated at the contract price, but any amount paid over the appraised value must be in cash. The amount of the loan is calculated as a percentage of the appraised value in such a case. Another frequently used option is to renegotiate the contract to reflect the appraised value.

Determining Value. HUD/FHA appraisals are made in the same manner as other appraisals with possibly one slight difference: Because of the volume of FHA activity, it retains substantial records of previous transactions that can be used for making good comparisons with other sales. HUD Field Offices can usually quote a current value per square foot of house in most of its neighborhoods.

However, the FHA has the same problem as VA and conventional loan underwriters with the impact of seller loan buy-downs on the price of a house that may be used as a comparable. Over a period of time, it is quite possible for a home builder to offer an attractive buy-down for a loan, add its costs to the price of the house, and develop an inflated "market value" that could be used as a sales comparable. HUD/FHA addresses this problem in two steps: (1) All appraisals must now include as additional information the amount of loan discount when the house was acquired, and (2) excessive buy-downs must be deducted from the value of any house used as a comparable.

••

EXAMPLE

Say that a $70,000 loan was made to the homeowner with an eight-point discount and buy-down tied in. Say that in the region involved, the FHA considers anything over five points to be "excessive." This would mean that three points, amounting to $2,100 of the $70,000 loan amount, is considered a reduction in the sales price for that property. Thus, if the listed sale price had been $76,000, its true price for use as a comparable would be $73,900 ($76,000 minus $2,100 equals $73,900).

••

Scope of Appraisal

The HUD/FHA appraisal contains other important information. In addition to placing a dollar value on the property, an appraiser also determines what repairs may be needed to restore the property to acceptable FHA standards. Special inspections may be called for to examine the roofing, plumbing, electrical system, the heating/air conditioning system, and the water heater.

If deficiencies are found, the property must be brought up to standard before the loan can be funded. The seller may make the repairs or, in some cases, the buyer may do the work as part of the buyer's cash contribution—a "sweat equity" contribution.

In 1995, HUD advised its underwriters to delete "conditions that have little or nothing to do with safety or soundness of the property" from repair requirements stipulated by an appraiser.

DEPARTMENT OF VETERANS AFFAIRS (VA)

The Veterans Administration was elevated to cabinet rank in 1989 as the **Department of Veterans Affairs.** Title and mortgage documents now reflect conveyance to the "Secretary of Veterans Affairs" rather than the "Administrator of Veterans Affairs." The historic abbreviation for the agency as "VA" remains in place.

While the VA administers a number of programs for the benefit of eligible veterans, our interest is confined to the home loan program that was created in 1944 as a part of the so-called "GI Bill of Rights." Section 501 of this act provides for a first-mortgage real estate loan that is partially guaranteed by the VA and is subject to strict rules covering all phases of the loan: the borrower, the lender, the property, the loan charges, the term and loan amount, collections, and foreclosures. The primary interest of the VA is to assist the veteran, and to this end the rules are directed.

While HUD/FHA insures 100 percent of its approved loans, the VA guarantees only a portion of the loan amount. Since the guarantee reduces the risk exposure for a lender, it has been an acceptable loan. The VA does not have a cash requirement for a veteran to qualify, meaning no down payment is required. Even the VA funding fee can be added to the loan amount rather than paid in cash. However, the "no cash" rule describes what is acceptable to the VA for its loan approval. It does not apply to a lender who may require a down payment and an origination fee paid by the veteran. Thus, even though a VA loan may be found with no cash required of the veteran, many lenders believe some investment on the part of a borrower makes a more acceptable loan and this is permitted by the VA.

Not all veterans are eligible for a home loan guarantee. They must meet certain minimum requirements of time served on active duty. Eligibility for a loan is different from "entitlement," although the terminology is often confused. The differences between what is meant by these two terms are more fully described next.

Eligibility of a Veteran

To be eligible for a home loan guarantee, the veteran must have served on active duty a minimum amount of time that varies during different periods—lesser time during periods of "hot wars" and longer for others. Table 8–2 lists the time periods and duration of active duty required for **eligibility.** Unmarried surviving spouses of persons who died as a result of service-connected disabilities or while on active duty in the armed services may also be eligible. Since 1988, members of the Merchant Marine are included as eligible veterans. The most recent addition for eligibility are individuals who have completed a total of at least six years in the Reserves or National Guard.

TABLE 8–2 Veteran Eligibility

Era	Minimum Service Required
WW II, 9/16/40–7/25/47	90 days
Peacetime, 7/26/47–6/26/50	181 days
Korean War, 6/27/50–1/31/55	90 days
Post Korean, 2/1/55–8/4/64	181 days
Vietnam War, 8/5/64–5/7/75	90 days
Post Vietnam, 5/8/75–9/7/80	181 days
Enlisted personnel after 9/7/80	24 months
Commissioned officers after 10/16/81	24 months
Persian Gulf War, 8/2/90–Present	90 days
Reserves or National Guard after 10/28/92	6 years
If a veteran is still on active duty	181 days

For any veteran considering the purchase of a home and the use of a VA loan, it is a good idea to ask the VA Regional office to confirm eligibility. This is done by submitting VA Form 26-1880, "Request for Determination of Eligibility and Available Loan Guaranty Entitlement." The VA response to this request answers two questions: Is the veteran eligible? and if so, How much is available in the entitlement?

The Loan Guaranty Entitlement

The amount of money that the VA will guarantee for a veteran is called an **entitlement.** At its origin in 1944 the maximum entitlement amounted to $2,000. As housing prices increased over the years, Congress has periodically adjusted the entitlement limit as shown in Table 8–3.

TABLE 8–3 Entitlement Increments

Date of Increase	Maximum Entitlement
Original Act, 1944	$ 2,000
December 28, 1945	4,000
July 12, 1950	7,500
May 7, 1968	12,500
December 31, 1974	17,500
October 1, 1978	25,000
October 7, 1980	27,500
February 1, 1988	36,000
December 18, 1989	46,000
October 13, 1994	50,750

Sliding Scale Guaranty

Prior to 1988, the VA applied the same maximum permissible amount as the guaranty portion of a loan regardless of the amount of the loan. As the size of loans continued to increase, the single-figure guaranty became disproportionate for a smaller loan as compared with larger loans. The VA introduced a sliding scale of loan guarantees on February 1, 1988, when the limit was increased to $36,000. The new guaranty limits are a mix of loan percentages and fixed amounts as shown in Table 8–4.

∙∙∙

EXAMPLE OF GUARANTY CALCULATION

If a veteran has not previously used an entitlement and now wishes to purchase a home that would qualify for a loan of $64,000, the loan would fall in the guaranty category of 40 percent (see Table 8–4). To calculate:

64,000 × .40 = 25,600 (guaranty applied to the loan)

∙∙∙

Partial Entitlements

If a veteran sells a house with assumption of a VA loan, the Department of Veterans Affairs remains liable to the holder of that note (the lender) until it is paid off. This is true whether or not the selling veteran has obtained a release of liability from the obligation to the VA. So when this occurs, the veteran's entitlement for that existing loan remains committed insofar as the VA is concerned. This means that the amount of entitlement previously committed cannot be used to acquire another property. However, when the entitlement limit itself is increased, the additional amount becomes available for further use. Thus, under such circumstances, a veteran may be eligible for partial entitlement.

TABLE 8–4 Sliding Scale Guaranty

Loan Amount	Guaranty
$45,000 and less	50% of loan
$45,001 to $56,250	$22,500
$56,251 to $90,000	40% of loan
$90,001 to $144,000	$36,000
$144,001 to $184,000	25% of loan
Maximum loan guaranty	$50,750

....

EXAMPLE

Consider a veteran who purchased a home in 1977 using a VA guaranty that amounted to $17,500 at that time (refer to Table 8–3). The home is sold in 1992 with an assumption of the old loan by the new buyer. If the veteran seller did not obtain a restoration of full entitlement at the time, there is still a new entitlement that can amount to the difference between the $17,500 that remains committed and the current limit of $46,000. But there is now a limit on partial entitlements.

....

Limit on Partial Entitlements. Except in the case of eligible loans in excess of $144,000, the maximum amount of the guarantee remains $36,000. For example, a veteran who previously used a $17,500 entitlement that has not been restored has $18,500 available (36,000 minus 17,500 equals 18,500) for use in connection with any eligible purpose. However, in the event of a new loan in excess of $144,000, the remaining entitlement used to guarantee the loan amount will be based on the difference between $46,000 and the previously used guaranty amount. Thus, the same veteran with a previously used guaranty amount of $17,500 would have a $28,500 entitlement for use if the purpose of the new loan is to acquire a home or condominium with a loan in excess of $144,000.

Practical Value of an Entitlement. In the marketplace, the amount of entitlement is a key determinant of the maximum size of a VA loan. The reason is that almost all VA loans are now sold into Ginnie Mae loan pools. It is a Ginnie Mae requirement, not VA, that states for any VA loan to be accepted into a Ginnie Mae-underwritten pool it must have guaranty and/or cash covering at least 25 percent of the loan amount. Since VA loans can be approved with no cash down, the market puts emphasis on the amount of a veteran's entitlement, meaning at least 25 percent of the loan amount must be a VA guaranty. This number easily translates into market jargon that "a VA loan cannot exceed four times its guaranty." The VA's limit on loan amount is quite different: the loan cannot exceed the appraised value of the property. The appraised value in VA terminology is the **Certificate of Reasonable Value (CRV).**

Restoration of Entitlement

Restoration of entitlement is often confused with a release of liability. They are quite different and require two separate procedures if both are to be accomplished. One way of distinguishing between the two is to think of restoration of entitlement as help in obtaining a new loan. Release of liability, as will be explained later, has to do with responsibility for an old loan. Restoration is important for a veteran desiring to purchase a new house and this question should be considered in any contract when a veteran sells a house that has a VA loan.

There are two ways that a veteran can regain the right to full entitlement. These are:

1. Pay off the loan through sale of the property. This means not allowing an existing VA loan to be assumed. Once the loan is paid off, the obligation of the VA terminates for that loan and the veteran's entitlement rights can be restored. One further requirement: The house must be vacated as a veteran can only own one house, which must be his or her principal residence.

2. Substitute another veteran's entitlement. To qualify under this procedure, the veteran may sell his or her home on an assumption basis, but only to another qualified veteran. The purchasing veteran must (a) have at least as much entitlement as the selling veteran, (b) meet the normal income and creditworthiness requirements, and (c) agree to permit the entitlement to be substituted.

For many years the VA also required that there be a compelling personal reason for the sale, such as a job transfer, to restore a veteran's entitlement. This is no longer necessary.

Assumption of a VA Loan

Prior rules allowed the assumption of a VA loan by any purchaser, veteran or nonveteran, without approval by the VA. What became lost in the long upswing in the housing market into the early 1980s was the fact that the seller remained primarily liable for repayment of that assumed loan; the loan could be transferred, but not the responsibility for its repayment. Unless the selling veteran took the available steps to find a creditworthy buyer and then obtain a release of liability, the obligation remained. When the economy in certain areas of the country began to decline in the mid-1980s, defaults and foreclosures became far more prevalent. Many problems resulted when a private mortgage lender was forced to foreclose on properties that had been conveyed to buyers unknown to the VA or the lender.

A claim for repayment of a defaulted VA loan is a debt owed to the federal government (as is an FHA claim) and subject to collection from the debtor(s) through the U.S. government's right of indemnification and/or subrogation. To reduce any recurrence of this kind of problem, the VA changed the assumption rules for all VA-guaranteed loans underwritten after March 1, 1988.

Assumption by Creditworthy Buyers Only. For loans underwritten after March 1, 1988, assumptions are not permitted without prior underwriting approval by the lender or VA. This rule is not retroactive and does not apply to loans underwritten before that date, meaning older loans may still be freely assumed. But without a release of liability from the old loan, the seller remains fully liable.

Veterans holding VA loans underwritten after March 1, 1988, must follow specific procedures if a loan assumption is anticipated. A selling veteran must notify the mortgagee before the property is transferred. The mortgagee must then determine if the prospective buyer meets credit standards. If the selling veteran fails to notify the mortgagee before transferring the property, or if the property is transferred to a buyer who has failed the creditworthiness test, the lender has the right to accelerate the note. There is a right of appeal for the selling veteran. Should the lender determine that the prospective buyer is not creditworthy, the seller has 30 days to appeal the decision. If the VA overrides the lender's determination, the lender must then approve the assumption.

To protect the veteran and to make sure assumption requirements are fully disclosed, mortgage instruments underwritten after March 1, 1988, must show in large type on the first page the following sentence: "THIS LOAN IS NOT ASSUMABLE WITHOUT THE APPROVAL OF THE DEPARTMENT OF VETERANS AFFAIRS OR ITS AGENT."

A transfer fee of one-half of 1 percent of the balance due on the loan shall be payable at the time of transfer to the loan holder, or its authorized agent, as trustee for the Secretary for Department of Veterans Affairs. In the event the fee is not paid, it shall be added to the debt secured by this instrument.

Release of Liability

The above-stated rules underline the importance of selling a house to someone who is capable of making payments on the loan if it is to be assumed. While it will take many years for the older, more easily assumed loans to work their way out of existence, selling veterans continue to have the right to obtain a release of liability in a sale with a loan assumption. A selling veteran is entitled to a **release of liability** if the following conditions are met:

1. The loan must be paid currently.
2. The purchaser/assumptor must qualify from the standpoint of income and be an acceptable credit risk.
3. The purchaser must agree to assume the veteran's obligations on the loan.

The veteran need not sell the house to another veteran in order to obtain a release of liability for a loan assumption. The purchaser need only meet the above-listed requirements. Release of liability is a separate form and should be completed at the time the transaction is closed.

Loan Default and Foreclosure

Even though the VA guarantee covers only a portion of the loan amount, historically, in the event of foreclosure, VA followed a policy of paying off the principal balance with interest due and taking title to the property. This practice enhanced the value of a VA guaranty for the lender. However, as foreclosures escalated in the late 1980s, increased losses were sustained by the VA. To better protect the programs and reduce potential cost to taxpayers, VA changed its procedures when faced with a foreclosure.

Similar to the practice followed by HUD/FHA, the VA now requires notification of a pending foreclosure so that it can have the property appraised. On a case by case basis, the VA then decides what action is in the best interest for VA; that is, to decide whether or not it is best for the VA to pay off the loan and take title to the property or simply pay only the guaranty amount to the lender. If the latter method is followed, the VA pays the guaranty and declines to bid for the property at foreclosure, or "no bids" the property. This means the lender takes title in foreclosure and must arrange for whatever disposition it can find.

The "no bid" procedure has substantially altered the risk level of a VA loan and is one of the reasons lenders encourage veteran applicants to consider competitive conventional loans.

Funding Fee

Initially, the VA home loan program was handled as part of the country's ongoing commitment of service to veterans. For many years, there was no charge for processing the loan application or for issuing the guaranty certificate. However, increasing costs and growing losses caused Congress to add a 0.50 percent funding fee in 1982 for issuance of a VA guaranty. Since then, the fee has been raised and lowered several times, the latest increase becoming effective on October 1, 1993. There are now three categories of eligible veterans with differing fees. The fee is reduced as down payment is increased as shown in Table 8–5.

The fee is payable at closing and may be included in the amount of the loan. There are a few exceptions. For example, the fee is not paid by veterans receiving compensation for service-connected disabilities or surviving spouses of veterans who died in service or as a result of service-connected disabilities.

Fees apply to all types of VA-guaranteed loans, but do vary for different categories. For instance, the fee for interest rate reduction refinancing loans was reduced to 0.50 percent as of October 28, 1992. The VA accepts the possibility that the addition of a funding fee may make the loan in excess of the property value.

TABLE 8–5 VA Funding Fees (Effective October 1, 1993)

Down Payment	Veterans	National Guard & Reservists	Multiple Users
No down payment	2.00%	2.75%	3.00%
Down payment at least 5%	1.50	2.25	1.50
Down payment 10% or more	1.25	2.00	1.25

Negotiated Interest Rate and Discount

In an historic change for VA, Congress passed legislation in 1992 to allow market interest rates and discounts to be applied to VA loans. (FHA made this change in 1982.) Before this change, the VA set a maximum permissible rate for issuance of its guaranty and allowed no discount to be paid by a veteran borrower. Even though the VA interest rate was changed periodically to stay abreast of market fluctuations, the cost of a loan to the borrower was adjusted by lenders to meet current market yields through a change in the discount. The burden was placed on the seller who was required to pay any discount and this cost was often shifted into the price of the property.

The new law, which became effective October 28, 1992, allows loans to be guaranteed by the VA at an interest rate agreed upon between the veteran and the lender. In addition, discount points as agreed between veteran and lender may be paid by the veteran, but may not be added to the loan amount.

Adjustable-Rate Mortgage (ARM)

A three-year test period to underwrite ARM mortgages expired on September 30, 1995. The program was not renewed. The reason announced was that the program had cost the VA money.

Interest Rate Reduction Refinancing Loans (IRRRLs)

In times of low interest rates, as occurred in the 1990s, both the FHA and VA take steps to encourage refinancing existing loans. It is not their money that is at stake, but their underwriting guarantees of loan repayment. The easier it is for their borrowers to repay loans, the lower the risk for the underwriting agencies. Refinancing loans to obtain lower interest rates results in lower monthly payments and easier repayment.

Inducements to refinance include eliminating an appraisal, extending loan terms, and reducing funding or insuring fees. For VA loans closed after January 21, 1988, the term may be extended for up to 10 years longer than the remaining term of the original loan but not longer than a maximum of 30 years and 32 days. The veteran need not occupy the house to secure refinancing but must certify that the house had been occupied by the veteran when the loan was secured. The funding fee for refinancing has been reduced to 0.50 points.

The rules applicable to refinancing a VA-guaranteed loan at a lower interest rate were modified in May 1999. In a final rule on the issue, VA will not permit refinancing if a loan is delinquent. Further, the payment must be reduced on the refinanced loan and the veteran seeking refinancing must meet certain credit standards. The purpose of requiring a payment reduction is to prevent lenders from lowering the interest rate but packing the refinanced loan with excessive fees so that the payment is actually increased.

Other VA Requirements and Procedures

To assure the veteran that the home loan will be properly handled and that the government guaranty will not be abused, the VA has a number of specific requirements relating to the loan and how it is handled. Essential areas of VA concern are discussed next.

The Lender. To protect against an unscrupulous lender, the VA distinguishes between supervised and nonsupervised lenders. A *supervised* lender is one who is subject to periodic examination and regulation by a federal or state agency. Savings associations, commercial banks, savings banks, and insurance companies all qualify as supervised lenders. As such, they can process loans on an automatic basis.

Under this procedure, the supervised lender takes all the necessary steps to qualify a borrower, asks for a VA appraisal, and then makes its own underwriting decision. If favorable, the information is submitted to the VA in a Loan Report that the VA is obliged to honor with the issuance of a guaranty certificate.

A *nonsupervised* lender is anyone who does not qualify as a supervised lender. Mortgage companies, fraternal associations, and individuals are examples of nonsupervised lenders. To obtain a certificate of guaranty from the VA, the nonsupervised lender must first obtain approval from the VA to make a loan to the veteran applicant, and would have to submit all required information to the VA office for their underwriting approval.

A third category of lender is a *nonsupervised lender that qualifies for automatic loan processing.* Mortgage companies that are wholly owned subsidiaries of a supervised lender subject to the same periodic examination as their parent firm are listed in this category. If the VA qualifications are met, the nonsupervised lenders may submit their own approved applications for guaranty in the form of a Loan Report and receive the same automatic issuance of a VA guaranty certificate as a supervised lender.

Owner-Occupied. The VA guaranty can be used by a veteran only to buy a house to live in as the principal residence. The guaranty cannot be used to purchase rental property, except an approved one-to-four-family dwelling that is also occupied by the veteran buyer. The definition of an owner-occupant has been expanded to include a qualified veteran's spouse during the time a veteran may be on active duty out of the country.

Term of the Loan. A VA home loan can be obtained for up to 30 years. Shorter terms are approved by the VA if required by the lender and accepted by the veteran. The veteran has the right to repay all or any part of the principal balance due on the loan at any time with no additional interest charges or penalties.

Loan Servicing. The administration of a VA loan is not prescribed by the VA. Approved lenders are expected to follow the normal standards and practices of prudent lenders. The VA expects a veteran-obligor to meet the obligations fully and on time; however, it does encourage reasonable forbearance on the part of the lender with enforcement of its collections. The lender is required to notify the VA of a default within 60 days after nonpayment of an installment. Failure to file the default notice within the prescribed time limits can result in a reduction of the guaranty allowed for the lender.

Default and Foreclosure. Once notification of default has been filed with the VA, there is no time limit on when a lender must take action to foreclose the property. If foreclosure does become necessary, the VA must first appraise the property and set a "specified value." This value becomes the minimum amount for which the property can be sold and serves as a protection for all parties involved.

In years past, the VA has followed the practice of paying a lender in full on a foreclosed loan and taking title to repossessed property. It was not legally obligated to do this but believed assurance to a lender of full recovery of its loan balance with interest provided greater credibility for the VA guaranty. And certainly it did so.

More recently, as foreclosure problems escalated, the VA altered its policies into what is commonly called a "no-bid" action in foreclosure proceedings. This means that the VA now appraises the property's net value to the VA prior to a lender foreclosure action. If it would cost the VA less to pay off the guaranty to the lender (rather than the balance due on the loan) it simply chooses to not bid at the foreclosure auction (no-bid) and forfeits any further claim to the property. This possibility has lessened the value of a VA guaranty for many lenders.

Manufactured Home Loans

The Veterans Housing Act of 1970 (updated 1974) authorized the VA to guarantee loans made by private lenders to veterans for the purchase of new and used mobile homes. (Mobile homes constructed on or after June 15, 1976 are called *manufactured homes* as defined by HUD.) The same VA rules apply to a manufactured home as for a site-built house; it must be occupied by the veteran as the principal residence. The unit so acquired may be a single-wide or a double-wide, and the authorization to guarantee also covers a lot suitable for a manufactured home.

Because the status of a manufactured home as real versus personal property is not always clear, the VA now offers two categories under which lenders may request guarantees. The older procedure, identified as Section 1819 (of Title 38), offers a guaranty at the lesser of 50 percent of the loan amount to a maximum of $20,000. Effective on March 2, 1984, a new provision was added to Section 1810 increasing the maximum guaranty for a manufactured home permanently affixed to a lot provided the manufactured home is considered real property under laws of the state where the lot is located. A Section 1810 loan allows longer repayment terms and may be guaranteed on the same sliding scale entitlement as for site-built houses.

Section 1810 permits a veteran to purchase a manufactured home already permanently affixed to a lot or a home and a lot to which the home will be permanently affixed, or to refinance an existing loan secured by a manufactured home permanently affixed to a lot. The veteran is allowed to pay a reasonable discount on the refinancing portion of the loan. The term of these loans can be for as long as 30 years and 32 days. Interest rate and discount can be negotiated between the veteran and lender.

Manufactured home loans are not an additional entitlement for the veteran as the privilege is reduced by the amount of entitlement already committed, similar to a regular home loan. The same rules that apply to regular VA house loans regarding a veteran's entitlement, negotiated interest rate, and liability for repayment also apply to a manufactured home loan.

Analyzing the Loan Application

Both the property to be pledged as collateral and the veteran applicant must meet VA qualification standards. Because both HUD/FHA and the VA have similar underwriting goals (that is, a sound building as collateral and a creditworthy borrower), their qualification standards are similar. And both agencies now accept the other's qualifications of applicants with a few exceptions. Property qualification is considered next. The process of qualifying a veteran applicant is examined in the next chapter to allow comparisons with other loan-qualifying procedures.

Qualifying the Property

The VA uses both its own staff and approved independent fee appraisers to inspect and evaluate property that may serve as loan collateral. While the appraisal form has been standardized (see Appendix for an illustration), the VA refers to its appraisal analysis as a Certificate of Reasonable Value (CRV). A CRV represents the maximum amount a lender may loan and still obtain an underwriting guarantee from the VA. A veteran may purchase a house at a price exceeding the CRV, but any amount in excess of the CRV must be paid in cash. Or, if the CRV comes in at less than the agreed price, the veteran has the right to withdraw from the contract and recover the earnest money in full.

The requirements mentioned are for VA qualification and are not necessarily the same as a lender might require. Lenders are not required to make a loan at the VA-permissible limits. Simply, a lender cannot exceed those limits and still obtain a VA guaranty. But if the lender's policy is more limited than that allowed by the VA, it is free to apply its own limitations and still obtain a VA guaranty commitment. For instance, many lenders will not accept 100 percent loan-to-value loans regardless of VA permission. Nevertheless, so long as the loan does not exceed VA limits, the guaranty can be issued. The same concept applies to all other underwriting programs—FHA, GNMA, and all conforming loans—and the lender is free to offer a loan at lower than the designated limits and may still qualify the loan for whatever underwriting program is sought. The point is that loan applicants should not expect government agency maximum limitations to be uniformly accepted by all private lenders.

Scope of the VA Appraisal. Like the HUD/FHA appraisal procedure discussed earlier in this chapter, there are other pieces of information needed beyond the property evaluation. VA is the only agency that still requires information on the maintenance and utility costs of the house to be acquired. Both of these costs are considered in an applicant's income qualification under the residual guideline method, as more fully described in the next chapter. And like the FHA, VA appraisers are expected to make the necessary adjustments in valuation that will more closely reflect the property's real value rather than an inflated value caused by excessive financial inducements.

The appraiser's responsibility extends to inspecting the property to make sure that it meets VA minimum property standards. If not, repairs may be required to upgrade the property before the loan can be funded.

Questions for Discussion

1. How has the FHA achieved the goals for which it was established?

2. Explain the two different dollar limits that apply to HUD/FHA-insured commitments.

3. In HUD/FHA settlement requirements, what rules apply to the handling of the down payment? The closing costs?

4. Explain the difference between loan underwriting commitments made by the VA and by HUD/FHA.

5. What charges must a borrower pay for a HUD/FHA-insured commitment?

6. How are interest rates determined on HUD/FHA loans? On VA loans?

7. Explain the assumption requirements now in effect for HUD/FHA loans. For VA loans.

8. Distinguish between the release of liability for a veteran and the restoration of entitlement.

9. What is the purpose of the HUD/FHA 203(k) Rehabilitation Home Mortgage Insurance program?

10. What charges, if any, must a veteran pay for a loan guaranty?

Chapter 9

Borrower Qualification

KEY WORDS AND PHRASES

Residential loan • Equal Credit Opportunity Act (ECOA) • Loan application • Credit scoring • Production-related income • Assured income • Liabilities • Assets • Willingness to pay • Credit report • Fair Credit Reporting Act • Percentage guideline method • Effective income • Housing expense • Residual method (VA) • Cost-of-living expenses (VA) • Income ratio method (VA) • Conforming loan • Private mortgage insurance (PMI)

INTRODUCTION

For the purpose of analysis, mortgage loans may be divided into two categories: those made to individuals and families to buy homes and those made to individuals and companies to acquire commercial properties. Because the basic source of loan repayment is not the same, the analysis differs in emphasis. For a home loan, the analysis focuses first on the applicant's income. It is the buyer's personal income, essentially income unrelated to the property itself, that will be used to repay the loan. For a commercial property loan, the lender normally expects repayment from income produced by the property, and that source takes priority in the analysis.

This chapter examines, first, the individual as borrower for the purpose of buying a home. **Residential loans** comprise over two-thirds of the mortgage loan market and may be classed in four major categories: (1) HUD/FHA, (2) VA, (3) conventional/conforming, and (4) other conventional. (A conventional loan is one without government underwriting.) Of the four, both HUD/FHA and VA offer fairly clear standards and guidelines for the industry and the consumer.

The third category mentioned, conventional/conforming, covers loans made with the expectation of selling them to either Fannie Mae or Freddie Mac. Both of these secondary-market purchasers have developed uniform documents and some common limitations (but not always the same standards) on the loans they can accept.

The fourth category, other conventional, offers few uniform procedures with many minor variations. A recent variation of a conventional loan is designed to better fit the needs of lower income families and will be explained later under the umbrella term of *affordable housing loan.* Summing up, the field of loan qualification does not offer standards used by everyone! (Some of the variations can be found in Table 9–2 later in this chapter.)

To enable a student to better understand the similarities and the differences between the four major categories of borrower qualification, all are presented in this chapter. Examples are given for each using the same basic applicant's income and loan amount. Generally, the analyses arrive at similar conclusions but use slightly different methods to reach that point.

A requirement for all borrowers is to furnish a credit report. The information found in these reports is explained in this chapter. Also, some information is given on qualification of corporate borrowers. Finally, because private mortgage insurance has become an essential part of mortgage lending practices, this kind of underwriting is reviewed.

Loan analysis begins with the loan application. Lenders no longer have the freedom to ask whatever questions they may wish of an applicant. This practice in the past has led to some discrimination in lending practices. As a step toward reducing discrimination in all kinds of credit transactions and to more sharply focus the questions that may be asked, Congress passed the Equal Credit Opportunity Act. How this act has affected mortgage lending procedures is discussed next.

EQUAL CREDIT OPPORTUNITY ACT

The basis for analysis of a borrower starts with the loan application. As a step toward equalizing the availability of credit, the **Equal Credit Opportunity Act (ECOA),** passed in 1974, limits information that may be required in an application. Questions that could lead to discriminatory lending practices have been eliminated and new questions have been added that need only be answered on a voluntary basis. The act was implemented under the direction of the Federal Reserve Board and is administered by the Consumer Affairs Office of the Federal Reserve.

Initially, the act prohibited discrimination in the granting of credit on the basis of sex or marital status. On March 23, 1976, the ECOA was amended to expand the prohibition against discrimination in credit transactions by adding race, color, religion, national origin, age, receipt of public assistance income, and the exercise of rights under the Consumer Credit Protection Act, of which the ECOA is a part, as protected categories.

The restrictions covering information on sources of an applicant's income do not apply if the applicant expects to use that income as a means of repaying the loan. For example, no questions may be asked regarding alimony, child support, or separate maintenance payments *unless* the borrower plans to use this money to make the loan payments.

No discounting of income is allowed because of sex or marital status or because income is derived from part-time employment. In earlier years it was not uncommon to discount the income of a wife of child-bearing age by as much as 50 percent. In regard to a credit history, an applicant must be permitted to show evidence that facts in a joint report do not accurately reflect his or her individual ability or inclination to repay the loan. If credit is denied, the lender must provide the reasons for denial upon request of applicant.

The act preempts only those applicable state laws that are inconsistent with the federal requirements. Lenders in states that may impose additional requirements, such as additional prohibitions on what may be in a loan application, must also comply with state laws. It should be noted that the act's requirement for separate liability for separate accounts (married persons can demand that separate credit records be maintained in either a married name or a maiden name) cannot be changed by state laws. However, any action taken by a creditor in accordance with state property laws directly or indirectly affecting creditworthiness will not constitute discrimination.

In general, the law does not specify how or to whom loans should be made, but does call for lenders to be much more specific with reasons for rejection of a loan applicant. Generalizations and categories of persons not eligible for credit are no longer permissible. For example, at one time a married person who was separated could be denied credit by lenders as a customary policy. Or, simply, a single person might not be accepted as a loan applicant. This kind of blanket denial is no longer permitted because each person must be considered as an individual and judged by the same standards as any other person. There can be a difference in the standards that a lender may use for long-term mortgage credit as opposed to a short-term installment-type of credit, but the standards must be applied uniformly to all applicants.

THE LOAN APPLICATION

A mortgage **loan application** offers information for qualification of both the borrower and the property. If the loan is residential, as explained earlier, the information requested on an application must conform with the requirements of ECOA. For this purpose, the Federal Reserve has prepared model application forms for five different types of credit, one of which is residential real estate. On the basis of the Federal Reserve model, Fannie Mae and Freddie Mac designed their own standard form (FNMA 1003 and FHLMC 65, respectively). As the need for greater standardization developed, this form became mandatory for use after November 15, 1986, by all lenders with all residential loans. The latest revision, dated October 1992, is illustrated in the Appendix.

The information required in a residential loan application may be summarized as follows:

1. Identification of borrower (and co-borrower).
2. Employment and income data.

3. Anticipated monthly housing expenses.
4. Cost of house, down payment, financing requested.
5. List of assets and liabilities.
6. Credit references.
7. Applicant's certification as to accuracy of information.

Commercial Loan

If a loan is for commercial property, the lender is more likely to use its own application form because considerably more information is needed. Further, federal laws regarding application information designed to better protect an individual generally do not apply to commercial loans.

Since most commercial loans are expected to be repaid from the property income rather than from the borrower's personal income, specific information is needed on that property. An appraisal, market information with a review of competition, and substantial financial data on anticipated operations would be required. More detailed information on commercial loans will be considered after the examination of residential loan qualification next.

FINANCIAL EVALUATION OF THE BORROWER

The high loan-to-value ratios (LTVR) often found in residential loans place a premium on an accurate examination of the borrower's repayment ability. In the event of default the conventional lender, or the private mortgage insurance company covering only a portion of the loan, would be hard pressed to make full recovery from disposition of the collateral in case of an early foreclosure. Proper analysis of the borrower to determine total available income, any claims against that income, as well as the credit record is important for a home loan.

A borrower's other assets are helpful as additional security for a loan and can result in a lower rate of interest, but other assets cannot always be counted on for use in repayment. The lender knows that in many cases of actual default in payments the borrower has met with financial problems that were beyond his or her control. Accidents, job layoffs, or serious illness in the family can deplete most of a family's financial assets, leaving the lender with few means of recourse beyond the house that has been pledged as loan collateral.

No two borrowers ever present the same credit picture. Even so, analysis of a borrower can be handled two different ways: (1) by a human underwriter, called *manual underwriting*, or (2) by a computer, called *automatic underwriting*. Software programs have been developed for computers that use artificial intelligence and reference to a variety of information that enables the computer to give loan approval when it is justified. However, the machine does not provide a rejection of the applicant. Such questions that should be answered are referred back to the lender's underwriter for further work.

Because a computer is more number oriented, it also uses **credit scoring,** which is a method of giving a default probability number based on an individual's credit record. The method has been available for nearly 50 years but has received publicity recently because of its wider use. A more detailed explanation of the procedure will be given in Chapter 14 as a part of the discussion on automated underwriting.

There are some guidelines and general rules, mainly based on common sense, that are helpful in determining whether or not a borrower should be able to make a loan repayment. One popular rule is to always follow the "Three Cs" of good underwriting. These are:

1. **C**apability—evaluating a borrower's capacity to make the required payments.
2. **C**redit—assessing the borrower's credit reputation (willingness to pay).
3. **C**ollateral—determining that the property is adequate collateral for the mortgage loan.

Thus, to make a sound prediction, the underwriter must consider the three basic questions: (1) What is the applicant's ability to pay? (2) What is the applicant's willingness to pay? (3) Does the property provide enough collateral (which is the subject of the next chapter)?

Ability to Pay

More than for any other type of loan, the residential lender looks to a family's income as the basic resource for repayment. Assets are important, but are used in part to determine the spending or saving patterns practiced in the use of that income. Therefore, a careful review of the employment record, present income, and future potential is important. The following are some of the income elements considered by a lender, with a commentary on each.

Types of Income

Lenders make a broad distinction between **production-related income** and **assured income.** Production-related income means commissions, bonuses, and, in some cases, piecework pay. It does not have the certainty of assured income such as wages or a salary and normally requires a longer record of earnings to qualify. Following are major types of income and comments on their acceptability.

1. **Salary.** A salary, particularly from a major company or institution, is highly acceptable for loan qualification. It can be easily verified from IRS W-2 reports.
2. **Bonus.** A bonus should not be counted on unless a regular pattern can be established for several successive years.
3. **Commission.** A straight commission job can be very lucrative, or it can be a complete bust. Only a past record of income culled from several years of tax returns can be accepted as factual.

4. **Hourly wages.** An hourly wage is a solid basis for continuing income and one that can usually be confirmed by an employer.

5. **Overtime wages.** This is an uncertain basis for making a long-term loan as most employers try to avoid overtime, using it only for an emergency situation or as a temporary practice. Again, a consistent pattern of overtime payments for several years would make this an acceptable addition to an applicant's gross income.

6. **Second job.** Many persons today hold more than one job on a full- or part-time basis. Teachers, police officers, and skilled hourly workers all can have other capabilities and may spend extra hours augmenting their income. If the second job has been held over a period of several years on a regular basis, it provides a substantial lift to the regular income.

7. **Unreported income.** A few people accept extra work, or even become involved full-time, in jobs that pay in cash and on which income is not reported for tax purposes. Such income, if not reported, is illegal and cannot be used under any condition to justify a loan. This "borrower" could lose this income abruptly and spend some time in prison.

8. **Co-borrower's income.** Prior to enactment of the Federal Equal Credit Opportunity Act, it was a fairly common practice to reduce the effective income that could be accepted from a working wife. The reasoning then was that young married couples were also interested in rearing families. And earlier customs generally assigned more of the problems concerned with family emergencies, sickness, pregnancies, and child care to the wife. The new laws recognize changing customs, and a lender is now required to apply the same qualification standards to each borrower without questioning marital status or gender.

9. **Income from children.** While many young men and women living with their parents earn substantial money at full- or part-time jobs, these earnings are not generally a recognized addition to the family income for loan purposes. The obligation on the part of children to contribute to family finances for support of the home is not a continuing one. Normally, children will leave home to set up their own household within a few years. Thus, temporary income supplied by grown children lends no real weight to most loan requests. There is another qualification pattern that considers children's income differently. Many state and local housing authorities offer loan assistance programs using lower cost "bond money" that limit eligible income. Generally, for qualification, eligible "family income" is the combined income of all persons who will live in the house to be financed. Similar provisions apply to the more recently designated category of affordable housing loans.

10. **Pension and trust income.** In years past, not many have enjoyed pensions, retirement funds, or other work benefits at a sufficiently early age to apply them toward a home purchase. However, this pattern is changing. For instance, many veterans of military, government, or corporate services have completed 20 or 30 years of employment before the age of 50 and are eligible for further lifetime benefits. These benefits are one of the most reliable forms of income.

11. **Child support and alimony.** Some states do not permit alimony in divorce actions but provide child support as a matter of court decree. Other states permit both alimony and child support. Such payments can be considered as regular income for a divorced spouse or remarried person, depending on the court ruling. However, the record of payment must show dependability over a period of time before it would constitute an acceptable addition to total income. ECOA restricts information that must be provided on this source of income if it is not to be counted as income for repayment of the loan.

12. **Self-employed persons.** Many people operate their own businesses or work as self-employed individuals in professional capacities. This type of income is one of the more difficult to evaluate because of the flexibility in accounting procedures that define such income. Some small business owners are able to pay certain living expenses from their business (car expenses, entertainment, travel, etc.), but weight can only be given to the individual's income that is reported as taxable. Without an employer to verify income, lenders must rely on several years of federal income tax returns. Certified copies of these returns can be obtained from the Internal Revenue Service for a small fee upon application by the taxpayer only.

13. **Interest and dividends.** This type of income derives from investments that may, or may not, provide an ongoing source. If the assets can be held as an investment, they represent stable income. However, losses can occur and the assets might be sold, which would eliminate that particular source of income. Again, the past record would give some indication of how investment assets have been managed.

14. **Part-time employment.** In the past, income derived from part-time work was not accepted at full value toward a person's income applicable to repayment of a mortgage loan. The concern was about the future stability of this source of income. ECOA requirements now permit no discounting of income from part-time employment. However, the lender may still require that an applicant show evidence of stability and reasonable assurance that part-time work will continue.

Stability of Income

Along with the size of an applicant's income, the assurance that it will be continued must be investigated. Two measures are most commonly used: (1) time on the job and (2) type of work performed.

Length of Time on Job. While standards vary, some length of time on the same job is a measure of stability. The changing nature of job tenure has brought a reduction in the former three-year standard to a more common one-year requirement. There is a basis for this restriction in that any new job may or may not work out due to personality factors, lack of accomplishment, or dissatisfaction with the work.

With the more rapid changes in jobs today, tenure may be more fairly judged from the individual's job history. Has the applicant made a record of "job hopping" without noticeable improvement in income? Is the present job one of greater responsibility and growth potential than the previous job? Has the applicant maintained a record of employment in a chosen field of work, or is the present job an entirely new type of work? The lack of standards makes this question a judgment call for an underwriter.

Type of Work. While a person with a long record of steady employment provides a very good answer to the question of income stability, many seeking loans cannot provide such a record. So an additional standard is helpful in analysis of an applicant: the type of work.

Persons with salaried jobs employed by major companies or institutions rate very well. So do professional people with job tenure of various kinds. Hourly workers, some with the protection of union contracts, can be more stable (and often more highly paid) than lower level management and clerical staff workers. Government employees carry good security as do teachers, police officers, and other service workers.

On the lower side of the scale, new sales representatives enticed by stories of high commissions, entertainers, and seasonal workers give poor evidence of continued stable income. To some lenders, socially unacceptable types of work carry unduly low ratings. It might be noted that laws do not protect persons against credit discrimination due to type of work.

Liabilities

For residential loan qualification, fixed liabilities must be reported on the application. If **liabilities** are excessive, an applicant can be rejected (a judgment call). The standard measure applied is a conversion of liabilities to a per-month basis. Not all liabilities are included or measured in this manner, only those that are required by the lender to be listed. The key determinant is whether or not the required monthly payments could prevent making a mortgage payment. However, that determinant is limited. For instance, cost of food, clothing, transportation, and income taxes need not be listed even though they are all rather essential.

To qualify an applicant's income, certain monthly obligations should not exceed guideline percentages of the applicant's income. The obligations that fall under this criteria are housing costs as reflected in the monthly mortgage payment plus other fixed obligations such as installment payments and revolving account payments. In general, more than half of an applicant's income is open to use for unlisted obligations. Each of the major categories of loans (FHA, VA, conforming/conventional, and other conventional) apply slightly different guideline standards for listing liabilities. These will be more fully explained later in this chapter.

While there are some differences between lenders and types of loans as to which monthly obligations must be listed, caution should be taken before incurring other debt prior to qualifying for a mortgage loan. A recent study indicates that a major cause of loan rejection is not the housing payment itself, rather it is heavy monthly installment obligations for other items such as cars, computers, video equipment, and similar purchases that might well be postponed.

Assets

Unlike an applicant for a commercial loan, residential applicants need not show substantial **assets** to qualify. Many home buyers are younger people who have had little time to accumulate much in other assets yet still qualify for suitable home loans. However, there is an advantage if assets other than a home are held by an applicant. Ownership of stocks, bonds, real estate, savings funds, and other such assets does indicate an ability to live prudently and conserve a portion of one's income. If this is the case, the applicant should find qualification of income much easier as the percentage guidelines that limit the amount of obligations will most likely be relaxed a bit.

As a commentary on how lenders might look at other assets, life insurance is both an asset in its cash value and protection features and a liability in its cost. Cars and boats represent some trade-in value but usually discounted. Furniture and personal property are often overvalued in an applicant's statement of assets because of the owner's personal attachment and these values are not given much weight by lenders. Employee trust and pension funds can represent value if the interest is a vested one; that is, if employees can take the funds with them should they leave the job. An interest in one's own business is best determined by an audited financial statement of that business. Accounts and notes receivable should be detailed for proper valuation.

Willingness to Pay

The element of **willingness to pay,** sometimes called *credit character,* is the most difficult to analyze and judge. Yet this factor alone can be the cause of loan rejection. An underwriter's judgment is crucial in making this decision as it can involve questions of credit discrimination.

Creditworthiness is judged from an applicant's previous record of meeting obligations. The most common source of information to make this determination comes from credit reports as issued by credit bureaus. Information for mortgage loans is also obtained from public records covering litigation, judgments, or criminal actions. Conversations with persons involved in the house sale transaction can sometimes bring to light information on the applicant's manner of living, personal attitudes, and activities that might give cause for a more detailed investigation.

Some lenders prefer to take loan applications at the borrower's place of residence as a person's manner of living can be helpful in judging credit character. There is a question as to when personal inquiry becomes an invasion of one's privacy. But lenders are obligated to exercise prudent judgment and need information to make sound decisions. The true picture can be just as advantageous for the borrower as for the lender and is mandatory in making proper judgment on any loan. Individuals asking to borrow someone else's money should be willing to provide complete and accurate information about themselves within the requirements of the Equal Credit Opportunity Act.

Under the category of willingness to pay, lenders have always tried to assess an applicant's motivation for owning a home. Lenders in the past have felt that the strongest incentive for owning a home came from a family unit committed to the rearing of children. But lifestyles have changed, and many persons today are not interested in having a family but do want houses. Even prior to the enactment of the Equal Credit Opportunity Act, lenders were enlarging qualification standards and making loans to single persons, both men and women, and nonfamily units where there was reasonable assurance of continuity of interest in owning a house. ECOA has eliminated gender and marital status as a basis for loan rejection, but it has not foreclosed the lender's right to exercise judgment as to the continuing need to repay a mortgage loan. This is an area that does not lend itself to clear-cut definitions and presents problems for a responsible loan officer.

Credit Reports

Most adults in this country have **credit reports** compiled by the more than 1,100 credit bureaus, whether or not they are aware of it. Information is routinely submitted to local credit bureaus by their members who normally are those extending credit within the community. Credit bureau members consist of local merchants, financial institutions, gasoline retailers, providers of medical services, taxing authorities, and possibly utility companies. (Utility companies may not exchange credit information as they have very effective constraints if payment becomes delinquent!)

Records of credit card accounts are generally kept separately in huge computer data banks, not in local credit bureaus. Information in credit files is classed as proprietary, available only to approved credit bureau members and to individuals seeking information on their own records. Those who pay bills only in cash are not likely to have credit records anywhere, which can create some problems when seeking a mortgage loan. However, to properly handle such people wanting to obtain credit, the fairly new credit criteria allowed under "affordable housing loans" recognizes insufficient credit records and accepts timely cash payments as proof of sound payment practices.

Keepers of Credit Records

Before applying for any loan, it is wise for an individual to review any credit information that he or she may have on file. The Fair Credit Reporting Act grants individuals the right to do this. Errors can be corrected and this is best handled before a loan officer examines the record. The place to begin is with the local credit bureau which is listed under "Credit Reporting Agencies" in the Yellow Pages. Large cities have multiple bureaus and usually one will dominate mortgage loan information—the one commonly used by FHA, VA, and mortgage companies generally. Individual credit reports cost about $15, may take several weeks for delivery, but are free if a bad report is the reason for denial of credit.

Three major national credit data companies (also called national repositories) hold credit information on individuals and may be contacted. Most mortgage lenders now require reports from at least two of the three in addition to the local credit bureau report as part of the loan documentation. The three do not share credit information and their reports can differ. Contacts are as follows:

EQUIFAX
Box 740241, Atlanta, GA 30374-0241
Phone: 800-685-1111

EXPERIAN
Box 949, Allen, TX 75013
Phone: 800-682-7654

TRANS UNION
Box 390, Springfield, PA 19064-0390
Phone: 800-916-8800

Credit Information

Credit bureaus provide records of credit accounts and payment histories of those accounts. Each creditor makes the decision as to whether or not to grant credit. The information contained in a report covers the past seven years (10 years for bankruptcy filings). If an individual files a complaint against a credit reporting company, the law requires that an answer be provided within 30 days. Disputed information may be removed from the credit record while an investigation is made to the original creditor. If the information is accurate, it is returned to the record. If it is inaccurate, the information must be deleted and the individual can instruct the credit bureau to send a correction to all creditors who reviewed the file in the previous six months. If unfavorable credit information is on the record and there are mitigating circumstances (such as a serious injury causing delay in making payments), an individual can file a statement with the credit bureau of up to 100 words in explanation.

Responsible Federal Agency. The basis for the preceding information on consumers' rights stems from the **Fair Credit Reporting Act** passed in 1970. This act is administered by the Federal Trade Commission headquartered in Washington, D.C., with regional offices in major cities.

Credit Reporting Problems

Almost all credit information is now maintained in computerized systems. Large creditors send data to their own bureau on computer tapes, minimizing the possibility of errors. Nevertheless, there remain the problems of confusion with persons of similar name, changes of married names, and just plain errors in the recording of data. Confusion over names is not always simplified by the use of Social Security numbers. The reason is that creditors may not demand a Social Security number when considering granting credit. The Social Security Act itself classifies an individual's number as private. However, depository institutions must record a depositor's number in order to report any payment of interest to the IRS. But the refusal to disclose a Social Security number to a creditor cannot be used as a basis for denial of credit.

Credit Scoring. The increased use of computer analysis has brought greater use of credit scoring to mortgage lending. Credit scoring is the assignment of a numerical rating to consumers based on their credit history. It is not new as it has been used for over 30 years by auto lenders, credit card issuers, and other extenders of credit. Credit scoring is calculated by credit bureaus using information from one or more of the three major credit repositories: Equifax, Experian, and Trans Union. Therefore, they can report different ratings.

A number of other factors enter into judging a person's creditworthiness—scoring is just one. Further information on this subject may be found in Chapter 14, "Technology Advances in Mortgage Lending."

QUALIFYING THE APPLICANT

All lenders have the same underwriting goal: a borrower capable of repaying the loan plus a property providing adequate collateral. As examined earlier in this chapter, more than income is involved in borrower qualification for a residential loan. This is only one of the elements that falls under "ability to pay," albeit a crucial one. Greater emphasis is being given to income qualification today as it involves numbers that provide easier comparisons between applicants. Comparison between applicants is one method of screening the mortgage market for discriminatory practices.

A residential loan applicant's personal income is examined carefully since that is where the money will come from to repay the loan. Other obligations against that income must be weighed to determine if an additional burden can be undertaken. It does neither party, the lender nor the borrower, any good to place an overload of debt on a home buyer. Several different paths are used to reach a judgment on qualification, but in the final analysis, the decision has to be a "judgment call." The decision can be made by a human underwriter or by a computer with a software program that uses artificial intelligence to evaluate the information submitted.

Following are explanations of the qualification guidelines—income and other measures—as applied to each of the four principal kinds of home loans: (1) HUD/FHA, (2) VA, (3) conventional/conforming, and (4) other conventional loans, with special attention given to affordable housing loans. While each procedure differs slightly from the others, the thrust is the same: set a measure that limits other obligations to a percentage of the applicant's effective income. An underlying problem is defining what should be included as "other obligations."

HUD/FHA Borrower Income Qualification

HUD/FHA uses a percentage guideline method to measure the adequacy of an applicant's income. As part of an ongoing effort within the industry to standardize residential loan procedures, the measures used to qualify FHA loan applicants have been simplified and are now similar to those used for conventional loans.

To give an idea of former requirements, older procedures required an applicant's Social Security and withholding taxes to be deducted before determining effective income. Also, the costs of maintenance and utilities for the new house were classed as housing expense items and had to be deducted. None of these are deducted today. Taxes, maintenance, and utilities are now considered payable from "residual income"—that income remaining after the required mandatory expenses have been deducted.

Percentage Guideline Method

The **percentage guideline method** considers an applicant's monthly liabilities in two separate categories and measures each amount against the applicant's effective income. The two categories and limits applied are:

1. Housing expense should not exceed 29 percent of the applicant's effective income.
2. Housing expense plus other recurring charges are identified as fixed payments and should not exceed 41 percent of effective income.

How HUD/FHA defines the measures that are used is important. A brief explanation of the major items considered follows.

Effective Income. This includes gross income from all sources, including borrower and co-borrower, that can be expected to continue for the first three years of the mortgage. (This measure was changed in 1995 from five years to three years.) Even though an applicant's income is properly verified, HUD/FHA reserves the right to adjust, or disallow, unacceptable income. A bonus or unusually large commission should be supported by a record of equivalent previous earnings. The owner of a business would be allowed the amount he or she withdraws as salary, provided this amount does not exceed actual earnings. Money reimbursed for travel expenses cannot be accepted, nor any repayment of principal on a capital investment.

Housing Expense. These expenses include the mortgage payment of principal, interest, real estate taxes, and hazard insurance plus flood insurance if applicable. (In conventional loans, this payment is often identified simply as PITI.) Housing expense also includes the FHA annual premium charge and homeowners' association or condo fees if any are applicable.

Recurring Charges. These include any debt that matures in more than 10 months (changed in 1995 from a six-month requirement) or is continuous in nature, such as child support as ordered by a court and installment plus revolving accounts. Child care is no longer counted as recurring debt. In addition, any large monthly debt that matures in less than 10 months must be given underwriting consideration.

Fixed Payment. Fixed payment is the sum total of the housing expense and the recurring charges.

Residual Income. This is gross effective income minus fixed payment. Because residual income is affected by tax liabilities, Social Security deductions, and utility and maintenance expenses, HUD/FHA does not establish a required residual income amount as is found in VA procedures.

Ratios

The measure of adequacy is determined by ratios. By dividing the housing expense by the applicant's gross effective income, a ratio is determined. Housing expenses should not exceed 29 percent of income. The second ratio is for the total fixed payment. By dividing fixed payment by gross effective income, the ratio should not exceed 41 percent.

These ratios are guidelines and subject to an underwriter's judgment. If compensating factors are present, the ratios may be exceeded by one or two percent. An example of compensating factors is a borrower who:

- Invests 25 percent or more in a down payment.
- Owns substantial reserves for contingencies.
- Is a limited user of credit.
- Has no automobile.

To illustrate the key elements of an applicant's income qualification, a simplified example is offered next.

· ·

EXAMPLE

Percentage Guideline—Monthly Basis

Gross effective income			$3,000
Housing expense			
Mortgage principle and interest	$660		
Taxes and insurance	165		
Total housing expense		$825	
Recurring charges			
Car payment	$240		
Revolving account payment	90		
Total recurring charges		$330	
Total fixed payment			$1,155
Ratios:			
Housing expense	825/3,000 = 27.5%		
Fixed payment	1,155/3,000 = 38.5%		

· ·

In this example, the housing expense shows 27.5 percent of effective income, which falls within the HUD ceiling of 29 percent. The other measure, fixed payment, shows a 38.5 percent ratio of effective income, which also falls within the HUD 41 percent guideline. If either exceeds the guidelines, the underwriter would look for other compensating factors that might justify the granting of an insurance commitment.

Borrower Rating

Income qualification alone is not the final determinant. One further judgment must be made by a HUD/FHA underwriter, and that is a *borrower rating*. An older method using a five-point gradient scale (from excellent to reject) has been replaced with only two grades: acceptable or rejection. A rejection on any one of the ratings is cause for denial of the loan commitment. The four elements that are rated are:

1. Credit characteristics
2. Adequacy of effective income
3. Stability of effective income
4. Adequacy of available assets

VA Borrower Qualification

How the VA qualifies property offered as collateral was discussed in the previous chapter. This section examines the methods used by the VA to qualify an applicant-veteran. In addition to meeting the requirements for eligibility and entitlement stated in Chapter 8, the applicant must show an income adequate to repay the loan and have an acceptable credit record with other creditors. To qualify an applicant's income, the VA requires two separate sets of calculations. One, called the **residual method,** has been used for many years. The other, a procedure using income ratios, became effective October 1, 1986. Explanations, examples, and guidelines for each of the two methods follow.

Residual Method of Income Qualification

The VA's residual method of qualifying an applicant's income might be called a summation process. It starts with the applicant's *gross monthly income,* which means gross pay before any deductions are taken. Then, mandatory deductions start with the applicant's monthly tax liabilities, continue with shelter expenses and other fixed obligations, and result in what the applicant has left. What remains after the applicable mandatory obligations have been deducted is called *residual income.* How the VA underwriter defines the various items is discussed next.

Gross Income. The recognized income of both borrower and spouse are added together, and that income should have a reasonable expectation of continuing.

Tax Liabilities. The applicant's tax liabilities include federal and state income taxes, Social Security tax, and any other tax liabilities that may be due. The amount of tax is based on that shown by tax tables applicable to an applicant's recognized income and may not be the same as what the taxpayer pays. Tax liabilities are deducted from the gross income, resulting in the applicant's net take-home pay. Take-home pay is not a critical number with the VA as it is not used as a basis for qualification.

Shelter Expenses. For the residual method only, the VA adds certain shelter expenses not found in either FHA or conforming loan qualification calculations. In addition to the standard mortgage payment (principal, interest, taxes, and insurance, PITI) and any special assessments, the VA adds estimated costs of maintenance and utilities for the house to be acquired. (These two expenses are not included in the VA's income ratio method.) The costs of maintenance and utilities are developed by the VA Regional Office from experience with various neighborhoods.

Other Monthly Obligations. Under other monthly obligations, the VA lists installment obligations (such as a car payment) with six or more monthly payments still due, revolving account payments, alimony and/or child support, and job-related expenses (such as union dues). If the applicant is obligated for other state and local taxes or life insurance premiums, these should also be listed.

Residual Income. After deducting the taxes, shelter expenses, and other monthly obligations from the applicant's gross monthly income, what remains is called *residual income*. For qualification, the residual income must be sufficient to cover the applicant's required minimum residual income. The minimum residual income is a cost of living amount that varies by region, by family size, and by loan amount. It is adjusted periodically by the VA to meet changing conditions.

Cost of Living Expense. Unlike any other underwriting procedure, the VA residual method uses a calculated figure for determining the cost of living. These costs include food, clothing, transportation, personal and medical care, and other consumption items. Since 1986, these costs have been determined by the standards for the four Census Bureau regions: West, South, Midwest, and Northeast. The actual figures are developed by the VA from Department of Labor data on consumer expenditure surveys.

Table 9–1 gives the cost of living figures for the four regions by family size and loan amount. The applicant's residual income (that remaining after total monthly obligations have been deducted) must be sufficient to cover the applicable cost of living amount.

Whatever amount remains from the applicant's income after total obligations and cost of living expenses are deducted is called *excess residual income*. The "excess," if any, may be used to help qualify marginal applicants, as will be shown later.

TABLE 9–1 Veterans Administration—Table of Residual Incomes by Region (Effective April 1994)

LOAN AMOUNTS OF $69,999 AND BELOW

Family size*	Northeast	Midwest	South	West
1	$375	$367	$367	$409
2	629	616	616	686
3	758	742	742	826
4	854	835	835	930
5	886	867	867	965

*For families with more than five members, add $75 for each additional member up to a family of seven.

LOAN AMOUNTS OF $70,000 AND ABOVE

Family size*	Northeast	Midwest	South	West
1	$ 433	$424	$424	$ 472
2	726	710	710	791
3	874	855	855	952
4	986	964	964	1,074
5	1,021	999	999	1.113

*For families with more than five members, add $80 for each additional member up to a family of seven.

••

EXAMPLE

Residual Guideline Method—Monthly Basis

Gross salary or earnings		$3,000
LESS:		
Federal income tax	330	
Social Security tax	205	
Total tax liabilities		535
Net take-home pay		2,465
LESS:		
Principal and interest	660	
Realty taxes	105	
Hazard insurance	60	
Maintenance	55	

Utilities	125	
Total monthly shelter expenses		1,005
LESS:		
Installment obligation	240	
State and local taxes	90	
Total other obligations		330
Applicant's residual income		$1,130

•••

If the applicant in the example is a family of two living in the South region and the loan amount is less than $69,999, the minimum required residual (from Table 9–1) amounts to $616. Since the applicant has a residual income of $1,130, it is adequate to meet the requirements. It might be noted that the VA process favors single persons and small families. Applying the cost of living table, as the family members increase, an applicant is less likely to qualify.

Excess Residual Income. There is one more piece of information to be derived from this method of calculation, and that is how much the applicant's residual income exceeds the minimum required amount. To continue using the same example, the *required* residual amounted to $616. Subtracting that amount from the applicant's residual income of $1,130 leaves an "excess residual" of $514 ($1,130 minus $616 equals $514). It is not the amount but the ratio that is significant. To achieve this, divide the applicant's excess residual by the minimum required residual to determine the *excess residual ratio*. In the preceding example, dividing $514 by $616 gives a ratio of .83, or 83 percent. This ratio fits into the qualification measure if there is a problem with the income ratio qualification calculation. If the excess residual ratio is 20 percent or greater, the applicant may still qualify even though the income ratio guidelines are not met. The income ratio method of calculation is explained next.

VA Income Ratio Method of Qualification

As of October 1, 1986, the VA introduced the **income ratio method** of qualifying an applicant's income. It is used in conjunction with the residual method: If the income ratio is not met, an applicant may still be approved, providing the excess residual is at least 20 percent of minimum required residual. The income ratio method uses some different measures, one being the applicant's income is gross income; income taxes and Social Security taxes are *not* a recognized deduction. Other differences in definitions for the income ratio method follow.

Shelter Expenses. The same expenses apply for the income ratio method as for the residual method with the exception of utility and maintenance costs. These are not included when calculating the income ratio method. Unlike either FHA or conforming-loan guideline procedures, VA draws no line that requires any percentage limit on shelter expenses.

Other Monthly Payments. There is no difference in defining other monthly payments between the two methods. Recurring monthly obligations include other loan repayments, installment obligations, and such other obligations as child support. Federal tax obligations are not included in this method as they are expected to be paid from income remaining after all mandatory deductions are taken.

Income Ratio. The sum of housing expenses plus other monthly payments (as briefly defined above), is then compared with the applicant's gross income. The limitation is 41 percent. That is, the listed expenses should not exceed 41 percent of gross income.

••

EXAMPLE

Income Ratio Method—Monthly Basis

Applicant's total gross income		$3,000
LESS: Housing expense		
Mortgage principal and interest	$660	
Taxes and insurance	165	
Other monthly payments		
Car payment	240	
State and local taxes	90	
Total monthly obligations		$1,155
Ratio:		
Gross income	$3,000	
Total monthly obligations	$1,155/3,000 = 39%	

••

In this example the total monthly obligations amount to 39 percent of the applicant's gross income. Since this is within the VA's 41 percent guideline, the applicant would meet the test for adequate income.

Comparison with Residual Guideline. As a final step in qualifying an applicant's income, the underwriter must review the results of the residual method qualification. This becomes most important if the income ratio method exceeds the 41 percent guideline limit. Should that occur, the underwriter then reviews the amount that the applicant's residual exceeds the minimum residual as required by the VA cost-of-living figures. As explained earlier, if the excess residual ratio is 20 percent or greater, the applicant may still qualify.

Other Qualification Considerations

While the VA considers the income available for family support a significant factor, it is not the sole criterion for approving or rejecting a loan. Other important considerations for qualification are:

1. Applicant's demonstrated ability to accumulate liquid assets such as cash and securities.
2. Applicant's ability to use credit wisely and refrain from incurring excessive debt.
3. Relationship between proposed housing expenses and the amount applicant is accustomed to paying.
4. The number and ages of applicant's dependents.
5. The likelihood of increases or decreases in income.
6. Applicant's work experience and history.
7. Applicant's credit record with other obligations.
8. The amount of any down payment made.

Conventional/Conforming Loan Qualification

A **conforming loan** is a conventional loan that meets the requirements of either Fannie Mae or Freddie Mac. Both of these secondary-market agencies, while publicly owned, are subject to a HUD oversight committee and must have congressional approval for any major change in their operating procedures. Congress has set the policy on the maximum loan amount that these agencies may purchase, which amounted to $240,000 in 1999 for a single dwelling unit. Because Fannie and Freddie are continuously in the market to purchase mortgage loans, this loan limit has set a benchmark for pricing loans: Loans that do not exceed the limit are more readily salable and can be delivered at lower cost than larger loans.

While Fannie Mae and Freddie Mac use the same basic documents (application, verification forms, mortgage, and note) in processing their loan applicants, there are some differences in the standards applied and the kinds of repayment plans that are acceptable. For instance, Fannie Mae will not accept either ARMs with negative amortization or GPMs if combined with ARMs, while Freddie Mac will accept both but requires at least a 10 percent down payment. There are no restrictions on who is eligible for a conforming loan other than meeting the minimum standards set by each agency. What makes the procedures a bit confusing is that loan originators may set requirements more stringent than those acceptable to the agencies but they cannot exceed the limitations if the loan is to be sold through either agency.

Like both FHA and VA, a conforming loan must meet certain percentage guidelines covering an applicant's income. The mortgage payment cannot exceed 28 percent of an applicant's gross income, and other obligations when added to the mortgage payment cannot exceed 36 percent. *Note:* For conforming loans, the applicant's gross combined income is used to measure adequacy.

Mortgage Payment. For a conforming loan, the mortgage payment amount is defined as principal, interest, taxes, and insurance (PITI), plus any special assessments that may hold the power of a lien right on the property.

Other Monthly Payments. Recognized obligations include installment debt that extends for six months or longer, revolving account payments, and other payments that represent a fixed claim on the applicant's income. Like both FHA and VA, the definition of what comprises a fixed claim on an applicant's income is subject to some interpretation. Many real demands on income, such as food, clothing and taxes, are not included. This does not mean these costs are overlooked. It is simply that these costs represent considerable flexibility and are expected to be paid from the 64 percent of an applicant's income that is not designated for mandatory payments.

....

EXAMPLE

Conforming Loan Qualification

Applicant's total gross income		$3,000
Mortgage payment (PITI)		
Mortgage principal and interest	$660	
Taxes and insurance	165	
Total mortgage payment		$825
Other monthly payments		
Car payment	240	
State and local taxes	90	
Total other payments		330
Total mortgage plus other payments		$1,155
Ratios:		
Total mortgage payment		$ 825/3,000 = 27.5%
Total mortgage and other payments		$1,155/3,000 = 38.5%

....

The figures in this example would disqualify an applicant from a conforming loan. The total mortgage payment ratio of 27.5 percent is within the 28 percent limit for a 90 percent loan. However, the total of mortgage payment plus other monthly payments at a 38.5 percent ratio exceeds the 36 percent limit for total fixed payments. If either ratio exceeds the limit, the applicant's income does not qualify.

Other Conventional Loan Qualification

With the exception of a fairly new set of standards for "affordable housing" loans, there are few fixed guidelines for conventional loan qualification. When a lender is offering its own deposit assets to fund a loan, it is free to set standards that meet its own requirements. There are some general limitations such as nondiscrimination laws and state usury laws, but perhaps the biggest restraint is the need to attract borrower-customers. Borrowers usually investigate more than one source for loans, and if the qualification standards are unreasonable, there are other sources available. Even when making conventional loans intended to be held in portfolio, many lenders prefer to follow the guidelines for conforming loans in case there may be a need to sell the loans at a later date.

Affordable Housing Loans

The Financial Institutions Reform, Recovery and Enforcement Act (FIRREA) passed in 1989 expanded the 1977 Community Reinvestment Act to target both regulated and nonregulated lenders. FIRREA sharpened the performance ratings for regulated institutions and required disclosure of what each is doing to meet local credit needs.

Grades ranging from "outstanding" to "substandard compliance" are issued periodically by an institution's regulatory authority and publicized locally. Satisfactory ratings are a prerequisite to regulatory approval of activities including mergers, acquisitions, expansions, and siting new branches.

While satisfactory compliance involves a number of activities, one is to offer a range of residential mortgage, housing rehabilitation, and small business loans. One result of the act's application is the creation of a new category of conventional loan that targets low- and moderate-income people. The generally accepted definition of *low income* is 80 percent of the local area's median income and 115 percent for *moderate income*. Loans are limited to low- and moderate-income families. Some programs limit the maximum purchase price of the house and all include a home buyers' education course. The education course is usually six hours of instruction that covers the functions of brokers, appraisers, title companies, and mortgage lenders. The course also explains the responsibilities of owning a home.

Strong support for affordable housing loans has been given by both Fannie Mae and Freddie Mac as well as private mortgage insurers, such as GE Capital Mortgage Insurance and Mortgage Guaranty Insurance Corporation. All four of these organizations sell their services to regulated lenders and are interested in assisting them in this particular activity. All have developed special programs for this purpose. For instance, Fannie Mae has a variety of "Community Homebuyers Programs" and Freddie Mac calls its operation the "FHLMC Affordable Gold Program."

The purpose is not to make risky loans to unworthy borrowers. Rather, the purpose is to recognize that many people simply follow different living practices. Studies have indicated that lower income families normally pay a higher percentage of their income for housing than others do. So an affordable housing program allows a higher ratio of income applied to housing, such as 33 percent of gross income instead of the 28 or 29 percent found with other kinds of loans. These families do not normally commit to an overload of other debt, so total fixed obligations are limited to 38 percent of income, somewhat less than the 41 percent found in FHA and VA qualification.

Many lower income people prefer to pay bills with cash instead of using checking accounts. To accommodate this practice, these programs accept timely payment of rent and utility bills as evidence of creditworthiness. Cash requirements for closing, a special problem when income is low, can be reduced by allowing some borrowing or acceptance of grants from others. A number of housing agencies and local communities offer support programs that include cash grants.

What has become evident from this particular program in its few years of existence is that the credit experience has been excellent. Low income does not mean poor payment; higher default rates seem to stem from higher income people! It is a viable market that may have been overlooked in the past.

Comparison of Qualification Guidelines

The following table gives a summary of the percentage guidelines found in the four types of loans just discussed.

	Housing Ratio	*Fixed Payment Ratio*
HUD/FHA	29%	41%
VA	(Not limited)	41
Conforming/conventional	28	36
Affordable housing	33	38

COMMERCIAL LOANS

As explained earlier, commercial loans follow a different pattern than residential loans. In most instances, repayment of the loan is expected from the property's income rather than from the borrower's personal income. A creditworthy borrower is still important, but greater emphasis is placed on the property. Further, commercial loans are made primarily to businesses rather than individuals and detailed financial statements are normally required. These are scrutinized as to profitability and the accumulation of assets over a period of time. Ownership of the company must be examined and information submitted on the principal owners and/or officers and directors. A loan agreement is usually required that spells out certain limitations on the company's operations during the term of the loan. Even though quite different, like all loans, the beginning is a loan application.

Commercial Loan Application

No consumer-based protective restrictions on what questions may be asked apply to commercial loan applications. Lenders may develop their own forms to fulfill their need for information since there are no standards. This is one of the reasons commercial lenders often specialize in the kind of loans they will undertake. Knowledge of a particular kind of property and the business operation involved is crucial in making sound commercial loans. So knowing what kind of information is necessary is reflected in the application's questions.

The general areas of information covered in a commercial loan application may be listed as follows:

1. Company name, address, and business structure
2. Information on owners or corporate officers and directors
3. Name of contact person
4. Purpose of the loan requested
5. Financial statements for past three to five years:
   - Balance sheet
   - Profit and loss statement
   - Pro forma statement showing impact of loan on profitability
6. Names of suppliers and banks for credit references
7. Appraisal of property to be pledged as collateral
8. An environmental assessment of the property
9. Possibly a feasibility study if project is new construction

The listed information would suffice for a preliminary review of the loan application but more detail may be required later.

With commercial loans, it is normal for a lender to require an upfront charge to review the application. Some set a rather high fee for new applicants simply to discourage frivolous requests. All costs of information are paid by the borrower.

The review necessary for a commercial loan can be very broad, covering management, sales, production, purchasing, research and planning, and personnel policies plus the physical plant and equipment. The loan underwriter expects to have current, preferably audited, financial statements presented with the loan application. An *audited statement* is one in which all pertinent data is verified by the certified public accountant preparing the report.

When examining a financial statement, the underwriter looks for a record of profitable use of existing assets; the accumulation of cash, property, and other assets versus outstanding obligations; and the very important working ratio of current assets to current liabilities. A favorable ratio would be at least $2.00 of assets for every $1.00 of liabilities. The ratio indicates both the manner of operation and the immediate cushion of assets available to protect the company against a temporary reversal.

Creditworthiness of a commercial loan applicant can be determined by contacting the firm's suppliers and bank references (must have applicant's permission to do so). Also, various credit reporting agencies are sources of commercial credit information. One of the largest is Dun & Bradstreet, which can provide something of a history on some companies as well as a credit rating.

To evaluate the results of the loan on the company's finances, it is customary to prepare pro forma statements: both a balance sheet and a profit and loss statement. These statements are a projection of what the loan will do for the company—such as enable it to increase the investment in productivity, add a new product line, provide an additional service, or enter a new market—as well as an estimate of the expected effects on profitability. It is the long-range ability of a company to operate profitably that is the real key to the trouble-free recovery of a loan.

Loan Agreement. Since the ownership and/or management of a company may change during the term of a commercial loan, a separate agreement is usually a part of the loan commitment. The agreement may state how the proceeds of a loan are to be used and can provide penalties for noncompliance. In addition, certain restrictive covenants are often added that limit company policies during the term of the loan. This would include such actions as loans or advances to officers or employees, control over the amount of salary increases, restrictions on the payment of dividends, and limits on any other borrowing. Further, the agreement might require lender approval before any major assets, patents, or leasehold interests could be sold. All terms of a loan agreement are negotiable and are designed primarily to protect a lender's interest in the company until the loan is repaid in full.

PRIVATE MORTGAGE INSURANCE

Many, many years ago, in the jargon of the mortgage industry, an "insured loan" was simply another name for either an FHA or VA loan. These government-backed insurance programs created a standardization of loan practices and uniform documentation that produced loans readily salable to investors throughout the country. Investors knew in advance what they were buying. Conventional loans, those not covered by government insurance, were not standardized. They remained localized in their procedures and documentation for many years.

In that time period, the lack of standardization was no big handicap as prior to the 1980s, major funding for conventional loans was found in local savings associations and a few banks. As this source of funds declined in the early 1980s, the need for alternate sources to fund conventional loans helped fuel the growth in private mortgage insurance. As sources of funds became national and thus further removed from the geographic location of a mortgage loan, the need for protection against loan default increased.

History of Private Mortgage Insurance

The idea of writing an insurance policy to protect a lender against loss in the event of loan default began with the creation of the Federal Housing Administration in 1934. It was not until the 1950s that several entrepreneurs began testing the market for private default insurance coverage for conventional loans. Progress was slow at first as few lenders required the coverage; after all, if an insured loan was needed, just contact the FHA or VA!

It was not until 1971 that private mortgage insurance became a requirement for higher ratio conventional loans. In that year, regulatory authorities expanded lending limits for conventional residential loans and required the use of default insurance coverage. The new limits allowed federally chartered savings and loan associations to make loans up to 95 percent of appraised value of a house, compared with 90 percent previously, provided that loans over 90 percent were insured. The result was a tremendous growth in private mortgage insurance.

One major pioneering insurance company, Mortgage Guaranty Insurance Corporation (MGIC, picking up the acronym Magic) based in Milwaukee, increased its loan coverage volume from almost nothing in 1970 to $7.5 billion in 1972 with about 40 percent in 95 percent loans. The private sector topped the FHA coverage in that year and has retained its lead ever since.

By the end of the 1970s, private mortgage insurance companies had become popular growth companies on the nation's stock markets. More growth meant higher stock values, and many companies overlooked loan quality in the competitive surge for more premium income. The fallout came in 1982 and 1983 when loss ratios increased dramatically due to more foreclosures. A few companies withdrew from the mortgage insurance market, but most tightened their loan qualification requirements and raised premium rates to rebuild their resources.

Private Mortgage Insurance Companies

The very specialized nature of default risk has limited the number of companies offering this kind of coverage. About 15 companies are currently in the business. Two companies dominate the market: General Electric Capital Mortgage Insurance Co. in Raleigh, North Carolina, and Mortgage Guaranty Insurance Corporation in Milwaukee. Each holds about 25 percent of the market. The insurance companies work through various loan originators to sell their coverage. The originator must meet company requirements to be designated as an agent. Agents obtain the necessary qualifying information from a loan applicant for submission to the insurance company underwriter.

Qualifying Information Required

Loan originator/agents use information taken from a borrower's application to prepare a request for coverage to the private mortgage insurance company. The decision to approve or disapprove is made by the insurance company's own underwriters. The insurance company relies on loan originators to submit complete and accurate information on an applicant as response is fast, within 24 hours, allowing no time for verification. A request for coverage includes submitting (1) a copy of the loan application, (2) a property appraisal made by an approved appraiser, (3) a credit report on the borrower, (4) several verifications, and (5) any other data helpful in analyzing the loan.

Amount of Coverage Offered

While private mortgage insurers, FHA, and VA all offer protection against the same risk of default, the amount of coverage differs. HUD/FHA insures 100 percent of the loan amount while VA guarantees only a portion of the loan. Private mortgage insurance carriers issue a variety of policies for residential loans that range from a low of 12 percent of the loan amount insured to a high of 35 percent. For example, a 12 percent insurance commitment limits the insurer to paying only 12 percent of the original loan amount should default occur.

Term of PMI Insurance. Further, there is a difference in the term of insurance coverage. HUD/FHA and VA offer their commitments for the life of a loan while private mortgage insurers limit their coverage to a shorter term of years. The range varies from 3 to 15 years. This means that insurance coverage would terminate at the end of the term regardless of the balance due on the loan.

Type of Property That Can Be Covered. Private mortgage insurance is available for a greater variety of property than with government programs. Residential loans that can be insured include primary residences, second or leisure homes, multifamily properties, mobile homes (if permanently secured and classed as real estate by state law), and modular housing. Commercial loan coverage is available for hotels, motels, shopping centers, office buildings, warehouses, and others. The loans may be participation loans, loans secured by junior liens, and seller-financed mortgages. Each insurance company may set its own standards for the loans it will cover as there are no national requirements.

Premiums Charged

Because private mortgage insurance usually covers less than the full amount of a loan for a shorter term, the premiums are less than those found with a HUD/FHA loan. As a type of insurance, PMI comes under the regulation of state insurance commissions in those states with that kind of authority. These states determine insurance premiums, including PMI, as a protective measure for their citizens. The state in which the property is located controls.

Premiums on PMI may be paid as a single premium at time of closing or in installments as an annual premium plan. The premium amount is expressed as a percentage of the original loan amount, measured in "points." If the premium is paid in installments, the charge is simply added to the interest rate.

As a type of insurance, it has been customary to treat PMI premiums the same as other insurance charges; that is, require two months of premium paid at closing plus the cost for one year placed in escrow. By 1993, competition brought a change in this policy. In an effort to reduce the upfront cash requirement for some loans, several companies began offering to drop the one-year escrow requirement and make charges only on a monthly basis.

The normal PMI policy has allowed for payment of premiums for the life of the loan. This has been true even though the coverage may no longer be needed. Lenders have been able to legally collect premiums even though Fannie Mae, for one, has had a rule that allows dropping the insurance when a mortgage balance is paid down to 80 percent of the original value of the property. A U.S. District Court ruled in 1996 that the Fannie Mae rule is a set of instructions from a lender-principal to a servicer-agent, not a contract between borrower and lender.

This policy has been changed by federal legislation passed in 1998, effective July 29, 1999. The law exempts FHA and VA loans and does not preempt any state statutes in effect before January 2, 1998. Lenders are required to notify consumers of their right to cancel PMI when the equity in their homes reaches 20 percent if requested by the borrower. In addition, the law provides for automatic cancellation of PMI when the loan reaches 78 percent LTVR.

Who Determines the Need for PMI?

The answer is lenders, not borrowers. The need is based on risk—the more down payment, the lower the risk. A general rule of lenders is that loans with 20 percent or more down payment (80 percent loan-to-value) are not required to carry PMI. (The federal regulator limit is that loans over 90 percent loan-to-value must carry PMI.)

In practice, the borrower has little voice in the selection of coverage or the insurance carrier, as that decision is made by the loan originator. The reason is that it is the lender who is protected by the insurance, not the borrower. What the borrower gains is an easier qualification for perhaps a larger loan and a lower down payment than might otherwise be available.

PMI Obligations in the Event of Foreclosure

Even though PMI coverage is limited to a percentage of the loan amount, insurance companies have generally followed a practice of reimbursing the lender in full on their mortgage loan should a foreclosure become necessary. By then taking title to the foreclosed property, the insurance company relieves a lender of any further problems. It is one of the settlement options offered by PMI carriers. The purpose, of course, is to make the insurance coverage more competitive in a market that places a high value on service. As foreclosure problems escalated in some parts of the country, many insurers were forced to limit their exposure to the legal obligation contained in the insurance contract; that is, reimburse the lender for the amount of the loan actually covered.

Indemnification Clause. Another obligation often overlooked, and not very well understood by borrowers, is the indemnification clause in many private mortgage insurance policies. What this clause means is that if the insurance company suffers a loss in the settlement of a claim with a lender (when the loan balance due exceeds the value of the property), the borrower is liable for reimbursement of the loss. Remember, the insurance protects the lender against loss. And unlike many other kinds of insurance, the insurance company holds the borrower responsible for repayment of any loss. While the indemnification clause is clearly stated in the body of policies, it is not usually carefully explained to a possibly unwary borrower. However, recovery of such a loss against a borrower/debtor who has just lost his or her home is not always feasible.

Questions for Discussion

1. How does the Equal Credit Opportunity Act reduce discrimination?
2. List the essential information that a prospective borrower must provide in a residential loan application. For a commercial loan.
3. Discuss "ability to repay" a loan as may be indicated by type of income and stability of income.
4. How is the income of self-employed persons verified?
5. Define *willingness to pay* and how it can be evaluated.
6. What information is normally obtained from a credit report?
7. In analyzing corporate credit, what further investigation would an underwriter employ beyond a careful study of the company's financial statements?
8. What is the risk insured by private mortgage insurance?
9. Discuss the principal features of an affordable housing loan qualification.
10. How are liabilities usually measured in the analysis of an applicant seeking a home loan?

Chapter 10

Property Analysis

INTRODUCTION

The process of analyzing and approving a loan is called **underwriting.** The individual who assembles and analyzes the necessary data and is authorized to give a company's consent to a specific loan is referred to as the *underwriter.*

Properly underwriting any loan requires a complete analysis of all pertinent factors, including: (1) the borrower's ability and willingness to pay; (2) the property's condition, location, and usage; (3) all relevant economic influences; (4) laws controlling foreclosure procedures and assignments of rent; and (5) any unusual conditions that may exist.

An underwriter must examine the future, estimate the continued stability of the borrower, and try to judge the future value in a specific property. The underwriter must look beyond a normal appraisal, which provides an estimate of past or present value, and weigh the forces that affect the future based on his or her experience in this field. It is a daunting task.

A loan analysis covers a wide assortment of information and, from these diverse elements, an underwriter must determine the degree of risk involved. There is no such thing as a risk-free mortgage loan. It is the underwriter's prime responsibility to determine the magnitude of the risk and to compensate for it in the terms and conditions of the loan. The degree of risk determines the ratio of loan to value, the length of time for repayment, and the interest and discount points required by the lender.

As one of the essential elements in underwriting any mortgage loan, the property to be pledged must be examined for suitability. As discussed in the previous chapter, for a residential loan, it is the borrower's personal income that is expected to repay the loan. For commercial loans, it is the income from the property that becomes more important. So the analysis of property that will be pledged as collateral for a loan differs somewhat between residential and commercial types of loans. For a residential loan, the property serves as a backup, a pledge of something of value that better assures repayment of the loan. But it is not something the lender expects to use for repayment of the loan. So the thrust of a property analysis for a residential loan is simply to determine the market value and if that serves as adequate collateral for the loan.

For a commercial loan, the property analysis must look further. Generally, the loan is expected to be repaid from income generated by the property. While the property does serve as collateral—a backup in case of loan default—it is more important for the underwriter to make sure the property income can sustain loan repayment. While the underlying purposes differ, both rely on professional appraisals as a starting point for property analysis.

PROPERTY APPRAISAL

An appraisal may be defined as an *estimate* of value of an adequately described property as of a specific date. It is the considered opinion of a knowledgeable and qualified professional supported by an analysis of relevant data. An appraisal can be an evaluation of a full ownership, a partial ownership interest, or leasehold rights.

A **property appraisal** provides information that has several uses in financing real estate. It is used as an important measure of loan amount. Lenders limit loan amounts to a percentage of property value. However, for commercial loans, the loan amount may have an alternate limit as a percentage of the property's income. But a property's income is also a direct reflection of the property's value. In addition, an appraisal serves as a support document for institutional lenders when they undergo regulatory examinations.

Determination of appraised value is made by persons specially qualified in the field. In the not-too-distant past, a lending institution's loan officer might have estimated the property value based on personal knowledge and experience in the area. However, as mortgage lending increased in volume and complexity, almost all appraisals were shifted to professionals who specialize in this work. Some work as employees of a lending institution and some as independent fee appraisers.

Federal/State Certification

Qualification of what can be considered a professional appraiser and determining what comprises acceptable content in an appraisal in the past have been the province of various independent appraiser associations. These are primarily peer groups organized to develop quality standards among themselves and to award designations to eligible members meeting their requirements. Prior to 1989, there was no federal regulatory involvement in this field.

While many must share the blame for the collapse of savings and loan associations in the 1980s, Congress felt the quality of appraisals carried some of the responsibility. As a result, legislation was passed creating a system for setting proper standards for both appraisers and the content of appraisals.

In 1989, Congress passed the Financial Institutions Reform, Recovery and Enforcement Act (FIRREA) in which Title XI spelled out a system for setting federal appraiser and appraisal standards to be used as guidelines for each state to develop its own system of qualification. FIRREA established a council called the Federal Financial Institutions Examination Council with a subcommittee known as the Appraisal Subcommittee. The law applies to a loan made by a federally related lender and is applicable to both residential and commercial loans.

The purpose of the Subcommittee was to develop suitable criteria for state licensure of appraisers and standards for appraisals that would assure credible information for federally related lenders. *Federally related* is a broad-brush definition of any lender with some relation to the federal government, including those carrying federal deposit insurance, or quasi-government related, such as Fannie Mae and Freddie Mac.

Since its creation, the Appraisal Subcommittee has set standards that are now reflected in every state's requirements for certification and licensing of individuals qualified to perform appraisals in federally related transactions. The Subcommittee continues to monitor requirements of federal regulatory agencies in respect to appraisal standards. In addition, it maintains a national registry of state certified and licensed appraisers eligible to appraise for federally related transactions.

Standards for Appraisers

FIRREA's Title IX calls for the qualification of appraisers through appropriate testing and experience requirements established by state law. As of January 1, 1998, new appraiser criteria became effective as announced by The Appraisal Qualifications Board of The Appraisal Foundation. It should be noted that state requirements may exceed AQB minimums. Four categories of appraisers and their qualifications are identified as follows:

1. **Certified general appraiser.** Qualified to evaluate both residential and commercial property of any size. A general appraiser must demonstrate knowledge of the profession and understand the documents involved. To qualify, the appraiser must have 165 hours of education, including 15 hours of USPAP, plus 14 hours per year of continuing education and 2,000 hours of experience during the past 30 months.

2. **Certified residential appraiser.** Qualified to evaluate all one- to four-family properties. To qualify, the appraiser must have 120 hours of education, including 15 hours of USPAP, plus 14 hours per year of continuing education and 2,000 hours of experience during the past 24 months.

3. **Licensed appraiser.** Qualified to evaluate properties in transactions of $250,000 or less. A licensed appraiser must have 90 hours of education, including 15 hours of USPAP, plus 14 hours per year of continuing education and 2,000 hours of experience during the past 24 months.

4. **Trainee.** An appraiser trainee must take 75 hours of education, including 15 hours of USPAP, plus 14 hours of continuing education in the third and successive years. Trainees are not required to pass a state exam (as all other categories are).

Standards for Appraisals

FIRREA's Title XI requires that the content of appraisals meet standards set by the Appraisal Standards Board which is a part of the Appraisal Foundation. The Appraisal Foundation was created in 1987 by eight active private appraisal associations. Prior to passage of federal legislation in 1989, professional appraisers recognized a need for better qualification for both appraisers and appraisals and established the Appraisal Foundation to develop practical standards and requirements. Federal recognition of their good work was indicated in FIRREA's acceptance of their standards.

Federal standards require appraisals to conform with the Uniform Standards of Professional Appraisal Practice (USPAP) as adopted by the Appraisal Standards Board. A standardized appraisal form has been developed in a cooperative effort between the industry working group, Fannie Mae, Freddie Mac, HUD, and VA. The form, called the Uniform Residential Appraisal Report (URAR), is a revision of Fannie Mae Form 1004/Freddie Mac Form 70 and became mandatory for use after January 1, 1994. (A copy of the form is reproduced in the Appendix.) Federal requirements also set a minimum level of certification based on the value and kind of property appraised.

Appraisal Associations

Federal certification standards for appraisers have not changed the existence of a number of private professional organizations offering appraisal designations to those who qualify under each organization's standards. These are peer groups made up of appraisers who are interested in maintaining and improving the quality of their profession. Each organization offers certain designations which indicate qualification in a particular area of appraisal work. The requirements differ somewhat but all are based on a minimum prescribed level of education and experience plus passing some rather difficult tests. Following is a brief listing of some of the better-known organizations and the designations granted by each:

The Appraisal Institute
  MAI—Member of Appraisal Institute
  SRA—Senior Residential Appraiser

American Society of Appraisers

    ASA—Senior Member of the Society

    FASA—Fellow of the Society

American Society of Farm Managers and Rural Appraisers (the oldest group in the United States)

    AFM—Accredited Farm Manager

    ARA—Accredited Rural Appraiser

American Association of Certified Appraisers

    CA-R—Certified Appraiser, Residential

    CA-S—Certified Appraiser, Senior

    CA-C—Certified Appraiser, Consultant

    CA-F&L—Certified Appraiser, Farm and Land

International Association of Assessing Officers

    CPE—Certified Personality Evaluator

    AAE—Accredited Assessment Evaluator

    CAE—Certified Assessment Evaluator

National Association of Independent Fee Appraisers

    IFA—Independent Fee Appraiser, Member

    IFAS—Independent Fee Appraiser, Senior Member

    IFAC—Independent Fee Appraiser, Counselor

National Association of Master Appraisers

    MRA—Master Residential Appraiser

    MFLA—Master Farm and Land Appraiser

    MSA—Master Senior Appraiser

National Association of Real Estate Appraisers

    CREA—Certified Real Estate Appraiser

    CCRA—Certified Commercial Real Estate Appraiser

Peer designations are good indicators of expertise in a specialized area of appraisal work. And they give some assurance of an appraiser's interest in maintaining professional standards. But there is no requirement that a person belong to any peer group in order to qualify as a state-certified appraiser.

Principles of Appraising

How do appraisers approach their problems? What are they looking for in determining values? What analytical details should lenders or borrowers expect to find in professional appraisals? Considerable study has been given to the theory that underlies all sound appraisals. The theories have been developed into specific **appraisal principles** that guide professional thinking in evaluating property. Following are descriptions of several of the more important principles:

1. **Supply and demand.** The same theory underlying all economic practice is that scarcity influences supply and that what people want and can purchase controls the demand.

2. **Substitution.** The value of replaceable property will tend to coincide with the value of an equally desirable substitute property.

3. **Highest and best use.** It is the use of land at the time of the appraisal that will provide the greatest net return. This requires the proper balance of the four agents of production (labor, coordination, capital, and land) to provide the maximum return for the land used.

4. **Contribution.** This principle applies to the contributory market value added by an improvement, such as an elevator in a three-story building, or the value added to a building lot by increasing the depth of that lot.

5. **Conformity.** To achieve maximum value, land use must conform to the surrounding area. An overimprovement, such as a $200,000 house built in a neighborhood of $60,000 homes, will lower the value of the larger house.

6. **Anticipation.** Since value is considered to be the worth of all present and future benefits resulting from property ownership, the anticipation of future benefits has to be evaluated.

TYPES OF APPRAISALS

In 1994, the Uniform Standards of Professional Appraisal Practice (USPAP) was changed to allow a Departure Provision. This provision permits a limited appraisal and the rules are classified as specific guidelines rather than binding requirements. The burden of proof is placed on the appraiser to decide before accepting an assignment that the departure from the Uniform Standards will not confuse or mislead those relying on the appraisal.

The appraiser must advise the client that the assignment calls for something less than a full appraisal and that departures will be explained. The client must agree that a limited appraisal would be appropriate.

The Departure Provision of USPAP now lists two types of appraisals:

1. A *complete appraisal,* which is defined as the act of estimating value without invoking the Departure Provision.

2. A *limited appraisal,* defined as the act of estimating value resulting from invoking the Departure Provision.

USPAP now defines three different levels of reporting requirements. These are:

1. The *self-contained appraisal report,* which is the most detailed and encompassing of the report formats. The length and descriptive detail in such a

report should fully support, in a self-contained format, the conclusions of the appraiser.

2. The *summary report,* which is less detailed than a self-contained report. The information and the appraisal procedures may be summarized rather than reported in detail.

3. The *restrictive report* is the least detailed of the reporting options. There is a minimal presentation of information and it is intended for the client only. The report must contain a use restriction that clearly limits reliance on the report to the client and warns that it cannot be properly understood without additional information from the appraiser.

The three levels of appraisals may be found in practice in roughly the following formats:

1. The restrictive report: *Letter form.* In its simplest form, an appraiser can submit a letter to the client detailing only the most important points and reaching a conclusion of value. No background information or supporting data are given, although the appraiser must have developed it prior to issuing the estimate.

2. The summary report: *Standard form.* For residential appraisals, a standard printed form is now required. It is Freddie Mac Form 70/Fannie Mae Form 1004, most recently revised in June 1993. It is called the Uniform Residential Appraisal Report and became mandatory for use on January 1, 1994.

3. The self-contained appraisal report: *Narrative report.* The most detailed of all appraisals. The narrative report gives background data, substantiation of information, and an explanation of why certain conclusions were reached.

Narrative Appraisal Report

To better explain major information found in an evaluation of property, the narrative, or self-contained appraisal report, is detailed in the following section.

Description of Property

The property should be defined in accurate legal wording, and the precise rights of ownership must be described. The rights may be a leasehold interest, mineral rights, surface rights, or the full value of the fee simple rights in the land and buildings thereon.

The Date and Purpose of the Appraisal

Appraisals can be made for times other than the present, such as when needed to settle an earlier legal dispute. The date of the appraised value must be clearly shown. Also, the purpose of the appraisal should be stated as it will influence the dominant approach to value. In professional appraisals there is no such thing as the buyer's or seller's value; this is not a "purpose" as identified here.

An example of purpose would be to estimate value for an insurance settlement, which would emphasize a cost approach to value as claims are adjusted on the basis of cost. If the purpose is a condemnation action, the most relevant approach would be the market value.

The Background Data

While the standard form and simple letter report will not provide any economic background data, the narrative report discloses economic information as clues to value. An overall study of the market region, which may be as large as an entire state, is made. The focus is then narrowed down to the local area—the town or that portion of a city where the property is located. From there the analysis narrows even further to the specific neighborhood and then to the actual site under appraisal.

The Approaches to Value

Appraisers use three common approaches to estimate value: (1) cost, (2) sales comparison, and (3) income. All approaches should be used wherever possible, and all should reach approximately similar values, although these values are seldom the same. In certain appraisals, only one approach may be practical, such as valuing a city hall building for insurance purposes. In such an analysis only a cost approach would be practical as there is not much buying or selling of city halls to provide sales comparison data, nor is there a true income from the building itself to provide figures for an income approach. A single-family residence may appear to lack any income for analysis, but certain neighborhoods have sufficient houses rented to provide enough data to reach an income approach conclusion. The three approaches to value are discussed in greater detail later in this chapter.

Qualifying Conditions

If, in the analysis of property, the appraiser discovers any material factors that will affect the property's value, these can and should be reported as further substantiation of the value conclusion.

Estimate of Value

This is the real conclusion of the study, the figure most people turn to first when handed a finished appraisal. Each of the approaches to value will result in a firm dollar valuation. Then, it is the purpose of this estimate to explain why one of the approaches to value is favored over the others. For example, with an income property such as a motel, the value judgment would rest most heavily on the income analysis. The final conclusion is a single value for the property and represents the considered knowledge and experience of the appraiser making the report.

Certification of the Appraiser and His or Her Qualifications

The professional appraiser certifies to his or her opinion by signature and disclaims any financial interest in the property being appraised that could influence a truly objective conclusion. A recitation of the appraiser's educational background, standing within the profession as indicated by professional ratings, and previous experience such as appraisals previously made and for whom. The certification serves to substantiate the quality of the appraisal for an underwriting officer.

Addendum

Depending on the need for clarification, the appraisal will include maps of the area under consideration with the site pointed out, plus the location of comparable properties referred to in the analysis. Charts may be used to indicate such things as the variables in a market analysis. Photos of the subject property are usually mandatory.

THREE APPROACHES TO PROPERTY VALUE

To understand more clearly the use of the three approaches to value, which is the essence of an appraisal, each is discussed in the sections that follow.

Property Value as Estimated by Cost Approach

The **cost approach** is developed as the sum of the building reproduction costs, less depreciation, plus land value. The reproduction costs can be developed the same as a builder would prepare a bid proposal by listing every item of material, labor, field burden, and administrative overhead. Reproduction cost estimates have been simplified in active urban areas through compilation of many cost experiences converted to a cost-per-square-foot figure. The offices of active appraisers collect such data in depth for reference.

Depreciation, by definition, detracts from the value and must be deducted from the reproduction costs. However, external **obsolescence,** as described next, can be either a deduction or an addition, depending on its nature. Three separate types of adjustments must be made in the cost approach:

1. **Physical deterioration.** The wear and tear on the building is the type most commonly associated with the word *depreciation.* Examples would be the need for repainting, a worn-out roof needing new shingles, and rotting window casements. These are curable items and under the breakdown method should be deducted from value as a rehabilitation cost. Other items of physical deterioration are incurable, meaning not economically feasible to repair. An illustration would be aging of the foundations or of the walls,

and this kind of deterioration should be charged off as a certain portion of the usable life of the building. Another method of handling physical deterioration, in contrast to the breakdown method, is the engineering or observed method wherein each major component of the building is listed and a percentage of its full life is charged off. This method recognizes that each major component of a building may have a different life and the percentage of depreciation would vary at any point in time.

2. **Functional obsolescence.** Equally as important as physical deterioration is that category of loss in value resulting from poor basic design, inadequate facilities, or outdated equipment. These elements, too, can be curable or incurable. An example of incurable functional obsolescence would be an aging building that no longer meets the needs of modern business with its demands for greater flexibility in its office arrangements. There could be an excess of walls or partitions in an office building, which would cost money to remove and modernize, but might be curable. Lack of air conditioning in a hotel or office building is an older example of curable functional obsolescence.

3. **External obsolescence.** The third type of depreciation has a more elusive quality and really is not in the building at all. External obsolescence is that set of factors outside and surrounding the property that affect its value, requiring the determination of the plus or minus effect of these forces. Some are very obvious influences—a new freeway bypassing an existing service station, the construction of an undesirable industry in an area adjacent to residential property—and would certainly lower value. However, the bridging of a stream to open new land for development would create a substantial increase in value. A more difficult problem is ascertaining economic impact of a possible decline in a specific neighborhood. While landowners are able to exercise some voice in protest or encouragement of these outside forces, for the most part what is done with neighboring properties is not controllable and is not curable. And it will always be a latent force that can affect the value of an individual property.

After determining building reproduction cost, then depreciation adjustments, the third factor to be considered under the cost approach is value of the land. Land value, which varies with local economic conditions, affects demand, and to a lesser extent, supply. More recently, environmental problems have affected the value and availability of land. Land value is best determined through an examination of recent sales of similarly located properties—the sales comparison method as discussed in the next section.

However, there are sometimes specific reasons for changes in the appraised value of land. Buildings can and do deteriorate, while land can continue to increase in value due to the same outside factors noted in the preceding discussion of external obsolescence. For example, as urban areas expand, certain intersections become more and more valuable, new throughways and freeways concentrate greater flows of traffic, and huge shopping centers add to the value of all surrounding land. As the suburban sprawl moves outward, former farmland increases in value as it becomes potential residential subdivisions.

Another example can be found in some older sections of a city when the land becomes more valuable than the building. The building may represent such poor usage of the land that it becomes a liability to the property value, and its removal costs should be deducted from the stated value of the land. By ascertaining these fluctuations in land value, the appraiser can bring a cost analysis into step with a changing market value.

Property Value as Estimated by Sales Comparison Analysis

Also known as a market analysis, the estimated value by a **sales comparison approach** is determined by prices paid for similar properties in the neighborhood. This approach is most commonly used with residential property because it offers sufficient sales information to make comparisons useful. Since no two properties are ever precisely **comparable,** much of the analysis under this method concerns itself with detailing major characteristics and whether these add to or subtract from the value of the property. For example, if a similar property was sold two years earlier, the appraiser could assume that the subject property would show an increase, or decrease, in that time span, depending on the nature of the neighborhood. A fireplace in the subject property would give it a plus factor in comparison with a similar property lacking a fireplace. Comparisons are comprehensive, covering such points as location, size, physical condition, and amenities.

Some confusion does exist in the relationship between sales prices and asking prices. An appraiser is primarily concerned with completed sales and with sales uncomplicated by extraneous pressures such as forced sales, estate disposals, or transfers within a family. The willing-buyer and willing-seller standard of a free market sale is lacking in a forced sale. An asking or offering price is considered by most to represent a ceiling or maximum value for the property. Appraisers usually recognize the inherent inaccuracy of an asking price, especially one set by homeowners. This figure is often arrived at by adding the original purchase price, plus the full cost of all improvements that have been made, plus the selling commission, plus the owner's amateur notion of general market appreciation. But every so often an owner actually receives such a sales price from a willing buyer, and this makes the professional feel a bit foolish!

Sales price as a sound basis for comparing market values of property came under question in the mid-1980s. By that time, it had become common for home sellers, particularly home builders, to offer attractive financing plans as a sales inducement. By paying a lender part of the interest cost up front as in a buy-down, a seller could offer lower-than-market "effective" interest rates to a buyer during the early years of a mortgage. The lower payment amount made loan qualification easier, which attracted more buyers. The cost of the buy-down of interest was usually added into the price of the house. Since the sales price then included a built-in finance cost, it was no longer an accurate indication of true market value. Most lenders have since added a requirement that any market value used as a basis for sales comparisons be adjusted downward to reflect any excessive finance costs. Both Fannie Mae and Freddie Mac have revised their definition of *market value* to "the most probable price which a property should bring."

Property Value as Estimated by Income Approach

Because the **income approach** examines the actual return per dollar invested, it is the most important method for any investment property. When people buy investment property, they normally expect to recover, or "recapture" in appraisal terminology, their money with a profit. They do this from two sources: (1) the annual earnings (excess income over all costs) and (2) the proceeds from a resale at the end of the term of ownership, called the *residual value*.

There are several acceptable methods used to estimate value with an income approach. However, any method based on the value of future income suffers from the same problem: Real estate does not offer the certainty of future income that other kinds of investment may provide. Nevertheless, once an income stream has been developed for analysis purposes, two methods are more widely used to convert the income stream into a value of the income-producing asset: the capitalization method and the discount analysis method, described next.

Capitalization Method

Probably the oldest, and simplest, method of converting an income stream into an asset value is **capitalization** of the income. This is done by using the following formula:

$$\frac{\text{Income stream}}{\text{Rate of return}} = \text{Value}$$

In the formula, the income stream is the expected profit derived from the property for the year. The rate of return is the return, expressed as a percentage, that the investor expects to receive from the property. The return is determined by the investor, or the analyst, as one commensurate with current market conditions and the degree of risk involved.

••

EXAMPLE

Say the subject property shows an income stream[1] of $20,000. A fair rate of return for the present market, including comparable risks involved, is, say, 9 percent. Using the formula:

$$\frac{\$20,000}{.09} = \$222,222$$

[1]The term *income stream* is not precisely defined; it can mean different things to different analysts. However, when comparisons between properties are made, whatever measure is used, the same measure must be applied to each property.

So, if you are offered a property showing the foregoing returns, you can place a value of $222,222 on the cash flow. Add to that amount the residual value of the property at the end of a holding period, and it will give the property value by one income approach. Thus,

Value of income stream	$222,222
Value of residual (estimated)	85,000
Total value	$307,222

Discount Analysis Method

Another analysis method, this one derived from financial markets, is **discount analysis.** This procedure takes each year's future cash flow and reduces it to its present worth. The investor receives a return on the investment delivered at intervals in the future. Yet payment for the income-producing asset is expected at time of purchase, either in cash or by borrowing money to deliver the cash at closing. So the question is: How much are the future cash flows worth in dollars today? By referring to a "Present Worth of a Dollar" table, the discount can be easily calculated. Using the same numbers as in the previous example gives the result shown in Table 10-1.

The figures in Table 10–1 are hypothetical and are intended only to illustrate the discount calculation. In practice, the holding period would most likely be much longer. And the annual cash flows would be projected with such variations as might be anticipated in occupancy and rental rate adjustments. This kind of calculation can be made easily with a computer using any of several software programs that are available.

TABLE 10–1   Present Worth of Cash Flow Plus Residual

At End of Year	Annual Cash Flow		Present Worth of a Dollar Factor* at 9% Rate		Present Worth of Cash Flow
1	$20,000	×	0.91743	=	$ 18,349
2	20,000	×	0.84168	=	16,834
3	20,000	×	0.77218	=	15,444
		Sum of annual cash flows		=	50,627
At the end of year 3, the property is sold for $250,000, +					
discounted to its present worth equals $250,000 × 0.77218				=	193,045
Total present worth of cash flows plus residual				=	$243,672

*Present worth factors are obtained from financial tables, such as "Ellwood Tables for Real Estate Appraising and Financing," L. W. Ellwood, Ballinger Publishing Co., Cambridge, Mass.

PROPERTY CHARACTERISTICS

Property analysis extends beyond an appraisal and includes some of the conditions discussed in the following sections. Most of this information refers to residential loans. When dealing with this type of loan, there is often a similarity in neighborhoods that precludes a detailed study of each house. But with commercial loans, the property is almost always considered on a case-by-case basis. Because of its greater emphasis on property analysis, commercial lending is considered in more detail in later chapters.

Physical Characteristics

There are several considerations concerning the property's **physical characteristics** that may be used as "go: no-go" determinants in the approval of a mortgage loan. Commentary follows on several of the more common distinctions.

Dwelling Units. Statistical references class one- to four-family housing as residential. However, many lenders in the conventional loan market separate this group into single-family housing, which qualifies for prime loan rates, and multiunit commercial property, which is rated for higher risk loans. Both the FHA and VA issue commitments for two-, three-, and four-family housing, but the requirements are not as favorable as those for single-family units.

Number of Bedrooms. Conventional lenders no longer consider the number of bedrooms an important consideration. Years ago it was not unusual to restrict loans to housing that had more than one bedroom. But the market has changed so that a number of buyers prefer limited bedroom space. As long as the lender believes a reasonable market exists for the property should foreclosure become necessary, the collateral is acceptable. (The FHA does base some of its loan limits in certain programs on the number of available bedrooms.)

Square Footage. Minimum house size based on square footage is no longer used as a loan determinant. As builders have endeavored to reduce housing costs, the size of houses has been reduced. The old standard of "not less than 1,000 square feet of living area" is simply not applicable in today's markets. Actually, the importance of square footage is more relevant to the value of the house in an appraisal.

Paved Streets. While most cities have managed to pave their streets, there are some smaller communities and new subdivisions that have not. Lenders have used the lack of paving as a "no-go" situation for a loan if it can result in a lessening of the collateral value. For example, the cost of paving is often handled in the form of an additional assessment on the property fronting the new pavement. If the assessment's amount is unknown, it is difficult to make adequate provision for the charge.

Utilities. A loan application may be rejected if the property offered as collateral does not have adequate sewer and water facilities. Top preference is given to a municipally operated or a regulated private operation furnishing both sewer and water services. The use of septic tanks or private water wells may be a cause for rejection. Some lenders will permit a septic tank if the percolation tests of the soil surrounding it meet certain minimum requirements. Also classed as utilities are the services of electricity, natural gas, and telephone. Lack of electricity would be a negative factor for urban and suburban properties but could be accepted in rural areas. Lack of natural gas or telephone is not detrimental for a loan. Also, there are no requirements for electricity or phones to be furnished through underground systems at the present time.

Building Materials. As important as building materials would seem to be, only the use of asbestos is considered a negative factor in underwriting a loan. Whether the building is sheathed in aluminum, wood, brick, or stone is important to an appraiser in evaluating the building, but not to a lender in determining a "go; no-go" situation. The quality of building materials is expressed in both terms of value of the building and in its estimated life or apparent age.

Amenities. The extra niceties that exist in some buildings are reflected in the value of the property but are not considered critical for the underwriter. A swimming pool, fine landscaping, exterior lighting, a neighborhood club, or recreational area are all added features that increase property value but are never considered a requirement for loan approval.

Hazardous Waste Areas. A more recent concern in the evaluation of real property as collateral for a loan is whether or not the land is on, or near, a hazardous waste area. While the problem is more likely to be found in a commercial area, residential developments may also be involved. The importance of all environmental requirements has become a major factor in loan determination and will be discussed more fully in a later chapter.

Location of Property

Lines are drawn by most conventional lenders among urban, suburban, and rural housing. The differences are not always clearly delineated, but they do provide a broad classification that is useful in describing packages of loans.

Due to the sprawl of metropolitan areas, the term suburban now means almost any location in a recorded subdivision of land in the general area surrounding cities—still the region of greatest growth in our country. *Urban* means the downtown and near-downtown areas of our cities. *Rural* identifies farm housing and, to many lenders, houses existing in the smaller towns. Rural may also be used to identify housing without access to a central water and sewer system.

Neighborhoods. Lenders no longer specify areas or neighborhoods within a city as acceptable or unacceptable for making loans. The practice is known more commonly as **red-lining,** from lines drawn on city maps to guide loan officers. Such identification has been interpreted as leading to possible discrimination in violation of the Fair Housing Act. Obviously, a neighborhood that is allowed to deteriorate does not make an attractive location for a 30-year loan. Nevertheless, lenders are asked to qualify houses on their individual merit rather than on the neighborhood in which they are located.

As assistance in monitoring compliance with these rules, federally regulated lenders are required to disclose the geographic areas in which they have made loans by census tract or by postal ZIP code number.

Flood-Prone Areas. The federal government has designated certain areas of the country as flood plain zones. These are areas that have been flooded in the past 100 years, or that, if records do not exist, are calculated to have a 1 percent chance of being flooded. Flood plain elevation lines have been determined by the U.S. Geological Survey: land at lower elevation comprises a flood plain area. While houses may be built in a designated flood plain, they may not be financed by lenders subject to any federal regulatory body unless minimum elevation requirements are met. Essentially, this means that buildings in flood-prone areas must either be flood-proofed or have the ground floor raised at least one foot above the elevation of the 100-year flood plain line.

Since 1968 the federal government has offered assistance to property owners with subsidized flood insurance through the National Flood Insurance Program. For a homeowner to be eligible for such coverage, the community must agree to participate in flood management and regulate development in its flood-prone areas. The subsidized insurance is offered in cooperation with selected private insurance companies in approved areas.

In 1973 Congress passed the Flood Disaster Protection Act as a stricter set of rules. This required communities to participate in the National Flood Insurance Program as a condition for receiving federal financial assistance. And it required property owners in flood hazard areas to purchase flood insurance as a condition of obtaining financing through a federally regulated, supervised, or insured financial institution. Even so, many borrowers, probably believing they would not be flooded, stopped paying premiums during the term of the loan.

To help make such nonpayment of premiums more difficult, the National Flood Insurance Act of 1994 imposes new obligations on lenders and servicers that include mandatory escrow requirements for flood insurance and mandatory provisions for "forced placement" of flood insurance if the borrower fails to pay premiums. The borrower must be notified if the required coverage is not purchased and kept in force. If no action is taken within 45 days of notification, the lender or servicer must purchase the insurance on behalf of the borrower, charging the cost to the borrower. Lenders and servicers may now rely on a determination by the Director of the Federal Emergency Management Agency (FEMA) stating whether or not the building is in a special flood hazard area.

Other Disaster-Prone Areas. As new real estate developments increase in areas that are subject to certain kinds of natural disasters, many lenders are refusing to consider loans for such properties. The potential for disasters includes earthquakes, volcanic eruptions, swelling soils, subsidence of the land, landslides, firestorms, and geographic faulting. Where adequate hazard insurance is available, however, most lenders will make the loans.

Age of Property

The age of a house is a simple, frequently used criterion for determining acceptable and unacceptable loans. The range varies from an insistence by a lender on exclusively new houses, which is unusual, to no fixed limit. Many lenders couple the age of property with the location of the house. Some neighborhoods maintain their desirability over the years, and 30- to 40-year-old homes may qualify for prime loans. Older houses that are not in prime neighborhoods may still qualify for mortgage loans but at higher interest rates and for shorter terms. The originator of a loan must always keep in mind the specific requirements of various secondary-market sources of money in regard to property age.

Conventional loans are handled in two ways regarding the question of age. One is the actual age of property; the other is its years of remaining useful life. If actual age is the criterion, a "no-go" limit is set at a specific maximum age, such as 15 years, for example. A lender may commit to take loans on new houses only, or perhaps on houses not over 3 years old, or not over 20 years old. Determining the actual age is the responsibility of an appraiser and some flexibility is allowed in his or her professional opinion. It is not necessary, in most cases, to report the date of a building permit or the exact day of commencement of construction. Rather, the appraiser can make a judgment call on the **apparent age** of the house. Obviously, a well-kept house and yard would indicate a lower "apparent" age than would one that had been allowed to deteriorate.

The second method of using the age of a property as an underwriting guideline for a conventional loan is the appraiser's judgment of its **remaining useful life.** For this purpose, both FNMA and FHLMC use the same standard as the FHA and VA to qualify loans that they will purchase: The term of the loan cannot exceed 100 percent of the remaining useful life of the property pledged as collateral. Prior to 1986 the limitation was 75 percent of remaining useful life, which is why many older appraisals show an estimate of 40 years for remaining life rather than the 30-year estimate now in more common usage.

Usage of Property

Residential properties can be said to fall into four categories of usage insofar as mortgage loans are concerned. These are:

1. **Owner-occupied.** This usage of property is considered the best and generally commands lower interest rates and discount than apply to other usages.

2. **Tenant-occupied.** For loan purposes, rental property is classed in the commercial loan category. The rationale is that rental property would not have a first call on the owner's personal income should a troubled financial situation occur. This means a loan at a little higher interest rate and discount and for a shorter term than that for owner-occupied property. This is true even though residential rental properties classify as "residential loans" for savings association tax purposes and insofar as banking regulations are concerned.

3. **Resort housing.** Not too many years ago, resort houses could be described as cottages, sometimes poorly built of nonpermanent materials and generally not acceptable as security for loans. The locations often lacked proper fire and police protection, were subject to vandalism and excessive storm damage, and were often not connected to municipal utility systems. In recent years, the growth of new, higher class subdivisions in lakefront or mountainous areas has greatly improved the quality and thus the acceptability of these homes as collateral. Lenders do, in fact, make many resort home loans, but they adjust the loan amount downward ranging from, perhaps, 90 percent to as low as 65 percent loan-to-value ratio.

In resort-type developments, it is not unusual for a developer to buy a loan commitment, paying the discount fee necessary to provide potential customers with a dependable, economical source of mortgage money.

4. **Second homes.** Second homes are a close corollary to resort homes, though they differ in several ways. The more affluent society has produced a growing number of families financially able to own and utilize two different houses. On occasion, the house in the city might be less lived in and less occupied, on the whole, than the so-called second home in the country. In financing these homes, a lender usually makes a careful determination as to which house might be considered the primary housing entitled to preferential treatment and which one should be downgraded as a second home, receiving an 80 percent or smaller loan. A decision such as this would be required where the borrower was making a purchase based primarily on a substantial annual income and not much in other assets. The lender must then consider risk from the viewpoint of a sudden decrease in income due to job loss or working disablement. Which house, then, would most likely have to be forfeited under adverse circumstances?

CONDOMINIUMS

Changes in lifestyles have supported a growth in demand for **condominiums** in place of free-standing houses. The advantages include less maintenance responsibility, access to more amenities, and the same tax advantages that go with all homeownership. Those most interested in this type of dwelling are singles, young marrieds, and senior citizens, together comprising over half the adult population.

To classify a unit of space remote from attachment to the land as a piece of real estate has required new state property laws. All states passed such enabling legislation prior to 1960, making it possible to pledge such property as collateral for mortgage loans. Generally, these laws state how condominiums can be legally described so that they can be classified as real property. Nevertheless, from a lender's viewpoint, a condominium loan involves more questions than does a free-standing house loan because of **common areas** usually owned jointly by all unit owners

Management of common areas is generally handled by a **homeowners' association,** or perhaps through a management agreement. Lenders need to know how maintenance costs are managed and how they are allocated to the unit owners. The reason is that with an imprecise agreement or under inadequate management, costs could suddenly escalate creating an early loan default. One example of possible problems is with new properties. A developer may hold maintenance costs to a minimum during the sell-out period, but this may leave an overload of maintenance costs for unit owners later on.

While a lender has little voice in the continuing operation of a condominium project, careful screening of the management agreement may point out other troublesome provisions. Besides maintenance costs themselves, the rights associated with collecting these charges can present real problems. In some states, a maintenance assessment may carry lien rights similar to those of property taxes; that is, they can take priority over a mortgage lien.

Lenders generally require a copy of the management agreement, or the homeowners' association operating contract, for the condominium as part of the loan documentation. A review of this agreement takes time, so to spread the cost lenders usually require more than one loan in a project before undertaking examination of a condominium loan application. To avoid this problem, some builders ask a lender for project approval prior to offering any units for sale.

Several pitfalls occurred in some of the earlier condominium projects and with better understanding have been fairly well overcome. These involved problems with both apartment conversions and new developments in which developers held onto management control too long. Examples of this kind of problem are retention of exclusive rights to all future sales of the units, controlling distribution and resale of utilities to the individual units, and holding an unlimited right to expand the project that could overburden existing amenities.

While property qualification for a condominium differs as outlined, qualification for a borrower buying a condo is the same as for any other mortgage loan.

Commercial Condominiums

While the condominium concept has been most widely applied to residential units, a number of applications have been made for use of condos as rental properties or as business locations. In some condo projects, a number of the dwelling units are owned by investors and are subject to rental. This has caused additional problems in that the motivation among occupants differs. Those owning their own condos consider the entire project, including common areas, as an asset to be maintained and protected to assure future value. Those renting units may consider occupancy a temporary situation and have little interest in maintaining the property's future value. Differing motivations present difficult problems for a homeowners' association. This conflict of interests is sometimes created unintentionally when a developer is unable to sell all finished units and resorts to rentals as preferable to vacancies.

The economic advantages of a multiple-occupancy building have encouraged groups of businesspeople to utilize the condominium concept for owner-occupied office space. The group can be one with similar interests such as doctors, or it can be a diverse group of professionals or possibly a variety of sales offices. Whatever the makeup, a developer or builder may undertake such a project, generally emphasizing presale of the units to assure acceptable construction or rehabilitation financing. Individual condos used for business purposes may be purchased with long-term financing at commercial loan rates and conditions. They are eligible for the same basic tax treatment as any freestanding building used for business.

COOPERATIVE APARTMENTS

A **cooperative apartment** is one in which the ownership of the entire project is vested in an occupant-owned corporation or trust that leases the dwelling units. The concept originated in the eastern part of this country before condominium ownership was fully developed. It provides the advantages of multifamily dwellings along with certain ownership rights. In addition, co-op apartments offer owners some degree of control over who may occupy the units and a legal means to enforce compliance with its rules. This is accomplished through control over the ownership of its stock.

To purchase an apartment unit, it is first necessary to buy shares of stock in the owning corporation or a beneficial interest in the trust, depending on how the ownership is held. Then the apartment is leased from the corporate owner. The purchase price of the stock covers the basic cost of acquiring the unit while the lease payment covers ongoing maintenance costs. Thus, the occupant holds no title to the apartment unit. To sell a unit, an occupant must sell the stock held in the ownership entity which would be subject to certain restrictions on this right to sell. The difficulty of freely marketing a co-op unit has made this type of ownership less desirable than that of a condominium. In contrast, a condominium unit is classed as real property and legal title can be conveyed to an owner upon acquisition. The right to sell is not subject to approval by other condo owners.

Nevertheless, cooperative apartments may offer an owner similar tax advantages to those available to the owner of a condominium. There are some minor differences in tax questions, though, as the common areas of a co-op are owned by the corporate owner rather than jointly by the unit owners as would be true of a condominium unit.

Financing the construction of a cooperative apartment (or a condominium project) has the disadvantage of requiring a number of units to be built with the initial commitment of money. Unlike a single-family housing development, which allows houses to be constructed at about the same rate as they are sold, the cooperative apartment must be planned and built as a complete project. One method that is sometimes used to assure a construction lender of loan repayment is to presell (or prelease) a certain number of the units. Release of construction funding can be made contingent on the presale of a specified number of units.

MANUFACTURED HOUSING/MOBILE HOMES

The only difference between a mobile home and a manufactured home is that the latter is constructed on or after June 15, 1976. Otherwise, the same description applies. The date for the change of names derives from the Federal Manufactured Home Requirements inposed by the U.S. Department of Housing and Urban Development. The HUD description of such a unit is that it must be transportable in one or more sections not less than 8 feet wide and 40 feet long. When assembled, such a home must contain no less than 320 square feet. It must be built on a permanent chassis and may, or may not, have a permanent foundation.

Unless the unit can be classed as real property, it does not qualify for a regular mortgage loan. Financing for these units when considered other than real property may be accomplished with a chattel mortgage as security for the loan. However, in most areas, the chattel mortgage has been replaced by a bill of sale with a security agreement that is regulated by the Uniform Commercial Code.

Conversion of Manufactured Home to Real Property

State laws control definition of real property and there are some differences. Nevertheless, a manufactured home is initially sold by a manufacturer as personal property with an instrument asserting title similar to that of a car. Liens may be included in the title instrument to accommodate purchase financing. Conversion of the unit to real property normally requires several steps. First, liens attached to the initial title normally must be released. The initial title must be canceled which, in effect, releases the unit from its title as personal property. Then, to become real property, the unit must be permanently attached to the land. Depending on state law, in general, prior liens on the manufactured home do not attach to the land, but liens against the land will attach to the manufactured home upon permanent attachment.

SURVEYS

One of the recurring problems in passing land titles and in making sure that a lender is actually receiving a mortgage on the proper land is the identification of that land. Improper identification of the property to be mortgaged, through field error or typographical error, will invalidate the mortgage instrument (but not the obligation to repay the loan). It is to identify physically a parcel of land that a survey is made. A **land survey** is an accurate measurement of the property, not a legal description of it.

An example of an error in property description occurred in a motel loan several years ago. In this case, the property described in the mortgage was identified by the perimeter of the building rather than by the boundaries of the land on which the building stood. The parking areas surrounding the building, which provided the only access to the premises, were not included in the mortgage indenture. When it became necessary to foreclose, the mortgagee learned the hard way that there was no access to the building!

For our purposes, a survey is the physical measurement of a specific piece of property certified by a professionally registered surveyor. In processing a mortgage loan, no lender will accept any measurements other than a professional's. It is a precise business, and the loan package requires an accurate description of the land being mortgaged.

When a licensed surveyor physically defines a piece of property, it is customary to drive stakes or iron rods into the ground at the corners and to "flag" them with colored ribbons. It is not unusual for a lending officer to physically walk the land, checking corner markers, thus making sure of the shape of the parcel and whether or not there might be any encroachments that could infringe on the mortgage lien. Any purchaser of land is well advised to follow the same procedure: Walk the land prior to closing as a prudent exercise. However, the prime responsibility for locating encroachments belongs to the surveyor, which is one of the reasons why a survey is necessary.

LEGAL DESCRIPTIONS

A completed survey is a map showing each boundary line of the property with its precise length and direction. A survey should not be confused with a legal description. A legal description describes property in words, while a survey describes by illustration. Legal descriptions are most commonly found in the following three formats.

Lot and Block

Probably the best-known type of legal description is that found in incorporated areas that have established procedures for land development. To obtain city approval to build streets and connect utilities, a developer will submit a master survey of the entire tract of land, showing how the area is to be divided into lots. The lots are each numbered and may be grouped into "blocks" for easier identification. Once the subdivision plat is approved, it can be recorded in the county offices and becomes a readily available legal reference to any lot in the plan.

For lending purposes, where the need is to identify a specific property over a period of 30 or even 40 years, the recorded subdivision plat is a much better method than a street address. Street names change and numbers can be altered, but the lot and block numbers remain secure because they are recorded. It may be argued that a street address gives a much better picture of where the property lies in discussing various houses or properties, but such identification is not sufficiently accurate to be acceptable to a lender. The common method of clearly identifying property in real estate transactions is, first, to give the legal description, followed by a phrase such as "also known as," and then to provide the street address. To illustrate, a property identification might be spelled out as, "Lot 6, Block 9, Nottingham Addition, Harris County, Texas, also known as 1234 Ashford Lane, Houston, Harris County, Texas."

Metes and Bounds

When recorded plats are not available for identification of land (and sometimes when plats are available), it becomes necessary to use an exact survey of the boundary lines for complete identification. This might be true of a recorded lot that has a stream or river as one boundary, the precise boundary being subject to change through erosion or realignment.

The method used is to define a starting corner with proper references to other marking lines, then note the direction in degrees and the distance to the next marking corner, and so on around the perimeter of the property back to the starting point. These descriptions can be quite lengthy and involved. An example of the wording used to describe several boundary lines might be ". . . and thence along said Smith Street south 61 degrees 32 minutes 18 seconds west 948 and 25/100 feet; thence continuing along said Smith Street south 64 degrees 45 minutes 51 seconds west 162 and 80/100 feet to the point of beginning."

It is obvious that considerable accuracy is required to figure the necessary directions down to a second of a degree and to measure the distances over highly variable and often rough terrain in order to close the boundaries properly. Such a description is acceptable only if certified by a registered surveyor.

In some rural areas, land is identified in the form of metes and bounds by the use of monuments. A *monument* may be something tangible, such as a river, a tree, rocks, fences, or streets, or an intangible, such as a survey line from an adjoining property. Physical monuments such as these are subject to destruction, removal, or shifting and do not provide lasting identifications for long-term loans.

U.S. Geodetic or Government Survey

As long ago as 1785, the federal government adopted a measurement system for land based on survey lines running north and south, called *meridians*, and those running east and west, called *base lines*. The system eventually applied to 30 western states with the exception of Texas. A number of prime meridians and base lines were established. Then the surveyors divided the areas between the intersections into squares called *checks*, which are 24 miles on each side. These checks are further divided into 16 squares, each measuring 6 miles by 6 miles, called *townships*. The townships are then divided into one square-mile

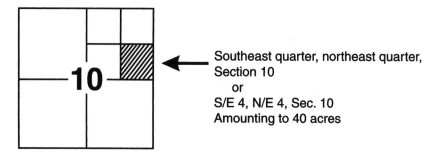

Southeast quarter, northeast quarter, Section 10

or

S/E 4, N/E 4, Sec. 10
Amounting to 40 acres

FIGURE 10–1 Section of Township Divided into Quarters

units (36 to a township), called *sections,* which amount to 640 acres each. These sections are then divided into halves, quarters, or such portions as are needed to describe individual land holdings. An example is shown in Figure 10–1.

During the growth years of this country, much of the western land was laid out in this fashion by contract survey crews. Marking stakes were duly placed to identify corners, and these same markers are frequently used today. The fact that many of the surveys accumulated errors, including the failure to close lines, has created some confusion. It is a concern primarily for oil and mining companies which must identify their land rights, and ranchers claiming property lines against a neighbor. However, these faulty descriptions have not constituted a serious problem for lending institutions. Land described, for example, as "Section 16, Township 31 north, Range 16 east, New Mexico Prime Meridian," could effectively collateralize a farm or ranch loan. A minor inaccuracy in describing such a tract would not undermine the basic security of the collateral.

In pledging property where there is the possibility or probability that some slight inaccuracy has occurred as to the exact amount of land involved, it is customary to use a qualifying term such as "comprising 640 acres, more or less." Any variation in property size should be considered in the light of what might be termed "reasonable." A few acres out of line among 640 acres would not matter a great deal, but a few feet in a downtown city property could well be of critical importance.

Questions for Discussion

1. Define an *appraisal.*
2. What qualifications does a mortgage lender require for an appraiser?
3. What is meant by the "highest and best use" of land?
4. Describe each of the three approaches to value and give examples of the property type for which each would be most applicable.
5. Identify the three categories of depreciation associated with real property.

6. How would you capitalize an income stream so as to show a property value? What is the advantage of a discounted or present-worth analysis over capitalization?
7. Discuss the two methods of using age of property as criteria for loan approval.
8. Why is a loan for a condominium more difficult to analyze than one for a free-standing house?
9. Distinguish between a survey and a legal description.
10. Give an example of a physical characteristic of a house that could cause loan rejection.

Chapter 11

Commercial Loans: Construction and Land Loans

···

KEY WORDS AND PHRASES

Commercial loan • *Balance sheet* • *Profit and loss statement* • *Operating statement* • *Net operating income* • *Pro forma statement* • *Certified public accountant* • *Audited statement* • *Feasibility study* • *Land loans* • *Land development loans* • *Release clauses* • *Office of Interstate Land Sales* • *Construction loans* • *Takeout commitment*

···

INTRODUCTION

In mortgage financing, the term **commercial loan** has a broad and ill-defined meaning. One major discrepancy in the standard, accepted definition is that an apartment loan is considered a commercial type of loan. Yet, for tax purposes such as calculating depreciation, an apartment is classed as residential property. Perhaps the best definition of a commercial loan would be a very generalized "those loans that are not classed as residential." It is a broad category with considerable variety in the handling of each major class of property.

A practical distinction between residential and commercial loans can be drawn from the anticipated source of loan repayment. A residential loan is expected to be repaid from the personal income of the borrower—income unrelated to the property offered as collateral. The commercial loan is a business loan and in most instances repayment is expected from income generated by the property pledged as collateral. The individual involved with seeking a commercial loan is certainly important, but not crucially so as with a residential loan. Indeed, in many large commercial loans there may not be any personal liability for the principals as individuals. For it is the property that provides both the loan collateral and the anticipated source of loan repayment.

Consequently, commercial loan evaluation focuses first on the property, then on the business applicant who expects to own the property. The following section discusses the type of information needed for commercial loan analysis and several of the tools that are used to make an analysis.

INFORMATION SOURCES

The underwriter of a commercial loan has more sources of information than are normally found with home loans. The home loan evaluation is based primarily on an applicant's personal income and a market appraisal of the property offered as collateral. Proper underwriting of a commercial loan usually involves a business operation and property expected to produce sufficient income to repay the loan. So, to evaluate a commercial loan, the underwriter examines the financial statements offered by the business (or individual) applicant, studies the income-producing capability of the property offered as collateral, and conducts an examination of the local market for that property's particular product or service. In addition, analysis of a commercial loan application can include extensive interviews with the principals involved in the business operation and a thorough inspection of the property itself.

THE LOAN APPLICATION

All loans commence with an application. However, unlike residential loans, a commercial loan application is not a standardized form. It is designed by lenders to suit their own specific requirements. Often, the application has specialty sections that focus on different classes of properties, such as the distinctive information needed for a hotel loan that differs from that needed to evaluate an apartment loan application. Knowing what questions to ask about specific kinds of properties is one reason commercial lenders tend to specialize in their lending practices.

Generally, application information identifies the applicant and the individuals involved, the amount and purpose of the loan, and the source of loan repayment. The detailed information is furnished in separate exhibits that would include complete financial statements, a property evaluation, a projection of how the loan is expected to be repaid, and any supplemental information such as building plans and specifications if construction is involved.

It is normal for the lender to charge a reasonable nonrefundable application fee for several reasons. One is to defray the cost of studying an extensive, and usually "one of its kind," body of information that supports sound applications. Another reason is simply to discourage frivolous applications.

Information Required for a Commercial Loan Application

How financial information is presented has a few standards and little regulation. What is close to a standard is the design of the principal kinds of statements, but the information can vary considerably. Regulations that apply to this type of information are directed almost entirely to those real estate companies that offer securities to the general public. The specific information most likely required in a real estate loan application is further described next, followed by information on the professionals who prepare such information.

Operating Statements of Property

If the property has been operating, statements for the past two or three years are required. These would include annual balance sheets and profit and loss statements. A third statement, an operating statement, reports an individual property and does not show income tax or depreciation figures. While tax and depreciation figures are very important, they are not considered to be operating expenses but costs that vary with the owner's personal situation. Following is more detail on the three principal financial statements.

Balance Sheet. A **balance sheet** is the most standardized of all the financial statements. It is a listing of a company's (or individual's) assets in a column at the left of the page, and a listing of the liabilities plus the net worth in a column at the right of the page. The difference between the assets (what is owned) and the liabilities (what is owed) amounts to the net worth of the company. This makes the sum of liabilities and net worth on one side of the sheet equal in amount to the assets listed on the other side—thus, a "balance" sheet.

Figures that are of concern to an analyst of the balance sheet are the valuation of assets. This is particularly important when major assets consist of real estate. A distortion in value can easily present an erroneous picture of true worth. The careful underwriter will need to know how asset values, particularly land and buildings, are derived: Is it a book value representing the original cost of the property? Is it based on a professional appraisal? Could the value be an owner's concept of market value? Most other figures found in a balance sheet are more easily verified with simple auditing procedures.

Profit and Loss Statement. The **profit and loss statement** is a statement of income and expense; it has nothing to do with assets and liabilities. The basic format is simple: Start with the income, then deduct expenses, and the bottom line shows a profit or loss for the time period covered. The figures may be presented in excruciating detail covering several pages or can be reduced to three lines: one for gross income, one for total expenses, and the third representing the difference between the two, which is the profit (or loss). Most statements fall in between the extremes.

Normally, the P & L statement gives some detail as to what items comprise the operation's income as several sources are often involved. The same is true of expenses which provide information on where the money has been spent. By subtracting the operating expenses from income the result is commonly called **net operating income.** Operating expenses are those costs necessary for the day-to-day operation of the business. They do not include such important deductions as debt service, depreciation, and reserves for payment of income taxes. This is why net operating income best reflects the true operation of a property.

To explain further, the other costs mentioned (debt service, depreciation, and tax reserves) are determined by the owner's decisions and have little to do with the efficiency of day-to-day management of operations. Debt service is the cost of financing and has nothing to do with operations. To put it another way, if the property is overloaded with debt, firing the manager is not a solution. As identified on a P & L statement, debt service is the payment of principal and interest only. It does not include insurance premiums and property taxes (these are deducted as expenses) as is customary with home loans. (Home loans identify this cost as a *mortgage payment* which includes principal, interest, taxes, and insurance—or PITI.)

The choice of depreciation procedures allows an owner some flexibility and reflects tax decisions rather than operations. And in today's world of income taxes, there is no standard that can be applied to any particular income. Such taxes, particularly when real estate is involved, must reflect all sources of income. Thus, identical dollar amount of income no longer results in identical taxation.

Because of the questions just raised, a profit and loss statement should deduct debt service, depreciation, and tax reserves from the net operating income after that figure has been determined. This gives an important "bottom line" for an owner or analyst to make informed decisions on future property rehabilitation, expansion, possible disposition, and tax matters. This information is often considered proprietary and not readily available to potential buyers of the property. Instead, for potential buyers, a shortened form of the P & L is commonly used, better known as an *operating statement.*

Operating Statement. Because it is similar in format, an **operating statement** is often confused with a profit and loss statement. As a shortened P & L, it limits information to income and expenses: no debt service, no depreciation, and no income taxes. Further, both income and expenses should be presented in sufficient detail to give a reader good knowledge of the property's operation.

An operating statement contains the kind of information most commonly found in real estate transactions. It gives some detail on the income that can be made (the potential gross income), reduced by vacancy and credit losses. Operating expenses are then listed as a deduction from income. The expenses are given in considerable detail and include property taxes and insurance premiums. As explained earlier, these items are not included in debt service when considering commercial loans. The information, subject to verification, can be used as part of an offering package for prospective buyers.

A helpful addition found on some operating statements is a percentage column that gives the ratio of an expense to the property's gross operating income. For example, to use round figures for simplicity, if a property shows a gross operating income of $100,000 and the cost of electricity is $8,000, that would represent an 8 percent (8,000 divided by 100,000 equals .08) measure.

Key expenses should be shown in a percentage column as it is helpful for two purposes: (1) for comparison of operating expenses between potential acquisitions, and (2) to single out those expense items that appear inordinately high compared with local norms. Percentages are a more accurate reflection for comparing costs than dollar amounts because of variation in size of properties. It helps show whether or not expenses may be increasing because of increased revenue or for some other reason.

Pro Forma Cash Flow Statements

A pro forma statement is a projection of both income and expenses. It is not a record of what has happened, but what might be expected. Pro forma statements are most frequently used as an analysis for new developments. They may be found in a prospectus for an offering of a real estate security. Because the figures are all projections, a pro forma statement should be very clearly labeled. In the hands of a professional analyst, the pro forma can provide very helpful information on a proposed investment project. In the hands of a sales enthusiast, however, it can be misleading.

Business Financial Statements

If the real estate borrower has a business, or is a business, lenders will require two or three years of signed and dated statements. Audited statements are usually preferred but some lenders accept those that are client prepared.

Personal Financial Statements. The principals involved are expected to furnish statements for the past two or three years.

Business and Personal Income Tax Returns. A complete loan package will include two or three years of tax returns for both a business and the principals involved.

Current Rent Roll. The rent roll is a list of the space available for rent and, if available, should include current tenants, vacancies, current rent (gross and effective rate per square foot per year), escalation clauses, maturity of rent contracts, options for renewal, type of rent (net lease, net net lease, or triple net lease), rent concessions and their timing, and square footage currently under lease. Copies of all leases are normally required. Creditworthiness of current tenants is reviewed and the lender may require an assignment of leases and rental agreements as additional collateral.

Accounts Receivable and Accounts Payable Aging Reports. Some lenders may require this information to help analyze the overall financial health of the business.

Purchase Contract or Warranty Deed. If the property is to be purchased, the lender will want a copy of the purchase contract and all addendums. If the property is already owned, the lender will want a copy of the recorded warranty deed.

Insurance. Lenders require that the property have hazard and general liability insurance. Depending on the location of the property, other types of insurance (such as flood insurance) may be required.

Current Real Estate Appraisal. Lenders usually order the appraisal since they have their own list of acceptable appraisers. A narrative type of appraisal is normally required, giving cost, market, and income approaches to value.

Survey. Lenders require a current survey of the land made by a registered surveyor.

Property Tax Bill. Some lenders require a copy of the tax bill to verify the legal description, the owners, and the tax assessment on the land and any buildings.

Résumés of Principals. The borrower should supply a lender with a brief résumé of all principals' work history. Also, if a business is involved, a brief history is helpful.

Articles of Incorporation. If the borrower is a corporation, the lender will require a copy of the articles of incorporation and a corporate borrowing resolution.

Authorization to Release Information. A commercial loan package should contain an authorization for the lender to request credit information on all principals and the business if one is involved.

Environmental Audit. All commercial loans require an environmental site assessment. The audit should be made by a professional acceptable to the lender.

PREPARATION OF FINANCIAL STATEMENTS

The most important assurance of receiving complete and accurate information on a financial statement is the caliber of the person preparing the statement. The highest professional designation in this field is **certified public accountant (CPA),** which may be granted by each state. Some states offer lesser designations such as "public accountant" for those meeting certain requirements, usually preparatory to reaching the CPA level. The requirements vary somewhat among the states, but all demand completion of educational courses, some experience in the field, and the passing of exhaustive qualification tests.

In practice, only a CPA may prepare an **audited statement.** This means that the information contained therein has been prepared in accordance with accepted accounting practices and that the numbers used have been verified by the preparer. The preparer then certifies that the statement accurately represents the financial condition of the subject. CPAs can also prepare statements without audit that do not offer the substantiation of data provided with an audit. For larger commercial loans, lenders may insist on audited statements.

The initial presentation of most commercial property investments as found in sales brochures often offers financial information that has not been compiled by professional accountants. If the preparer is an owner or a sales broker, the information given may be suspect because of the vested interest of the preparer. Nevertheless, such information can be verified to some degree by an interested investor and does provide a point of beginning. A major problem with these statements is that they lack consistency, do not have uniform account identification, can reach conclusions that defy easy comparison, and are not always accurate.

Prudent investors normally take the financial information supplied, verify essential details, and then restate all of the figures onto a standard form. A standard form is used to shift income and expense items into uniform accounts that allow easier comparison. The standard statement procedure also shows up accounting information that may be lacking, such as how replacement costs are handled. By restating information onto a standard form, an investor, or analyst, can make a better comparison between properties offering investment opportunities.

PROPERTY EVALUATION

In commercial loan analysis, the evaluation of property offered as collateral involves more than determining its present value. In most instances, it is the income produced by that property that is expected to repay the loan, so the study involves its potential for producing sufficient income to handle timely repayment. Each kind of property presents a different set of circumstances that affects its cash flows. Because of this, many lenders simply limit their participation in commercial lending to the types of properties they know best. Experience is a valuable teacher.

The specialized problems of the major classes of income properties are discussed in the next chapter. More generalized information can be obtained from an appraisal and a feasibility study, as explained next.

Appraisal

Unlike residential loans, there are no standardized forms and few regulations that apply to how an appraisal must be prepared for a commercial loan. The most common practice is for a lender to require a narrative-type appraisal prepared by a recognized professional. If the loan is destined for handling by any federal-related lender, such as a multifamily housing loan, a state-certified appraiser must be used. It is most important that the appraiser be acceptable to the lender. Lenders sometimes will provide a list of appraisers that are known to them and have a sound record of performance. Or the lender requirement might be given as a minimum level of appraiser designation, such as "an MAI appraiser or the equivalent with state certification."

For a lender, an appraisal represents several things. It is used to confirm an applicant's opinion of value. It provides a professional opinion of what the property actually comprises in land and buildings. And it gives regulated lenders an acceptable basis for meeting maximum limits on loan-to-value ratios. An appraisal should be recognized as an estimate of value at approximately the time of loan origination, and not an assurance that value will remain unchanged over the life of the loan. Nevertheless, the appraisal industry has come under increasing scrutiny by regulatory authorities (see Chapter 10).

Feasibility Study

A **feasibility study** is a variation of the more standardized appraisal techniques in that it places much greater emphasis on a market study of the products and services offered by the subject property. Further, while appraisers are professionally recognized with designations offered by various peer groups and state certifications, those who prepare feasibility reports are not. Even so, feasibility studies are usually prepared by various professionals such as appraisers, property managers, real estate brokers, and market analysts.

As its name implies, a feasibility study attempts to determine whether or not a proposed investment is likely to be successful. It estimates the cost of the project, whether new construction or rehabilitation. Potential income is measured with a market analysis of competing properties in the area. This involves a study of occupancy, amenities offered by the competition, and rental rates. Based on the proven experience of similar properties, the analysis will include a pro forma statement of the expected income and expense of the operation. Also, problems associated with environmental questions are examined as they relate to the subject property. In its conclusion (which is often presented at the beginning of the report), the study attempts to answer the practical question of whether or not the project will be successful. Obviously, the knowledge and ability of the preparer is critical in reaching reasonably accurate conclusions.

LAND PURCHASE LOANS

Considered as a class, raw land acquisition loans are probably the most difficult of all mortgage loans to obtain. Undeveloped land offers no income that might be used to repay the loan. There is further concern in the need for additional cash each year to pay property taxes, possibly insurance, and various "standby" charges. A hindsight view of the serious decline of real estate values and the collapse of many savings institutions in the late 1980s point a heavy finger at raw land as the most serious real estate problem. As a result, not too many lenders will even entertain an application for a **land loan.**

Lenders who do make this kind of loan are likely to restrict approval to those with (1) a good track record of repayment of other land purchase loans, (2) substantial other assets available, or (3) an assurance with some written commitment of a future resale of the land. Effective in March 1993, new loan-to-value limits were placed on regulated lenders at 65 percent for raw land loans. However, lenders can, and do, apply even lower limits as prudent policy.

Any mortgage loan that is expected to be repaid through the sale of its collateral carries a higher risk for the lender. A future sale is not always an assured condition. In certain situations, a future sale or use of the land might be known when the land is acquired yet final disposition is not immediate. For instance, the land may be purchased for a housing development, or perhaps a shopping center, requiring more time to complete plans and permanent financing. If such conditions exist, the attraction for a lender to assist in the immediate purchase of raw land is the potential to make the construction and permanent loans.

Sometimes a land broker or developer will locate a tract of land highly suitable for a particular purchaser. It could be a small tract for a service station or a larger parcel on which to erect a retail store outlet. But at the time the property becomes available, the ultimate user may not be in a position to consummate the land purchase. In such a circumstance, a binding letter of intent by a creditworthy buyer issued to a real estate broker or developer would greatly facilitate a raw land loan to acquire the chosen site. The land broker would be presenting the lender with a reasonably sure sale for the land within a specified time period, with the land itself as collateral.

LAND DEVELOPMENT LOANS

The next logical step after purchase of raw land is its development. Land development for loan purposes means the building of streets and utilities to prepare lots for resale as home sites. In contrast, the land development work associated with the construction of an apartment or office building project is in the category of site development, or land preparation, and is an integral part of the project's construction costs. For such projects, separate **land development loans** are not needed. Since the work called for in land development plans can easily identify the project for residential purposes, such a loan is much more acceptable to a savings association than the land purchase itself. The reason is that the development loan classifies as "residential," which for regulatory and tax purposes may receive more favorable treatment for the lender than strictly commercial loans.

A development loan is limited for regulated lenders to a maximum of 75 percent of the property value. The property value normally used for this measure is the appraised value of the finished lots. This is one of several types of loans that generate what might be called a certain distortion in values due to the fact that the very development being financed greatly enhances the value of raw land. Normally, the appraised value of completed lots based on an existing market would be substantially greater than the development costs. In such a case, a 75 percent loan could permit the developer to borrow an amount in excess of the actual costs. In lending jargon, the amount of a loan that exceeds a borrower's actual costs is called *walking money*—money the borrower can walk away with upon completion. The prudent lender is reluctant to permit a borrower to obtain a cash "profit" from a development loan since this has a tendency to lessen the incentive to sell the property as intended.

Release Clause

An integral part of a land development loan agreement is the **release clause.** This is the clause that spells out when, how, and at what price any lot or lots may be released from the mortgage pledge of the initial tract of land. The release terms may call for an order of priorities by which the land can be developed and will state in what manner lots may be released. The purpose of this kind of mandate would be to assure overall development in a manner that realizes the most efficient utilization of the entire tract that is pledged.

Another important clause specifies the amount of money from each lot sale that must be paid to the lender to release that lot. The release itself is a specific release of the mortgage lien on the lot or lots being sold and is intended to permit delivery of a clear title to the lot purchaser, usually the home builder. The amount of money required to release a lot may be a percentage of the sales price of the lot, such as 75 percent, stating a minimum sales price. In this procedure, any increase in sales price over the minimum would increase the payment to the lender and amortize the loan more rapidly.

Another method is to set a flat sum on each lot for release and let the developer sell at whatever price he or she can. The flat sum per lot is usually calculated to repay the development loan with interest in full when somewhere between 60 and 75 percent of the lots have been sold. Lenders are not interested in waiting for the last, perhaps least desirable, lots to be sold in order to recover the loan.

Office of Interstate Land Sales

Since 1968, the Department of Housing and Urban Development (HUD) has had an **Office of Interstate Land Sales** charged by Congress with the responsibility of establishing guidelines and procedures for land developers in an effort to minimize deceptive practices and outright frauds. Sales of lots, developed and undeveloped, have grown substantially in this country and have brought out some unscrupulous operators. Basically, the rules require a full disclosure of the essential facts for the land buyer and serve as a protection for both buyer and seller. As one explanation goes, a developer can still sell a lot that is completely under water but must state in writing that it is under water! The rules apply to any development with over 50 lots for sale, of less than five acres each, and on which no construction is required. Failure to comply with HUD regulations can involve a fine and imprisonment for the lender, the developer, and the sales agents.

CONSTRUCTION LOANS

The construction industry is a major employer in this country and much of it depends heavily on the availability of lendable funds. However, several large segments of the construction business are not so dependent on the regular commercial loan market. These are mostly government projects such as streets, highways, dams, and public buildings, which can be paid for from tax revenues. To finance these projects, various types of bonds can be sold that are often collateralized with a pledge of tax revenues. Another large segment of the construction market is the building of industrial plants and utility systems by large corporations. These projects are often financed from their own revenues, or perhaps through the sale of corporate securities, including mortgage bonds.

The type of construction lending discussed in this section concerns a building loan: the money needed to construct a house, an office building, or a shopping center. While these loans vary substantially in size, there is a similarity in the risks involved. All are secured by a mortgage on the land and the building to be constructed, all are funded only after each stage of construction has been completed, and almost all require a permanent loan commitment or takeout of some kind to assure repayment of the construction loan immediately upon completion of the project. So where is the big risk?

The risk to the construction lender is whether or not the building can be completed with the available money and whether it meets all required specifications. Many factors that are difficult to foresee enter into the successful completion of a building. Some of the problems are the weather, labor difficulties and strikes, delays in the delivery of materials, and changes in the plans or specifications. A more recent requirement has been the meeting of sometimes difficult to define environmental stipulations. These can result in time-consuming meetings, additional paperwork, and even litigation.

Definition

The definition of a **construction loan** focuses on the special requirements for this type of financing. A construction loan is initially a loan commitment that provides for the money to be disbursed at intervals during construction in a manner that ensures payment of all construction costs and finance charges. It requires completion of the building in accordance with the plans and specifications so as to deliver a valid first mortgage upon completion. Further explanation of each part of the definition follows.

Disbursement During Construction

Unlike other types of loans, a construction loan is not funded when the borrower signs the note. All the borrower has at the beginning is a commitment that funds will be released as construction progresses. There are two basic ways that progress payments are released: one is on a time-interval basis and the other is on a by-work-completed basis.

With the time-interval method (usually monthly), the building progress is inspected at specified intervals and the amount of work completed is duly noted. The lender then releases that portion of the loan that has been allocated to the work accomplished. Under the by-work-completed plan, the lender and borrower agree at the outset on about five stages of progress which, when reached, will release that amount of the loan proceeds. An example of a first stage might be the completion of all underground work and the pouring of the foundation.

Assurance of Payment of Costs

While it is the borrower's prime responsibility to use the loan proceeds for the payment of charges on the construction, the lender has an important stake in making sure that all labor and materials are paid as the money is released. Every so often, a builder, by design or in error, may mix the records and use the proceeds from one construction loan to pay charges accruing from another project. The result can be labor liens and material suppliers' liens filed on the property for which loan funds have already been released to cover those claimants.

Lenders can minimize the risk of improper disbursement in several ways. One is for the lender to handle the payments to contractors and subcontractors. Another is to require proof of payment for costs incurred by the borrower before any funds are released from the loan. Another is to require a waiver-of-lien form signed by each contractor involved with every progress payment. Perhaps the most important protection for the lender in this regard is to know the borrower's reputation for handling building projects, then to make close inspection a standard procedure.

Completion in Accordance with Plans

Again it is the borrower who is primarily concerned that the building is constructed according to the plans and specifications. But the lender also has a real interest in this question, as failure to meet the plans can be a cause for refusal by the permanent lender to release the loan for payoff of the construction loan. The problems are mostly technical, such as the size of pipes and wiring, the grade and thickness of concrete, the amount of reinforcing used, the compaction of foundation and parking areas, and many others.

On small projects, the lender may rely on its regular staff for inspection approvals. On large projects, it is more common to employ an independent firm or professional to serve as the inspector. Architects and engineers are both used for this purpose, and the decision of the professional is usually accepted by both the borrower and lender as final determination of the acceptability of the project as it is built.

Delivering a Valid First Mortgage

Insofar as the lender is concerned, the goal of a successful construction loan is to complete the project within the money allocated, all bills paid, and no liens filed. The construction loan can then be repaid through funding of a permanent loan or the sale of the property.

Additional Comments

In a construction loan it is customary for the lender to withhold 10 percent from each progress payment until final completion. The purpose is to provide a reserve against unexpected claims. Some lenders will hold this reserve until the statutory lien period has expired after completion before releasing it to the borrower. If an unexpected cost is encountered that was not allowed for in the loan amount committed, the lender will ask, or demand, that the borrower make such payment. The same procedure is used if the borrower decides to make some changes in the plans after the loan has been committed. Such changes must be approved by the lender, and if they should cause an increase in the anticipated cost, the borrower will be expected to use his or her own funds for payment. The lender does not want to have a building only partially completed with all loan funds exhausted.

Personal endorsement by the borrower-owner is almost always required on a construction loan. The same lender may agree to make a long-term permanent loan with no personal endorsement required, but will refuse to do so on the construction loan for the same project. The reason is not just the added security given by another endorsement; it is to place personal responsibility on the borrower-owner who is in a controlling position during construction to insist on changes in the plans or create costly problems that can upset orderly construction work. The lender just wants to make certain that the borrower-owner carries a full share of responsibility.

The principal sources for construction money are commercial banks with specialized construction loan departments, savings associations, and mortgage companies that represent life insurance companies. The commercial banks' interest is in the higher yields and short terms represented in construction lending; savings associations and mortgage companies prefer the higher yields, but also are usually in a position to pick up permanent loans at a minimum of expense to themselves.

Construction Loans for Residential Properties

Single-family detached houses and some townhouse projects are financed by builders on both a contract basis and a speculative basis.

Contract Basis

A house built for an owner under contract represents a reduced risk to the construction lender. The normal sales contract to the home buyer is a firm commitment by the purchaser and includes a permanent loan commitment for closing. Often the permanent commitment is made to a home buyer by the same lender handling the construction financing as a sort of package deal, which minimizes paperwork. On such a loan the risk to the construction lender is primarily in the builder's ability to complete the house within contract terms. The builder's track record must be known to the lender.

In smaller communities and rural areas, houses are often constructed under contract by a local builder, who may also operate a lumberyard or other supply facility, with the builder providing the construction financing from personal resources. A nearby savings association will have already agreed to make the permanent loan when the house is completed.

Speculative Basis

Many builders, mostly in the growing suburban areas, build houses with the expectation of selling them by the time they are completed. To the risk of being able to complete the house within the projected cost figure is added the risk of selling the house at a profitable price upon completion. A lender must look at the strength and capability of a speculative builder before accepting such a loan. As a builder proves satisfactory ability to the lender, the construction line of credit can be expanded.

When the housing market fluctuates downward, the speculative builder is the first to be hurt. He or she can be caught with many unsold houses on which the high interest of a construction loan can continue to eat at any profits. More and more, construction lenders are seeking to protect themselves against a soft market by demanding a takeout commitment before they will agree to the construction loan.

Takeout Commitment

A **takeout commitment,** sometimes called a standby commitment, is a promise to the home builder by an acceptable mortgage lender to make a permanent home loan directly to the builder in the event the subject house is not sold within a certain time limit, commonly one year. The commitment is usually in the form of a simple letter agreement and costs the builder at least one point payable upon delivery of the letter agreement. The amount of the commitment would be the same as the construction loan, normally 80 percent of the sales value of the house.

However, the commitment is not really expected to be used. It serves more as an insurance policy to protect the construction lender's loan. To encourage the builder to sell the house, rather than rely on the takeout commitment, the rate of interest on the takeout is set at one to three percentage points over the going rate, and the term much shorter, probably 10 years, than if the loan had been made to the intended occupant-buyer. The builder still has the problem of selling the house but has a little breather in facing a monthly amortization payment rather than full repayment of the construction loan, while the construction lender is clear with all money repaid.

Construction Loans for Income Properties

Apartments, office buildings, shopping centers, and warehouses all use construction financing, sometimes termed *interim financing,* to accomplish the building of the project. As pointed out earlier, only the strongest builder-developers are capable of commanding construction financing for any income property without a permanent loan commitment to pay off the construction loan at completion. The terms of the permanent loan influence the manner in which the construction money can be handled. Special requirements for funding the permanent loan, such as an 80 percent lease-up before release of the loan proceeds, place the construction lender in a far riskier position. If a permanent lender is currently unavailable, the developer may resort to a takeout commitment within the same framework as described earlier for a home builder. The construction lender must have a closing date for the takeout within a reasonable period (one to three years) for proper recovery of the construction loan.

Construction lending calls for highly experienced personnel who can work with builders and who understand construction progress and procedures, so as to make timely releases of the loan proceeds. Most lenders will not release a progress draw without physically inspecting the project or having an independent architect inspector submit an estimate of work accomplished. The trick is to be able to complete the project within the money available and still have 10 percent of the loan amount retained at completion to protect the lender against any unforeseen contingencies. When the lender is satisfied that all bills are paid and that no valid liens can be filed, this 10 percent retainer can be released.

Questions for Discussion

1. Discuss the differences in the loan application for a commercial loan and a home loan.
2. Describe the risk involved in a raw land purchase loan.
3. What type of work is covered in a land development loan?
4. Describe the information normally found in a profit and loss statement. An operating statement.
5. What is a pro forma statement?
6. What is an audited statement and who can prepare one?
7. Describe the function of the Office of Interstate Land Sales.
8. Define a *construction loan*.
9. How is a takeout commitment normally used?
10. List two ways a lender can be assured that release of construction money is delivered to the right contractor.

Chapter 12

Commercial Building and Farm Loans

....

KEY WORDS AND PHRASES

Special-purpose buildings • Endorsement • Future purchase contract •

Apartment buildings • Term lease • Fair Housing Amendments Act of 1988

• Retail store buildings • Net lease • Shopping centers • Anchor tenant

• Neighborhood center • Community center • Regional center •

Percentage lease • Office buildings • Warehouse buildings •

Office/Warehouses • Miniwarehouses • Farm and ranch loans •

Family-resident farm loans • Agricorporate farm loans

....

INTRODUCTION

Commercial loans deal with a wide variety of properties and businesses. Major categories of buildings are identified in this chapter with some information on the special conditions that lenders must examine to properly underwrite each loan. With certain categories of commercial buildings, different forms of leases are normally used. The leases are explained along with the buildings that use them. For instance, a term lease is normally used for apartment rentals, net leases are often used in free-standing store buildings and warehouses, while percentage leases dominate shopping centers.

The chapter closes with some information on farm and ranch loans, which are not classed as commercial loans. While they are a most important category of loans and follow different guidelines, this text only gives some generalized information and does not address this kind of loan in any depth.

The following commentary points out major differences in the various categories of commercial loans for buildings.

SPECIAL-PURPOSE BUILDINGS

In a sense, all buildings are special purpose as their design generally restricts use to a specific kind of occupancy. However, in the jargon of real estate, *special purpose* has a more precise meaning. **Special-purpose buildings** offer a specific kind of service and are more difficult to convert to any other usage. Examples of special-purpose buildings include fast-food restaurants, bowling lanes, service stations, recreational structures, theaters, and automobile dealerships. Because of the close relationship between the building and the specialized services offered, they are often owned by the business operator. But many are built by investors for lease to professional operators.

Another feature of a special-purpose building is a much greater dependence on the ability of the operator/manager to achieve profitable operation. While management is important in other kinds of income property, such as apartments and office buildings, it is less critical than with special-purpose property. For instance, an office building, once leased up, will continue to show a cash flow even with changes in the management. But an automobile dealership or a fast-food franchise is heavily dependent on the particular skills of management for its profitability.

Because of this emphasis on management, lenders must look beyond the building itself and examine the capability of those who will be managing the property. This is never an easy determination and is particularly difficult if the loan applicant is a newcomer to the business. To overcome some of these obvious problems, several alternative procedures may be used, as discussed next.

Earnings Record of Applicant

If the company requesting the loan has a record of steady earnings and is creditworthy, there is little further problem with approval. Examples of building owners seeking financing that would fall into this category are oil companies building service stations and fast-food franchisers expanding their operations.

Endorsement

A method of credit enhancement sometimes used to expand automobile dealerships or recreational facilities is manufacturer **endorsement** of the obligation. This means that the manufacturer agrees to accept a contingent responsibility for repayment of the mortgage obligation on the special-purpose building. The purpose of undertaking such a risk would be for the manufacturer to increase its sales outlets.

Future Purchase Contract

Yet another method of credit enhancement that has a broader application than just special-purpose buildings is a **future purchase contract.** Consider a situation where a large grocery chain desires assurance of a special product made or produced by a small local supplier. By offering the supplier a large continuing contract for its product, the supplier would have a proven source of cash flow to induce a lender's favorable decision on a loan. As additional security, the lender might ask that the purchase money for the product be paid through the lender's offices as delivery is made to the grocery chain. While such a contract, assigned to the lender or not, falls short of an endorsement of the obligation, it does give a lender some assurance as to how the loan will be repaid. And that is the key question of all lenders.

APARTMENT BUILDINGS

An **apartment building,** or multifamily housing as the federal government classifies it, represents an investment in residential property. In the past, residential property, particularly low-income housing, has enjoyed certain tax advantages and is subject to some restraints that serve to protect the rights of tenants. While tax advantages for a while tended to distort investment decisions, the principal determinant for sound apartment investment still remains the occupancy of such projects in each market area.

Underlying the achievement and maintenance of good occupancy are several qualifying factors. Experienced apartment operators judge three factors to be of almost equal importance in a successful operation: (1) location, (2) physical facilities, and (3) management. Obviously, a careful underwriting analysis must consider all three factors in determining the risk involved.

Location

Location is usually the first limiting requirement of an apartment seeker. A major consideration of location is easy access to jobs; freeways affect and broaden accessibility. Also important in judging location is proximity to schools and churches. The availability of recreational facilities, such as parks, golf courses, restaurants, and other entertainment, is also to be considered. Apartment dwellers, as a group, are not as burdened with housework and yard maintenance as single-family home residents would be.

Since location is a major determinant of the available market, it is necessary to evaluate the market in that area. For instance, does the proposed rental structure fit the requirements and will it be competitive? Do the size and type of units meet these demands?

Physical Facilities

The physical plant must meet the market requirements, not only in size of units but also in architectural style and amenities available. Amenities would include such factors as playground areas, tennis courts, swimming pool, club room, and entertainment facilities. If the market is primarily families, the two- or three-bedroom units would be the most popular choice; if intended for young singles, the one-bedroom and studio designs would be in greatest demand. The elderly, on the other hand, might prefer one or two bedrooms with a minimum of stairs to climb. Sometimes an assortment of units is used with the hope of covering all phases of the market. In smaller communities, an assortment may best fit local needs. However, in metropolitan areas, this "shotgun" approach is a poor substitute for careful analysis of the market as it may result in one type or style of unit easily rented and maintaining good occupancy while others go begging for tenants. Before building begins on an apartment complex, knowledgeable operators (developers) study the market for particular requirements, and then use their merchandising power to attract suitable occupants.

Management

Management is the third major factor in successful apartment operation, its importance known well to experienced owners but too often underestimated by newcomers to the field. Along with location and the physical plant, management, too, can be a "make-or-break" factor.

The larger cities throughout the country have companies that specialize in apartment management, offering a complete management service for a fee of 3 to 5 percent of the gross revenues. Good management involves maintaining routine cleanliness of the public areas, prompt repairs of equipment or damaged sections of the building, and fair enforcement of rules for the mutual well-being of the tenants; all are necessary to achieve and maintain a high occupancy rate. Experienced operators learn how to cope with the special requirements of rental properties such as initial screening of tenants, the most effective methods of collecting rents and keeping them current, the special problems created by domestic pets, and the handling of skip-outs and of tenants who create disturbances for other occupants. Consequently, an underwriter will look much more favorably, riskwise, on a property under the management of competent individuals or companies.

As apartment-style living proliferates in the cities, underwriters recognize that the better planned, better maintained facilities are those that will sustain occupancy in soft or competitive markets. And a continuous high occupancy rate is the key to survival in this business.

Analysis of Income and Expenses

On proposed apartment construction, a projected statement can be prepared to show anticipated gross revenues from each unit and all miscellaneous revenues (for example, from laundry rooms), less a vacancy factor and credit losses. This will produce an effective income from which deductions can be made for all expenses. Fixed expenses include such items as taxes and insurance, which do not fluctuate with occupancy rates. Operating expenses can fluctuate with occupancy rates and comprise the costs of utilities, maintenance, supplies, and labor. A special expense that is frequently overlooked or underestimated is replacement cost; items such as drapes and carpeting, equipment such as ranges or dishwashers, all in continuous use, have a tendency to wear out. Allowances must be set aside for their replacement. The cash remaining after these deductions then becomes available for debt service. Any remaining cash, after all expenses and debt service have been covered, serves as a cushion against a loss or a slow period.

It is apparent, then, that many variables among these figures are subject to interpretation. For example, what occupancy rate may be reliably projected? The FHA uses a percentage figure of 93. Conventional lenders generally tend to select an occupancy rate substantiated by actual rates prevailing in a particular area. Most lenders require proof of an occupancy rate near 90 percent before they will entertain an apartment loan application. Rental rates also must be in line with the going market. Expenses can be projected with reasonable accuracy. In general, total expenses range from 36 to 45 percent of the gross operating income, depending on the size of the operations and the efficiency of management.

As previously defined, *debt service* is the monthly or annual cost of the principal and interest payment and should be tailored to ensure timely retirement of the full loan. By careful analysis of the cash available for debt service, the underwriter can determine the most effective loan for the proposed apartment. Adjustable and negotiable factors are the term, which ranges from 15 years upward to 30 years, and the loan-to-value ratio, which determines the equity cash required. The interest rate may be adjustable or fixed, usually pegged to market rates, and less subject to negotiation.

Term Leases

Apartments are usually leased under the conditions of a **term lease**—a short-term lease that may or may not be in writing. While state laws control how leases may be handled, a general rule is that a lease for less than one year need not be in writing. The short-term nature of the lease allows the landlord to make periodic increases (or decreases) as the market may require. Occupancy is more volatile in an apartment property than in an office building or retail store and this can create a lack of stability in its continuing income.

Fair Housing Requirements

The **Fair Housing Amendments Act of 1988** extended the prohibitions against discrimination of the 1968 Fair Housing Act for all residential real estate transactions. Prior law considers unlawful any discrimination in housing because of race, color, religion, gender, or national origin. The new amendment added two new categories for protection against discrimination: disability and familial status. The additional restrictions are of particular importance in the rental of multifamily dwellings.

The new category of "disability" protection requires proper accommodation in the design and construction of multifamily dwellings. The building and its facilities must provide accessibility and usability for physically disabled people. This includes such items as doors and hallways wide enough to handle wheelchairs, light switches and elevator buttons at a level accessible to those in wheelchairs, and alarm signals in both light and sound to protect those with hearing and visual impairment. Persons with AIDS are now included in this protected category.

Protection for familial status prohibits discrimination because of family make-up. Housing must be open to persons with children 18 years and under. Parents with children or guardians with children cannot be denied housing. "Adults-only" apartments are no longer permissible. There are exceptions for housing occupied by elderly persons only.

Tax Deductions

As residential rental property, apartments have always offered some special tax advantages for investors. The purpose, of course, is to encourage suitable housing in this country. Under current law (the 1993 Tax Act), residential property retained its 27 1/2-year recovery period while nonresidential property was increased from 31 1/2 years to a 39-year recovery period. Another tax advantage is that since the building, not the land, is depreciable, an apartment offers a favorable combination of values. The building portion of the investment is relatively high compared with the nondepreciable land. Also, items classed as personal property such as drapes, appliances, and carpeting necessary for apartment operation are eligible for even greater depreciation deduction rates than the building, and the calculation can be made using accelerated rates.

Revisions in the 1986 Tax Act changed the tax nature of certain kinds of property formerly considered real estate to the class of "other tangible property" eligible for greater depreciation deductions. Such land improvements as roads, fences, and landscaping are now placed in the 15-year class and eligible for either straight-line or accelerated depreciation deductions. Another possible tax break is that sewer pipe is listed in the 20-year class.

While tax deductions have been diminished since the early 1980s, there remain important benefits for real estate investors. Depreciation deductions are based on the total value of a building, not just the equity interest in it. Since this kind of deduction represents a noncash item it protects cash flows, allowing more money for debt service if necessary. Nevertheless, it is true that lenders are skeptical of any cash flow that depends on the unstable nature of tax law.

RETAIL STORE BUILDINGS

The free-standing **retail store building,** or strip of stores, is an interesting investment for individuals as well as large companies. The more conservative way to handle such an investment would be to first obtain a lease for the premises, then build to suit the tenant. Nevertheless, many such buildings are constructed on strictly a speculative basis, expecting to attract tenants later.

Analysis of Income and Expenses

A retail store building rented to a business tenant for a fairly long term, say 10 or 15 years, offers a stability of income not found in apartment-type properties. A well-drawn lease agreement should allow periodic rental increases, either as a fixed amount every few years or as an escalation clause. The escalation clause ties an increase in rentals to increases in the landlord's operating expenses.

With this type of property, the payment of expenses is usually negotiable between the landlord and tenant and is spelled out in the lease agreement. A common division of responsibility for maintenance is that the tenant pays the costs of maintaining the interior of the building while the landlord is responsible for the exterior. And the landlord is responsible for handling building insurance coverage and payment of taxes.

Net Lease

Free-standing store buildings are often leased to major grocery chains and other retailers on a **net lease** basis. This means the tenant is responsible for maintaining the building, providing the insurance coverage, and paying property taxes. With the responsibility for paying maintenance, insurance, and taxes passed on to the tenant, this kind of lease is often identified as *triple net*. It is the kind of investment that is attractive to a person who wants to avoid management of the property; the rental rate is based on a fair return on the investment without the addition of a management cost. Financing for this kind of investment may be enhanced by the assignment of all or part of the rentals. A major tenant is an attractive source of loan repayment for lenders.

SHOPPING CENTERS

The development and leasing of **shopping centers** is a specialized business. Some developers not only build major centers but are retained to manage them. Many large retailers have entered the development business themselves to expand their own market reach. Probably more than for any other kind of property investment, shopping center owners endeavor to prelease the space. To attract tenants to a new project, the developer can undertake a careful market analysis of the area to be served. Such a market study includes potential sales volumes for the various commodities that will be offered at the center. With this information in hand, the developer can better prove the value for a merchant to open an outlet in the subject area. The market study would also be good assistance in obtaining a mortgage loan.

Anchor Tenant

Crucial to the successful operation of a shopping center is having a major or **anchor tenant.** The big merchant can attract shoppers that benefit the smaller merchant. Major retailers have learned that smaller stores can also attract customers on their own, thus benefiting all, as it offers greater convenience for the shopper.

The value of an anchor tenant is such that many major retailers have spearheaded their own projects. Some rely on experienced shopping-center developers to implement their plans and manage the center upon completion. Others, such as Sears, Roebuck & Company, have entered the development business themselves. Sears has built a number of major centers through its Homart Development Company subsidiary.

Classification of Centers

Shopping centers defy easy classification as most major developers try hard to be different. Something unique has an appeal not found in the commonplace and the intent is to attract the general public. Roughly, there are three classes based mostly on size and merchandise offered: neighborhood, community, and regional.

Neighborhood Center. Smaller **neighborhood centers** often consist of a large corner area with a strip of two or more stores. Merchandise offered is mostly daily essentials such as food, drugs, hardware, and other everyday services.

Community Center. A **community center** offers all the services found in the neighborhood center plus an anchor tenant offering general merchandise, apparel stores, furniture outlets, professional services, and some recreational facilities.

Regional Center. The largest category, a **regional center** offers a full range of merchandise and services. It would contain at least two anchor tenants, scores of lesser shops, a variety of restaurants, theaters, and other recreational facilities. Often there is a large mall that offers various kinds of entertainment to attract the general public. Around these centers are found hotels, office buildings, and apartment complexes. Regional centers have become an attraction for business meetings of all kinds since they offer easy access to "off-duty" activities for those attending (or those not attending) the meetings.

Income and Expenses

The income from a shopping center depends to a considerable degree on the success of its tenants. High-volume sales attract and retain tenants. Management expertise can add to the success with advertising and crowd-attracting displays and entertainment. The reason for the tie between center profitability and tenants' success is that most leases are based on a percentage of the tenants' sales. To enhance promotion of the center, management usually organizes and spearheads a tenant/management association that meets regularly to plan and arrange financing for various sales events. Larger shopping malls are capable of offering rather lavish seasonal entertainment spectacles that boost sales. Some malls actively encourage senior citizen walking clubs that use the climate-controlled areas for exercise and perhaps spend a few dollars with the merchants as well.

Operating Expenses

The costs of operating and maintaining a shopping center are divided between landlord and tenant. There is no standard procedure as negotiation plays an important role in attracting larger tenants. A simple rule is that the more costs borne by the tenant, the lower the rental. A common practice is that all exterior maintenance of the building, grounds, and common interior areas is the responsibility of the landlord, while the tenant pays for interior maintenance of its space. Janitorial service normally follows the same pattern: The landlord pays for cleaning public areas while the tenant services its own space.

Utility service is usually separately metered to tenants. However, a recent trend in larger centers is to install their own electric generating plants, even selling surplus power back to the local utility under a co-generation agreement.

Heating and air conditioning may be either centrally furnished or supplied by each tenant with its own equipment. Shopping center management prefers that the tenant furnish such equipment and take responsibility for its operation for several reasons. One is that maintenance and operating costs are not easily predictable, and providing the proper temperature often causes problems. Another reason is the potential for liability if sales are lost through failure of the equipment to maintain comfortable temperatures.

A growing practice is to separate the base rent from many of the operating costs. This is accomplished by billing such operating expenses as a separate "service fee" to the tenant. It allows a more stable rental structure yet provides the landlord with some protection against the uncertainty of future operating costs. An alternative method of allowing for fluctuating costs is to include an escalation clause in the lease agreement that allows an annual rental adjustment based on changes in operating costs.

Percentage Leases

Shopping centers lease space at percentage rates based on the nature of the tenant's business, normally not a flat percentage for the entire center. The rates vary from a low of 1 to 1 1/2 percent of gross monthly sales for large volume stores such as supermarkets and discount stores, to a high of 10 to 20 percent for smaller shops and boutiques.

Percentage leases usually require a base, or minimum, rental payment each month. Otherwise, it would be possible for a merchant to achieve a profitable operation on high-margin merchandise that could produce too low a gross volume for the landlord to pay its own expenses. The minimum may be stated as a rental "amounting to 6 percent of gross sales each month but not less than $1,500." Or the base rental could be separated from the percentage with language such as "rental shall be $1,500 each month *plus* 3 percent of gross sales."

The minimum rental payment may be subject to an escalation clause based on a landlord's cost experience.

Verification of the tenant's monthly sales volume is usually a requirement in the lease terms. It can be achieved through submittal of a copy of the tenant's state sales tax report to the landlord each month. Or the landlord may require a periodic audit of the tenant's sales records.

Financing of Shopping Centers

Three categories of retail store facilities must be considered separately for loan purposes. The differences are based on whether or not a merchant wants to own or lease its premises. It is a top policy decision and major retailers differ on the answer. Some prefer to lease their store space and use that capital for other business purposes, which is fairly common for grocery chains. Others see an advantage in anticipating a market growth area and building their own facilities to maintain a better control of operating costs. Following is a discussion of the three categories: (1) owner-occupied buildings, (2) preleased space, and (3) speculative projects.

Owner-Occupied Buildings

An owner-occupant merchant seeking financing to buy or build a new facility has several options to work with. The company may use its own cash flow as a source of funds, or, if the company is large enough and well recognized, it may obtain funding through the sale of mortgage bonds in the financial markets. If the decision is to seek financing from a mortgage lender, the financial record of the company itself becomes as important as the value of the property pledged as security. While the property serves as collateral, the success of the company's operations would be a key factor in loan approval.

Preleased Space

The method used by most shopping center developers is to prelease as much space as possible, and certainly this would include the major tenants. With leases in hand, the developer can show a lender exactly what kind of stores will be operating in the center and, more importantly, that there will be a commitment of rental income. It is not unusual for a lender to base the loan amount on the value of the leases rather than the value of the buildings as collateral. Thus, the better the quality of leases, the greater the loan commitment, which reduces the equity cash required up front. Few centers are able to fully prelease their space and usually include some additional, speculative space. This space is easier to lease if the smaller merchants know who the other tenants will be and what kind of competition will be encountered.

Speculative Projects

Only financially strong builders/developers are able to construct speculative store space, either as free-standing buildings or neighborhood centers. The larger shopping centers cannot be financed without obtaining leases with substantial tenants. The risk of leasing speculative space is considerable, and the quality of the tenant is unknown to the lender. Nevertheless, a number of developers are quite capable of erecting smaller projects and have proven successful. One key is to maintain close touch with the growth in market areas and select appropriate building sites. Another key is to maintain a sound list of prospective clients—merchants who have proven records of success and are aggressively expanding their operations. A track record of successful development is an essential for any loan approval in this field.

OFFICE BUILDINGS

The owners of all types of **office buildings,** ranging from the largest to the smallest, acquire or construct them for one of two purposes: (1) their own occupancy, or (2) for lease to others.

Owner-Occupied Buildings

Many owner-occupied office buildings are bought or built by companies or persons with a financial history that makes the decisions on underwriting such a property somewhat easier for the lender. This is because the credit reputation of the owner is the major qualifying factor under consideration, whereas the real estate that is to be pledged is of secondary importance. Ultimately, the source of loan repayment is closely tied to the owner-occupant's record of profitability and the manner in which previous financial obligations have been met.

In financing large owner-occupied buildings, an alternative choice to straight-mortgage financing would be the sale of first-mortgage bonds (a pledge of the property collateralizes the bond issue) through an investment banker or a mortgage banker. Acquisition of large office buildings by investing institutions, such as banks or insurance companies, is a common practice. To accomplish this, owners may simply finance the property from their own investment funds.

Various local, state, and federal governments and their agencies build office buildings for their own use with legislative appropriations or through the sale of various types of bonds. Some government buildings, such as post offices, are built by private investors under long-term lease contracts and are financed through private sources.

Office Buildings for Lease to Others

The underwriting of buildings intended for lease to others calls for some specialized techniques of real estate mortgage financing and requires extensive analysis of the property involved. In this category there are three main groups: (1) a builder-investor with preleased office space to build, (2) a speculative builder-investor hoping to attract tenants before the building is completed or soon thereafter, and (3) an owner-occupied building with extra space for lease.

Preleased Office Space

A substantially preleased building is the more conservative method of making an office building investment. For financing, it provides the underwriter with a lease to analyze, a tenant to examine for creditworthiness, and a building and location to study. If the building is specialized to meet the tenant's unusual requirements (such as heavy electrical gear, raised or lowered floors, or special wall patterns), the term of the lease should be sufficient to recover the extra investment. Most underwriters will limit loans to a percentage of the total lease payments as this is the main source for loan recovery.

Similar to a shopping center, a preleased office building faces an inflexible situation in regard to an overrun on construction costs. The building must be designed and constructed in a manner that meets projected costs, and the contractor must have the ability to complete the project within the contract terms. Bonding of the contractor is a normal requirement. Preleased office buildings for single tenants are usually "bare-wall" leases; that is, the tenant pays for finishing the interior (not added to the rental payment) and provides future maintenance.

Speculative Office Buildings

The speculative builder presents a greater risk to an underwriter, and this limits loans to only the more experienced and creditworthy builders. In addition to the usual analysis of the building and its location, consideration must be given to the market and the regional economic pattern. What are the chances of the speculative building becoming fully leased? The underwriter, however, is not in the business of chance by choice, so a protective restriction is sometimes applied that would require the building to have a 75, 80, or perhaps 85 percent occupancy with bona fide tenants before the permanent loan would be released. A clause that might be found in a speculative building loan is a minimum rental provision to protect the lender's repayments. Of course, restrictions based on lease-up throws a real burden on construction financing and usually means that the builder of a speculative building must have the credit strength or cash reserves to build and lease the building without an assured permanent commitment.

It is not unusual for a knowledgeable builder-contractor to build and lease a moderate-sized office building with its own funds, then mortgage out for more than the costs. In such a case, the loan security rests as much on an assignment of the lease income as on the mortgage pledge. One method of measuring loan size based on lease assignments is to calculate the present worth of future lease payments and loan 80 percent of that value.

Owner-Occupied Building with Space to Lease

A building constructed or acquired for owner-occupancy is often larger than needed at the time. The expectation, of course, is allowance for future expansion. This would mean offering leases to others of shorter duration, like two-to five-year, or even including cancellation clauses in anticipation of future needs. Such limitations on occupancy could mean lower rental rates.

In periods of downsizing, owners may reduce their own use of office space. In an effort to attract new tenants, favorable rental rates may be offered in an effort to further reduce overhead expenses.

Regardless of how multitenant occupancy is created, owners tend to use contract management companies to handle operations rather than self-managing the property. Management is a specialized business and building owners generally recognize the advantages of having experienced personnel handling lease-up and operation of a property.

WAREHOUSE BUILDINGS

Another type of income property that is preferred by many investors because of its relatively low maintenance and management requirements is the **warehouse building.** The demand for warehouse space has grown substantially in the past decade for several reasons. Many types of companies use general warehouse space to store merchandise in peak seasons, to keep a product closer to its ultimate market, or to house an unusually large stock of a particular raw material.

Somewhat like office buildings, this type of facility can be built for use by an owner, such as a grocery chain operator; it can be built for use in part by an owner, such as a light manufacturer, with portions available for lease to others; or it can be built for speculative leasing as commercial warehouse space. It is the speculative warehouse that requires the most careful loan evaluation of the property. Owner-occupied or partially occupied buildings provide an established business with a source of income to substantiate and undergird the loan analysis. Warehouses are built fully preleased and partially preleased in much the same way as office buildings and shopping centers, so the analysis of the different types is similar.

General Warehouse

There are several basic requirements for general warehouse space that would make it more easily rentable during the life of a loan. Like all other income properties, location is of paramount importance. Location should include accessibility by roads running in several directions and capable of handling large trucks. The land need not be in high-density traffic zones as required by shopping centers and some office buildings, but neither should it be locked into small street patterns that limit the size of the truck that can be accommodated. The warehouse should also be accessible to rail spurs, if possible. Availability of a rail siding is not essential to every user, but lack of this facility may limit future marketability.

Because general warehouses may be built in older or lesser developed areas of a community, it is important to check out the availability of adequate water lines and pressures to support proper fire extinguisher installations. Without adequate fire protection, insurance rates skyrocket and greatly increase storage costs for the prospective tenant.

In the construction design of the building itself, provision should be made for loading docks capable of handling truck and freight-car loadings at the proper heights. The ceilings must be high, generally over 15 feet, for more efficient stack storage of merchandise. The costs of construction of a warehouse building are similar to those for a shopping center building inasmuch as both are fairly high-ceiling buildings with little or no interior finishing provided by the builder. Warehouses require heavier floors to support more weight but use much less parking space than a shopping center building. Further, the cost of land suitable for a warehouse is much lower than that required for freeway-accessible shopping sites.

Net Lease

Warehouse leases often provide for a triple net return to the owner, which means the tenant pays all maintenance and operating costs, plus all insurance and taxes on the building. In such a lease, management expenses would be held to a bare minimum. The cash available for debt service is thus very easy to calculate. On general warehouses with multitenant occupancy, the owner may provide some services and, most likely, will be responsible for taxes and insurance costs.

Office/Warehouses

A variation of the general warehouse is the type of building that combines an office facility in front and larger warehouse-type space in the rear. These **office/warehouses** have many uses: as sales and storage offices for such items as parts or distribution of equipment, small manufacturing operations, repair facilities, and others. Office/warehouses should be more accessible to general traffic than general warehouses and are more likely to be attractively landscaped with parking available for the tenants' customers. Construction costs are about the same as for a general warehouse except for finish work in the office area.

Miniwarehouses

A growth segment of the warehouse market has developed in the building of one-story structures partitioned into small rental spaces. The market for these **miniwarehouses** comes from the more affluent and mobile citizens who accumulate material goods but are unable to accommodate them in small apartments and houses. The structures usually contain from 100 to 300 rental spaces, each ranging in size from 5 × 5 to 20 × 20 feet. The management requirement, depending somewhat on size, ranges from almost nil to full-time administrative personnel and security guards. Returns on investment have been good. Owners have reported that a completed warehouse averages about one-half the cost per square foot as that for an apartment building, and the rental rates per square foot are about the same.

FARM AND RANCH LOANS

Farm and ranch loans are distinctive and should not be classified as commercial loans. They require a very specialized knowledge of both the borrower and the property pledged to make a sound underwriting judgment. Almost all of these loans are analyzed in the local area. There are few, if any, national guidelines, as each local area presents its own distinctive soil, weather, crops, and markets. Because of the great importance of agriculture to the national economy, federal and many state governments have undertaken a number of helpful loan programs to support some stability within the industry. Government land and crop loans are the single most important source of farm loans, accounting for about half of all farm mortgage debt outstanding. The other half of the market is covered by commercial banks in rural communities and life insurance companies dealing through mortgage companies. The creation of Farmer Mac by Congress in 1989 and its expansion of powers in 1996 enhanced the willingness of regulated lenders to undertake farm loans. Farmer Mac is now authorized to buy agricultural loans and create its own mortgage pools very similar to Fannie Mae and Freddie Mac.

The term of a farm loan varies as to need and may run from 10 to 40 years with 33 years a popular term, partly because the Federal Land Bank formerly used 33 years. More leniency is given in the repayment of farm loans than other real estate loans. A farmer's income is subject to greater variation, and a rigid payment schedule can be self-defeating. But any long-term farm loan should have full amortization as a goal.

Some of the major government agencies handling direct farm loans were discussed in Chapter 3 as a part of the primary-mortgage market. This section comments on some questions that would be involved in conventional underwriting of farm and ranch loans. Two general categories of farm loans are (1) the family-resident loan and (2) the agricorporate loan.

Family-Resident Farm Loans

The **family-resident farm loan** has not changed a great deal in the past 30 years. It is still based on the three legs of any good mortgage loan: (1) a creditworthy borrower, (2) a property of sufficient value to provide good collateral, and (3) the ability of the property and the borrower to produce an income, assuring repayment of the loan. Judgments on farm land value require good knowledge and experience in the local area. A single-crop farm is the most vulnerable to failure and subsequent loan default. A diversified crop operation, plus some livestock, gives the best security. So the ability of the farm to produce a continued income, regardless of an occasional crop failure or a fluctuating market, is a prime consideration in making a sound farm loan.

The land value itself may be distorted by outside pressures such as a city developing nearby, a large neighboring farm desiring to expand, or possibly a new freeway providing much frontage acreage. But the farm underwriter should confine the analysis to the producing factors—soil conditions, weather, available irrigation, type of crops, nearness to markets, and condition of the markets—that will produce the income from which the loan can be recovered. To give any substantial weight to possibly increasing land values takes the loan into the speculative category of land development.

Agricorporate Farm Loans

Agricorporate farm loans show some similarity to special-purpose property loans. Large commercial farm companies control much of the nation's agriculture today and usually provide good business records to assist an underwriter in making an evaluation. Studies of land productivity with various crops and fertilizers, of the most effective methods of breeding and feeding livestock, and of management techniques in cost control have developed economies of operation. Equipment can be more fully utilized and better maintained than on smaller holdings. But, along with the advantages, a word of caution: The dependency on hired labor and fixed management costs make commercial farms less flexible and more difficult to retrench in periods of declining prices.

Ranch Loans

A ranch presents only slight variations to a farm loan in that it produces livestock as a principal source of revenue. Because ranches are predominantly in the water-short southwestern regions, an underwriter must take care to analyze the water situation. Often water rights can be of greater value than the land since without water the land may be worthless. A common practice in ranching is to lease public lands for grazing. The acreage so leased becomes of value to the ranch only in the productivity it can add to the ranch, and this can be limited by the term of the lease. But leased land or grazing rights do add value and should be included in the appraisal for loan purposes. Sometimes ranches produce additional revenues from the sale of timber rights, from mineral leasing, and even from hunting leases and dude ranching. All income has its value, but must be considered according to its tenure and stability.

Questions for Discussion

1. Describe a *special purpose building.*
2. How can a commercial loan be enhanced?
3. Discuss each of the three factors in the operation of a commercial building: location, physical facilities, and management.
4. What part of the federal Fair Housing Act is applicable to an apartment project?

5. Describe a *net lease*.
6. Why does a shopping center management promote shopper-attraction activities?
7. How does a shopping center utilize percentage leases?
8. Discuss who builds office buildings and why.
9. Evaluate preleased space as a factor in obtaining a building loan.
10. Distinguish between management requirements for a warehouse property and an office building.

Chapter 13

Other Financing Practices

INTRODUCTION

While practices in the real estate business do vary across the country, there are a number of conditions, terms, and procedures that are commonly used. This chapter explains many of these practices.

HOME BUILDER COMMITMENTS

When a new home is purchased directly from a builder, the builder may already hold a commitment for mortgage money that can be used by the home buyer. Some of the ways these commitments are handled are discussed in the sections that follow.

Competitive Method. The small- to medium-sized builders may have their construction money secured without any commitment for the permanent loans. For example, a commercial bank carrying the construction financing may not be interested in making a permanent loan to a buyer. If there is no commitment, the purchaser is free to seek whatever source of mortgage money may be found.

Commitment Method—Construction. When any builder obtains construction money, the lender may request a first-refusal right to all permanent loans on the project. The construction lender thus ties up a good source of loans for the future, which is one of the incentives to make the construction loan in the first place. To enforce this right, the lender can add a penalty provision in the construction loan agreement that provides for an extra one-half or 1 percent of the construction loan to be paid for a release of the construction mortgage if the loan is not handled through the same lender.

A purchaser cannot be required to borrow money from a particular lender, but it can be a bit more costly to go elsewhere.

Commitment Method—Purchase. Some of the larger builders who can qualify for the lowest rates on their construction money, or use their own funds for this purpose, may purchase a future commitment for money direct from a savings association or other major source to protect future customers needing loans. The builder will pay at least 1 percent of the total commitment amount to hold the money or may pay additional fees to ensure the future home buyers a lower, more competitive interest rate. This expense, which in effect is a prepayment of interest by the builder for the benefit of the buyer, is charged back to the cost of the house. This is how builders can advertise lower-than-market interest rates and obtain a competitive advantage in the housing market.

Associated Companies. A few of the larger builders that are basically national in scope may own affiliated mortgage companies or money sources to provide permanent loans. The tie-in is generally competitive with market rates for money and is intended as a convenience for the buyer. Associated companies are subject to a 1992 HUD rule that requires full disclosure of ownership in related companies. The rule applies to any affiliation with service providers within the real estate industry. These companies are not permitted to require the use of an affiliate's service as a condition for closing a transaction, nor are they allowed to pay each other fees for referrals. However, they carry a competitive edge by being available at the proper time and place to consummate a deal.

LOAN-TO-VALUE RATIO (LTVR)

The **loan-to-value ratio** is the amount of a loan as a percentage of the property's value. For this purpose, the property value is the lesser of the appraised value or the sales price. An exception is VA's valuation that accepts only their own appraised value for property offered as collateral, called the Certificate of Reasonable Value or CRV. Of course, if a sale is not involved such as in refinancing, the appraised value would be the proper measure.

The LTV ratio is an important standard for mortgage lenders. It is used by the industry in the following ways:

1. **As a standard for pricing a loan.** The higher the ratio, the greater the risk, which requires a higher price. A borrower offering 5 percent down has a lesser stake in the property than one offering 20 percent down. Lender experience indicates that those with greater equities are less likely to allow a default to occur. Thus, a 95 percent LTVR loan would require the highest interest rate and the greater number of discount points. Generally, the price distinction levels out at an 80 percent LTVR. A buyer offering more than 20 percent down achieves only marginally better pricing.

2. **As a standard for default mortgage insurance.** (Also called Private Mortgage Insurance or PMI.) Federal rules require that residential loans greater than 90 percent LTVR must be insured against default. Most lenders apply their own rules which may require such insurance on loans greater than 80 percent LTVR. Buyers making down payments of more than 20 percent can usually obtain loans with no default insurance required. Also, the price of mortgage insurance varies with the LTVR.

3. **As a standard for quality of loan.** The role of an LTVR in setting standards for most conventional residential loans has been diminished by the growth of no-down-payment loans and even home loans made at 125 percent of the value of the house. Nevertheless, prudent lenders still class a 95 percent LTVR conventional loan as a high-risk loan. In 1998, the Federal Reserve issued a warning to banks under its authority to tighten credit standards. While commercial banks do not make many home loans with their deposit assets, the warning is a caution to all lenders. Federal bank examiners are expected to use LTVR as one standard of loan quality.

DOLLAR AMOUNT OF LOAN

There are some **dollar limitations** on the amount of residential loans. HUD/FHA and VA set their own limits, as described in Chapter 8. For conventional loans, the various regulatory agencies can set limits. Most of these involve a limitation on the amount of any single loan as a percentage of the lender's total assets and limits on the amount that can be loaned to any individual. In years past, states have set limits on dollar amounts for single-family residential loans, but most of these have since been eliminated.

Fannie Mae/Freddie Mac Limits

A widely used standard for loan limits is that applied by secondary-market investors Fannie Mae and Freddie Mac. Each January, the two federal underwriting agencies adjust the limit on the dollar amount of a loan that they can purchase (or allow into a mortgage pool) in accordance with federally mandated guidelines. The limit can be adjusted each year by the amount of change in the average purchase price of a single-family house financed by a conventional mortgage as determined by the Federal Housing Finance Board. The change is based on the 12-month period prior to the end of October each year. The limit becomes the conforming/conventional loan limit. Further, the limit on FHA loans is calculated each year as a percentage of the conforming loan limit. An increase is not mandatory but cannot exceed the calculated limit.

The Fannie Mae/Freddie Mac single-family loan limit for 1999 was $240,000, which was nearly a 6 percent increase over the previous year's limit.

The 1999 conforming loan limit for the number of dwelling units follows:

Number of Units	Loan Limit
1	$240,000
2	$307,100
3	$371,200
4	$461,350

Loan limit for second mortgages is $120,000.

Limits are 50 percent higher for properties in Alaska, Hawaii, the U.S. Virgin Islands, and Guam.

Minimum Loan Limits

There are no regulatory minimums for mortgage loans but there are some practical limits. Compare, for instance, the fee for servicing a $100,000 loan with one for $20,000. Normally, the servicing fee amounts to one-quarter percent; thus, for a $100,000 loan, the servicer would make $250 per year or $20.83 per month. For a $20,000 loan the quarter-point earns $50 per year or $4.16 per month. Because the cost of servicing can exceed the fees earned on a smaller loan, any sale of the loan requires substantial discounting. For these reasons, some conventional lenders set minimum dollar amounts for loans they will make at the risk of being charged with discrimination. HUD/FHA has never allowed its approved mortgagees to set minimum amounts for acceptable loans.

The problem arises from the fact that smaller loans are most likely to be needed by lower income families. If a mortgage lender sets minimum limits on acceptable loans it could be discriminatory. In fact, in 1993 several conventional mortgage lenders were charged with violation of the Fair Housing Act by refusing to make loans for less than $50,000.

Large Residential Loans

As the average cost of homes increases in certain areas above the $200,000 level, the need for larger loans becomes more important. Loans that exceed the conforming loan limit (Fannie Mae/Freddie Mac limit as described earlier) are more difficult to sell. While there is a growing secondary market for so-called "jumbo loans," the yield requirements are slightly higher. Attracted by higher yields, some of these larger loans are held in portfolio by lenders. Even so, the amounts may exceed the lender's own limits for a single loan. To overcome this problem, two or more lenders may combine to fund the loan. This is called a **participation loan.** One lender services the loan and accounts to the other participants as their percentage of the loan may require.

LAND LEASES

While most developments are built on land owned by the developer or builder, there is a growing use of **land leases** for development purposes. There are several reasons for leasing land instead of buying it outright, as explained next.

Land Not for Sale. In some areas of the country such as Hawaii; Orange County, California; and certain high-density downtown areas, land is simply not available for purchase. Land ownership in these areas may be limited to large holders and they see greater value in leasing than converting the land asset into cash that is subject to capital gains tax.

Leasing May Be Lower Cost. It is quite possible to negotiate a multiyear lease on land at a lower cost than financing the purchase price. Lease payments are tax deductible (provided the land is used for business purposes), while land is nondepreciable as an asset.

Separating Ownership. Another purpose for a land lease might be to separate the ownership of improvements from the land ownership. The separation allows either one to be sold without capital gains tax assessed on the other. And a sale of either one, rather than both, could reduce the financing requirements.

Financing Development on Leased Land

When a lease on land is consummated between a landowner and a builder/developer, the contract is generally known and referred to as a *ground lease.* The landowner's interest is termed the *underlying fee,* and the lessee's (builder's) interest is known as the *leasehold.* Ground leases are usually net leases that create a tenancy for years, typically with terms of 55, 75, or 99 years. The 99-year limit derives from some early state laws that held that leases of 100 years or longer were transfers of title rather than leases.

Financing construction on land that is leased has some limitations as the builder can pledge only the leasehold interest, not the underlying fee, as collateral. This can cause a problem for lenders accustomed to working with mortgages that include a pledge of the land itself. While the legal terminology varies a bit, there are two basic ways to handle loans involving property where the land is leased: an **unsubordinated ground lease** and a **subordinated agreement lease.**

Unsubordinated Ground Lease

Under this procedure, the landowner does not subordinate the ownership (fee title) to the leasehold interest. This means that if the ground rent is not paid, the landowner can foreclose and terminate the leasehold rights. In such a case, improvements could be claimed by the landowner, thus defeating any claim by a lender holding only a pledge of the leasehold interest. To minimize such a consequence, with this kind of lease the lender would normally require that the borrower pay the ground rent in escrow to the lender as a part of each mortgage payment. The lender would then pass the ground rent on to the landowner when it becomes due, or even advance the ground rent, if necessary, to protect the lender's collateral position. Handling of the ground rent as part of a mortgage payment may be likened to the handling of property taxes: Usually one-twelfth of the annual tax assessment is paid into escrow for future timely remittance by the lender.

Subordinated Agreement Lease

With a subordinated agreement lease, the landowner grants the lease and then encumbers the fee title with a subordination agreement. This means that the landowner subordinates the ownership of the land in favor of the mortgage holder. With this kind of lease, the developer, with only a leasehold interest, can pledge title to the land itself as part of the collateral to secure a development loan. The reason is that the subordination agreement signed by the landowner grants a priority claim to the lender which is similar in effect to granting a first lien with a mortgage instrument.

The concept is often used in the development of motel properties and some fast-food operations. It is true that the landowner places valuable property at risk with a subordination agreement, but would be encouraged to do so if a greater return can be realized than simply holding unimproved land. If the mortgage loan for the development is not paid, the mortgagee has the right to take both the land and improvements in a foreclosure action. To protect the landowner against such a consequence, the subordination agreement would normally require timely notification to the landowner of any act in default on the mortgage loan. If such should occur, the landowner would then have the right to step into the position of tenant/borrower with rights to the property's cash flow and the obligation to pay the balance due on the mortgage note.

Build-to-Lease

A popular investment with lesser risk to the investor is for the lessor to agree to construct a building to certain tenant specifications in return for a lease commitment from the prospective tenant. The procedure is also called **build-to-suit** or *build-to-let*. The builder/investor has an assured tenant upon completion of the building and an immediate cash flow. Advantage for the tenant is obtaining a specially designed building that meets its needs more precisely. Examples of how this procedure is used would be free-standing store buildings for a tenant such as Safeway Corporation (grocers) and service stations built for major oil companies. This method is also used by the U.S. Post Office for outlying facilities. The Post Office leases buildings built to their specifications based on open bidding of projected rental rates.

Sale and Leaseback

Another financing technique that involves lease procedures is for an owner-occupant to sell his or her property to an investor and simultaneously lease it back for continued occupancy. For the owner/seller, the advantage is the cash realized from the sale that can be used for further expansion of a company. The continued occupancy of the facilities allows an uninterrupted operation. And the lease payments are tax deductible if they are for a business purpose. The investor/buyer obtains a sound real estate property with an immediate cash flow presumably calculated to yield a fair return.

While the procedure is most commonly used with commercial properties, it also has an application for a homeowner. A homeowner, perhaps a parent, might sell his or her house to a son or daughter and lease the premises for continued occupancy. While the lease payments are not tax deductible for the tenant (it classifies as property used for personal purposes), the son or daughter would own the property as an income-producing asset subject to all deductions available for rental property, including depreciation. (*Caution:* Any transaction between family members must be at fair market value or the tax treatment may be disallowed.)

The **sale-and-leaseback** technique is also used in certain instances of company acquisition. To reduce the up-front cash needed to acquire a company, a buyer may arrange a sale and leaseback of property owned by the company to be acquired. Simultaneously, with the closing of the acquisition, the buildings are sold to an investor and the cash is applied to the purchase of the company. At the same time, the buildings are leased back to the acquired company with no interruption in its operation.

SALE OF EQUITY INTERESTS

Two types of equity investment have become popular as methods for financing real estate: syndications and realty funds.

Syndication

Syndication is a term that describes land or property acquisition and ownership by a group of participants. A syndicate is not a type of business organization; rather, it is a name applied to any group set up to pursue a limited objective in business. The participants may be individuals, partnerships, or corporations. While a number of different types of business organization may be used to form a syndicate, the most popular is the **limited partnership.** As a form of business organization, the limited partnership is recognized in all states. Essentially, it provides for one or more general partners who are responsible for the management and are personally liable for the partnership's obligations. Another class of partner is also recognized: the limited partners, who are not permitted to participate in management decisions and whose liability is limited to the amount of their invested capital. A limited partnership must file its chartering agreement with the state in accordance with the applicable laws.

Real estate syndicates operate by two basic methods:

1. **Sale of interests in existing properties.** Under this method, the property is identified for the participants. For example, a builder or developer (usually called a *syndicator*) owns or controls (by option or contract of sale) a suitable investment property. The syndicator then sells participating interests to raise the money to develop the land, or possibly to complete the acquisition of an existing building.

2. **Sale of interests in property to be acquired.** A syndicator sells interests to raise money for the acquisition of property as determined later by the syndicator. This procedure is also referred to, quite accurately, as a *blind pool*. Because it allows so much freedom to the syndicator in the use of other people's money, many states forbid its use.

Since a participating interest in a syndicate can be classed as an investment in securities, most states place limits on the number of people who can be offered participating interests without a complete registration under the state's security laws. If sales are made across state lines, or the number to whom participations are offered exceeds 35, then a registration must be made with the federal Securities and Exchange Commission. Failure to comply with the law can result in felony action against the syndicator for the sale of unregistered securities.

Realty Funds

Whenever a larger group (generally more than 35 persons or companies) is formed to participate in a real estate venture, registration with federal and state regulatory agencies is necessary. The participation can be in the form of "units" purchased in a realty fund, which is usually organized as a limited partnership.

Realty funds are organized by persons or companies wishing to raise equity money for real estate projects, such as the purchase of raw land, a construction project, or the purchase of existing income properties. The interests are sold in the form of participation certificates at a fixed price per unit. A unit generally costs anywhere from $100 to $5,000, depending on the plan of organization, and represents a certain percentage of interest in the total fund. Federal and most state laws classify the sale of such participating interests as a sale of securities that must be registered and approved before any sale can be made.

The participant is actually a limited partner and may share in the tax losses and depreciation as well as in the profits generated through the fund's investments. The organizer of the fund is usually the general partner, or a company controlled by the general partner is so designated, and also serves as managing agent for the fund's properties.

SEC REGULATIONS FOR REAL ESTATE TRANSACTIONS

As mentioned briefly in Chapter 1, the Securities and Exchange Commission (SEC) was created during the 1930s Depression years. It is charged with correcting possible abuses in the sale of securities to the general public plus overseeing market activities. There are several ways that real estate transactions can become involved with **SEC requirements.**

Sale of Mortgage Bonds

Large, well-known corporations have an alternative method of raising money not generally available to an individual. This consists of borrowing in the financial markets through the sale of bonds. If the purpose of the money is to build a commercial or industrial building, the builder might sell mortgage bonds. Such an issue of bonds would be secured by a pledge of the real estate being developed. If such an issue is sold to the general public, it would be subject to registration with the SEC. SEC examination of any proposed security issue is directed toward ensuring accuracy of the information distributed for the protection of the general public. It does not, however, assess the risk of any issue.

Advance Payments on Real Estate

There are many ways of offering real estate for sale, but only a few present any possible problems with the SEC. In general, the SEC considers suspect transactions designed to raise money from the general public through the sale of "paper" that may evidence receipt of cash rather than delivery of a contract giving a clear right of title to property. Under certain circumstances, the paper could be construed as a security and consequently subject to SEC registration requirements. The sale of securities in violation of SEC regulations is a felony offense.

The kinds of real estate transactions that may be subject to SEC registration include the sale of predevelopment certificates for lots, the sale of condominium units in a building yet to be constructed for which a down payment is required, and the sale of limited partnership interests, if offered publicly. In these instances, where the line between selling real estate and selling a security is difficult to draw, it is best to consult with competent legal counsel.

SUPPLIER FINANCING

Under certain conditions it might be possible for a builder/developer to obtain **supplier financing** assistance. It is a tool sometimes used by a supplier to gain an advantage in a competitive market. Such assistance may be obtained in two ways: (1) extended terms that allow later payment or (2) a direct loan by the supplier. Both are discussed next.

Extended Terms

Most companies selling a service or product need their accounts receivable paid promptly and often offer cash discounts for timely payments. A few companies utilize credit terms as an incentive to do business with them and, in so doing, provide additional financing for the customer. For instance, in building an apartment, an office building, or even a house, a major supplier such as a lumber dealer, cement company, or electrical or plumbing contractor may agree to extend payment terms for 60 or 90 days or, in some cases, until the project is finished and sold.

This method does conserve cash for the builder/developer, but usually comes at a higher price—an increase in the product or service price plus interest. And the supplier may be exposed to a payment delay that could mean forfeiture of lien rights, which limits a supplier's willingness to use the procedure. The extended terms method of auxiliary finance should not be confused with slow payment or nonpayment of material suppliers' bills; both are very poor procedures. Building supply companies are fully aware of the 90- to 120-day time limits within which to file liens for nonpayment and, without a specific agreement allowing delay in payment, they normally make sure their interests are protected.

Supplier Loans

In recent years some of the major appliance companies and, in a few cases, utility companies, have given larger builder/developers financial assistance with outright loans secured by second mortgages. The ulterior motive in supplier financing is always to ensure the use of the lender's products. This could be heating and air conditioning equipment or a full range of kitchen equipment, or it could be a utility company seeking a competitive advantage.

SELLER-FINANCED HOME MORTGAGES

Market conditions, with adequate money at reasonable interest rates, have diminished the need for seller financing. Nevertheless, **seller-financed mortgages** should be examined as a possible sales tool. While a large majority of property sellers want the cash generated by a sale to use for other purposes, there is a growing group who may think otherwise. These are mostly older people whose financial obligations have dwindled—the term *empty nesters* has been applied—and sound investments are important. An assured source of income could be more important than a top-dollar sales price. In spite of some publicity to the contrary, home mortgages carry very high ratings as credit-worthy investments. On average, at any given time less than 5 percent of home mortgages are delinquent and less than 1 percent suffer default. For those selling houses to seek smaller accommodations, accepting all or part of the sales price in the form of a secured note can be a wise investment.

Because structuring a mortgage loan and qualifying applicants require specialized knowledge of the business, consideration should be given to using a reputable mortgage company to handle a seller-financed transaction. Mortgage companies are familiar with the documentation needed, can provide private mortgage insurance where necessary, and have access to secondary-market purchasers should it be necessary for the seller to convert the loan into cash. If a seller-financed loan is handled by an approved seller-servicer with uniform documentation, Fannie Mae is able to purchase the loan should an emergency need for cash arise. Any discount at time of loan purchase would be only what it takes to match the seller-financed interest rate with current market yield requirements. However, no premium would be paid should the seller-financed interest rate exceed market yield requirements.

REFINANCING

A decline in interest rates usually brings many property owners back to the mortgage market to refinance loans at lower rates. Some homeowners have taken this step two and three times as rates continued to decline. In 1997, **refinancing** accounted for about 40 percent of all loan originations. (Most lenders consider refinancing the payoff of an existing loan from the proceeds of a new loan.)

The benefits of refinancing differ for each borrower. It involves the amount of rate reduction, the costs of renegotiating the loan (new closing costs and discount), the effect of tax laws on the borrower, and possible new lender requirements such as an adjustable-rate instead of a fixed-rate loan. There are no real standards for refinancing and costs can vary substantially between lenders. A discussion of the major questions involved with refinancing follows.

Where to Refinance. The best place to start a refinance search is with the holder of the existing mortgage note. Most lenders (but not all!) are aware that mortgage notes can be refinanced when rates drop and would rather accept a lesser rate than lose the customer. The market is very competitive and most borrowers have access to more than one source. If the note holder will not reopen a loan for refinancing in a lower interest market, other lenders may be willing to consider such an application.

Rate Reduction. An earlier guideline for refinancing was that a rate reduction of 2 percent or more was worth taking. However, rate reduction alone may not save money if the costs exceed the savings. So a more practical approach is to add the costs of refinancing, then compare that with the savings to see how many months it will take to recover the costs.

Calculation of the savings is shown in the following example.

....

EXAMPLE

A property financed at 10 percent on a 30-year, fixed-rate loan is compared with an 8 percent fixed-rate loan. (Reduction in principal balance is not considered.)

At 10%, $120,000, 30 years: Monthly payment	$1,053.10
At 8%, $120,000, 30 years: Monthly payment	880.55
Monthly savings	$ 172.55

....

The important question is: How long will it take to recover refinancing costs? Several lenders should be contacted because their charges can vary substantially.

Refinancing Costs. No specific regulations apply to the charges that may be assessed in a refinancing transaction. Most lenders consider refinancing in the same category (costwise) as a new loan. They may require a new application fee, title insurance, attorney's fees, and an appraisal. Most require some discount that may be a cash requirement. Add up the costs assessed by each lender contacted and an easy comparison can be made.

For an example, say the lowest cost offered amounts to $6,300. By dividing that sum by the monthly savings from the preceding example, the number of months it takes to recover the expenditure calculates as follows:

$$6,300 \div 172.55 = 36.51 \text{ months}$$

If occupancy of the house is expected to continue longer than 36.5 months, a savings can be achieved.

Effect of Tax Laws. Tax law treats refinancing differently from a new loan in terms of deductibility of a discount. Even though a discount may be paid in cash for refinancing, the IRS ruled in May 1986 that a discount for refinancing a home loan must be amortized over the life of the loan. This differs from a discount paid by the buyer at the time of purchase of the house, which may be deducted in the year paid, the same as interest. Another tax question that should be considered concerns the tax value of deducting interest on a home loan. The benefit differs with the taxpayer's tax bracket. Thus, a taxpayer in a higher bracket would have greater possible deductions and would need a lower refinance rate to achieve the same benefit as a person in a lower bracket.

Restructuring the Loan. Refinancing is a negotiable transaction. If a lender agrees to an interest rate concession, it is possible that one bargaining chip would be a change from a fixed-rate to an adjustable-rate repayment plan. The lender is accepting a lower rate and may insist that the rate be adjustable, should the market rise in the years ahead.

Appraisal Problems. One major problem that some homeowners have encountered in attempting refinancing is that the market value of the house has declined to an amount something less than the balance due on the loan. Or, in the case of some graduated payment designs, the balance due on the loan, which increased with negative amortization in the early years, has exceeded the market value of the property. In general, a refinanced conventional loan cannot exceed 95 percent of the current market value of the property. This means that additional cash may be required at closing in order to reduce the loan amount to an acceptable level based on the newly appraised value of the property.

Another escape from possible appraisal problems is available for holders of FHA and VA loans. Both agencies encourage their borrowers to seek refinancing if lower interest rates can be achieved. An appraisal is not required and agency fees have been reduced. As underwriters of these loans rather than lenders, the agencies benefit from anything that makes loan repayment easier for borrowers.

TITLE PROTECTION

A standard requirement for approval of a mortgage loan is that the title to pledged property be valid. The lender wants some assurance that the parties granting the mortgage are the true owners and hold valid title to the property pledged. Many problems can occur in a chain of title ownership that may impair present ownership rights. These include the possibility of forged documents, undisclosed heirs, mistaken legal interpretation of wills, misfiled documents, confusion resulting from similarity of names, and incorrectly stated marital status. It is most important that a purchaser of real property take the necessary steps to assure good title whether or not a mortgage loan is involved.

Three methods are commonly used to protect both a purchaser and a lender from future title problems. One is an opinion by a qualified attorney based on the research of an abstract; another is the purchase of title insurance; and the third is a land registration system, used in a few areas of the country, called the *Torrens system.* Each will be discussed further.

Attorney's Opinion Based on Abstract

The older method, and still the only one available for assuring valid title in oil and gas sale or lease transactions, is a research of the abstract by a qualified attorney.

Abstract of Title. The chronological collection of all recorded documents that affect land title is called an **abstract of title.** It is prepared by an abstracter who specializes in researching county land records. Early recorded instruments affecting land title were all handwritten and provide a fascinating history of the people and events involved with a particular tract of land. Modern abstracts can be drawn from computerized files. The record includes conveyances, wills, judicial proceedings, liens, and encumbrances that affect title to land. It is simply a history of the instruments that affect title and, by itself, does not assure the validity of title. The status of title comes from an opinion given by a qualified attorney.

Attorney's Opinion. After careful research of an abstract, a qualified attorney can issue an opinion as to the validity of title. By examining the chain of events that affect title, the attorney can reach a conclusion as to who the present owners are and report any instruments that have an adverse effect on the ownership rights. Further, the attorney may state what curative steps must be taken to clear the title if there is an adverse claim or a break in the chain of ownership. An attorney's favorable opinion may be accepted by a lender as adequate proof of title.

In large real property transactions, an attorney's opinion may be a lower cost procedure. In recent years, some large office buildings have been conveyed based on an attorney's opinion of title as lower cost than the purchase of title insurance. This is more likely when no mortgage loan is involved. However, there are some disadvantages. This method provides no insurance against an adverse claim, leaving the purchaser with only the seller as recourse against future loss. Further, it can take more time than the issuance of a title policy, since title insurance companies usually maintain continuous records of all recorded documents subject to rapid recall.

Title Insurance

The most popular method used to assure valid title in real estate transactions is the purchase of **title insurance.** It is a specialized type of insurance that protects a policyholder against loss from something that has already happened, such as a forged deed somewhere in the chain of title. Title companies examine the chain of title to make sure the title is insurable (that there are no defects that could cause a subsequent claim). This is important because the title company also agrees to defend the policyholder's title in court should any lawsuits arise with adverse claims.

Title insurance policies normally list certain exclusions that are not covered by the insurance protection. These exclusions include such things as the rights of parties in possession, unrecorded easements, encroachments, zoning laws, and other governmental restrictions. What is insured is sometimes called a *marketable title*, meaning one not necessarily perfect, but free from plausible or reasonable objections. There are two different kinds of title insurance; one indemnifies an owner against loss; the other indemnifies a lender against loss.

Owner's Policy

An owner's policy protects him or her as long as the insured has an interest in the property. This protection can extend beyond the period of actual possession. When an insured owner sells the property, it is often conveyed with a general warranty deed. The warranty clause in that kind of deed makes the seller liable to "forever defend" against possible defects in the title at the time of conveyance, even though the claim may not arise until long after the property has been conveyed. State limitation statutes normally limit this exposure to a period of 20 to 30 years, after which time the insurance policy itself lapses. The important point is that the owner's title insurance does not "run with the land"—it does not transfer to a new owner and is not assignable. The reason is that the previous owner remains liable and holds the protection of that policy.

An owner's policy is issued in the amount of the property value at the time of the transaction. In certain instances, it is possible to increase the coverage should substantial improvements be made or appreciation occur in the property value.

Lender's Policy

At the time that an owner's policy is issued, the same property can be insured against the same defects for the benefit of a lender. It is a different kind of policy, however. The lender's, or mortgagee's, policy is issued in the amount of the mortgage loan and declines with each reduction in the principal balance. When the loan is paid off, the lender's policy becomes void. Also, unlike the owner's policy, a lender's policy automatically transfers to whomever holds the mortgage note. If the property is foreclosed and purchased by the mortgagee, the policy automatically becomes an owner's policy.

Who Pays for Title Insurance?

Practice varies throughout the country in regard to who pays for an owner's title policy. A fairly common procedure is for the owner selling the property to pay. The reasoning is that it proves the seller is delivering valid title, even though the coverage protects the buyer. In some parts of the country, the buyer pays for title insurance as the one gaining protection. It is the lender's policy that is most consistently paid for by the buyer as a cost of borrowing money.

Torrens System

In those states that permit the use of the **Torrens system,**[1] it provides a method of registering the ownership of land and encumbrances, except for tax liens. It might be compared with the registration system used for automobiles.

---

[1]The Torrens system co-exists with regular recording procedures in Colorado, Georgia, Hawaii, Illinois, Massachusetts, Minnesota, New York, North Carolina, Ohio, Virginia, and Washington.

The system was developed in 1857 by Sir Robert Torrens of Australia who took the idea from how title to ships were registered.

To initiate a Torrens system registration, the landowner petitions a state court to register the subject property. Necessary title information must be filed with the court and notice given to all interested parties. The court's determination is made in the form of a decree somewhat similar to that used in a quiet title suit. Once a property is registered following the court's decree, title cannot pass to another, nor are encumbrances or conveyances effective until they also are registered on the certificate of title. Initial use of the Torrens system is optional, but once property is registered, all subsequent transfers must follow the registration procedures. In some states, Torrens registered property is not subject to general judgment liens, nor can title be lost through adverse possession.

One of the problems with the use of the Torrens system as a method of protecting one's title to property is that the cost of court action to simply register a title may easily exceed the cost of purchasing title insurance.

FORECLOSURE

Foreclosure is a legal procedure by means of which property pledged as collateral is sold to satisfy the secured debt. A mortgage grants a lender the right to foreclose in the event of default. While default most often occurs because of nonpayment, there are other reasons that can trigger such action. For instance, the debtor must maintain the property in good condition, keep it free of liens, and comply with all local laws that affect the property. If an act in default occurs, the lender may take such action as is authorized by applicable state laws to protect its interests. In the foreclosure process, title passes at an auction to the highest bidder. This is usually the holder of the mortgage note (the lender), but it could be to a third party who may purchase it at the foreclosure auction sale. If the price paid at foreclosure is more than the debt to the lender, the lender is entitled only to the money due on the note. In the unlikely event of any surplus money, that is paid to the foreclosed owner.

Foreclosure is a step that lenders want to avoid, if at all possible. There are seldom any winners in this action. For the lender, it is costly, time consuming, and may require additional funds to be advanced for payment of various foreclosure costs. If the property is vacated, there is danger of vandalism. Also, it brings up the additional problem of future disposition of the property.

Foreclosure for the borrower results in the loss of property, possibly the homestead. It is a traumatic experience and will result in a negative report on one's credit record. For a borrower facing default, the first step should be to discuss the problem with the lender. Most lenders recognize the fact that various personal and business problems, beyond the control of a borrower, can cause default. While the lender is not always able to modify a repayment agreement, it is possible that a moratorium on payments could be granted for a limited period of time. Or possibly the release of some tax escrow funds could provide temporary assistance to the debtor.

Lenders do not normally seek out borrowers to offer assistance, as their responsibility is to the holder of the note and to pursue timely repayment of the loan. So it falls to the borrower to initiate any move to delay payments or to rework the mortgage obligation. The earlier a repayment problem can be called to the attention of a lender, the more likely it is to be resolved with forbearance for the borrower.

Types of Foreclosure

Foreclosure practices are determined by state laws. They fall into three categories: judicial, nonjudicial, and strict foreclosure.

Judicial Foreclosure

A judicial foreclosure is normally used when a regular mortgage is the security instrument. A default is handled by filing the required notices to the debtor followed by a suit in court to foreclose the mortgage claim. If the court agrees with the claim, it can order that the property be sold to satisfy the debt. The sale is handled through a public auction, usually called a *sheriff's sale.*

Nonjudicial Foreclosure

A nonjudicial action is the method by which foreclosure is accomplished when a power of sale clause is contained in a mortgage or deed of trust. No court action is required as the instrument contains a clause granting power of sale to a third-party trustee. The lender notifies the trustee of a default and requests foreclosure action to protect the lender's interest. Depending on the applicable state laws, proper notification must be given to the debtor prior to the property being offered for sale. Then, the trustee, who is the third party in a deed of trust, may sell the property at public auction. The trustee is authorized to bid for the property on behalf of the lender (called the *beneficiary* in a deed of trust), usually up to the amount of the mortgage debt. Title to the property can be transferred to the winning bidder by the trustee with no court action involved.

Strict Foreclosure

Strict foreclosure is possible in only a few states as the borrower loses all equity invested in the property. After appropriate notice is given to a delinquent borrower and proper papers are filed in court, the court establishes a specific time period during which the entire defaulted debt must be paid. If full payment is not made within the time period, the borrower's redemption rights are waived and the court awards full legal title to the lender. There can be no deficiency judgment claimed under strict foreclosure.

DEFICIENCY JUDGMENTS

The sale of property at a foreclosure auction may or may not produce sufficient recovery to satisfy all claimants. The lender is entitled only to the defaulted debt (principal balance plus interest) and costs incurred. If, for example, the debt at foreclosure amounts to $42,000 and the property is sold for $35,000, there remains $7,000 due to the lender. Since the borrower may be obligated to the lender for the balance due on the note, the lender may have the right to seek a **deficiency judgment** for the remaining $7,000. However, some states limit the lender's right to a deficiency claim if the property is a person's homestead. In such a case, the lender could only recover the amount realized in the foreclosure sale.

Another protective law found in some states is granting a foreclosed debtor the right to cite the market value of foreclosed property as a defense against a deficiency claim. This kind of protection forces a lender to bid more realistically on the value of foreclosed property and not resort to deficiency judgment claims that can be abusive.

Relief of Debt

There can be unpleasant tax consequence for the borrower after foreclosure. This can occur if a borrower is granted relief from payment of any unsatisfied obligation. Income tax law treats relief of debt as income to the person granted relief. If a lender grants such relief, a Form 1099 must be filed with the IRS reporting the amount that the debtor is no longer obligated to pay. To a homeowner who has suffered the loss of a home, an additional tax obligation seems particularly unfair. Nevertheless, present IRS rules consider borrowed money that is not repaid as simply another source of income for the relieved debtor.

OBLIGATIONS INVOLVED WITH DEFAULT INSURANCE—INDEMNITY

When a foreclosure occurs and losses are sustained, who bears the cost? The party holding the secured note undertakes foreclosure action if there is a default and bears the initial cost. But if the loan is insured against default, the note holder can claim reimbursement for the loss. Exactly how the claim is handled depends on the type of default coverage. This can be private mortgage insurance, a HUD/FHA insured commitment, or a VA guaranty.

Regardless of the type of default protection, all kinds insure the lender against loss, not the borrower. This is true even though it is the borrower who pays the insurance premiums. It is often misunderstood since, unlike other kinds of insurance, the party paying for the coverage is not the one insured. What the borrower is paying for is an assurance to the lender that the loan will be paid should the borrower suffer a default. The benefit to a borrower is in obtaining a loan that might otherwise not be available.

There is another major difference between this coverage and other kinds of insurance: As a qualification requirement for coverage, the borrower must indemnify the insurance company against loss. This means that if the insurance company must reimburse a lender for a loss, then the insuring company (or federal agency) has a right to demand reimbursement from the defaulted borrower. This right applies to all three major types of coverage: private mortgage insurance, HUD/FHA, and VA.

Until late 1986, there was little action taken against borrowers who might owe a deficiency claim after foreclosure had been taken. There were two practical reasons for this seeming leniency. First, during most of the 1970s and the early 1980s, property generally increased in value, thus limiting the potential loss for a lender; second, in that time period, people tried to hold onto their mortgaged property as it increased in value, enlarging their equity. If a default did occur, the debtor seldom had sufficient other assets to allow collection of such a claim.

This situation began to change in the mid-1980s. Substantial loss in real property values in certain areas of the country caused some debtors to "walk away" from both their property and the obligation to pay the remaining debt. With property value substantially less than the balance due on a mortgage note, continued payments seemed to be a bad deal to some. As losses mounted, lenders began to take steps to enforce their claims. In October 1986, all federal agencies involved with underwriting home loans required that mortgagees report defaults and foreclosure action to credit bureaus. A further stipulation was that deficiency judgments must be pursued if the debtor holds other assets that may be subject to attachment.

If the claim against a defaulted borrower is made by a private mortgage insurance company, a deficiency judgment must be sought against the debtor through the courts. This judgment, when filed of record, operates as a general lien on the debtor's assets and is collectible in the same manner as any other judgment. As such actions became more common by the early 1990s, debtors fought against such claims, primarily on the basis that the indemnity obligation to the insurer was not fully disclosed when the policy was issued. Results so far have been mixed and the amounts involved have not been great enough to justify much litigation.

The problem is different if the loss is sustained by either HUD/FHA or VA. Since both are federal agencies, an obligation to them becomes an obligation to the government, allowing a federal lien to be filed against a debtor. Recent Justice Department rules consider federal debt as preempting all other claims to property, including first mortgage liens. And such debt is more difficult to wash through bankruptcy. Further, the 1992 expansion of HUD's Credit Alert Interactive Voice Response System (CAIVRS) added a number of government lending agencies to the list with access to the files. This means that default on any of these government-related loans will be on record with CAIVRS and prevent use of government credit until acceptable resolution is made.

Settlement of a federal lien depends on the debtor's circumstances and is handled on a case-by-case basis. Generally, the obligation can be mitigated only in cases of proven hardship.

Questions for Discussion

1. Discuss methods a builder might use to assist with a home buyer's permanent financing.
2. Discuss maximum and minimum dollar limits on loan amounts.

3. When is refinancing a mortgage loan practical? Why?

4. Describe two of the three ways that title to property is protected against adverse claims.

5. How is loan-to-value ratio used in lending practices?

6. What kind of real property transaction might fall under jurisdiction of the SEC?

7. Who benefits from a sale-and-leaseback deal, and how?

8. What is the risk involved in an unsubordinated leasehold mortgage and how might protection be obtained?

9. What is a syndication? A realty fund?

10. Describe a judicial foreclosure proceeding. A nonjudicial foreclosure.

Chapter 14

Technology Advances in Mortgage Lending

....

KEY WORDS AND PHRASES

Computerized loan origination (CLO) • *Manual underwriting* • *Automated underwriting* • *Loan Prospector* • *Collateral assessment* • *Desktop Underwriter* • *Desktop Originator* • *Credit score* • *FICO* • *Subprime loans* • *Internet loan applications* • *Online real estate services* • *Risk-based mortgage loan pricing* • *Universal account*

....

INTRODUCTION

Advances in computer technology helped make possible the handling of data necessary to organize and manage mortgage loan pools and their cash flows into mortgage-backed securities. One of the results was broadening of the loan market by adding many newcomers. New software has been developed that uses artificial intelligence to analyze a loan application and give an approval, if justified. Decisions on loan applications can be made with much greater speed than previously. The new technology has brought greater depth in the data available on the creditworthiness of borrowers which gives lenders more precision in loan analysis. This enlarged database has encouraged the subprime loan market.

COMPUTERIZED LOAN ORIGINATION (CLO)

One of the early applications of computer technology to mortgage lending was **computerized loan origination (CLO).** As a method of transmitting information between computer terminals for analysis by human underwriters, this system was introduced nationally in 1986 by Citicorp, the New York bank company. Their *MortgagePower* software program was sold to loan originators across the country. Terminals were installed in offices of companies and people who had contact with home buyers. This included appraisers, lawyers, title companies, mortgage companies, and real estate agents.

Citibank expanded its *MortgagePower* program through the late 1980s to over 3,000 terminals around the country. In 1989 it became the nation's largest originator of mortgage loans with this system. However, Citibank has since withdrawn from its computer network although it remains very active in the mortgage market.

Almost from CLO's initiation, a controversy developed between the Mortgage Bankers Association (MBA) and the National Association of Realtors (NAR). The MBA saw an intrusion into their specialized field of mortgage loan origination, especially by real estate agents who had first contact with a potential buyer. The MBA's position was that the Real Estate Settlement Procedures Act (RESPA) prohibited a real estate agent from making a fee for a loan, which might be considered a kickback. If not that, such action amounted to "steering" the buyer to one lender, which is also prohibited by RESPA.

NAR felt that a real estate agent was allowed to earn a fee because it was a service provided the buyer, which is allowed by RESPA. Further, NAR wanted its members to offer a "one-stop-shopping" service to property buyers that would include assistance in arranging a mortgage loan.

A decision was sought from the Department of Housing and Urban Development (HUD), the monitor of RESPA. HUD looked beyond the immediate argument and saw advantages with computerized loan systems. They made mortgage money more available to potential home buyers and they could lower the cost of loan origination. Further, it offered a less-biased system as there was a minimum of human contact.

Nevertheless, it was not until June 1996 that HUD issued a final rule. An earlier rule that had allowed a CLO operator to charge any fee that seemed fair so long as it was disclosed and approved in writing by the borrower was eliminated. In its place, the final rule limited the CLO operator to charging a fee that was "reasonably related to the value of the services provided." Further, a listing of only one lender (which was formerly permitted) was considered to furnish "no or nominal compensable services."

As the market has evolved over the years, both mortgage brokers and real estate agents found that by working together it was possible to increase their sales with both parties earning a portion of the origination fee.

Real estate agents interested in utilizing a CLO system, now called **manual underwriting,** are generally resorting to intermediary companies that perform the loan services, via computer, of a loan broker or a mortgage company. By sending information on a potential borrower to the intermediary, the real estate agent is prompted if all information needed is not submitted. Further, the intermediary has contacts with lenders and is able to place acceptable loans rather quickly. An origination fee split is negotiable between the intermediary and the agent as both assist the borrower.

If there is an ownership interest of 1 percent or more between the parties involved with a CLO, it is considered a controlled business arrangement and must be disclosed to the consumer. Further, there can be no required use of the affiliated company and nothing of value may be given the affiliate other than a return on the ownership interest.

Larger mortgage companies either allow loan closing by agents using the mortgage company's name or buy loans from the agents. To pay the agents, mortgage companies often allow the agent to earn a portion of the interest rate that is charged. This is called a *yield-spread premium* or a *service-release premium*.

AUTOMATED UNDERWRITING SYSTEMS

More advanced use of the computer has been developed by larger lenders as more experience and better technology has become available. As reported earlier, in 1995 both Freddie Mac and Fannie Mae introduced separate **automated underwriting** systems for use by their seller/servicers. Each has developed advanced software with artificial intelligence capable of analyzing a loan application and approving it for funding if qualifications are met. Other lenders produced their own systems to assist analyzing loan applications.

About the same time, the Federal Reserve Bank Board announced its own software system, called *Partners*, that tells a potential borrower if he or she qualifies for a mortgage loan. It is designed to help professionals assist low- and moderate-income borrowers, but is accessible to anyone seeking help.

While they are not the only automated underwriting systems, a brief description on Freddie Mac's *Loan Prospector* system is followed by Fannie Mae's *Desktop Underwriter*.

Freddie Mac's *Loan Prospector*

Freddie Mac's automated underwriting system, called **Loan Prospector,** was released nationally in February 1995. It is limited for use by Freddie Mac's seller/servicers who are required to submit verification of the data submitted. The information submitted is that required by the Uniform Residential Loan Application (Freddie Mac Form 65) and the initial charge for an analysis was $100. Verification of the applicant's employment, income, and assets is required.

If the loan-to-value ratio is greater than 80 percent, the application is forwarded to a private mortgage insurer chosen by the lender. All major mortgage insurers are represented on the Freddie Mac system.

The computer classifies the applications in three categories: (1) accepted, (2) refer, and (3) caution. An accepted application is approved for purchase by Freddie Mac. At this writing, Freddie Mac is able to process about one-third of its applications by computer. Of this amount roughly one-half have met the necessary requirements for "accepted."

An application classified as "refer" is returned to the lender's underwriting department with a request for further information. If the classification is "caution," which is about 10 percent of those submitted, it, too, is returned to the lender's underwriters. Reasons given are that some serious issues are involved that disallow purchasing of the loan. The computer does not reject any loan but sends those applications that do not meet approval back to the lender for further human underwriting.

Credit Approval by *Loan Prospector*

A lender is allowed to choose among eight approved credit reporting companies. Credit reports are available that merge information from at least two of the three major databases. *Loan Prospector* also has the ability to access the credit card database to determine total credit available and the percentage of credit being used.

Collateral Assessments

Property evaluation is not called an "appraisal" by *Loan Prospector;* it is a **collateral assessment.** The program assesses whether or not the collateral is sufficient to secure the loan.

Two methods are offered to make this determination and it is up to the lender to select the most effective. The two are (1) nonexpedited and (2) expedited.

> **Nonexpedited.** This is a full appraisal and is offered in a time frame of 72 hours or less. Freddie Mac selects one of three appraisal management firms to handle the appraisal. The firm selects a local appraiser to make the assessment and report back to the lender.

> **Expedited.** If the lender selects an expedited assessment, it could be completed within two hours. The procedure involves a physical assessment of the property, primarily to see if any obvious problems exist. For instance, if the building is boarded up, the evaluation would be upgraded to a full appraisal. Expedited appraisals are intended to reduce unnecessary work and time expended when it serves no useful purpose.

To further expedite the appraisal process, Freddie Mac has created a software service called *GoldWorks* that links a lender directly with the appraiser. It eliminates the cost of overnight deliveries.

Fannie Mae's *Desktop Underwriter*

In April 1995, Fannie Mae released *two* programs to its seller/servicers. The basic program, called **Desktop Underwriter,** uses artificial intelligence and information from Fannie Mae's seller/servicer guide to properly analyze a loan application.

A second program, called **Desktop Originator,** is designed to allow an agent or a mortgage broker to take an application in a potential borrower's home with a laptop computer, relaying the information to the lender who is the seller/servicer.

Information on the loan and the applicant must come from the same form as used by Freddie Mac: the Uniform Residential Loan Application (Fannie Mae

Form 1003, Freddie Mac Form 65). The lender must verify the information and then submit it to Fannie Mae through its *Desktop Underwriter*. A response can be provided within 60 seconds on "approved" applicants. The lender is responsible for notifying the broker or agent who originated the loan, who in turn notifies the applicant.

While Fannie Mae is seeking better and faster ways to handle its appraisals, it still uses many of the traditional methods. As for credit reporting, Fannie Mae now works with two providers: (1) Credco and (2) Information Research.

Studies are seeking other ways of satisfying lender requirements, particularly in regard to property evaluations. A study has been made of using pictures taken from satellites to determine only if a building actually exists on the property. Probably a more logical approach is to use tax data currently found in county tax offices that can be accessed by a computer.

CREDIT SCORING

A **credit score** is a snapshot that objectively assesses a borrower's credit history and current usage at a given point in time based on credit bureau reports. An individual borrower's credit score may vary somewhat across repositories if there are differences in amount or content of information contained in credit records. A credit score may be generated even if a repository's file includes only one tradeline. So lenders try to make sure that multiple files are included, probably at least three.

While credit scoring has recently received greater publicity, it is not new. One of the principal procedures was begun in 1956 by Fair, Isaacs Company of San Rafael, California, known as **FICO**. What has brought credit scoring to wider usage is its easy adaptability to computerized loan analysis. The "score" is a number that shows a person's credit history and helps the analysis of a borrower's probability of paying off another loan. Or, as some lenders interpret, the score is indicative of the risk of foreclosure.

Today, credit scoring is offered under two major methods. Both methods are approved and recommended for use with either manual or automated underwriting of mortgage loans. Both have shown a good predictive power in loan analysis. One is the FICO "bureau scores" that run from about 400 to 900 with the *lower* number showing the greater risk of default. Scores over 660 will generally have credit histories acceptable to Fannie Mae, but it is not a cutoff point as lower scores can be approved. Freddie Mac recommends a cautious and detailed review for loan files that score less than 620.

The other credit score method is the "bankruptcy score" developed by CCN-MDS which runs from about 0 to 1,300 with the *higher* MDS number showing a greater risk of default. It is recommended that underwriters use only one type of credit scoring to analyze borrowers as use of both can cause some confusion.

Credit scoring is used in conjunction with many other criteria, such as an applicant's income, other assets, total indebtedness, and future possibilities. It is only one criterion that shows good predictive powers but is seldom used by itself for underwriting purposes. It has been a big help in setting prices for subprime loans.

SUBPRIME LOANS

Subprime loans are those made to persons who do not have a top-grade credit record as is required to qualify for a regular mortgage loan. While subprime loans are not connected to automated underwriting, the many credit details that can be handled by computer analysis are one reason many lenders have undertaken loans in this field. Another reason is that subprime loans command higher interest rates and discounts which add profitable business to a lender providing it is careful in analyzing the higher risks involved.

With a conforming loan, rates are posted in newspapers and elsewhere. But subprime lending uses risk-based pricing. Rates are not publicly quoted; rates are found, or negotiated, to fit the risk profile. To determine a risk profile, start with a prime loan. A prime loan is made to a good-to-excellent borrower who has perfect credit, which means no derogatories and no 30-, 60-, or 90-day delinquencies in his or her mortgage history, or has very few derogatories/delinquencies.

Below this level of risk are the subprime borrowers. To underwrite this type of loan, the underwriter is not examining whether or not the borrower is worthy of credit but where he or she belongs on the risk scale. Credit scoring is a helpful factor in this determination. Also, appraisals are critical. It takes an astute underwriter to sort out the various risks involved and to properly evaluate the greater risk.

The borrower is matched to one of a series of risk profiles. Unfortunately, lenders differ in defining these profiles as it involves some gray areas. Following is an example of what may be included in determining the risk of an A, A-, B, C, D, or F mortgage borrower by a typical mortgage lender. Comparisons can be made to an "A" borrower who has a delinquency rate of 1.20 percent as rated by many lenders.

"A" borrower. No late mortgage payments and no credit card payments over 30 days delinquent in the last year. "A" borrowers have a low default rate and underwriters can allow a higher loan-to-value ratio. (Current delinquency rate, according to Mortgage Information Corporation: 1.19%.)

"A-" borrower. No late mortgage payments and one or two credit card payments 30 days late. (Delinquency rate: 2.04%.)

"B" borrower. Thirty days late on a mortgage payment and 60 days late on one or more charge account debts. Has satisfactory credit but high debt ratios. Reasons for delinquencies are important as the record may indicate problems that can, or have been, overcome. This borrower may be self-employed and has trouble documenting income. The underwriter first looks for explainable delinquencies, then at secondary credit and revolving credit over a two-year period. (Delinquency rate: 3.88%.)

"C" borrower. Thirty days late two or three times on a mortgage payment and several charge accounts 60 days or more in arrears. Has only fair credit and high debt ratios. A 500 credit score is typically a "C" borrower. These borrowers may have had employment problems or health and accident problems and are over their heads in debt. They want to consolidate the indebtedness. Underwriters look for both the willingness and ability to repay. (Delinquency rate: 5.19%.)

"D" borrower. Has poor credit and high debt ratios. These borrowers are not likely to become "A" borrowers very soon. Such loans have a good chance of going into foreclosure and the lender must depend on the collateral to guarantee repayment. (Delinquency rate: 8.05%.)

"F" borrower. Currently in bankruptcy or foreclosure.

With the help of state-of-the-art information-gathering systems, subprime lending is burgeoning. Some lenders are doing very well with this category of loans; others are not showing good results. While the growing field has not had enough time to develop quality experience factors, preliminary analyses show results not much different than in the past: The average delinquency and foreclosure rates are about what has been predicted from past experience. In 1997, A loans had serious delinquency rates of 1.96 percent, B loans were 3.73 percent, C loans 4.99 percent, and D loans 8.07 percent.

MORTGAGES ON THE INTERNET

The use of computers in mortgage lending has expanded so that a borrower can negotiate a loan on the Internet. An increasing number of Web sites are offering mortgage loans directly to consumers who qualify, but there are a few caveats.

There are several reasons for the growing interest in **Internet loan applications.** Many applicants live in rural areas and want to avoid traveling long distances to branch offices in metropolitan areas. Even though the usual time-consuming verifications are required, people who are pressed for time look to the Net to expedite the loan process. Another lure is anonymity. People with tarnished credit histories don't have to face a skeptical loan officer. Even people with good credit records sometimes feel more comfortable with impersonal vending devices than face-to-face encounters.

Mortgages negotiated through the Internet may have lower origination fees, like three-eighths of a point compared to 1 to 1 1/2 points with regular mortgage brokers. But the other fees and interest rates are about the same as regular mortgages. There is also a problem in not having a real person to talk through financial needs. Because anonymity works both ways, the Internet has its share of shady operators who can take advantage of unwary borrowers.

Many companies offer an **online real estate service** that allows consumer access to information on a full range of services. In 1998 software giant Microsoft stepped into this field. The company offers consumers a service that gives them the opportunity to search for homes, find builders, compare mortgage products, and apply for loans. The service gives a consumer access to information that has been the special province of real estate agents and mortgage brokers.

Companies offering these services deny any intention to replace existing agents who are given a broader market to work with. Microsoft has stated that it is partnering with present real estate settlement providers. All the service expects to provide is information on what is available and a comparison of prices. To close any deal, the consumer must contact an agent in that business.

Technology brings rapid changes that create better and more information along with faster response. For an idea of how diverse is the information currently offered on the Internet, following is a very brief review of several Web sites.

www.hsh.com Offered by the financial publishing company HSH Associates of Butler, New Jersey, the site surveys 2,500 lenders across the country and updates daily. It doesn't make loans or accept consumer advertising, which makes it an excellent source of objective data on interest rates and terms.

www.keystroke.com The site was created by Keystroke Financial Inc., a Seattle mortgage brokerage firm which has built partnerships with two hundred lenders. The application process and fees involved are explained simply and without jargon.

www.iown.com A San Francisco online mortgage brokerage firm, I-own has 23 lending partners. On visiting the site, one can receive a list of up to 10 lenders ranked by whatever aspect of the loan matters most—closing costs, interest rates, or monthly payments—and receive a complete breakdown of closing costs and fees, including the half-point fee that I-own charges to process the loan.

www.homeadvisor.msn.com The site created by Microsoft Corporation, Redmond, Washington, features 11 lenders and has an easy-to-use, 10-step application process with helpful worksheets. If the applicant fails to qualify, the program suggests ways to meet the qualification requirements. As an attraction, if a loan is applied for online, the applicant receives a hand-held computer free.

www.eloan.com A Palo Alto, California, online mortgage brokerage firm, E-Loan, Inc., offers prequalification and preapproval for home equity loans, as well as first mortgages and refinancing. The site has a link that helps a user compare values of different homes in the neighborhood. It even has a feature that allows the user to hold out for a particular interest rate and to receive an e-mail when the rate becomes available.

USING COMPUTERIZED INFORMATION IN THE FUTURE

As technology advances, indications are that by early in the next century, mortgage loans will move to a **risk-based mortgage loan pricing** system where lenders assess borrowing costs loan by loan. This will be possible with computerized loan evaluation systems capable of forecasting the default risk dictated by each applicant.

In addition, secondary-market companies will be able to adjust the guarantee fees charged to lenders to more accurately reflect the risks represented by the individual mortgages within a loan pool that an originator wants to sell. As lenders pay varying guarantee fees, market forces may prompt them to pass the distinctions on to borrowers in the form of similarly varying mortgage fees.

The ongoing adoption of automated underwriting systems has given the lending industry the ability to measure risk more quickly and accurately than ever before. For years, the country's main residential market, sometime referred to as the *prime market,* has relied primarily on average cost pricing. Every mortgage interest rate includes a premium to cover the risk of default with all prime borrowers paying the same interest rate. With risk-based pricing, the alignment of risk and reward is more closely met by giving lower interest rates to less risky borrowers.

What this more accurate risk assessment may lead to in the future is a **universal account** that could make mortgages obsolete. The idea would be a combination of loans, such as a car loan, a personal loan, or a mortgage loan, in one account. Multiline financial institutions, such as commercial firms and stock brokerages, are already moving in this general direction in recognizing the value of cross-selling products, a concept that is key to giving this futuristic financial instrument its universal applicability.

Questions for Discussion

1. What is HUD's position on computerized loan origination?
2. Explain what is meant by the terms *manual underwriting* and *automated underwriting.*
3. Describe the principal features of Freddie Mac's *Loan Prospector.*
4. What does Fannie Mae offer in automated underwriting?
5. Explain how credit scoring operates.
6. What is the incentive for making loans to subprime-rated borrowers?
7. What roughly comprises a "C" borrower's credit risk?
8. Describe the kinds of people who want to arrange mortgage loans through the Internet.
9. Explain what is meant by offering real estate services online.
10. Describe risk-based pricing as it applies to mortgage loans.

Chapter 15

Environmental Issues

INTRODUCTION

In addition to a property appraisal, a fairly recent requirement for loan qualification is an **environmental site assessment.** This has become a necessary procedure due to the potential for massive liabilities that can be assessed against a property owner should environmental problems be discovered. There are a number of different kinds of environmental issues that affect property; some can change its value, some limit usage of the property, and some affect both value and usage. However, of all the environmental issues, the one that harbors the greatest potential for liability is the cleanup of toxic waste sites as addressed by the federal government under the Superfund Act. A further complication is that these problems are tackled by federal, state, and local laws which makes compliance somewhat complicated.

Environmental issues cover a number of important problems. This kind of assessment is commonly required for commercial loans but not in such detail for home loans. Owner-occupied dwelling units usually hold certain exemptions from environmental rules as explained next.

ENVIRONMENTAL ASSESSMENTS FOR HOME LOANS

Home loans are distinguished from residential loans in this section as the latter category includes multifamily properties which are treated as commercial loans. A broad exemption from liability for cleanup of toxic waste sites was granted homeowners by the **Environmental Protection Agency (EPA)** in 1991. It has eased some concern for lenders considering home loans on or near hazardous waste sites.

In its policy statement, "Policy Toward Owners of Residential Property at Superfund Sites," issued in July 1991, the EPA stated that it would not hold homeowners liable for cleanup costs unless that owner knowingly contaminated the property or failed to cooperate with the EPA in its cleanup efforts (such as not permitting the EPA access to a Superfund site). Homeowners are only protected if they use their property solely for residential purposes. The policy also protects lenders who acquire residential properties through foreclosure (defined as one- to four-family dwellings in this policy statement).

EPA's policy statement is not a statutory exemption. Rather, it is intended only as guidance for EPA enforcement employees. In other words, the EPA's policy does not amend the Superfund statute, meaning homeowners can still be held liable for cleanup costs. However, the EPA is indicating that it will not exercise its right to pursue homeowners, but it remains free to rescind the policy or take actions at variance with the policy.

ENVIRONMENTAL ASSESSMENTS FOR COMMERCIAL LOANS

Almost all commercial loan applications must now include an environmental site assessment. This includes multifamily dwellings. The normal requirement is for a "Phase I assessment," more fully discussed later as it is defined under the Superfund Act. A properly completed Phase I assessment can offer a new owner an acceptable defense against claims for toxic waste cleanup costs.

A big problem with Phase I assessments is that the law defining this procedure fails to set standards as to precisely what constitutes contamination or just what qualifications are necessary for a person to prepare an acceptable assessment. Education programs and certain standards are being developed so that future resolution of this problem is likely. Another problem with Phase I assessments is that critical environmental problems, such as the presence of asbestos or lead-based paints, are not covered inasmuch as these dangers do not subject an owner to the same broad liabilities that stem from the Superfund Act.

Efforts to overcome these limitations have resulted in requirements for an environmental site assessment that is intended to cover all environmental problems, such as wetlands, endangered species, and the presence or nearness of any hazardous materials. This is in contrast to the more limited definition of a "Phase I Assessment" which is defined in the Superfund Act and is identified as a possible defense against liabilities imposed for the cleanup of hazardous waste sites. While market jargon still uses both terms almost synonymously to identify the requirement, it is most important for a buyer or investor to clarify the terminology and to understand what the other party really means when an assessment requirement is made.

ENVIRONMENTAL REQUIREMENTS OF THE SECONDARY MARKET

While the secondary market is dominated by home loans, a few commercial loans, including multifamily loans, are moving into the hands of secondary-market investors. Since these investors place limits on the kind of loans that are acceptable, some requirements regarding environmental questions are in place and more will likely be forthcoming as the need arises. At this time, both Fannie Mae and Freddie Mac require that certain environmental information be included with any loan eligible for purchase. Primarily, both agencies rely on some added information derived from a property appraisal.

Freddie Mac requires that an appraiser comment on any known environmental conditions that may adversely affect a property's value. This includes asbestos and urea-formaldehyde foam insulation. Further information is required on the proximity of the mortgaged house to industrial sites or waste or water treatment facilities, as well as nearby commercial establishments using chemicals or oil products in their operations. While appraisers are not considered to be experts on environmental hazards, they are expected to provide "early warnings" of properties harboring potential environmental problems. And Freddie Mac also requires that an appraiser consider environmental factors in reaching a conclusion as to the property's value.

For multifamily loans, Fannie Mae requires its seller/servicers to perform an environmental assessment before submitting the loans for purchase. This assessment includes a review of available documents, interviews with people familiar with the site, and an actual site inspection. If the Phase I assessment indicates potential problems, a Phase II assessment is required. (Both Phase I and Phase II assessments are explained in a later section of this chapter.)

Loan Documents. It is becoming more common for both residential and commercial lenders to include environmental covenants in their mortgage documents. For instance, the documents could prohibit a borrower from using hazardous substances on pledged property.

The Freddie Mac/Fannie Mae revised single-family mortgage requires the borrower to promise to abide by state and federal environmental laws and to refrain from storing or using hazardous materials on the mortgaged property. Further, the borrower must promise to notify the lender if an investigation or lawsuit involving hazardous substances is filed against the property.

PRINCIPAL ENVIRONMENTAL PROBLEMS

The need for information on environmental problems is now crucial in any transaction involving commercial property. Some limits have been defined for homeowners, insofar as storing or using hazardous material. This brings up the questions: Exactly what comprises an environmental problem? What is the origin of these problems and what is being done to mitigate the dangers? The balance of this chapter is devoted to outlining the problems, explaining the principal federal laws and regulations that are being applied, and identifying the major impact these changes will have on lenders and property owners.

The principal laws, rules, and regulations designed to protect the environment that also have substantial impact on real estate transactions and future land value are categorized as follows:

1. Laws concerned with the cleanup of toxic waste sites.
2. Laws addressing indoor air pollution.
3. Lead poisoning rules including proper disclosure of lead-based paint in dwellings.
4. Regulations designed to protect wetlands areas.
5. The Endangered Species Act.
6. Laws and regulations governing the proper handling of underground storage tanks.
7. Electromagnetic forces.

Other Environmental Issues

To give perspective to the subject matter, many more categories than listed are part of the broad subject of environmental problems. Among them are air and water pollution resulting from automobile and industrial discharges, changes needed in mining and forestry practices, the need to filter storm water runoff, and the proper treatment and disposal of sewage. Important as they are, these issues have more to do with providing a cleaner, safer world to live in and go a step beyond the immediate problem of determining real property value. These problems, therefore, will not be further discussed in this text since the seven categories of laws and regulations mentioned earlier are the ones that most directly affect land value. Unfortunately, the information presented may raise as many unresolved questions as it answers. But that is the present state of the laws and knowledge of the problems.

TOXIC WASTE SITES

Poisonous contamination of land can occur without visible evidence on the surface since it can be located deep underground. If contamination is present, the cost of cleanup is the responsibility of all who might have had a hand in creating the problem plus any unfortunate purchaser who may have acquired the land even a day or two before. A landowner, both unaware of and innocent of creating any contamination, is equally liable for cleanup as the party actually responsible for the danger. With such broad liability, the burden normally falls to the party with the "deepest pockets," almost regardless of responsibility.

Unfortunately, thus far, much of the money spent on environmental problems has been consumed with litigation denying liability for any cleanup. The ill-defined liabilities are a major reason for uncertainty as to future land values, particularly in areas of the country that harbor chemical plants, oil refineries, tank farms, heavy manufacturing plants, mining operations, and government-owned nuclear manufacturing and storage facilities. Underground seepage of hazardous materials generated by this kind of activity can wreak havoc on neighboring properties.

Discovery of the Problem

The first national notice that **toxic waste sites** could endanger people's lives surfaced on August 3, 1978, in news reports on Love Canal, near Niagara Falls, New York. For many years the Hooker Chemical Company and others had dumped nearly 22,000 tons of chemical waste in what had once been Love Canal. The wastes included polychlorinated biphenyls (PCBs), dioxin, and long-lasting pesticides. In 1953, Hooker filled in the dump and sold it to the city of Niagara Falls for one dollar. Later, a road was built on top of the fill, making way for houses and a public school. Complaints of foul odors, the surfacing of a black sludge, and minor burn marks showing up on children in the area were not heeded until the late 1970s when New York State began an investigation.

First Federal Action on Toxic Waste Sites. The public shock created by discovery of massive health problems found near Love Canal finally brought federal government action. The first result was passage of the **Comprehensive Environmental Response, Compensation and Liability Act of 1980 (CERCLA).** The act set up a $1.6 billion Hazardous Waste Trust Fund, which became known as **Superfund.** Later, an amendment increased the Superfund to $8.5 billion. CERCLA, and subsequent legislation, provides a federal regulatory mechanism to identify, investigate, evaluate, and clean up inactive and abandoned waste sites throughout the United States. It further authorizes states and private parties to take appropriate action to clean up contaminated sites and to seek reimbursement from the responsible parties. Implementation of the act was assigned to the Environmental Protection Agency.

Environmental Protection Agency (EPA)

The EPA has defined over 700 **hazardous materials.** Wherever a concentration of such materials is found, the site can be designated for cleanup. Definition of what is hazardous and in what concentrations there is a danger is left to the judgment of EPA. The EPA is responsible for administering the cleanup of these areas and recovering its costs from the **responsible parties.**

CERCLA specifically excludes a number of hazardous materials that fall under other environmental laws. These include petroleum and its derivatives, natural gas, mining wastes, cement kiln dust, and wastes generated from the combustion of coal and other fossil fuels. These exclusions are important since damage from such sources is separate from and not part of the liabilities cited in the Superfund Act.

Liability for Cleanup Costs

Liability for cleanup as determined by the Superfund Act is broadly stated to cover the release, or threatened release, of hazardous substances from a facility that causes the incurrence of response costs (investigating and testing) and remedial action (removal, neutralization, or containment). Responsibility for cleanup with strict, joint, and several liability falls on all who may have been involved in the waste site. *Strict liability* means liable regardless of fault. *Joint and several* means each party is both singularly and jointly liable for all costs. Liability to the government for reimbursement of cleanup costs cannot be allocated. However, liability among the various responsible parties may be apportioned if there is a reasonable basis for doing so.

The act offers no limits on the amount of cleanup, removal, or containment costs for which a responsible party may be held liable. However, liability for damages to natural resources is limited to $50 million.

No Minimum Quantity Required

Whether or not Superfund Section 101(14) requires a minimum quantity of a substance to be present for it to be considered hazardous is not clearly stated. Courts have generally ruled that in the absence of specific legislation to the contrary, no minimum quantity of a substance is necessary for it to be hazardous. The industry complaint is that the rules are ill defined and require monitoring of many harmless materials at substantial additional cost.

Responsible Parties

There are four categories of persons or companies specifically liable for cleanup costs under Superfund Section 107(a) as follows:

1. Prior owner or operator of the facility.
2. Party who arranged for disposal or treatment of the hazardous material.
3. Party who transported the hazardous substance to the facility.
4. Current owner or operator of the facility.

The burden is heavy on the current owner or operator as the party most visible. However, there is no requirement that the current owner have any part in creating the hazard to be liable, only that the party be owner or operator of the designated hazardous site.

Lender Liability

CERCLA allows a lender some protection from liability under the **secured creditor exemption.** The intent is to permit lenders to make mortgage loans without being included as a responsible party should toxic waste cleanup become a problem. However, a few subsequent court rulings placed cleanup liability on lenders if they have the "capacity to influence" a borrower's business.[1] The result has been much greater interest and diligence on the part of lenders making commercial loans to require an environmental assessment as part of a loan application.

Defenses to Cost Recovery Actions

There are very few statutory defenses that might be raised in a Superfund cost recovery action. Those available include a challenge to the quality of government evidence, a claim that liability is for events occurring prior to effective date of the law, or that the statute of limitations applies. The act itself provides some defenses, including such claims as an act of God, an act of war or that the damage was caused by a third party with whom the defendant had no contractual relationship.

Innocent Landowner Defense

Another possible defense is available under the act if certain steps are undertaken prior to acquisition of a property through what is called an **innocent landowner defense.** Such a defense may be sustained if the landowner makes an appropriate inquiry into the previous ownership and usage of the property before taking title. This constitutes an *environmental due diligence assessment*, also called a **Phase I assessment.** The purpose is to ascertain if any prior use would indicate the presence of environmental contamination or hazardous substances. If an adequate inquiry is made with proper records maintained, and nothing of a hazardous nature is found, the buyer may be classed as an innocent landowner. This provides the landowner with a valid defense against future cleanup liability should contamination occur later through no fault of the landowner.

If a Phase I assessment turns up indications of actual or potential contamination, a **Phase II assessment** will be required. Unlike the Phase I assessment, the Superfund Act does not set specific requirements for Phase II. The purpose is to target those areas believed to be contaminated and includes the collection and chemical analysis of soil samples, surface, and groundwater samples and other relevant investigations and analyses. Sampling must be undertaken pursuant to EPA or state regulatory procedures, or both.

A **Phase III assessment** essentially calls for a definition of the extent of contamination, determining the remedial action necessary, then implementing the most appropriate cleanup procedures.

Environmental Assessment Standards

One problem with site assessments as a defense against future liability is that no federal standards are provided for determining what comprises contamination. Further, there are as yet no government requirements as to what

[1]*Chemical Manufacturers Association v. Environmental Protection Agency,* No. 92-1314.

authority might be qualified to make such an assessment. To help resolve these problems, a number of trade associations and other organizations have worked with the EPA Enforcement Council to develop better standards for enforcement actions. There is a need to protect property and also to clarify more precisely what comprises a contributing cause that creates liability. Several major universities have developed degree programs to provide qualified professionals who will be able to make more accurate environmental assessments.

American Society for Testing of Materials' Standards

Another major step toward creating standards for an environmental assessment has resulted from an extended study made by the prestigious **American Society for Testing of Materials (ASTM).** On March 16, 1993, ASTM released voluntary standards of practice for performing environmental assessments on commercial properties. The purpose of the standards is to better measure what is meant by an "appropriate inquiry" that would satisfy CERCLA's requirements to support an innocent landowner's defense. The standards give definition to the CERCLA phrase "good commercial or customary practice." For instance, how can it be proven at the time of acquisition that the landowner did not know or have reason to know of any contamination? CERCLA's broad terminology states that in order to pass the "reason to know" test, the landowner must have exercised "all appropriate inquiry into the prior history and uses of the property consistent with good commercial or customary practice in an effort to minimize liability."

ASTM Methods

ASTM has developed two alternative methods that set standards for an "appropriate inquiry." These are: (1) a transaction screen process and (2) a Phase I environmental site assessment.

The **transaction screen** comprises a series of 25 questions that examine a property's history. It is recommended that the preparer of the screen be an environmental professional, but this is not required. The screen requires answers from owners, occupants, and the preparer of the report and may be sufficient for small commercial transactions. It is not an assured defense under the "innocent landowner" standards but is a valid step in the right direction.

The much more extensive ASTM-named Phase I assessment must be prepared by a professional, defined as "a person possessing sufficient training and experience necessary to conducting activities in accordance with (the standard)." The report format contains seven sections covering past and current use of the property, studies of the surrounding properties, identification of information sources, and conclusions as to whether or not further inquiry is indicated.

One of the sections addresses "nonscope considerations." Since the purpose of a Phase I assessment is to limit potential CERCLA liability, the ASTM report is limited to only those substances that are included in CERCLA's definition of hazardous materials. ASTM suggests that further assessments might be needed on such problems as asbestos-containing materials, radon gas, lead-based paint, wetlands, and possibly others.

Environmental Consultants

A number of property appraisers are entering the field of **environmental consulting.** Their background in examining real property is helpful in making specific environmental assessments. However, much more analysis is involved than assessing value, so the need for specialized training becomes obvious. Persons seeking an environmental assessment from acceptable professionals should base selection on a review of the consultant's education, experience, and reputation rather than on a state certification as none presently exist in this specialized area. If the purpose of an assessment is to support a loan application, the person selected should be acceptable to that lender.

Private Insurance for Superfund Liabilities

Obviously, the risk level of toxic contamination is difficult to measure. Nevertheless, a few insurance companies have reentered the field and offer two kinds of limited coverage: (1) pollution coverage and (2) banker's environmental risk.

Pollution Insurance

After suffering substantial losses from earlier policies that were interpreted by courts to include coverage for environmental liabilities even though not intended to do so, newer, more limited policies have become available. The policies offer pollution coverage targeting low-risk operations, such as owners of office buildings, warehouses, and shopping centers. An example of the cost for a property valued at $1 million would be an annual premium of $10,000 to $12,000 for a three-year policy providing $2 million in protection.

Banker's Environmental Risk Insurance

Bankers have difficulty determining the risk level of loans that could entail environmental hazards. Extensive research on the property seemed to be the best answer. Recently, another option has become available with insurance that protects lenders when a loan goes into default and contamination is found on the property. The insurance covers either the cost of cleaning up the property or it pays off the balance due on the loan. This helps avoid foreclosing on contaminated property and thereby becoming liable for cleanup costs.

While the practice is not yet widespread, a few lenders have recently begun to require environmental insurance as a condition for commercial loan qualification.

Brownfields Program

In many areas of the country, land that has been contaminated lays untouched by any further development. Several approaches have been made to return this contaminated land to a useful purpose. Under a voluntary program in Texas, property owners can document their cleanup activities and, after inspection by state authorities, obtain a certificate that is placed on the property deed releasing future owners and lenders of liability. While it does not release the present owner from liability, it makes a sale possible by eliminating future liability to the purchaser.

The EPA initiated a **brownfields program** to remove about 25,000 sites from the federal Superfund program. This reduction in liability has brought dormant sites back to useful life, improving former eyesores and making good use of well-located tracts. In September 1996, Congress passed legislation that reformed the Superfund Act. Under the revised law, lenders can conduct preloan activities, loan servicing activities, workout, reorganization, and foreclosure without becoming liable for the cost of cleanup. This is true provided the lender does not participate in management activities prior to foreclosure.

The 1997 federal tax package included some relief for urban environmental cleanups in empowerment zones. Taxpayers are allowed to deduct the costs of cleaning up these brownfields. After cleanup, the sites may be used for new businesses that create jobs.

INDOOR AIR POLLUTION

Recent studies by the Environmental Protection Agency have indicated that indoor air can be several times more polluted than outdoor air. EPA has estimated that half of all illnesses are directly attributable to seven types of indoor air pollution:

1. Formaldehyde gas
2. Asbestos as used in building materials
3. Radon gas
4. Tobacco smoke
5. Biological pollutants such as bacteria, viruses, and fungi
6. Volatile organic compounds found in cleaning and repair work
7. Combustion byproducts from wood, coal, or oil

Of the seven types of indoor pollution, the first three—formaldehyde gas, asbestos, and radon gas—are among the most dangerous and difficult to assess. Further discussion will be limited to these three.

Formaldehyde Gas

Formaldehyde gas is colorless, toxic, and water-soluble with a strong, pungent, picklelike smell. It can be emitted by a number of household materials such as urea-formaldehyde foam insulation, formaldehyde-based adhesives used in pressed wood, particle board, plywood, shelves, cabinets, and office furniture. It can also be found in some draperies and carpeting. The gas can cause health problems ranging from minor eye, nose, and throat irritation to such serious effects as nasal cancer.

Urea-formaldehyde foam was a popular insulating material in the late 1970s and early 1980s. It was used as a foam (about the consistency of shaving cream) and pumped through a hose into a wall cavity where it hardened as insulation. By 1982 the health hazard was recognized and this kind of insulation is no longer in general usage. While the greatest danger of gas escaping is when the material is first drying, gas can also be released later if the material is dampened or exposed to high temperatures.

Such problems with insulation are not normally found in the average building, but urea-formaldehyde based adhesives can be found in wood paneling and other construction materials. It poses greater problems in manufactured or mobile homes, very high energy-efficient houses, tightly constructed newer office buildings, and even in schools. Only manufactured homes are required to carry warning labels if they contain products made with formaldehyde and buyers must sign statements acknowledging the presence of any such material. Other buildings have no such requirements.

Testing for formaldehyde may be done by a professional or by a commercial testing device. To remedy this type of problem, the gas-emitting material can be removed. A lower cost procedure is to increase ventilation or lower the temperature and humidity within the building. A common remedy for adhesive-induced gas is to seal particle board and other wood products with paints or veneers.

Asbestos as Used in Building Materials

Asbestos consists of naturally occurring mineral fibers found in rocks. For many years it has been added to such manufactured products as patching compounds, siding, roofing shingles, and vinyl floors. Asbestos has many advantages as a building material because it strengthens material, provides thermal and accoustical insulation, and fireproofs material. Its only real disadvantage is that it can kill you!

Asbestos can cause asbestosis, a noncancerous disease that scars the lung tissues. It can also cause several different kinds of cancer in the lungs, esophagus, stomach, and intestines. Yet it is a difficult type of pollution to accurately assess. It can produce a health hazard in schools, office buildings, and dwelling units.

Nevertheless, recent studies indicate that the real danger lies in so-called "loose" asbestos rather than that occurring in "hard" form. Asbestos becomes dangerous only when it breaks down and its fibers are released into the air to be inhaled. There have been no conclusive studies, to date, that a health hazard is caused from ingesting food or water containing asbestos or that fibers can penetrate the skin. Testing for its presence should be done by an EPA-certified asbestos inspector when possible.

Many building owners have had the asbestos removed to eliminate the hazards. However, this is costly and not always necessary. In July 1990, EPA released a document entitled *Managing Asbestos in Place: A Building Owner's Guide to Operations and Maintenance Programs.* The objective is to reinforce EPA's position that the most prudent option is in-place management rather than removal. EPA defines a management program as a plan of training, cleaning, work practices, air monitoring, and maintenance of asbestos-containing materials in good condition. Maintenance, custodial, and administrative staff must be trained in the problem and tenants must be informed of the presence of asbestos in the building.

Discovery of asbestos in a building can be a nightmare to its owner. Aside from the problems associated with federal and state laws regarding the handling of asbestos-containing materials, another problem lies in the economic results of its presence. If it is found in a building, one result can be the potential of health-related lawsuits and another is a substantial loss in value of the contaminated building. This is true of both commercial and residential buildings.

The renovation and the demolition of an asbestos-bearing facility falls under the National Emission Standards for Hazardous Air Pollution (NESHAP) administered by the EPA and possibly a state agency. NESHAP requires that certain notices be filed with the EPA *prior* to work on a facility containing friable (loose) asbestos. *Friable asbestos* is defined as any material containing more than 1 percent asbestos by weight that hand pressure can crumble, pulverize, or reduce to powder when dry. The threshold level for reporting to the EPA is when at least 260 feet of friable asbestos-containing material is found on pipes or at least 160 square feet of asbestos-containing materials is being stripped or removed.

Radon Gas

In 1989, the then head of EPA, William Reilly, pronounced radon "the second leading cause of cancer in this country." EPA estimates that radon causes as many as 20,000 deaths each year.

Radon is an invisible radioactive gas. You cannot smell it, feel it, or see it. Outside it is virtually harmless as it is dissipated. It only becomes a big problem inside a building when it can accumulate into dangerous concentrations. Radon comes from decaying uranium. Uranium can be found in many places—in the earth's soil, black shale, phosphatic rocks, and even granite. It can be found in areas that have been contaminated with industrial wastes such as byproducts of uranium or phosphate mining.

The danger arises when such materials are located directly underneath an inhabited building and the gas seeps inside. Entry into a building can be through cracks in the slab or openings found around pipes. The gas can also enter through well water. In buildings that lack adequate ventilation, such as a basement area, the gas can become concentrated and dangerous.

Testing for radon can be managed with an activated charcoal canister available at hardware stores or home centers. After four to seven days in a suspected location, the canister should be sent to a laboratory for testing. Remedies include sealing cracks and other openings. Ventilation devices alone may be sufficient to reduce radon concentrations to a minimal level.

LEAD POISONING

Lead is a heavy, relatively soft, malleable, bluish-gray metal. It cannot be broken down or destroyed. Because of the ease with which it can be shaped, it has been used for centuries in the form of pipe and other building materials. More recently it has been alloyed for use as solder that can secure pipe joints and as a component of paint. Paint containing high levels of lead was found to be more durable and looked fresher for a greater length of time.

Although lead has some advantages as a building material, its adverse effects for humans have been known as far back as early Greek and Roman civilizations. Lead has no beneficial function in the human body; its ingestion can only do harm. The damage from **lead poisoning** is most threatening to children in their formative years. Its symptoms are wide ranging and can easily go undiagnosed and even unnoticed. Lead was reported as a cause of encephalopathy (inflammation of the brain) in a number of children in the United States in 1917. By 1930, more data became available on lead poisoning in children.

Lead can be more damaging to children than adults because of their higher rates of respiration and metabolism. Their bodies handle lead differently as they are not as efficient at keeping lead in the bones which leaves a higher percentage circulating in the blood stream. Lead can be most damaging to the brain. Testing in the first and second grades found that children with the lowest IQs, academic achievement, language skills, and attention spans had the highest levels of lead.

In 1970, Congress passed the Clean Air Act which led to the creation of the Environmental Protection Agency (EPA). In 1971, Congress passed the Lead-Based Paint Poisoning Prevention Act. In 1975, under Court order, EPA evaluated atmospheric lead as a "criteria pollutant" as it was referred to in the Clean Air Act. That led to an examination of the lead problem everywhere in the environment.

Sources of Lead Poisoning

There are two ways that lead can be absorbed into the body: inhalation and ingestion.

Inhalation. Airborne lead is caused by emissions from certain industrial plants, internal combustion engines (primarily cars still using gasoline containing lead), and dust found in the household. Dust can derive from lead-based paint and other lead-containing items. Lead-containing dust can also be transported on clothing from the workplace. On the brighter side, the EPA reported in 1995 that about 88 percent of lead had been removed from the air because of various restrictive rules.

Ingestion. Household dust and the soil around a house can contain lead that may be ingested. Water passing through lead or copper pipes with soldered joints can contain lead. Lead-based paint flakes can be attractive to children. Other lead-containing nonfood items such as toys, cosmetics, and jewelry may end up in children's mouths as can hands covered with dirt.

Testing for Lead

Lead poisoning is caused by high levels of lead in the blood. Since the greatest risk is with children seven and under, it is logical to test them first. Since there is no known "safe level," any level of lead in the blood is positive. If positive, it means that lead is being released somewhere in the daily environment of that child and further testing is necessary.

How Lead Affects Property Value

The presence of lead on a property in any form can reduce its value. Generally, lead problems are curable and the cost of cleaning up the property can be determined. This contaminant is not included in definitions of toxic waste substances and cleanup is not yet mandatory. However, if found, prompt remedial action minimizes future problems. The necessary constraints on further use of lead-based materials falls under the Clean Air Act as administered by EPA.

Lead-Based Paint Rule

On March 6, 1996, HUD and the EPA issued a joint final rule that requires sellers and renters of houses *built before 1978* to disclose to potential buyers or renters the presence of lead-based paint hazards. The disclosure statement must be attached as a separate item to all sales and lease contracts on pre-1978 properties. A federal lead-hazard pamphlet on how to protect families must be distributed to potential buyers and renters. Buyers must be allowed an optional 10-day period before the contract is closed to conduct a lead-based paint inspection or risk assessment at their own expense. While real estate agents are not responsible for ensuring that people read or understand the brochure, they are responsible for compliance.

The rule does not require any lead paint testing, removal, or abatement. Nor does it invalidate leasing or sales contracts. Not covered under this rule is housing built after 1977 and zero-bedroom units such as efficiencies, lofts, and dormitories. Also not covered are leases for less than 100 days, housing for the elderly or handicapped (unless children live there), and foreclosure sales.

Handling Lead When Found

Following is information on ways to handle lead found in paint and in water.

Lead in Paint. Lead-based paint was used until 1978 when its disadvantages became better known. Such paint is still not considered an immediate hazard if it is smooth and intact. Only damaged surfaces are considered dangerous, inside or outside, where the paint is blistering, peeling, scaling, or powdering. If any lead-containing paint is suspected, it should be tested.

To limit further problems, lead-based paint may be removed with paint remover, a gas torch, sanding, or scraping. Another option is to remove the offending windows or doors and replace them with new ones. A third remedial method is to encapsulate the offending area. Plywood paneling, wallboard, or sheetrock can cover walls, floors, or ceilings as may be necessary.

Lead in Water. Because there are no safe levels of lead, all drinking water should be tested. This is especially important if the property has lead pipes (most likely if the house was built before 1930). Lead-content solder was banned in 1986, but many houses built prior to that time have copper pipes with soldered connections. Local water utility companies or health departments may offer water testing for free or at a nominal charge. Also, the EPA has a list of approved testing labs.

One way to remedy possibly contaminated water is to install a filter system. Filters normally also reduce the acid level of water, making it less corrosive. Also, a "point of use" treatment device may be installed. Distillation units are available commercially but can be a bit costly and must be maintained.

WETLANDS PROTECTION

In years past, swampy, marshy, or water-saturated soils were considered a source of sickness—a breeding place for disease-bearing mosquitoes. Farmers were encouraged to drain or fill such areas. In addition, large areas of wetlands were eliminated for federal flood control projects, canal building, and mosquito control projects. Too late in many cases, scientists learned that wetlands can help control flooding, filter out pollution, clean drinking water, and provide habitat for fish and other wildlife. Environmentalists were quick to expand the new intelligence with rather far-reaching and perhaps overextended results.

The law covering wetlands stems from the 1987 Clean Water Act which introduced a permit system to control the discharge of any pollutant into waters of the United States. This law does not define "waters of the United States." It is the Code of Federal Regulations (Section 328.3) that defines the term as including wetlands and adjacent wetlands. Both the Environmental Protection Agency (EPA) and the Corps of Engineers (Corps) share responsibility for administering the Clean Water Act and the issuance of permits. This authority has been extended to include the issuance of permits that allow a landowner to disturb a wetland.

Wetlands is not a scientific term and lacks good definition. A wetland may be natural or man-made. Decorative lakes or water hazards on golf courses, for example, may become protected wetlands. If an area containing a wetland is disturbed before discovering that it is so defined, the result can be enforcement action including the assessment of administrative, civil, and/or criminal penalties.

To help guide landowners and others, in 1987 the EPA and the Corps combined to produce the *Federal Wetlands Determination Manual* which explains the criteria for judging what comprises one. Essentially, three criteria are described for making this determination:

1. The area must be inundated by surface water, groundwater, or rainwater.
2. The land must contain a predominance of vegetation typically adapted for life in water-saturated soils.
3. The soil must be under water long enough during the growing season to develop anaerobic conditions (meaning absence of oxygen). This usually occurs when the soil is saturated for a week or longer.

It is not clear yet whether just one, or all, of the criteria must be in place to declare an area as a wetland and subject to a permit before it can be disturbed. No distinction is made between natural and man-made wetlands. Thus, a wet area in a corn field created by a farmer's leaky irrigation ditch would be classified in the same way as an ancient cypress swamp in the Florida Everglades.

The only way to be certain whether or not an area falls under the wetlands definition is to ask the Corps to make an inspection and issue its own determination. Each of the 26 Corps District Offices throughout the country is authorized to make these determinations which are final unless landowners bring suit in federal court to overturn them. There is no right of administrative appeal.

Rule Favoring Small Landowner

In October 1995, a change in the rules (not in the legislation) softened the impact on small landowners and vacation property investors. The rule applies only to residential property. If a small tract contains one-half acre or less of wetlands area, the landowner may use an expedited process. Instead of going through the process of filing an individual permit to disturb the wetland area, the landowner may file a "Nationwide Permit 29" with the nearest Corps of Engineers office. Approval can usually be granted within 15 days, or if no word is heard, approval is automatic in 30 days.

Effect of Wetlands on Financing

Concern over additional risk resulting from wetlands problems is limited to land development loans. Even then, a lender would be primarily interested in the developer's awareness of the need to comply with the Clean Water Act. A violation could be damaging to completion of the development and jeopardize loan repayment if the developer suffers substantial financial penalties.

In parts of the country, entrepreneurs have created wetlands areas, or banks, of 500 acres or more that are offered to developers as may be needed as an alternative to wetlands found on property to be developed. The developer may buy acreage in the newly developed wetland area—usually on a ratio of 1 1/2 acres of new wetland for every acre of wetland in the to-be developed area. The developer can offer the newly developed wetlands acreage to the Corps as a substitute for what is to be developed. The method is known as *mitigation banking* and is gaining recognition as it offers an opportunity for commercial real estate developers to go forward with projects that involve disturbing a wetland area.

ENDANGERED SPECIES ACT

Landowners have recently become more aware that the **Endangered Species Act** of 1973 can have a profound impact on the value of their land. One reason for the delay in recognizing its importance is that, since the initial act was passed, it has been substantially expanded by bureaucratic regulations. The 1973 act was limited to the protection of endangered species *on federal land* and passed Congress almost unopposed. Since then, regulators have focused on controlling land usage, including private land, if it might contain an endangered species' habitat almost without regard to the actual presence of such species.

The Endangered Species Act mandates that a protected species be determined by the "best scientific and commercial data available." Nevertheless, no standards were set and the responsible agencies make their own determinations without peer review. The agencies specifically require that economic consequences *not* be a consideration in making the determination. The result has been a tremendous expansion of protected species which by implication can include up to 16,000, including fungi, algae, flat worms, round worms, bacteria, and sponges.

Taking Is Prohibited

The act prohibits the "taking" of endangered species as listed by the federal government. Taking means the killing of any listed plant, animal, fish, or insect. Also, U.S. Fish and Wildlife Service regulations prohibit any harm or harassment of an endangered species, including modification, damaging, or destroying habitat even though the species may not be present.

Challenge to Development

The Endangered Species Act authorizes citizen suits to enjoin a violation of the act or to compel the Secretary of Interior to enforce its provisions. Anyone can sue the landowner for violations of this act. It also allows recovery of awards and attorneys' fees in connection with private actions. The effect, of course, has been a substantial increase in the risk for any new development with an added increase in cost that must eventually be borne by the consumer.

Endangered Species Act Net Effect on Loans

Similar to the question of wetlands, the risk falls primarily on a land development but it can also affect rehabilitation and expansion. If a building permit is needed, the door may be opened to activists' challenges. There is a difference between wetland problems and endangered species questions in that a wetland is something visible while an endangered species habitat can be very difficult to discover.

The risk of not being able to complete a land development or rehabilitation on schedule and within budget is substantially increased by the open door to private challenges permitted under this act. There are a growing number of areas in the country today that have been closed to development simply from fear of a shutdown even after a project is underway. Land development loans in these areas are close to nonexistent.

Recent Rulings Mitigating the Act

If an endangered species or its habitat is found on private land, it has been customary for the U.S. Fish and Wildlife Service to prohibit any further use of the land that might disturb the habitat. Because of this practice, it is believed that some landowners are encouraged to "shoot, shovel, and shut up." Recently, the Department of the Interior has offered a "safe harbor" procedure to reduce this possibility. For example, golf course developers in the Carolinas agreed to provide a habitat for the red-cockaded woodpecker, which likes the openness of a golf course, as long as the government promised to do nothing legally to impair the future use of their land. In Texas, a similar deal was arranged with Frank Yturria near Brownsville to encourage the return of the aplomado falcon on his 13,000-acre spread. Such safe harbor deals and a similar law-softening policy called "no surprises," have been encouraged. Interior Secretary Bruce Babbitt reported that by 1997 about 200 such deals would have been made with private landowners controlling more than 5 million acres.

In a 1997 case, the U.S. Supreme Court gave those hurt by an action to protect an endangered species the right to sue over how the federal law is enforced. In this case, the Supreme Court reversed a lower court ruling in an Oregon suit by ranchers and irrigation districts which claimed harm as a result of efforts to protect an endangered species. Because of a drought in 1992, the government had cut off irrigation water to farms and ranches near Oregon's Lost River to preserve two species of fish. Lower courts had ruled that those claiming economic harm had no legal standing to sue over how the federal law was enforced. Justice Antonin Scalia, in the Supreme Court opinion, said the lower courts were wrong and revived the lawsuit.

The underlying legal question resulting from this act and other such laws is: Can prohibitions of land usage entitle the landowner to undertake an inverse condemnation suit against the government entities involved? The 5th Amendment to the U.S. Constitution clearly states "nor shall private property be taken for public use without just compensation." Earlier opinion interpreted this clause as meaning compensation is due only when title to private property is taken under the right of eminent domain. The difficult-to-define gray area that has since arisen concerns partial taking that leaves the landowner with full title but only limited rights to usage of the property. Only recently have the courts begun to recognize that private property rights can be taken through regulatory action and that, while the right to regulate is not challenged, the need to compensate landowners in certain cases may be necessary.

UNDERGROUND STORAGE TANKS

For many years, hundreds of thousands of underground tanks have stored petroleum products or other hazardous materials and many have leaked. Using the "out of sight, out of mind" theory, little attention was given to possible contamination—until recently. Damage to the land became obvious with a focal point on petroleum product storage, particularly with service stations.

A later amendment to the Resources Conservation and Recovery Act of 1976 required the Environmental Protection Agency to develop a comprehensive program to prevent, detect, and correct releases from **underground storage tanks (USTs).** The EPA defined a UST as any tank that has 10 percent or more of its volume below ground and contains either petroleum or hazardous substances.

The EPA estimates that 2 million USTs are covered by the regulations and 95 percent are used to store petroleum products. There are some exceptions from the definition including farm and residential tanks of 1,100 gallons or less storing fuel for noncommercial purposes, septic tanks, wastewater collection systems, and storage tanks located in an enclosed underground area (basement). Even though excluded by EPA, state or local laws may cover these types of tanks.

EPA regulations require UST owners to provide certain safety precautions, including corrosion protection and leak detection by monthly monitoring or inventory control. Owners must also provide tank tightness testing plus spill and overflow devices. Compliance was phased in over five years with USTs installed after December 1988, having all requirements in place upon installation. Qualified contractors must install new tanks according to code and tank owners must provide EPA with certification of proper installation. The same is true for tank removal. Since October 1990, owners and operators of USTs must demonstrate responsibility for corrective actions and be able to compensate for injury or property damage from $500,000 to $4 million, depending on the number of tanks owned.

Discovery of an underground tank by a landowner or a prospective buyer can affect the value of that property. The first task is to find what it contains and what condition it is in. Some abandoned tanks have been filled with sand, gravel, or other inert material. If the tank contains a liquid, it is necessary to find out what it is so that it can be properly disposed of and to determine whether or not the tank has leaked or is leaking. A professional may be needed to perform a tank tightness test. If a hazardous substance is involved, a report to the EPA may be necessary.

UST Effect on Loans

Discovery of an underground tank always raises a warning flag until it is known what it contains and what condition it is in. Insofar as lenders are concerned, the presence of underground tanks must be reported in an environmental site assessment which would become a loan application requirement. The assessment examines the possible presence of contamination surrounding the tank or tanks. If found, the assessment would call for further testing of the soil around and below the tanks.

ELECTROMAGNETIC FORCES

Most environmental concerns are real and should always be considered when dealing with land and what may be built upon it. Yet there is no doubt that some people profit from environmental scares. Whether or not electromagnetic force is mostly a scare tactic or a real concern is not clear. Even so, enough reputable people are reporting that it is a carcinogen that it is necessary for anyone involved with real estate to know what it is.

Electromagnetic forces (EMF) are silent and invisible. They exist anywhere electrons zip through transmission lines or the innards of appliances or even electric blankets. So they are nearly impossible to avoid. Thus far, there has been no clear relationship between the strength of an electromagnetic field and the incidence of cancer, particularly leukemia. In November 1996, the National Research Council, after three years of examining more than 500 studies, stated: "The current body of evidence does not show that exposure to these fields presents a human-health hazard."

When examining electromagnetic fields, it is important to know that its strength is sharply reduced by moving a short distance away from the source. For instance, 12 inches away from a can opener or hair dryer, rather than 6 inches, reduces the field strength by 75 percent.

Electromagnetic fields are measured in gausses, which is the CGS unit of magnetic induction. CGS means centimeter-gram-second: centimeter is a unit of length, gram a unit of weight, and second a unit of time. For our purposes, magnetic fields are measured in milligaus. Following are examples of several different magnetic fields in milligaus at one foot from the source:

Ceiling fan	3
Dishwasher	10
Electric clothes dryer	2
Power saw	40
Washing machine	7

The federal government has researched problems with EMF but, so far, has issued no rules or regulations. Some states have released rules, primarily for power line construction and improvements. For real estate agents, it is a subject that must be given serious consideration. If EMF testing is required by a potential buyer, this can be done by going room-to-room and even to appliances with a small gauss meter.

Energy-Efficient Buildings

The secondary market recognizes the value of energy-efficient properties by offering easier loan qualification if such a building is the collateral. For residential properties meeting state code energy efficiency requirements, Freddie Mac allows 2 to 4 percent higher qualification guidelines, while Fannie Mae and FHA allow 2 percent stretches for their qualifying ratios (applies to fixed payment or "back-end" ratio). The premise is that these properties will have lower utility expenses, which allows homeowners more income to make mortgage and tax payments.

What is an energy-efficient building? The definition derives from the Comprehensive National Energy Policy Act which became law in October 1992. It is a sweeping piece of legislation that, among other things, mandates energy-efficiency standards for residential, commercial, and industrial buildings. It is part of an accelerating trend of environmentalism that has spawned a growing body of energy conservation programs.

The legislation requires states to establish minimum commercial building energy codes and consider minimum residential codes based on voluntary standards. There is a tie between the availability of federal mortgage assistance for new residential buildings and compliance with Model Energy Code requirements.

Currently, the most stringent energy-efficiency code is the Council of American Building Officials (CABO), Leesburg, Virginia, Model Energy Code 1992. In addition to establishing performance standards for heating, cooling, and ventilation components, the Model Energy Code defines performance standards for the building "envelope"—the barrier between the inside and outside of the building.

CONCLUSIONS

Environmental problems escaped the nation's attention for so many years, that it will take time to define the true extent of contamination. The rush to prevent further damage and begin restoration has resulted in steps taken that have not always been effective. However, various environmental laws are undergoing review and further improvements can be expected. An assortment of regulatory agencies has been seeking cooperative procedures to reduce the overlap of requirements. However, as yet there is no movement toward consolidation of agencies; rather, the trend appears to be creation of new oversight agencies charged with bringing greater uniformity when standards are in conflict.

The problems are new, they are serious, and landowners are in the forefront of managing their resolution.

Questions For Discussion

1. Define an *environmental site assessment.*
2. Discuss Fannie Mae/Freddie Mac environmental requirements as stated in their mortgage instruments.
3. Explain the innocent landowner defense as defined by CERCLA.
4. What is an ASTM transaction screen?
5. Discuss EPA's asbestos-managing plan for building owners.
6. Where is lead most likely to be found in a household?
7. Identify the criteria for determining existence of a wetlands.
8. What happens to land containing an endangered species habitat?
9. Discuss a landowner's rights in a regulatory taking of land.
10. Explain EPA regulations for installing or removing USTs.

Chapter 16

Settlement Procedures

....

KEY WORDS AND PHRASES

Settlement agent • *Escrow closing* • *Real Estate Settlement Procedures Act (RESPA)* • *Loan status report* • *Preliminary title report* • *HUD guidebook: Buying Your Home* • *Good faith estimate* • *Designated service providers* • *Kickbacks* • *Truth-in-Lending Act* • *Finance charge* • *Annual percentage rate* • *HUD-1 settlement statement* • *Prepaid items* • *Reserves* • *Title insurance* • *Recording fees* • *Closing instructions* • *Disbursement procedures*

....

INTRODUCTION

Since property laws involving ownership and conveyance of land are essentially determined by each state, differences are reflected in the methods used to close, or settle, real estate transactions. Customs and practices have developed in every region of the country that best suit its unique business and legal requirements. The person or company selected to bring together the instruments of conveyance, mortgages, promissory notes, and, of course, the monetary considerations to be exchanged between the buyer and seller of real estate is most generally known as the **settlement agent.** The agent can be a lender, a real estate broker, a title company, an attorney, or a company specializing in these procedures, called an *escrow company*. In most parts of the country, the settlement agent arranges for the principals involved in the transaction to meet at a location where all the documents needed to transfer title and to secure and fund a loan can be reviewed and executed. At the conclusion of this process, if all documents are in order, the instruments and the money are then distributed to the various parties entitled to receive them.

Another procedure, called **escrow closing,** is commonly used in some states. In this procedure, however, the parties involved do not meet around a table to sign instruments or exchange any cash or documents. Rather, at the time of entering a contract of sale, the parties sign an escrow agreement. The agreement requires the deposit of certain documents and funds with the escrow agent within an agreed time. The agent is responsible for meeting the requirements of the escrow agreement, which usually include the adjustment of taxes, insurance, and rentals, if any, between the buyer and seller. The agreement also includes the payoff of any existing loan if required, arrangements for hazard insurance coverage, the computing of interest, and any other requirements for a new loan. If all papers and monies are deposited within the agreed time limit, the escrow is considered closed. The appropriate documents are then recorded and delivered to the proper parties along with the money that each is entitled to receive.

It was this area of diverse procedures that Congress focused on in 1974 and began to regulate. The purpose of the proposed legislation, by its own findings, was to protect consumers from "unnecessarily high settlement charges caused by certain abusive practices that have developed in some areas of the country." The result of congressional efforts was enactment of the **Real Estate Settlement Procedures Act (RESPA).** A subsequent amendment in 1976 clarified some of the problems that developed from the initial act. Implementation was assigned to HUD which makes periodic changes in the rules to accommodate new requirements. RESPA does not change any local practices and sets no prices for settlement services. Mostly, it is directed toward providing better information on the settlement process so that a home buyer can make informed decisions.

PRELIMINARY INFORMATION

Two pieces of information are closely associated with the settlement of a real estate transaction: an existing loan status report and a preliminary title report. They are discussed separately because of their special usefulness in any property disposition. Many good real estate brokers arrange for both pieces of information at the time a property is listed for sale. In this way, if there are problems with either an existing loan or legal title to the property, they are discovered early on, allowing more time for resolution before the seller is faced with an impending closing date. Also, it is very important that the seller or agent have accurate information on these two subjects since they are of critical interest to any prospective buyer.

Loan Status Report

Several different names are used within the industry to describe the information contained in an existing mortgage **loan status report.** Some call it a *mortgagor's information letter,* some a *mortgagee's report.* Further confusion is added to the nomenclature because in some areas of the country a *mortgagee's information letter* means a preliminary title report on the land. What is referred to here is a report on the current status of an existing loan prepared by the mortgagee for the mortgagor. It is a statement, usually in letter form, giving the remaining balance due on the loan, the monthly payments required, the reserve held in the escrow account, and the requirements and cost of a loan payoff.

A request for this information must come from the mortgagor, although brokers often use form letters for the request that require only the mortgagor's signature. While this information is very helpful in providing accurate financial information, it is not normally used by the settlement agent in closing a real estate transaction. The agent must call for a current report immediately prior to closing so it reflects the loan status as of the date of settlement.

Preliminary Title Report

When an earnest money contract has been signed, it is a good idea to "open title" with whatever title insurance company has been selected to handle the closing. Under RESPA rules, the seller may not require that title insurance be purchased from a particular title company as a condition of the sale. However, the mortgage lender has a right to accept or reject a proposed title company as the insurance coverage must be adequate for the lender. To facilitate selection, lending institutions are required to submit a statement to the borrower listing acceptable title companies and attorneys, along with the charges the borrower might expect. Also, any business relationship between the lender and a settlement service provider must be disclosed. In practice, the title company selected is normally located in the same county as the property being sold.

A **preliminary title report** is normally furnished by the title company to both the real estate agent and the mortgage company. The information contained is a confirmation of the correct legal description, and it also includes the names of the owners of the property as filed in the county records, any restrictions or liens on the property, any judgments against the owners of record, and a listing of any requirements the title company may have to perfect title before issuance of a title insurance policy. The report is for information only; it is not to be confused with a *title binder*, which legally obligates the title company for specific insurance. Title companies normally make no charge for the preliminary report as it is part of their service in anticipation of writing the title insurance policy at closing.

RESPA REQUIREMENTS

As amended in 1976, RESPA applies to residential mortgage loans only. Commercial loans are not included in the provisions of the act. Residential mortgage loans are defined as those used to finance the purchase of one- to four-family housing, a condominium, a cooperative apartment unit, a lot with a mobile home, or a lot on which a house is to be built or a mobile home located. RESPA requirements can be divided into two general categories: (1) information requirements and (2) prohibited practices.

Information Requirements

Lenders are required to furnish certain specific information to each loan applicant and additional information to the borrower prior to closing a loan, as follows.

Information Booklet

At the time of a loan application, or not more than three business days later, the lender must give the applicant a copy of the 1997 revised HUD-prepared booklet entitled *Buying Your Home.* The booklet is prepared by the Office of Consumer Affairs and Regulatory Functions of the U.S. Department of Housing and Urban Development. The information provided is discussed in two parts.

> **Part One** describes the settlement process and the nature of the charges that are incurred. Questions are suggested for the home buyer to ask that might help clarify charges and procedures. It also lists unfair and illegal practices and gives information on the rights and remedies available to home buyers should they encounter a wrongful practice.
>
> **Part Two** is an item-by-item explanation of settlement services and costs. Sample forms and worksheets are included to help guide the home buyer in making cost comparisons.

Good Faith Estimate

Within three business days of accepting a loan application, a lender is required to submit a **good faith estimate** of settlement costs to the loan applicant. Settlement charges are estimated for each item anticipated, except for prepaid hazard insurance and cash reserves deposited with the lender. (Reserves are subject to RESPA restrictions, which are detailed later.) The estimate may be stated in either a dollar amount or as a range for each charge, and the information must be furnished in a clear and concise manner (no special form is required). A typical good faith estimate is illustrated in Figure 16–1, which uses the terminology and account numbers from Section L of the mandatory Settlement Statement (see Figure 16–3 later).

Designated Service Providers

If a lender designates settlement service providers, who perform such tasks as legal services, title examination, title insurance, or the conduct of the settlement, the normal charges for these specific providers must be used in the good faith estimate. Further, when such a designation occurs, the lender must provide, as part of the good faith estimate, additional information giving the name, address, and telephone number of each designated provider. Any business relationship between the lender and an affiliated service provider must be fully disclosed, including an ownership interest of 1 percent or more. A rule issued by HUD in December 1992 prohibits any fee paid between affiliated companies for a referral, and there can be no condition requiring use of an affiliated company in consummation of the transaction.

Disclosure of Settlement Costs

As a part of the RESPA requirements, use of form HUD-1 (Figure 16–3), a uniform settlement statement, has been made mandatory for residential loan clos-

LENDER:

GOOD FAITH ESTIMATE   (RESPA)
OF SETTLEMENT CHARGES

Listed below is the Good Faith Estimate of Settlement Charges made pursuant to the requirements of the Real Estate Settlement Procedures Act (RESPA). These figures are only estimates and the actual charges due at settlement, may be different.

This form may not cover all items you will be required to pay in cash at settlement, for example, deposits in escrow for real estate taxes and insurance. You may wish to inquire as to the amounts of such other items. You may be required to pay other additional amounts at settlement.

THIS ESTIMATE IS NOT A LOAN COMMITMENT.

Property To Be Mortgaged _____

Sale Price: $ _____   Estimated Monthly Principal
                                        And Interest Payment: $ _____

Down Payment: $ _____   Estimated Monthly Tax
                                        And Insurance Reserve: $ _____

Loan Request: $ _____   Mortgage Life Insurance $ _____

Maximum Anticipated Interest Charge: _____ %   Private Mortgage Insurance: $ _____

Term of Loan: _____ years   Total Payment: $ _____

SETTLEMENT ITEM		Estimated Charge
801	Loan Origination Fee	$ _____
802	Loan Discount	$ _____
803	Appraisal Fee	$ _____
804	Credit Report	$ _____
805	Lender's Inspection Fee	$ _____
806	Mortgage Insurance Application Fee	$ _____
807	Assumption Fee	$ _____
901	Interest	$ _____
902	Mortgage Insurance Premium for _____ mo.	$ _____
903	Hazard Insurance Premium for _____ yrs.	$ _____
1001	Hazard Insurance for _____ mo.	$ _____
1002	Mortgage Insurance for _____ mo.	$ _____
1003/1005	Property Tax for _____ mo.	$ _____
1101	Settlement or Closing Fee	$ _____
1102	Abstract or Title Search	$ _____
1103	Title Examination	$ _____
1105	Document Preparation	$ _____
1106	Notary Fees	$ _____
1107	Attorney Fees	$ _____
1108	Title Insurance	$ _____
1201	Recording Fees	$ _____
1204	Tax Certificates	$ _____
1301	Survey	$ _____
1302	Pest Inspection	$ _____
Other	_____	$ _____
Other	_____	$ _____
	TOTAL ESTIMATED	$ _____

THIS SECTION TO BE COMPLETED BY LENDER ONLY IF A PARTICULAR PROVIDER OF SERVICE IS REQUIRED

Listed below are providers of service which we require you use. The charges or range indicated in the Good Faith Estimate above are based upon the corresponding charge of the below designated providers.

Designated Charge Item No. _____   Item No. _____
Service Provided _____   _____
Providers Name _____   _____
Address and _____   _____
Telephone Number_____   _____
We ☐ do, ☐ do not have a business relationship with the above named provider.   We ☐ do, ☐ do not have a business relationship with the above named provider.

NOTICE: The Federal Equal Credit Opportunity Act prohibits creditors from discriminating against credit applicants on the basis of race, color, religion, national origin, sex, marital status, age (provided that the applicant has the capacity to enter into a binding contract); because all or part of the applicant's income derives from any public assistance program; or because the applicant has in good faith exercised any right under the Consumer Credit Protection Act. The Federal agency that administers compliance with this law concerning this creditor is: _____

_____

_____

The undersigned applicant hereby acknowledges receipt of the above Good Faith Estimate and Equal Credit Opportunity Notice.

Signature _____ Date _____

FIGURE 16–1   Good Faith Estimate

ings. Account numbers and terminology are standardized on the form, and it is expected that settlement charges, however designated in various parts of the country, be fitted into this form. A copy of the completed form must be delivered by the settlement agent to both the buyer and the seller at or before the closing. Since some of the information needed to complete the form may not be available until the time of actual closing, the borrower may waive the right of delivery at closing. However, in such a case, the completed settlement statement must be mailed at the earliest practical date.

Borrower's Right to Disclosure of Costs Prior to Closing

A borrower has the right under RESPA to request an inspection of the settlement statement one business day prior to closing. The form is completed by the person who will conduct the settlement procedures. If a buyer wishes to make such a request, it would be wise to do so several days prior to the closing date. Preparation of the information takes time and a late request may simply force a delay in the closing date. The act does recognize that all costs may not be available one day prior to closing, but there is an obligation to show the borrower what is available, if requested.

Prohibited Practices

The vast majority of settlement procedures have always been conducted in an ethical manner by qualified professionals. However, abuses do occur occasionally, and it is one of the purposes of RESPA to expose unfair practices and make them illegal. Two such practices are described next.

Kickbacks

The law specifically prohibits any arrangement in which a fee is charged, or accepted, when no services have actually been performed—known as a **kickback.** The requirement does not prevent agents for the lender, attorneys, or others from actually performing a service in connection with the mortgage loan or settlement procedure. Nor does it prohibit cooperative brokerage arrangements such as are normally found in multiple listing services or referral arrangements between real estate agents and brokers. The target for the prohibition is the arrangement wherein one party returns a part of the fee to obtain business from the referring party. The abuse involved here, of course, is that such an arrangement can result in a higher settlement fee for the consumer/borrower with no increase in the services rendered.

Title Companies

A seller is not permitted to require the use of a specified title insurance company as a condition of sale. The buyer has the right to compare the services and charges of competing title companies. In many states the rates for title insurance come under the regulatory authority of the state and are thus uniform. In such cases, competition would be in the quality of services offered. Also, lenders retain the right to reject title companies that do not meet their minimum requirements of financial strength.

TRUTH-IN-LENDING ACT

The **Truth-in-Lending Act** is a federal law that became effective in July 1969 as a part of the Consumer Credit Protection Act. It is implemented by the Federal Reserve Board's Regulation Z. The purpose of the law is to require lenders to give meaningful information to borrowers on the cost of consumer credit, which includes credit extended in real estate transactions. The credit covered must involve a finance charge or be payable in more than four installments. Credit extended for business purposes, which includes dwelling units containing more than four family units, is not covered by this law. No maximum or minimum interest rates or charges for credit are set by the law, whose purpose is primarily one of disclosure.

While the act contains a limited right allowing the borrower to rescind or cancel the credit transaction and covers in considerable detail all types of advertising to promote the extension of consumer credit, the principal features discussed here are the disclosure of the finance charge and the annual percentage rate (APR).

Finance Charge

The **finance charge** is the total amount of all costs that the consumer must pay for obtaining credit. These costs include interest, the loan fee, a loan-finder's fee, time-price differentials, discount points, and the cost of credit life insurance if it is a condition for granting credit. In a real estate transaction, purchase costs that would be paid regardless of whether or not credit is extended are *not* included in the finance charge, provided these charges are reasonable, bona fide, and not included to circumvent the law. Among these excluded purchase costs are legal fees, taxes not included in the cash price, recording fees, title insurance premiums, and credit report charges. However, such charges must be itemized and disclosed to the customer. In the case of first mortgages intended to purchase residential dwellings, the total dollar finance charge need not be stated, although the annual percentage rate must be disclosed.

Annual Percentage Rate (APR)

The **annual percentage rate** as determined under Regulation Z is not an "interest rate." Interest is one of the costs included in the finance charge. The APR is the relationship of the total finance charge to the total amount to be financed and must be computed to the nearest one-quarter percent. Figure 16–2 illustrates a typical form used in a real estate transaction prepared in compliance with Regulation Z.

FEDERAL TRUTH IN LENDING DISCLOSURE STATEMENT

Creditor: Borrower(s):

Date:

Property Address:

ANNUAL PERCENTAGE RATE The cost of your credit as a yearly rate. **(APR)**	FINANCE CHARGE The dollar amount the credit will cost you.	AMOUNT FINANCED The amount of credit provided to you or on your behalf.	TOTAL OF PAYMENTS The amount you will have paid after you have made all payments as scheduled.
e %	$ e	$ e	$

Your payment schedule will be:

Number of Payments	Amount of Payments	When Payments are due

CHECK BOX IF APPLICABLE

☐ Your loan contains a variable-rate feature and variable-rate disclosures have been provided earlier.

☐ ESCROWS: Added to your monthly note payments will be required amounts which will be put into an escrow account to ensure the payment of real estate taxes, hazard insurance premiums, mortgage insurance premiums (if this insurance is required by the lender), etc. The amount of your escrow payments will be determined by the lender and will be enough to ensure that there will be sufficient funds in the account to pay the items when due. The lender will periodically review the account to determine changes that may be required in your escrow payments and you will be notified in writing of the changes and when they are effective. If deficiencies occur in your account, the lender will prorate the deficiencies among your regularly scheduled payments, however, you may clear the deficiency in one lump-sum payment. If surpluses occur in your escrow account, you can decide to have the surpluses credited to your account, or receive a refund. If you fail to pay the escrow payments when due, the lender can immediately require you to pay the entire loan balance and other amounts owed on the loan in full. If the total amounts owed on the loan are not paid, the lender could begin foreclosure proceedings which could ultimately cause a forced sale of your home.

SECURITY: You are giving a security interest in: ☐ The goods or property being purchased   ☐ Other collateral
☐ Real property you own located at

LATE CHARGE: If a payment is   days late, you will be charged   % of the payment.
           Minimum Late Charge $
PREPAYMENT: If you pay off early, you
    ☐ may   ☐ will not   have to pay a penalty.
    ☐ may   ☐ will not   be entitled to a refund of part of the finance charge.
    ☐ ASSUMPTION: Someone buying your property
    ☐ may, subject to conditions   ☐ cannot   assume the remainder of your loan on the original terms.

See your contract documents for any additional information about nonpayment, default, any required repayment in full before the scheduled date, and prepayment refunds and penalties.

e means an estimate

I/We the undersigned Borrower(s) acknowledge that I/we received a copy of this Disclosure Statement on _____

WITNESS	SIGNATURE
	SIGNATURE
	SIGNATURE
	SIGNATURE

CMCA, L.P. 78006 (9/88)

FIGURE 16–2   Federal Truth-in-Lending Statement

SETTLEMENT PRACTICES AND COSTS

As noted earlier in this chapter, settlement practices vary considerably in different sections of the country. There is no federal requirement to change any basic practices for residential loans except where it is necessary to add some disclosure procedures and to eliminate any prohibited practices. RESPA set limitations on the amount of reserve, or escrow, accounts that may be held by lenders, and there is one mandatory form to be used in the settlement of residential loans.

The mandatory uniform settlement statement form is illustrated in Figure 16–3 and will be used as the basis for the following discussion of the various services involved with a loan closing. While the emphasis is on residential loan practices, the procedures used in closing commercial loans involve most of the same services.

Settlement Statement

The design of the **HUD-1 settlement statement** places all the costs chargeable to the buyer, or the seller, on the first page, and a detail of these costs on the second page. A cursory examination of the statement shows that the first section, A through I, contains information concerning the loan and the parties involved. Section J lists the amounts due from, or paid by, the borrower, and Section K details the same for the seller. The bottom line in each column indicates the cash due by the borrower-buyer on the left-hand side and that due by the seller on the right-hand side. Whatever money must change hands is clearly the result of the two figures. Section L on the second page of the form lists various settlement services that can be involved in a closing with some blank lines for any separate entries not otherwise clearly identified.

This particular form must be completed for the settlement meeting by the person conducting the settlement procedures. A copy of the completed form is either given to both the buyer and seller at the meeting or mailed as soon as practical after the meeting. If there is no actual meeting of the parties involved for settlement, the agent must still mail the completed forms after the closing has been finalized. This is the same form that a borrower has the right to inspect one business day prior to closing. It is not required that all information be filled in one day prior to closing, but the settlement agent must disclose whatever is available if requested to do so by the borrower.

A settlement costs worksheet is also available and is intended for use by the prospective borrower as a handy guide for making comparisons of the charges quoted by the various service providers.

Sales/Broker's Commission (Item 700)

The sales commission is usually paid by the seller and is listed on the settlement in the total dollar amount, then divided between participating brokers as the sales agreement may provide. The amount is negotiable and may be a flat fee for the sale or a percentage of the sales amount.

A.

CHICAGO TITLE INSURANCE COMPANY

SETTLEMENT STATEMENT
U.S. DEPARTMENT OF HOUSING AND URBAN DEVELOPMENT

B. TYPE OF LOAN		
1. ☐ FHA	2. ☐ FmHA	3. ☒ CONV. UNINS.
4. ☐ VA	5. ☐ CONV. INS.	
6. File Number:	SAMPLE	
	SAMPLE	GPS
7. Loan Number		
8. Mortgage Insurance Case Number		

C. NOTE: This form is furnished to give you a statement of actual settlement costs. Amounts paid to and by the settlement agent are shown. Items marked "(p.o.c.)" were paid outside the closing; they are shown here for informational purposes and are not included in the totals.

D. NAME OF BORROWER: Samuel S. Smith and Sally Smith
ADDRESS: 1234 Main Street
Houston   Texas   77777

E. NAME OF SELLER: Judy Jean Jones
ADDRESS: 24 Lovers Lane
Dallas, TX   Texas   75225

F. NAME OF LENDER: Second Mortgages, Inc.
ADDRESS: 55 Greenback Drive
Houston   Texas   77222

G. PROPERTY LOCATION: 1234 Main Street
Houston   Texas   77056

H. SETTLEMENT AGENT: Chicago Title Insurance Company
ADDRESS:

I. SETTLEMENT DATE: 7/20/94

PLACE OF SETTLEMENT: 1001 S. Dairy Ashford
ADDRESS: Houston   Texas   77077

J. SUMMARY OF BORROWER'S TRANSACTION		K. SUMMARY OF SELLER'S TRANSACTION	
100. GROSS AMOUNT DUE FROM BORROWER:		**400. GROSS AMOUNT DUE TO SELLER:**	
101. Contract sales price	200,000.00	401. Contract sales price	200,000.00
102. Personal Property		402. Personal Property	
103. Settlement charges to borrower (line 1400)	2,556.42	403.	
104. Escrow Balance	1,156.90	404. Escrow Balance	1,156.90
105.		405.	
Adjustments for items paid by seller in advance		**Adjustments for items paid by seller in advance**	
106. City/town taxes / / to / /		406. City/town taxes / / to / /	
107. County taxes / / to / /		407. County taxes / / to / /	
108. Assessments 07/21/94 to 01/01/95	114.81	408. Assessments 7/21/94 to 01/01/95	114.81
109. Hazard Insurance 07/21/94 to 07/21/95	244.07	409. Hazard Insurance 7/21/94–12/01/94	244.07
110.		410.	
111.		411.	
112.		412.	
120. GROSS AMT DUE FROM BORROWER	204,072.20	**420. GROSS AMT DUE TO SELLER**	201,515.78
200. AMOUNTS PAID BY OR IN BEHALF OF BORROWER		**500. REDUCTIONS IN AMOUNT DUE TO SELLER:**	
201. Deposit or earnest money	10,000.00	501. Excess deposit (see instructions)	
202. Principal amount of new loan(s)	63,000.00	502. Settlement charges to seller (line 1400)	13,872.00
203. Existing loan(s) taken subject to	96,943.00	503. Existing loan(s) taken subject to	96,943.00
		504. Payoff of first mortgage loan	
204.			
205.		505. Payoff of second mortgage loan	
206.		506.	
207.		507.	
208.		508.	
209.		509.	
Adjustments for items unpaid by seller		**Adjustments for items unpaid by seller**	
210. City/town taxes 01/01/94 to 07/21/94	364.93	510. City/town taxes 01/01/94 to 07/21/94	364.93
211. County taxes / / to / /		511. County taxes / / to / /	
212. Assessments / / to / /		512. Assessments / / to / /	
213. Interest on Existing Loan	484.72	513. Interest on Existing Loan	484.72
214. INTEREST ADJ. FROM / / TO / /		514. INTEREST ADJ. FROM / / TO / /	
215.		515.	
216.		516.	
217.		517.	
218.		518.	
219.		519.	
220. TOTAL PAID BY/FOR BORROWER	170,792.65	**520. TOTAL REDUCTIONS AMT DUE SELLER**	111,664.65
300. CASH AT SETTLEMENT FROM/TO BORROWER		**600. CASH AT SETTLEMENT TO/FROM SELLER**	
301. Gross amt due from borrower (line 120)	204,072.20	601. Gross amt due to seller (line 420)	201,515.78
302. Less amts paid by/for borrower (line 220)	(170,792.65)	602. Less reductions in amt due seller (line 520)	(111,664.65)
303. CASH (☒ FROM) (☐ TO) BORROWER	33,279.55	603. CASH (☒ TO) (☐ FROM) SELLER	89,851.13

I have carefully reviewed the HUD-1 Settlement Statement and to the best of my knowledge and belief, it is a true and accurate statement of all receipts and disbursements made on my account or by me in this transaction. I further certify that I have received a copy of the HUD-1 Settlement Statement.

Borrower
Samuel S. Smith

Seller
Judy Jean Jones

Sally Smith

The HUD-1 Settlement Statement which I have prepared is a true and accurate account of this transaction. I have caused or will cause funds to be disbursed in accordance with this statement.

Settlement Agent   Date

WARNING: It is a crime to knowingly make false statements to the United States on this or any other similar form. Penalties upon conviction can include a fine and imprisonment. For details see: Title 18 U.S. Code Section 1001 and Section 1010.

FIGURE 16–3   HUD Settlement Statement for Residential Loans

File Number: SAMPLE   **L. SETTLEMENT CHARGES**

	PAID FROM BORROWER'S FUNDS AT SETTLEMENT	PAID FROM SELLER'S FUNDS AT SETTLEMENT
700. TOTAL SALES/BROKER'S COMMISSION based on price $ 200,000.00 @ 6.000 %= 12,000.00		
Division of Commission (line 700) as follows:		
701. $ 6,000.00 to Uptown Realty		
702. $ 6,000.00 to Boomtown Properties		
703. $ to		
(Money retained by broker applied to commission $)		
704. Commission paid at Settlement		12,000.00
705. Other sales agent charges payable to:		
800. ITEMS PAYABLE IN CONNECTION WITH LOAN		
801. Loan Origination Fee 1.000 % Second Mortgages, Inc.	630.00	
802. Loan Discount %		
803. Appraisal Fee to Second Mortgages, Inc. POC		
804. Credit Report to Credco	45.00	
805. Lender's Inspection Fee to		
806. Mortgage Insurance Application Fee to		
807. Assumption Fee to E-Z Mortgage	970.00	
808. Application Fee to E-Z Mortgage	125.00	
809. Recording of Assignment to Second Liens, Inc.	25.00	
810.		
811.		
900. ITEMS REQUIRED BY LENDER TO BE PAID IN ADVANCE		
901. Interest from 7/21/94 to 4/1/95 @$ 14.2600 /day	242.42	
902. Mortgage Insurance Premium for 0 months to		
903. Hazard Insurance Premium for 0 years to		
904. 0 years to		
905.		
1000. RESERVES DEPOSITED WITH LENDER		
1001. Hazard insurance 0 month @$ per month		
1002. Mortgage insurance 0 month @$ per month		
1003. City property taxes 0 month @$ per month		
1004. County property taxes 0 month @$ per month		
1005. Annual assessments 0 month @$ per month		
1006. 0 month @$ per month		
1007. 0 month @$ per month		
1008. 0 month @$ per month		
1100. TITLE CHARGES		
1101. Settlement or Closing Fee (Escrow Fee) to Chicago Title Insurance	60.00	60.00
1102. Abstract or title search to		
1103. Title examination to		
1104. Title insurance binder to		
1105. Document preparation to		
1106. Notary fees to		
1107. Attorney's fee to Dewey, Cheatem & Howe	150.00	160.00
(includes above items numbers:)		
1108. Title insurance to Chicago Title Insurance	120.00	1,518.00
(includes above items numbers:)		
1109. Lender's coverage $ 63,000.00		
1110. Owner's coverage $ 200,000.00		
1111. State of Texas Policy Guaranty Fees	3.00	3.00
1112. Messenger Fees	50.00	50.00
1113.		
1200. GOVERNMENT RECORDING AND TRANSFER CHARGES		
1201. Recording fees: Deed $ 20.00 ; Mortgage $ 32.00 ; Release $	26.00	26.00
1202. City/county tax/stamps: Deed $; Mortgage $		
1203. State tax/stamps: Deed $; Mortgage $		
1204.		55.00
1205.		
1300. ADDITIONAL SETTLEMENT CHARGES		
1301. Survey to		
1302. Pest inspection to No Bugs, Inc	25.00	
1303. Structural Inspection to The House Inspector	85.00	
1304.		
1305.		
1306.		
1307.		
1400. TOTAL SETTLEMENT CHARGES (enter on lines 103, Section J and 502, Section K)	2,556.42	13,872.00

I have carefully reviewed the HUD-1 Settlement Statement and to the best of my knowledge and belief, it is a true and accurate statement of all receipts and disbursements made on my account or by me in this transaction. I further certify that I have received a copy of the HUD-1 Settlement Statement.

Borrower   Seller

Samuel S. Smith   Judy Jean Jones

Sally Smith

The HUD-1 Settlement Statement which I have prepared is a true and accurate account of this transaction. I have caused or will cause funds to be disbursed in accordance with this statement.

Settlement Agent   Date

HUD-1 (3/86) RESPA, HB 4305.2

FIGURE 16–3 (Continued)

Items Payable in Connection with Loan (Item 800)

As identified by RESPA, the costs of the loan are the fees charged by the lenders to process, approve, and make the mortgage loan.

Loan Origination Fee (801). This is the fee charged by the primary lender to assemble information necessary to evaluate a loan application, to determine its acceptability, and to prepare the completed loan package. The charge is negotiable and varies from 1 to 1.5 percent of the loan amount.

Loan Discount (802). The loan discount is not truly a fee in that it is not considered payment for services rendered. Rather, it is another cost of borrowed money similar to interest. The discount is expressed as a percentage of the loan amount, normally measured in *points;* one point is 1 percent of the loan amount. The purpose of a discount is to adjust the yield on a fixed interest rate certificate to a level of return that is commensurate with the current market rate for money loaned. By charging a discount for a loan, the lender increases the return, or yield. Six to eight points of discount give the lender about the same return on a loan as increasing the interest rate by 1 percent. The value of the discount depends on the rate of interest: the higher the market rate, the greater the value of a point of discount. As a cost of borrowed money paid at the time of loan settlement, a loan discount becomes one of the items payable for obtaining a loan.

Appraisal Fee (803). An appraisal of the property is necessary to establish the value basis for a mortgage loan. Depending on the size of the loan, regulated lenders may be required to use a state certified appraiser. If not, a qualified member of the lender's staff or an independent fee appraiser may be used to provide factual data on the value of the property offered as loan collateral. Since an appraisal is of value to both the buyer and seller of property, it may be paid for by either one. Often, the cost of an appraisal is included as part of the initial application fee.

Credit Report Fee (804). Applicants for mortgage loans are required to submit credit reports, usually from both a local credit bureau and a national repository of credit data. The information is normally obtained by the loan processor from local credit bureaus. This report is a necessary verification of information submitted in the loan application plus statistical data on the bill-paying record of the applicant. A credit report is one source of information that a lender uses to determine if the applicant is an acceptable credit risk. Payment for the report is most often made by the borrower.

Lender's Inspection Fee (805). The lender is permitted to assess a charge for an inspection of the property offered as collateral. The inspection can be made by the lender's personnel or by an independent inspector. The purpose is to examine the physical facilities and any mechanical equipment and possibly to report on environmental problems. This inspection is not to be confused with pest inspections, which are discussed later.

Mortgage Insurance Application Fee (806). Private mortgage insurance companies charge fees for the processing of a loan application. This fee sometimes covers both an appraisal fee and an application fee.

Assumption Fee (807). An assumption fee is essentially a paper-processing fee charged in transactions in which the buyer takes title to the property and assumes liability for payments on a prior obligation of the seller.

Items Required by Lender to Be Paid in Advance (Item 900)

There are certain items that must be **prepaid** in advance at the closing of a loan as follows.

Interest (901). Since mortgage loans extend for long terms, it is a common practice to adjust the monthly payment to a convenient date each month, most often the first of each month. The normal monthly payment on a mortgage loan includes a charge for interest paid at the end of the month, that is, after the borrower has had the use of the money loaned. So, to adjust the monthly payment to a date other than that of loan closing, the interest charge is computed for the time period from the date of closing to the beginning of the period covered by the first monthly payment. For example, if the settlement takes place on June 16, a prepayment of charges is needed through June 30. The period covered by the regular monthly payment begins on July 1, and the first regular payment is due on August 1.

....

EXAMPLE

Compute the interest charges for 15 days (June 16 through June 30) on a $45,000 loan at 10 percent interest as follows:

    $45,000 × .10   = $4,500 (annual interest cost)
    $4,500 / 360   = $12.50 (daily interest cost)
    $12.50 × 15 days   = $187.50 (prepaid interest due)

The prepaid interest amount of $187.50 would be due at closing and the full monthly payment on a 30-year loan amounting to $394.91 would begin on August 1.

....

Mortgage Insurance Premium (902). Almost all lenders now require private mortgage insurance on loans in excess of 80 percent of the property value. And the FHA has reinstated its annual mortgage insurance premium payable as a part of each monthly payment. The protection for the lender is against a borrower default in the payment of the loan. It enables a lender to make higher ratio loans (up to 95 percent for a conventional loan) than would otherwise be possible, and thus allows lower down payments for the borrower. The first premium charge for a conventional loan is always higher than the continuing annual payments as it includes an issuing fee and is payable in full at the loan closing. This type of mortgage insurance should not be confused with mortgage life, credit life, or disability insurance, which are designed to pay off a mortgage in the event of physical disability or death of the borrower. None of these types of insurance are a standard requirement for a mortgage loan.

Hazard Insurance Premium (903). Hazard insurance protects both the lender and the borrower against loss to a building by fire, windstorm, or other natural hazard. Such coverage is a requirement for mortgage loans that include any buildings as part of the collateral. In addition, loans in certain areas of the country with development land in designated flood plain zones require flood insurance. It is customary to name the lender as a loss payee (in addition to the homeowner).

The normal lender requirement is for insurance coverage in an amount not less than the loan amount. This standard does not necessarily recognize co-insurance clauses found in most states' insurance codes. Co-insurance requirements set a minimum insurance coverage amount (usually 80 percent of the building value at the time of loss) to assure the property owner full recovery of partial losses. So while the lender may set a minimum requirement to cover the loan amount, on a low-ratio loan the coverage could be insufficient to fully protect the property owner.

Most lenders require a full first year's premium of hazard insurance paid at the time of closing. Often, the paid-up policy is delivered at the closing table as proof of insurance. In addition to the first year's premium, lenders may require a reserve of up to two months of annual premiums deposited with them at closing.

Reserves Deposited with Lenders (Item 1000)

Almost all residential loans require cash deposited with the lender at the time of loan closing to be used for future payment of recurring annual charges such as taxes, insurance, and maintenance assessments. The identification of these accounts differs as they may be referred to as **reserves,** escrow accounts, impound accounts, or reserve accruals. The purpose of the initial deposits is to assure the lender enough cash to make the first annual payment that comes due after the closing date. Because real estate practices differ throughout the country, RESPA allows some variations in how deposits are handled. In some parts of the country, taxes are paid for a year in advance; in others, they are paid for at the end of the tax year. The same is true of maintenance assessments.

RESPA places a limit on the deposits that may be required to meet the first year's payments on residential loans. The amount cannot exceed a sum sufficient to pay taxes, insurance premiums, or other charges that would have been paid under normal lending practices up to the due date of the first full monthly installment payment. In addition, the lender is permitted to require a cushion of up to one-sixth of the annual charges for the escrowed expenses. Then, each monthly installment payment can include one-twelfth of the annual charges on a continuing basis. RESPA rules restrict the lender to collecting no more than one-twelfth of the annual taxes and other charges each month, unless a larger payment is necessary to make up a deficit in the reserve account. A deficit in the account may be caused, for example, by increases in the taxes and insurance premiums during the loan payment year.

Hazard Insurance (1001). Most home buyers elect to purchase new insurance policies to fit their own needs. To do this, the normal lender requirement, approved as being in compliance with RESPA restrictions, is for a one-year premium paid in advance, plus a deposit to a reserve account in an amount not exceeding two months of the annual premium. A buyer may purchase hazard insurance from whatever company he or she chooses, so long as the company meets the lender's minimum standards for financial responsibility. If the buyer opts to continue an existing insurance policy, an adjustment would be necessary to reimburse the seller for any portion of the premium not used by date of closing plus a reimbursement of the two-month premium cushion.

Mortgage Insurance (1002). The premium reserve requirement for mortgage insurance is negotiable with the lender. It may be required that a part of the total annual premium be placed in a reserve account, but no more than one-sixth of the annual premium may be held as a cushion by the lender.

City/County Property Taxes (1003–1004). A reserve is required so as to have sufficient cash on hand to make timely payment of property taxes when they come due. The reserve is determined by the time span between the date of closing a transaction and the date the next payment of taxes becomes due. An example of this calculation follows.

••

EXAMPLE

Initial Tax Reserve Requirement for a Settlement Date of June 30

First monthly payment due August 1
Taxes for prior calendar year due December 1
Annual taxes: $900 ($75 each month)

Initial reserve from previous December 1 to July 30
8 months × $75	= $600
Plus 2 months cushion: 2 months × $75	= $150
Escrow deposit required at closing	= $750

••

In considering this example, keep in mind that taxes due for the months prior to actual closing are the financial responsibility of the seller. This would mean that seven of the eight months' requirement, amounting to $525, would be paid by the seller. One month (from June 30 to July 31) plus the two-month cushion, amounting to $225, is the responsibility of the buyer. So the settlement statement would reflect the proration of the tax liability.

If the house is newly constructed, the tax assessment during the construction period would most likely be a lesser amount than that for the finished house. In areas where taxes are paid at the beginning of each tax year, the deposit requirement to meet the coming year's taxes would fall to the buyer.

Annual Assessments (1005). The reserve that may be required for assessments covers such charges as a homeowners' association fee, a condominium maintenance charge, or a municipal improvement assessment. The same previously described RESPA reserve limitations apply to all forms of reserves.

Title Charges (Item 1100)

In the uniform settlement statement, *title charges* designates a variety of services performed to conclude a real estate transaction properly. These include searching records, preparing documents, and acquiring insurance against title failure. While practices and terminology differ in some areas, the services needed are basically similar.

Settlement or Closing Fee (1101). These are the charges made by the person or company for the service of handling the settlement procedures. Payment of the fee is negotiable between buyer and seller and is often divided equally between them.

Abstract or Title Search, Title Examination, Title Insurance Binder (1102–1104). In a real estate transaction, it is reasonable to expect a seller to offer some solid proof of his or her right to convey the property with good title to the buyer. This can be accomplished through a search of all the recorded documents affecting the land title (an abstract of title). In some cases, an attorney will review the abstract and issue a title opinion. Buyers can accept the opinion if it proves good title and proceed with the transaction although such an opinion provides no insurance against future adverse claims. More commonly, proof of title is handled through a title insurance company, which continuously searches the records and, if justified, insures the title against adverse claims for a specified period of future time.

In some areas of the country, the obligation to prove that good title is being conveyed places the cost burden on the seller. However, in other areas the fact that title insurance protects the buyer against future claims indicates the cost should be borne by the buyer.

A *title insurance binder* is a preliminary assurance by a title company that the title is valid and that a title insurance policy will be issued at a later date.

Document Preparation (1105). The charge for preparing legal documents may be listed separately or may be included with other service fees, most likely as a part of the attorney's fee.

Notary Fee (1106). Instruments that are to be recorded in the public records usually require that all signatures be acknowledged by a notary public or properly witnessed. Settlement agents are often licensed for this purpose and may ask a separate charge for their official services.

Attorney's Fees (1107). Few lenders will permit a loan to be closed without the assurance of a qualified attorney that all instruments have been properly prepared and executed. In any real estate transaction, the buyer and the seller may each be represented by their own attorney and, in such case, each may pay the attorney outside the closing procedure. In the handling of residential loans, the title company or settlement agent involved may employ an attorney to handle the legal requirements and, if both parties agree, the charges are allocated equally between buyer and seller.

Title Insurance (1108). **Title insurance** offers protection to the policyholder/landowner against adverse claims to ownership rights. Contrary to a popular belief, it is not a guarantee of title so much as it offers a legal defense should an adverse claim arise. If title does prove defective, a prior owner may assert ownership while the policyholder may recover the value of the insurance coverage.

In most states, title insurance is classed as another type of insurance and falls under the regulatory authority of the state's insurance commission. Premiums can be set uniformly by the state, limiting competition to the kind of service that different companies may offer. Title insurance is available in two separate types: (1) an owner's policy, which protects the landowner, and (2) a mortgagee's policy, which protects the lender.

Lender's Title Policy (1109). The lender's policy runs with the mortgage. Its value declines as the mortgage is paid down and it transfers to whomever holds the mortgage note. Furthermore, a payoff of the loan automatically cancels the lender's insurance coverage. The lender's title policy is paid for as a single premium at closing. In many areas it is issued simultaneously with an owner's policy, since the same basic risk is covered. Local practice varies as to whether the lender's or the owner's policy must pay the major share of premium cost. If the lender's policy carries the major cost, the owner's policy is usually issued for a nominal amount. Payment for a lender's policy is most likely to be made by the buyer as it is clearly part of the cost of obtaining a loan.

Owner's Title Insurance (1110). An owner's policy protects against adverse claims up to a specified amount and for a given number of years, usually 20 or 25 years. It cannot be transferred to another owner. The owner's policy is purchased at closing with a one-time premium charge. The time period for title insurance coverage is determined by each state's limitation statutes. Even though an owner may hold actual title to property for only a short period, say, a year or so, liability may continue after disposition of the property. The reason is that the warranty deed normally used to convey title leaves the seller with responsibility. The wording of the deed reads that seller "will warrant and defend generally the title to the property against all claims and demands." So the owner's title policy protects the owner, not only while he or she is in possession of the insured premises, but also for the time period after it is sold as the seller is still liable for possible adverse claims.

Customs vary regionally as to whether or not the buyer or seller pays for owner's title insurance. Since the issuance of such a policy represents good proof of the validity of the seller's own title to the land to be conveyed, in some areas the cost is paid by the seller. In other areas, if the seller can prove good title to the property through an attorney's opinion based on the abstract of title or by the issuance of a title binder by a title company, then payment for the attorney's opinion or for the owner's policy falls to the buyer as the party who carries the future benefit.

Government Recording and Transfer Charges (Item 1200)

Recording fees and transfer fees are those charged by city, county, or state governments for recording services, or as a tax on the transaction. The fees may be based on the amount of the mortgage loan or on the value of the property being transferred. Payment of these charges is negotiable between buyer and seller but they are usually paid by the buyer.

Additional Settlement Charges (Item 1300)

Charges that are not easily classified within previous categories of costs can be listed in this section. Mostly, they include costs of a survey and inspections that may be required to determine adequacy of the structure and its equipment.

Survey (1301). Almost all lenders require that a survey of the property offered as collateral be included in the loan package. An acceptable survey, which can only be prepared by a registered surveyor, gives a picture description of the land with an outline of its perimeter boundaries. It should show the precise location of buildings as well as any easements or rights-of-way that may cross the land. The survey can disclose any encroachments on the land that may create a cloud on the ownership rights. It is not unusual for an attorney to require a survey before preparing a deed or mortgage instrument to make sure of the land and the rights being conveyed. Payment for the survey is negotiable; the seller has an obligation to prove exactly what land is to be conveyed while the buyer has a need for the survey to complete the loan requirements.

Pest and Other Inspections (1302). In certain areas of the country where termites or other insects infest buildings and can create damage, it is normal to require a separate pest inspection. In such areas, sales agreements may call for the property to be delivered free of infestation. The pest inspection, plus treatment if necessary, with a certified letter of proof, is the seller's method of fulfilling this requirement. Even though buyer and seller do not address this question, the lender may require a pest inspection to assure that property offered as collateral is free of pest-caused structural damage. In such a case, the cost may be paid by the buyer as part of the requirements for obtaining a mortgage loan.

Total Settlement Charges (Item 1400)

At the bottom of the page listing the various settlement charges, the totals for the borrower's and seller's charges are listed and transferred to the summary section of the first page.

FINAL CLOSING INSTRUCTIONS

How the proceeds of a loan are disbursed is of prime importance to the lender. General instructions are often kept on file with closing agents by major lenders to expedite handling. Another kind of instruction preparatory to closing is normally provided by the agents representing the principals in the transaction. Both are discussed further.

Mortgagee's Closing Instructions

Once a loan has been approved, the mortgage company prepares a sheet of instructions for delivery to the settlement agent handling closing procedures. The **closing instructions** detail such items as the correct legal name for the mortgage instruments, the name of the trustee if a deed of trust is involved, and the terms of the mortgage note. Any special requirements to be included in the mortgage or deed of trust (that is, if the mortgage company is not submitting its own forms, or standardized documents, for a note and mortgage) are itemized. The lender will ask that specific instructions on monthly payments be given to the borrower, along with details of the escrow requirements and details of **disbursement procedures.** Along with the instructions, the mortgage company will send the buyer-seller affidavits as may be required, which certify to the actual down payment (cash and/or property exchanged) and to the use of the loan proceeds, which must be acknowledged by the notarized signatures of all buyers and sellers. Also, a truth-in-lending statement is prepared for the purchaser-borrower's signature at closing. Some mortgage companies require certifications of occupancy (for homestead information). The instruments may vary between companies according to how their legal counselors interpret state laws.

The instructions of a mortgage company invariably call for a certain amount of work on the part of the settlement agent closing the loan, if only as a means of clarifying the loan requirements. This is in addition to other details of closing that a settlement agent must handle, such as assembling the title information, preparing or reviewing the note and mortgage, verifying tax requirements, and determining the insurance payments needed.

It is advisable to allow the settlement agent a reasonable amount of time for its work in preparing for a closing. A forced deadline can induce errors and omissions. Figure 16–4 gives an example of typical mortgagee's closing instructions.

Setting the Closing

When the mortgage company has approved the loan and prepared its closing instructions, it is usually the responsibility of the real estate agent, or agents, involved to arrange a mutually agreeable closing time. Practices vary in different parts of the country: in some areas all parties meet for the settlement procedures; in other parts, no actual meeting is required, and escrow agents are authorized to request that the necessary instruments be delivered to them for release after all escrow requirements have been met.

Whenever the local practices require a meeting of the parties involved, it is usually held in the offices of the company or person designated to handle the settlement procedures. This may be a title company, an attorney, a real estate agent, an escrow agent, or the lender itself. Whoever handles the loan closing must have the approval of the lender as it is its money that is generally most involved.

Closings can be accomplished with separate meetings, the buyer at one time and the seller at another, leaving the settlement agent to escrow the instruments and consideration until the procedure is completed and distribution can be made. It is easier for the agents involved, and provides greater clarity for both buyer and seller, to arrange for a single meeting. Although a closing is no place for negotiations, if a misunderstanding crops up, it can be more readily resolved if all parties are immediately available for decisions.

DISBURSEMENT OF FUNDS

In many parts of the country, a closing is just that: Instruments are signed and funds are disbursed before anyone leaves the closing table. In some areas, it is more common to execute and acknowledge the instruments at the closing, but delay disbursement of funds until later. The purpose for any delay in releasing funds is twofold: first, to give the lender an opportunity to make a second review of all instruments and to verify proper signatures and acknowledgments; and second, to allow the settlement agent time to clear any checks that may have been submitted by the parties involved before releasing its own disbursement checks. Because any delay in the delivery of executed documents and funds can create problems, there is growing pressure to not call for the parties to meet until all loose ends have been resolved and good money is available for distribution at the closing table.

The actual disbursement of funds at or following the settlement procedures is usually made to several different individuals and companies as well as the cash due to the seller. One of the reasons an escrow agent is employed in the closing process is to make sure that all parties with claims in the settlement

COMMONWEALTH MORTGAGE COMPANY OF AMERICA, L.P.   SCHEDULE OF CLOSING CHARGES

CMCA Loan Number	Borrower	CMCA Office
Settlement Date		

The sales price and down payment specified are not to be reduced by any credits or allowances. Any changes or adjustments to the financing terms will require CMCA approval prior to execution of the documents and disbursement of the funds.

If applicable, this loan transaction has been approved subject to the following financing terms:

Sales Price $_____   Interest Rate _____
Prepaid Earnest Money Deposit   _____
CMCA Mortgage Loan   _____
Secondary Financing   _____   P & I $_____
Balance of Down Payment   _____

☐ Commonwealth will fund this loan upon receiving the instruments later referred to in these instructions, in form and content acceptable to us. **Documents must be returned 24 hours prior to funding.** Prepaid interest is to be computed at a per diem rate of $_____.

☐ Our net check in the amount of $_____is enclosed.   **A funding number must be obtained prior to disbursement of proceeds by calling Commonwealth.**   The funding number is_____, obtained from _____at Commonwealth on _____.   The check is not to be deposited in advance of the actual closing. It is to be returned to the branch office within _7_ days in the event of a postponement and immediately if the closer is unable to comply with our instructions.

Our closing charges have been deducted or are to be deducted from the loan funding check and are itemized below and to be charged to the applicable party indicated.

801	LOAN ORIGINATION FEE	%		
802	LOAN DISCOUNT	%		
803	APPRAISAL FEE "POC" – $	COST – $		
804	CREDIT REPORT "POC" – $	COST – $		
805	LENDER'S INSPECTION FEE			
807	ASSUMPTION FEE			
808	APPLICATION FEE			
810	UNDERWRITING FEE			
811	BUYDOWN FEE			
812	COMMITMENT FEE			
813	MESSENGER FEE			
814	LONG DISTANCE CALLS			
815	AMORTIZATION FEE			
816	PHOTO FEE			
817	FLOOD CERTIFICATION FEE			
818	REVIEW FEE			
819	TAX SERVICE CONTRACT FEE			
820	DOCUMENT PREPARATION FEE			
821	ATTORNEY'S FEE			
822	DEPARTMENT OF HUD — ONE-TIME MIP/PMI FINANCED			
823	VA FUNDING FEE			
824				
825				
826				

901	INTEREST FROM	TO	AT $	/DAY	
902	FIRST YEAR'S MORTGAGE INSURANCE PREMIUM				
903	FIRST YEAR'S HAZARD INSURANCE PREMIUM				
904	FIRST YEAR'S FLOOD INSURANCE PREMIUM				
905					

1001	HAZARD INSURANCE	MONTHS AT $*	PER MONTH		
1002	MORTGAGE INSURANCE	MONTHS AT $	PER MONTH		
1003	CITY PROPERTY TAXES	MONTHS AT $*	PER MONTH		
1004	COUNTY PROPERTY TAXES	MONTHS AT $*	PER MONTH		
1005	ANNUAL ASSESSMENTS	MONTHS AT $*	PER MONTH		
1006	FLOOD INSURANCE	MONTHS AT $*	PER MONTH		
1007		MONTHS AT $	PER MONTH		
	*CALCULATE AT 1/12 ANNUAL PREMIUM				

1301			
1302			
1303			

Closing Agent Please Note:

1. Purchaser's costs not to exceed $_____. Seller's costs not to exceed $_____.
2. Purchasers to pay $_____closing costs.
3. FHA and Conventional Purchasers must pay prepaid items, including preliminary interest and insurance premiums.
4. Purchaser and Seller must not pay more than the discount and closing costs listed above.   Any excess will require investor and Commonwealth's approval before funding can take place.
5. Endorsements required:_____
_____
_____
_____

CMCA, L.P. 78006 (12 87)

FIGURE 16–4   Mortgagee's Closing Instructions

are paid. The mortgage lender wants to be certain that taxes are paid, that the insurance coverage is in force and has been paid for, and that no subsequent claims can be filed that might cloud its right to a valid lien securing the loan. Sales agents, inspectors, attorneys, and service agents all normally expect to receive their fees from the closing agent. After all required payments have been made, the necessary instruments are filed in the county records, the balance due the seller is disbursed, and the transaction is considered closed.

Questions for Discussion

1. Discuss the purpose of the Real Estate Settlement Procedures Act (RESPA) and its key provisions.
2. Why should a listing agent obtain a preliminary title report on the listed property?
3. Discuss the importance of a survey in the settlement procedure.
4. Describe the essential elements of a HUD-1 settlement statement.
5. What is the reason for a prepayment of interest at the time of settlement procedures?
6. Where are loan closings normally held in your community?
7. What information is normally furnished to the settlement agent (closer) by the mortgage lender just prior to closing?
8. Describe at least three RESPA requirements that call for disclosure of information to a borrower.
9. Discuss requirements of the Truth-in-Lending Act as it relates to finance charges for mortgage loans.
10. What are the limitations on reserve deposits that may be held by a lender for a residential mortgage loan?

Glossary

The following terms are those most frequently used in real estate financing and are considered essential in understanding the material presented in this text.

Abstract. The recorded history of a land title. A compilation of all instruments affecting the title to a tract of land.

Acceleration. A clause in a mortgage instrument that permits the lender to declare the entire balance due and payable in the event of a default on the mortgage terms.

Acknowledgment. For real estate purposes, a signature witnessed or notarized in a manner that allows an instrument to be recorded.

Adjustable Rate Mortgage (ARM). A mortgage design that permits the lender to adjust the interest rate at periodic intervals, with the amount of change generally tied to changes in an independent published index of interest rates or yields.

Alienation. The act of transferring rights in real property. Sometimes used to identify the clause in a mortgage that allows the lender to declare the balance due and payable if the mortgaged property is transferred to another.

Amortization. The systematic and continuous payment of an obligation through installments until such time as that debt has been paid off in full.

Annual Percentage Rate (APR). The cost of credit expressed as a percentage of the net amount borrowed calculated as required by Regulation Z implementing the Truth-in-Lending Act.

Appraisal. An estimate of property value by a qualified person.

Appreciation. An increase in value. In real estate, appreciation is considered the passive increase in property value resulting from population growth, scarcity, and/or the decreasing value of money.

Asbestos. A mineral fiber found in rocks; it can cause illness if inhaled.

Assessed Value. Property value as determined by a taxing authority.

Assessment. A levy against a property owner for purposes of taxation; that is, the property owner pays a share of community improvements and maintenance according to the valuation of the property.

Assets. Real and personal property that may be chargeable with the debts of the owner.

Assignment of Mortgage. Transfer by the lender (mortgagee) of the mortgage obligation.

Assumption Agreement. A contract, by deed or other agreement, through which a buyer acquires title to property and undertakes the obligations of an existing mortgage.

Balance Sheet. A financial statement that itemizes personal or company assets and liabilities, with the difference between the two being net worth.

Balloon Payment. A debt repayment plan wherein the installments are less than those required for full amortization of the loan, with the balance due in a lump sum at maturity. Technically, a final payment greater than two monthly payments.

Basis Point. A unit of measure amounting to one-hundredth of one percent.

Basket Provision. Regulations applicable to financial institutions that permit a small percentage of total assets to be held in otherwise unauthorized investments.

Beneficiary. The lender, or mortgagee, in a deed of trust transaction. The lender benefits from the note.

Biweekly Payment Plan. A loan repayment plan that calls for 26 half-month payments per year, which retires the loan earlier, reducing total interest costs.

Blanket Mortgage. A mortgage that is secured by more than one parcel of real estate as collateral.

Blind Pool. A syndicate organized to acquire property, the nature of which is not known or disclosed to the participants at the time of solicitation.

Bond. A debt instrument. A type of security that guarantees at maturity payment of the face value plus interest to the holder. It is usually secured by a pledge of property or a commitment of income; such as a tax revenue bond.

Borrower. A person or company using another's money or property; a borrower has both a legal and moral obligation to repay the loan.

Bridge Loan. A short-term loan to cover the period between the termination of one loan and the beginning of another. Also called *interim loan*.

Broker. An intermediary between buyer and seller, or between lender and borrower, usually acting as agent for one or more parties, who arranges loans or buys or sells property on behalf of a principal in return for a fee or commission.

Buy-Down Mortgage. A mortgage repayment design offering lower initial monthly payments achieved through the prepayment of a portion of the interest cost. The prepayment of interest is usually limited to the first few years and is normally paid by a seller to help attract buyers by allowing easier borrower qualification.

Call Provision. A provision in a mortgage instrument that allows the mortgagee to accelerate full payment of the debt on a certain date or the happening of specified conditions.

Capitalization. A mathematical process for conversion of an income stream into a property valuation as used for an appraisal.

Cash Flow. The amount of cash received over a period of time from an income property.

Certificate of Reasonable Value (CRV). An estimate of property value prepared in accordance with requirements of the Department of Veterans Affairs. A VA appraisal.

Chain of Title. The sequence of ownership interests in a tract of land.

Chattel. An article of property that can be moved; personal property.

Chattel Mortgage. An obsolete term defined as a mortgage secured by personal property. Under the Uniform Commercial Code, chattel mortgages have been replaced by security agreements.

Closer. The individual responsible for making final settlement of a property transaction and disbursement of the consideration.

Closing. The consummation of a real estate transaction wherein certain rights of ownership are transferred in exchange for the monetary and other considerations agreed upon. Also called *loan closing*.

Closing Costs. Expenses of a property sale that must be paid in addition to the purchase price.

Cloud on Title. A defect in the chain of title to property that obstructs, or prevents, good delivery.

Collateral.   Any asset acceptable as security for a loan.

Collateralized Mortgage Obligation (CMO).   A mortgage-backed security variation that segments cash flows from an underlying block of loans so as to retire different classes of bonds in a sequence based on the bond's maturity.

Commercial Loan.   An imprecise term generally applied to an obligation collateralized by real property other than that used as a residence.

Commitment.   As applied to mortgage loans, a promise of loanable funds.

Commitment Fee.   Money paid in return for the pledge of a future loan.

Common Area.   That part of condominium property owned jointly by all unit owners.

Community Property.   Property owned equally by a husband and wife.

Compensating Balance.   A minimum balance held on deposit in accordance with a loan agreement.

Compound Interest.   Interest paid on accrued interest as well as on principal.

Computerized Loan Origination (CLO).   Initiation of a mortgage loan through a terminal linked to a lender's computer. Subject to HUD limitations, the method allows real estate agents to assist in loan origination.

Conditional Sale.   An agreement granting possession of property to a buyer while title is retained by the seller until all required payments have been made.

Condominium.   A unit in a multifamily structure or office building wherein the owner holds title to a unit plus an undivided common interest in the common elements with the other owners.

Conforming Loan.   A loan written on uniform documents as required by Fannie Mae and Freddie Mac if purchased by them. The loans are subject to limitations set by the agencies and Congress on the size and kind of loan.

Consideration.   The cash, services, or token given in exchange for property or services.

Constant Payment.   A fixed payment amount, covering the interest due and a partial reduction of principal. Usually calculated in a manner that repays the loan within its term.

Constant Rate.   Also called *constant,* it is that percentage of the initial loan amount that must be paid periodically to repay the loan within the specified term.

Construction Loan.   A type of mortgage loan to finance construction, which is funded by the lender to the builder at periodic intervals as work progresses.

Contingent Liability.   The responsibility assumed by a third party who accepts liability for an obligation upon the failure of an initial obligor to perform as agreed.

Contract for Deed.   An agreement to sell property wherein possession is granted to the buyer while title remains with the seller for conveyance after payment has been made. Also called *land contract.*

Contract of Sale.   An agreement between a buyer and a seller of real property to deliver good title in return for a consideration.

Conventional Loan.   A loan that is not underwritten by a federal agency.

Conveyance.   The written instrument by which an interest in real property is transferred from one party to another.

Cooperative.   Ownership of real estate by a corporation or trust wherein the shareholders are also the tenants through leasehold agreement.

Cost Approach.   An approach to evaluation of property based on the property's reproduction cost.

Cost Recovery Period.   The time period over which tax deductions may be taken on a depreciable asset. Terminology stems from 1981 Tax Act that replaced *useful life* and *salvage value* as determinants of depreciation rates.

Covenant.   An agreement between two or more parties that pledges the parties to perform, or not perform, certain specified acts.

Creative Financing. A generalized term applied to many kinds of unconventional and innovative mortgage repayment plans.

Creditor. One who lends something of value to another.

Credit Report. A report giving the credit history on an individual or company; it reveals previous debt payment experience as well as other identifying data.

Curable Depreciation. Deterioration in property that can be corrected at a reasonable cost.

Debenture Bond. An unsecured pledge to repay a debt.

Debt. An obligation to be repaid by a borrower to a lender.

Debtor. One who owes something of value to another.

Debt Service. A term normally associated with commercial loans; it means the periodic payment of principal and interest.

Deed. A written instrument, which is signed, sealed, and delivered by the seller, transferring real property to another owner.

Deed of Trust. A type of mortgage that conditionally conveys real property to a third party for holding in trust for the benefit of a lender as security for repayment of a loan.

Deed Restriction. A clause in a deed that restricts the use of the land being conveyed.

Default. The failure to perform on an obligation as agreed in a contract.

Delinquency. A loan payment that is overdue but within the grace period allowed before actual default is declared.

Depreciation. The loss in value to property due to wear and tear, obsolescence, or economic factors. To offset depreciation loss, tax laws permit recovery of the cost of an investment through annual deductions from taxable income.

Development Loan. Money loaned for the purpose of improving land by the building of streets and utilities so as to create lots suitable for sale or use in building homes.

Discount. The difference between the amount paid for a note and the nominal, or face value, of that note. The reduction in the amount paid is normally measured in points as a percentage of the note amount.

Discount Rate. The interest rate charged by the Federal Reserve Bank for loans made to regulated savings institutions, credit unions, and commercial banks.

Disintermediation. The withdrawal of deposits from savings account held by intermediaries, such as savings institutions or commercial banks, generally for reinvestment in higher yielding investments.

Disposition. The right of a landowner to sell, lease, give away, mortgage, or otherwise dispose of, his or her land.

Due-on-Sale Clause. A mortgage clause that calls for the payoff of a loan in the event of a sale or conveyance of the collateral prior to maturity of the loan.

Earnest Money. A cash payment delivered to the seller of real property, or to an escrow agent for the transaction, as evidence of good faith to bind the purchase.

Economic Obsolescence. A loss of property value, normally incurable, resulting from factors outside the property itself, such as social, economic, or environmental forces.

Eminent Domain. The right of state or federal governments, agencies of governments, or companies designated by governments, to take private property for a necessary public purpose with just compensation paid to the owner.

Encroachment. Any physical intrusion upon the property rights of another.

Encumbrance. A claim against land, such as a lien or easement. Anything that affects or limits the fee simple title to, or value of, property; for example, a mortgage.

Environmental Protection Agency (EPA). A federal agency created in 1970 by consolidating various federal pollution control agencies. Its original authority has been substantially increased by adding responsibilities for the administration of subsequent environmental legislation.

Equal Credit Opportunity Act. Federal legislation passed in 1974 to ensure the fair and impartial granting of credit by various financial institutions.

Equitable Title. The right held by a purchaser under a contract for deed (and other similar agreements) to eventually obtain absolute ownership to property when legal title is held in the seller's or another's name.

Equity. The ownership interest—that portion of a property's value beyond any liability therein.

Escalation. The right of a lender to increase the rate of interest in a loan agreement.

Escrow. The process by which money and/or documents are held by a disinterested third party until all conditions of these escrow instructions, as prepared by the parties involved, have been satisfied; at which time delivery of the items can be made to the proper parties.

Execute. The act of signing a legal instrument by the involved parties, usually witnessed or notarized, so that it may be recorded.

Fair Credit Reporting Act. A federal law intended to protect the public from the reporting of inaccurate credit information by giving individuals the right to inspect information in their own file.

Fair Housing Act. Federal legislation passed in 1968 with subsequent amendments that prohibits certain kinds of discrimination in the sale or rental of most residential property.

Fair Market Value. The highest monetary price or its equivalent available in a competitive market as determined by negotiation between an informed, willing, and capable buyer and an informed and willing seller. Also called *market value*.

Fannie Mae. Popular nickname for the Federal National Mortgage Association, a quasi-government agency that plays a major role in the secondary mortgage market.

Federal Deposit Insurance Corporation (FDIC). An independent arm of the U.S. Treasury that insures deposits in banks and savings institutions.

Federal Funds Rate. An interest rate charged between banks for short-term loans that facilitate compliance with federal liquidity requirements. It is a rate used periodically by the Federal Reserve Bank as a guide in setting monetary policy.

Federal Housing Administration (FHA). A federal agency created in 1934, now a part of HUD, that insures high loan to value ratio residential loans.

Federal Reserve Bank System. A central banking system created in 1913 designed to manage the nation's monetary system and serve as a national bank for its member institutions.

Fee Simple. A legal term designating the highest interest in land that includes all the rights of ownership.

FHA Loan. A loan insured by the Insuring Office of the Department of Housing and Urban Development; a Federal Housing Administration commitment.

Finance Fee. The charge made by a lender for preparing and processing a loan package. Also known as *origination fee*.

First Mortgage. A mortgage on property that is superior in right to any other mortgage because of its prior time of recording.

Fixture. Personal property so affixed to the land as to become a part of the realty.

Forbearance. Refraining from taking legal action, even though a mortgage may be in default.

Foreclosure. Legal action to bar a mortgagor's claims to property after default has occurred.

Functional Obsolescence. A loss in value of an improvement, resulting from poor or inadequate design or possibly from age.

Funding Fee. A fee paid for a loan. Used to identify the fee paid to the VA for issuing their guarantee. Also may be applied to an additional fee paid for funding a conventional loan, typically a commercial loan, at closing.

Gift Letter. A letter or statement given to a lender or government agency stating that money advanced to assist the purchase of real property is a gift and there is no obligation to repay.

Ginnie Mae. Popular nickname for the Government National Mortgage Association, an agency under HUD authorized from time to time to subsidize housing assistance programs and to issue guarantees for approved pools of FHA, VA, and certain rural housing loans as a credit enhancement procedure.

Good Faith Estimate. A preliminary listing of the anticipated closing costs as required by the Real Estate Settlement Procedures Act.

Grace Period. An agreed upon time after an obligation becomes past due within which a party can perform without being considered in default.

Graduated Payment Mortgage. A repayment plan popularized by the FHA, but also approved as a conventional loan, that offers early-year monthly payments substantially lower than a constant-level plan, permitting easier qualification for a borrower. Payment amounts increase annually at a predetermined rate until reaching a level that fully amortizes the loan within its term.

Gross Income. The total money derived from an operating property over a given period of time.

Guarantee (vb). The act of pledging by a third party to assure performance of another.

Guaranty (n). A pledge by a third party to assume the obligation of another. Also applied to the government assured portion of a VA loan.

Hard Money Mortgage. Any mortgage loan funded in cash rather than given to finance the acquisition of real property.

Hazard Insurance. The insurance covering physical damage to property.

Homestead. A tract of land owned and occupied as the family home. Also a legal life estate in land created in differing ways by state laws devised to protect the possession and enjoyment of the owner against the claims of certain creditors.

HUD. The Department of Housing and Urban Development.

Hypothecation. A pledge of property without delivering possession; for example, a mortgage.

Impound Account. Money held for payment of an obligation due at some future time. Also known as *escrow account*.

Income. Money or other benefit received from the investment of labor or capital.

Income Property. Real estate capable of producing net revenue.

Index Rate. The rate to which the interest rate on an adjustable rate mortgage is tied.

Installment Note. A promissory note providing for repayment of the principal in two or more payments.

Instrument. A legal document in writing.

Interest. Payment for the use of money.

Interim Loan. A loan made with the expectation of repayment from the proceeds of another loan. Most often used in reference to a construction loan. Also called *interim financing*.

Junior Mortgage. A mortgage of lesser than first-lien priority.

Land Contract. Another term used to indicate a contract for deed.

Land Loan. Money loaned for the purchase of raw land.

Late Charge. A fee added to an installment as a penalty for failure to make a timely payment.

Leasehold. An estate in real property limited as to time, obtained and held with the consent of and by the payment of a consideration to the owner.

Leverage. The capacity to borrow an amount greater than the equity in property. The larger the loan in relation to the equity, the greater the leverage.

Lien. A legal claim or attachment, filed on record, against property as security for payment of an obligation.

Liquidity. The extent to which assets held in other forms can be easily and quickly converted into cash.

Loan. A granting of the use of money in return for the payment of interest.

Loan Pool. A block of loans held in trust and pledged as security for the issuance of a guarantee certificate, which is called a *mortgage-backed security.*

Loan to Value Ratio (LTVR). The ratio between the amount of a loan and the value of property pledged.

Lock-in Clause. A clause in a promissory note that restricts prepayment.

Maker. The person who executes a promissory note.

Marginal Property. Property capable of making only a very low economic return.

Maturity. The date that final payment is due on a loan.

Mechanics Lien. A claim for payment for services rendered or materials furnished to a property owner and filed on record in the county where the property is located. Also known as *mechanic's and materialmen's lien,* or *M & M lien.*

Merchantable Title. A salable title that is reasonably free from risk of litigation over defects and that would be accepted by a well-informed and prudent person. Also known as *marketable title.*

Mortgage. A conditional conveyance of property held as security for a debt.

Mortgagee. A lender of money and the receiver of the security in the form of a mortgage. (*Memory note:* Lender and mortgagee both have two *e*'s.)

Mortgage Note. A description of the debt and a promise to pay—the instrument that is secured by the mortgage.

Mortgage Payment. A term normally used to distinguish the monthly payment on a home loan, including principal and interest plus one-twelfth of the annual property tax and insurance premium. Also known as PITI.

Mortgage Pool. A specific block of mortgage loans held in trust as collateral for the issuance of a mortgage-backed security.

Mortgage Portfolio. The aggregate of mortgage loans held by anyone as an investment.

Mortgage Release. A disclaimer of further liability on the mortgage note granted by the lender. When used with a trust deed, it is a deed of reconveyance.

Mortgaging Out. Securing a loan upon completion of a project that is sufficient to cover all costs—a 100 percent loan.

Mortgagor. The borrower of money and the grantor of a mortgage as security. (*Memory note:* Borrower and Mortgagor both have two *o*'s)

Multifamily Mortgage. A government term designating an apartment or any property with more than four dwelling units.

Mutual Mortgage Insurance Fund. A fund established by the National Housing Act into which all FHA mortgage insurance premiums and other specified revenues of the FHA are paid and from which claims are met.

Mutual Savings Bank. A nearly obsolete term designating a state-chartered savings bank owned by its own depositors. As many shift to stockholder-owned institutions, the word *mutual* is being dropped from its name.

Negative Amortization. A periodic increase in the principal balance due on a mortgage loan, usually resulting from unpaid interest added to the principal.

Negative Cash Flow. When cash expenditures to maintain an investment exceed the cash income derived therefrom.

Negotiable Instrument. Any written instrument that may be legally transferred to another by endorsement or delivery, such as a check or promissory note.

Net Income. That portion of gross income remaining after the payment of all expenses.

Nominal Interest Rate. The stated, or named, interest rate in a note or contract; the nominal interest rate may differ from the true or effective rate.

Nonrecourse Loan. A loan on which the borrower is not held personally liable.

Note. A unilateral instrument containing a promise to pay a sum of money at a specified time. The evidence of a debt.

Open-End Mortgage. An expandable mortgage containing a clause that permits additional money to be advanced by the lender and secured by the same collateral pledge.

Option. The right to purchase or lease a piece of property at a certain price without the obligation to buy or lease for a designated period of time.

Origination Fee. The amount charged for services performed by the company handling the initial application and processing of a loan. Normally paid at the time of closing.

Package Mortgage. A mortgage pledge that includes both real and personal property.

Partial Release Clause. A mortgage clause that allows the release of certain parcels of land from the blanket mortgage. Commonly used by land developers selling lots to home builders.

Participation Loan. A loan funded by more than one lender and serviced by one of them.

Pass-Through Security. A bond, certificate, or other form of security collateralized by a block of mortgage loans. Monthly payments on the mortgage loans are "passed through" a trustee to the holders of the securities.

Permanent Loan. A mortgage loan granted for a term of 20 to 40 years, based on the economic life of a property.

Personal Property. A possession—any item of value that is not real estate.

PITI. An acronym used to identify the components of a mortgage payment: principal, interest, taxes, and insurance.

Planned Unit Development (PUD). A comprehensive land development plan employed primarily in the more efficient planning of residential areas.

Pledged Account Mortgage (PAM). A mortgage repayment plan that features lower initial monthly payments similar to a graduated payment design. With a PAM, the borrower deposits a portion of the down payment in an escrow account with the lender and allows the lender to withdraw enough money from the account to supplement the borrower's monthly payments. The result is a constant-level, fully amortized payment applied to the loan each month.

Point. A unit of measure of finance charges, including but not limited to a loan discount, that amounts to one percent of a loan. One point is one percent of the subject loan.

Possession. Occupancy—the highest form of "notice."

Prepayment Penalty. An amount disclosed in the terms of a note requiring an additional fee to be paid the lender if all or part of a loan is paid prior to maturity.

Prime Rate. A base interest rate, determined independently by banks, that generally is charged the bank's most creditworthy customers.

Principal. The amount of the mortgage debt. Also identifies a party to a transaction.

Private Mortgage Insurance (PMI). Insurance against default on repayment of a mortgage loan, as offered by private insurance carriers.

Promissory Note. A written promise to pay someone a given amount of money at a specified time.

Purchase Money Mortgage. A mortgage taken by the seller as all or part of the purchase consideration. Also identifies a mortgage wherein the proceeds of the loan are used to purchase the property.

Qualified Buyer. A buyer who has demonstrated the financial capacity and creditworthiness required to afford the asking price.

Radon. A colorless, odorless naturally occurring gas produced from the decay of uranium and other radioactive materials.

Raw Land. Land in its unused, natural state.

Real Estate. Land and that attached thereto, including minerals and resources inherent to the land, and any manufactured improvements so affixed as to become a part of the land. Also known as *realty*.

Real Property. In addition to the land and that attached thereto, real property includes the interests, benefits, and rights inherent in the ownership of real estate.

Recording. Filing a legal instrument in the public records of a county.

Recourse Note. A debt instrument allowing recovery against both the property and the borrower, or endorser, personally.

Refinancing. Obtaining a loan for the purpose of repaying an existing loan.

Reverse Annuity Mortgage. A mortgage designed to use the equity value of a home as collateral for a loan funded in installments intended primarily to supplement living costs. Also called a *reverse mortgage* and may be insured by the FHA.

Secondary Financing. Negotiation of a second mortgage, or a junior mortgage, to assist in the acquisition of property.

Secondary Market. A market for the purchase and sale of existing mortgages.

Security. As used in finance, an instrument evidencing ownership (stock) or debt (bond) in a corporate entity.

Seller/Servicer. Loan originators who are approved to sell loans to Fannie Mae or Freddie Mac and who also service the loans for them.

Servicing (Loan Servicing). The work involved with handling mortgage payments, comprising the collection of payments, remittance of principal and interest to the note holder, accounting for escrow funds with proper disbursement, and follow-up on delinquencies.

Settlement Procedure. The steps taken to finance the funding of a loan agreement and a property transfer. Also called *loan closing*.

Simple Interest. Interest computed on the principal only.

Solar Heating. An energy efficient system for heating buildings that utilizes the sun's energy.

Spot Loan. Money loaned on individual houses in various neighborhoods, as contrasted to new houses in a single development.

Statutory Redemption. State laws that permit a mortgagor a limited time after foreclosure to pay off the debt and reclaim the mortgaged property.

"Subject To" Mortgage. Taking title to mortgaged property that is subject to an existing mortgage without accepting the obligation on same.

Subordination. To make a claim to real property inferior to that of another by specific agreement.

Survey. The measurement and description of land by a registered surveyor.

Sweat Equity. An ownership interest in property earned by the performance of manual labor on that property.

Syndication. A group of individuals or companies joined together in pursuit of a limited investment purpose.

Takeout Loan. A type of loan commitment—a promise to make a loan at a future specified time. Most commonly used to designate a higher cost, shorter term back-up commitment as a support for construction financing until a suitable permanent loan can be secured.

Teaser Rate Mortgage. An adjustable rate mortgage with an initial rate well below existing market rates.

Term. The time limit within which a loan must be repaid in full.

Term Loan. A loan that requires interest-only payments until maturity.

Time Deposit. Money held on deposit that is not subject to demand withdrawal.

Title. The right to ownership in land.

Title Insurance. Protection against adverse claims to ownership arising from defects in the chain of title.

Torrens Certificate. A certificate issued by a public authority in the few states that recognize the Torrens system, which establishes an indefeasible title for the registered owner of the land.

Tract Loan. An individual mortgage loan negotiated for houses of similar character located in a new development.

Trust Deed. An agreement in writing under seal conveying property from the owner to a trustee for the accomplishment of objectives set forth in the agreement. Sometimes used to describe a deed of trust mortgage instrument.

Trustee. One who holds property in trust for another to secure performance of an obligation. Also identifies the third party holding a conditional title to property held as collateral under a deed of trust mortgage.

Trustor. One who borrows money under the terms of a deed of trust mortgage.

Underwriter. The person or company taking responsibility for rating risks and approving mortgage loans. Also used to identify those who provide credit enhancement for mortgage loans, such as Fannie Mae and Freddie Mac.

Unit. That part of a property intended for any type of independent use and with an exit to a public street or corridor.

Unsecured Loan. A loan made without the benefit of a pledge of collateral.

Usury. Interest paid or accepted in excess of that permitted by state law.

VA Loan. A loan made by private lenders that is partially guaranteed by the Department of Veterans Affairs.

Variable Rate Mortgage. A nearly obsolete term for a mortgage that allows the periodic adjustment of the interest rate during the term of the loan. More commonly called *adjustable rate mortgage.*

Vendor's Lien. A lien securing the loan by a seller that is used to purchase the property.

Warehousing. The practice, mostly by mortgage companies, by pledging mortgage notes to a commercial bank for cash used to fund originated mortgage loans. A line of credit.

Wetlands. Water-saturated land areas that cannot be disturbed without a permit from the Corps of Engineers.

Whole Loan. A term used in the secondary market to indicate that the full amount of a loan is available for sale with no portion or participation retained by the seller.

Wraparound Mortgage. A junior mortgage that acknowledges and includes an existing mortgage loan in its principal amount due and in its payment conditions. Payment is made to the holder of the wrap, or his or her agent, who in turn makes payment on the existing mortgage. The purpose is to gain some advantages in lower interest cost on an existing loan, to hold the mortgage priority of an existing loan, and to retain an element of control over the loan payments.

Yield. The total money earned on a loan for the term of the loan, as computed on an annual percentage basis. Also known as *rate of return.*

Appendices

Uniform Residential Loan Application

This application is designed to be completed by the applicant(s) with the lender's assistance. Applicants should complete this form as "Borrower" or "Co-Borrower", as applicable. Co-Borrower information must also be provided (and the appropriate box checked) when ☐ the income or assets of a person other than the "Borrower" (including the Borrower's spouse) will be used as a basis for loan qualification or ☐ the income or assets of the Borrower's spouse will not be used as a basis for loan qualification, but his or her liabilities must be considered because the Borrower resides in a community property state, the security property is located in a community property state, or the Borrower is relying on other property located in a community property state as a basis for repayment of the loan.

I. TYPE OF MORTGAGE AND TERMS OF LOAN

Mortgage Applied for:	☐ VA ☐ FHA	☐ Conventional ☐ FmHA	☐ Other:	Agency Case Number	Lender Case No.

Amount $	Interest Rate %	No. of Months	Amortization Type:	☐ Fixed Rate ☐ GPM	☐ Other (explain): ☐ ARM (type):

II. PROPERTY INFORMATION AND PURPOSE OF LOAN

Subject Property Address (street, city, state, & zip code)	No. of Units

Legal Description of Subject Property (attach description if necessary)	Year Built

Purpose of Loan	☐ Purchase ☐ Refinance	☐ Construction ☐ Construction-Permanent	☐ Other (explain):	Property will be: ☐ Primary Residence ☐ Secondary Residence ☐ Investment

Complete this line if construction or construction-permanent loan.

Year Lot Acquired	Original Cost $	Amount Existing Liens $	(a) Present Value of Lot $	(b) Cost of Improvements $	Total (a + b) $

Complete this line if this is a refinance loan.

Year Acquired	Original Cost $	Amount Existing Liens $	Purpose of Refinance	Describe Improvements ☐ made ☐ to be made Cost: $

Title will be held in what Name(s)	Manner in which Title will be held	Estate will be held in: ☐ Fee Simple ☐ Leasehold (show expiration date)

Source of Down Payment, Settlement Charges and/or Subordinate Financing (explain)

III. BORROWER INFORMATION

Borrower	Co-Borrower
Borrower's Name (include Jr. or Sr. if applicable)	Co-Borrower's Name (include Jr. or Sr. if applicable)
Social Security Number / Home Phone (incl. area code) / Age / Yrs. School	Social Security Number / Home Phone (incl. area code) / Age / Yrs. School
☐ Married ☐ Unmarried (include single, divorced, widowed) ☐ Separated / Dependents (not listed by Co-Borrower) no. ages	☐ Married ☐ Unmarried (include single, divorced, widowed) ☐ Separated / Dependents (not listed by Borrower) no. ages
Present Address (street, city, state, zip code) ☐ Own ☐ Rent ___ No. Yrs.	Present Address (street, city, state, zip code) ☐ Own ☐ Rent ___ No. Yrs.

If residing at present address for less than two years, complete the following:

Former Address (street, city, state, zip code) ☐ Own ☐ Rent ___ No. Yrs.	Former Address (street, city, state, zip code) ☐ Own ☐ Rent ___ No. Yrs.
Former Address (street, city, state, zip code) ☐ Own ☐ Rent ___ No. Yrs.	Former Address (street, city, state, zip code) ☐ Own ☐ Rent ___ No. Yrs.

IV. EMPLOYMENT INFORMATION

Borrower	Co-Borrower
Name & Address of Employer ☐ Self Employed / Yrs. on this job / Yrs. employed in this line of work/profession	Name & Address of Employer ☐ Self Employed / Yrs. on this job / Yrs. employed in this line of work/profession
Position/Title/Type of Business / Business Phone (incl. area code)	Position/Title/Type of Business / Business Phone (incl. area code)

If employed in current position for less than two years or if currently employed in more than one position, complete the following:

Name & Address of Employer ☐ Self Employed / Dates (from - to) / Monthly Income $	Name & Address of Employer ☐ Self Employed / Dates (from - to) / Monthly Income $
Position/Title/Type of Business / Business Phone (incl. area code)	Position/Title/Type of Business / Business Phone (incl. area code)
Name & Address of Employer ☐ Self Employed / Dates (from - to) / Monthly Income $	Name & Address of Employer ☐ Self Employed / Dates (from - to) / Monthly Income $
Position/Title/Type of Business / Business Phone (incl. area code)	Position/Title/Type of Business / Business Phone (incl. area code)

Freddie Mac Form 65   10/92
PRINTED IN USA
Printed on recyclable paper.

Form DL 1002 R 6/95

Page 1 of 4 pages

Fannie Mae Form 1003   10/92

DATA LEGAL FORMS™
Easy toll free ordering 1-800-748-0235 • 1-616-459-3411
24 hour fax 1-616-459-5317

V. MONTHLY INCOME AND COMBINED HOUSING EXPENSE INFORMATION

Gross Monthly Income	Borrower	Co-Borrower	Total	Combined Monthly Housing Expense	Present	Proposed
Base Empl. Income*	$	$	$	Rent	$	
Overtime				First Mortgage (P&I)		$
Bonuses				Other Financing (P&I)		
Commissions				Hazard Insurance		
Dividends/Interest				Real Estate Taxes		
Net Rental Income				Mortgage Insurance		
OTHER (before completing, see the notice in "describe other income," below)				Homeowner Assn. Dues		
				Other:		
Total	$	$	$	**Total**	$	$

*Self Employed Borrower(s) may be required to provide additional documentation such as tax returns and financial statements.

Describe Other Income *Notice:* **Alimony, child support, or separate maintenance income need not be revealed if the Borrower (B) or Co-Borrower (C) does not choose to have it considered for repaying this loan.**

B/C		Monthly Amount
		$

VI. ASSETS AND LIABILITIES

This Statement and any applicable supporting schedules may be completed jointly by both married and unmarried Co-Borrowers if their assets and liabilities are sufficiently joined so that the Statement can be meaningfully and fairly presented on a combined basis; otherwise separate Statements and Schedules are required. If the Co-Borrower section was completed about a spouse, this Statement and supporting schedules must be completed about that spouse also.

Completed ☐ Jointly ☐ Not Jointly

ASSETS Description	Cash or Market Value	Liabilities and Pledged Assets. List the creditor's name, address and account number for all outstanding debts, including automobile loans, revolving charge accounts, real estate loans, alimony, child support, stock pledges, etc. Use continuation sheet, if necessary. Indicate by (*) those liabilities which will be satisfied upon sale of real estate owned or upon refinancing of the subject property.	Monthly Payt. & Mos. Left to Pay	Unpaid Balance
Cash deposit toward purchase held by:	$	**LIABILITIES**		
		Name and address of Company	$ Payt./Mos.	$
List checking and savings accounts below				
Name and address of Bank, S&L, or Credit Union				
		Acct. no.		
		Name and address of Company	$ Payt./Mos.	$
Acct. no.	$			
Name and address of Bank, S&L, or Credit Union				
		Acct. no.		
		Name and address of Company	$ Payt./Mos.	$
Acct. no.	$			
Name and address of Bank, S&L, or Credit Union				
		Acct. no.		
		Name and address of Company	$ Payt./Mos.	$
Acct. no.	$			
Name and address of Bank, S&L, or Credit Union				
		Acct. no.		
		Name and address of Company	$ Payt./Mos.	$
Acct. no.	$			
Stocks & Bonds (Company name/number & description)	$			
		Acct. no.		
		Name and address of Company	$ Payt./Mos.	$
Life insurance net cash value	$			
Face amount: $				
Subtotal Liquid Assets	$			
Real estate owned (enter market value from schedule of real estate owned)	$	Acct. no.		
Vested interest in retirement fund	$	Name and address of Company	$ Payt./Mos.	$
Net worth of business(es) owned (attach financial statement)	$			
Automobiles owned (make and year)	$			
		Acct. no.		
		Alimony/Child Support/Separate Maintenance Payments Owed to:	$	
Other Assets (itemize)	$	Job Related Expense (child care, union dues, etc.)	$	
		Total Monthly Payments	$	
Total Assets a.	$	**Net Worth** (a minus b) ▶ $	**Total Liabilities b.**	$

Freddie Mac Form 65 10/92
PRINTED IN USA
♻ Printed on recyclable paper. SOY INK

Page 2 of 4

Fannie Mae Form 1003 10/92

DATA LEGAL FORMS™
Easy toll free ordering 1-800-748-0235 • 1-616-459-3411
24 hour fax 1-616-459-5317

VI. ASSETS AND LIABILITIES (cont.)

Schedule of Real Estate Owned (If additional properties are owned, use continuation sheet.)

Property Address (enter S if sold, PS if pending sale or R if rental being held for income)	Type of Property	Present Market Value	Amount of Mortgages & Liens	Gross Rental Income	Mortgage Payments	Insurance, Maintenance, Taxes & Misc.	Net Rental Income
		$	$	$	$	$	$
	Totals	$	$	$	$	$	$

List any additional names under which credit has previously been received and indicate appropriate creditor name(s) and account number(s):

Alternate Name	Creditor Name	Account Number

VII. DETAILS OF TRANSACTION

a. Purchase price	$
b. Alterations, improvements, repairs	
c. Land (if acquired separately)	
d. Refinance (incl. debts to be paid off)	
e. Estimated prepaid items	
f. Estimated closing costs	
g. PMI, MIP, Funding Fee	
h. Discount (if Borrower will pay)	
i. Total costs (add items a through h)	
j. Subordinate financing	
k. Borrower's closing costs paid by Seller	
l. Other Credits (explain)	
m. Loan amount (exclude PMI, MIP, Funding Fee financed)	
n. PMI, MIP, Funding Fee financed	
o. Loan amount (add m & n)	
p. Cash from/to Borrower (subtract j, k, l & o from i)	

VIII. DECLARATIONS

If you answer "yes" to any questions a through i, please use continuation sheet for explanation.

Borrower Yes No / Co-Borrower Yes No

a. Are there any outstanding judgments against you?

b. Have you been declared bankrupt within the past 7 years?

c. Have you had property foreclosed upon or given title or deed in lieu thereof in the last 7 years?

d. Are you a party to a lawsuit?

e. Have you directly or indirectly been obligated on any loan which resulted in foreclosure, transfer of title in lieu of foreclosure, or judgment? (This would include such loans as home mortgage loans, SBA loans, home improvement loans, educational loans, manufactured (mobile) home loans, any mortgage, financial obligation, bond, or loan guarantee. If "Yes," provide details, including date, name and address of Lender, FHA or VA case number, if any, and reasons for the action.)

f. Are you presently delinquent or in default on any Federal debt or any other loan, mortgage, financial obligation, bond, or loan guarantee? If "Yes," give details as described in the preceding question.

g. Are you obligated to pay alimony, child support, or separate maintenance?

h. Is any part of the down payment borrowed?

i. Are you a co-maker or endorser on a note?

j. Are you a U.S. citizen?

k. Are you a permanent resident alien?

l. Do you intend to occupy the property as your primary residence? If "Yes," complete question m below.

m. Have you had an ownership interest in a property in the last three years?

(1) What type of property did you own–principal residence (PR), second home (SH), or investment property (IP)?

(2) How did you hold title to the home–solely by yourself (S), jointly with your spouse (SP), or jointly with another person (O)?

IX. ACKNOWLEDGMENT AND AGREEMENT

The undersigned specifically acknowledge(s) and agree(s) that: (1) the loan requested by this application will be secured by a first mortgage or deed of trust on the property described herein; (2) the property will not be used for any illegal or prohibited purpose or use; (3) all statements made in this application are made for the purpose of obtaining the loan indicated herein; (4) occupation of the property will be as indicated above; (5) verification or reverification of any information contained in the application may be made at any time by the Lender, its agents, successors and assigns, either directly or through a credit reporting agency, from any source named in this application, and the original copy of this application will be retained by the Lender, even if the loan is not approved; (6) the Lender, its agents, successors and assigns will rely on the information contained in the application and I/we have a continuing obligation to amend and/or supplement the information provided in this application if any of the material facts which I/we have represented herein should change prior to closing; (7) in the event my/our payments on the loan indicated in this application become delinquent, the Lender, its agents, successors and assigns, may, in addition to all their other rights and remedies, report my/our name(s) and account information to a credit reporting agency; (8) ownership of the loan may be transferred to successor or assign of the Lender without notice to me and/or the administration of the loan account may be transferred to an agent, successor or assign of the Lender with prior notice to me; (9) the Lender, its agents, successors and assigns make no representations or warranties, express or implied, to the Borrower(s) regarding the property, the condition of the property, or the value of the property.

Right to Receive Copy of Appraisal: I/We have the right to a copy of the appraisal report used in connection with this application for credit. To obtain a copy, I/we must send Lender a written request at the mailing address Lender has provided. Lender must hear from me/us no later than 90 days after Lender notifies me/us about the action taken on this application, or I/we withdraw this application.

Certification: I/We certify that the information provided in this application is true and correct as of the date set forth opposite my/our signature(s) on this application and acknowledge my/our understanding that any intentional or negligent misrepresentation(s) of the information contained in this application may result in civil liability and/or criminal penalties including, but not limited to, fine or imprisonment or both under the provisions of Title 18, United States Code, Section 1001, et seq. and liability for monetary damages to the Lender, its agents, successors and assigns, insurers and any other person who may suffer any loss due to reliance upon any misrepresentation which I/we have made on this application.

Borrower's Signature	Date	Co-Borrower's Signature	Date
X		X	

X. INFORMATION FOR GOVERNMENT MONITORING PURPOSES

The following information is requested by the Federal Government for certain types of loans related to a dwelling, in order to monitor the Lender's compliance with equal credit opportunity, fair housing and home mortgage disclosure laws. You are not required to furnish this information, but are encouraged to do so. The law provides that a Lender may neither discriminate on the basis of this information, nor on whether you choose to furnish it. However, if you choose not to furnish it, under Federal regulations this Lender is required to note race and sex on the basis of visual observation or surname. If you do not wish to furnish the above information, please check the box below. (Lender must review the above material to assure that the disclosures satisfy all requirements to which the Lender is subject under applicable state law for the particular type of loan applied for.)

BORROWER

Race/National Origin: ☐ I do not wish to furnish this information
☐ American Indian or Alaskan Native ☐ Asian or Pacific Islander ☐ White, not of Hispanic Origin
☐ Black, not of Hispanic origin ☐ Hispanic
☐ Other (specify) _____

Sex: ☐ Female ☐ Male

CO-BORROWER

Race/National Origin: ☐ I do not wish to furnish this information
☐ American Indian or Alaskan Native ☐ Asian or Pacific Islander ☐ White, not of Hispanic Origin
☐ Black, not of Hispanic origin ☐ Hispanic
☐ Other (specify) _____

Sex: ☐ Female ☐ Male

To be Completed by Interviewer This application was taken by:	Interviewer's Name (print or type)	Name and Address of Interviewer's Employer
☐ face-to-face interview	Interviewer's Signature Date	
☐ by mail		
☐ by telephone	Interviewer's Phone Number (incl. area code)	

Freddie Mac Form 65   10/92   Form DL 1002 R 6/95   Page 3 of 4   Fannie Mae Form 1003   10/92
PRINTED IN USA
Printed on recyclable paper

Continuation Sheet/Residential Loan Application

Use this continuation sheet if you need more space to complete the Residential Loan Application. Mark **B** for Borrower or **C** for Co-Borrower.	Borrower:	Agency Case Number:
	Co-Borrower:	Lender Case Number:

I/We fully understand that it is a Federal crime punishable by fine or imprisonment, or both, to knowingly make any false statements concerning any of the above facts as applicable under the provisions of Title 18, United States Code, Section 1001, et seq.

Borrower's Signature:	Date	Co-Borrower's Signature:	Date
X		X	

Freddie Mac Form 65   10/92

PRINTED IN US

Printed on recyclable paper.

Page 4 of 4

Fannie Mae Form 1003   10/92

FannieMae

Request for Verification of Deposit

Part I - Request

1. To (Name and address of depository)	2. From (Name and address of lender)

I certify that this verification has been sent directly to the depository and has not passed through the hands of the applicant or any other interested party.

3. Signature of Lender	4. Title	5. Date	6. Lender's No. (Optional)

7. Information To Be Verified

Type of Account	Account in Name of	Account Number	Balance

To Depository: I/We have applied for a mortgage loan and stated in my financial statement that the balance on deposit with you is as shown above. You are authorized to verify this information and to supply the lender identified above with the information requested in items 10 through 13. Your response is solely a matter of courtesy which no responsibility is attached to your institution or any of your officers.

8. Name and Address of Applicant(s)	9. Signature of Applicant(s)

To Be Completed by Depository

Part II - Verification of Depository

10. Deposit Accounts of Applicant(s)

Type of Account	Account Number	Current Balance	Average Balance For Previous Two Months	Date Opened
		$	$	
		$	$	
		$	$	
		$	$	

11. Loans Outstanding To Applicant(s)

Loan Number	Date of Loan	Original Amt.	Current Balance	Installments (Monthly/Quarterly)		Secured By	Numbers of Late Payments
		$	$	$	per		
		$	$	$	per		
		$	$	$	per		

12. Please include any additional information which may be of assistance in determination of credit worthiness. (Please include information on loans paid in full in Item 11 above.)

13. If the name(s) on the account(s) differ from those listed in item 7, please supply the name(s) on the account(s) as reflected by your records.

Part III - Authorized Signature
Federal statutes provide severe penalties for any fraud, intentional misrepresentation, or criminal connivance or conspiracy purposed to influence the issuance of any guaranty or insurance by the VA Secretary, the U.S.D.A. FmHA/FHA Commissioner, or the HUD/CPD Assistant Secretary.

14. Signature of Depository	15. Title (Please print or type)	16. Date

17. Please print or type name signed in item 14	18. Phone No.

FannieMae

Request for Verification of Employment

Instructions:
Lender - Complete items 1 through 7. Have applicant complete item 8. Forward directly to employer named in item 1.
Employer - Please complete either Part II or Part III as applicable. Complete Part IV and return directly to lender named in item 2.
The form is to be transmitted directly to the lender and is not to be transmitted through the applicant or any other party.

Part I - Request

1. To (Name and address of employer)	2. From (Name and address of lender)

I certify that this verification has been sent directly to the employer and has not passed through the hands of the applicant or any other interested party.

3. Signature of Lender	4. Title	5. Date	6. Lender's No. (Optional)

I have applied for a mortgage loan and stated that I am now or was formerly employed by you. My signature below authorizes verification of this information.

7. Name and Address of Applicant (Include employee or badge number)	8. Signature of Applicant

Part II - Verification of Present Employment

9. Applicant's Date of Employment	10. Present Position	11. Probability of Continued Employment

12A. Current Gross Pay Base (Enter amt. and Check Period)

☐ Annual   ☐ Weekly   ☐ Other (Specify)
$ _____   ☐ Monthly   ☐ Hourly

13. For Military Personnel Only
Pay Grade _____

14. If Overtime or Bonus is Applicable, is its Continuance Likely?
Overtime ☐ Yes ☐ No
Bonus ☐ Yes ☐ No

12B. Gross Earnings

Type	Year To Date	Past year 19	Past Year 19
Base Pay	Thru ___ 19 $	$	$
Overtime	$	$	$
Commiss.	$	$	$
Bonus	$	$	$
Total	$	$	$

Type	Monthly Amount
Base Pay	$
Rations	$
Flight or Hazard	$
Clothing	$
Quarters	$
Pro Pay	$
Overseas or Combat	$
Variable Housing Allowance	$

15. If paid hourly - average hours per week.

16. Date of applicant's next pay increase.

17. Projected amount of next pay increase.

18. Date of applicant's last pay increase.

19. Amount of last pay increase.

20. Remarks (If employee was off work for any length of time, please indicate time period and reason.)

Part III - Verification of Previous Employment

21. Date Hired	23. Salary/Wage at Termination Per (Year)(Month)(Week)
22. Date Terminated	Base _____ Overtime _____ Commissions _____ Bonus _____

24. Reason for Leaving	25. Positions Held

Part IV - Authorized Signature
Federal statutes provide severe penalties for any fraud, intentional misrepresentation, or criminal connivance or conspiracy purposed to influence the issuance of any guaranty or insurance by the VA Secretary, the U.S.D.A., FmHA/FHA Commissioner, or the HUD/CPD Assistant Secretary.

26. Signature of Employer	27. Title (Please print or type)	28. Date
29. Print or type name signed in item 26	30. Phone No.	

Printed by The Loan Handler - Contour Software Inc.
For Employer software to complete this entire form call 800-CONTOUR

Fannie Mae
Form 1005 Mar. 90

GIFT LETTER

TO WHOM IT MAY CONCERN:

This is to certify that I / we _____
(donor /s)

hereby give to my / our _____, _____
(relationship)   (name of recipient)

_____, the sum of $_____ in order to aid in the

purchase of a home. This sum is given freely as a gift and no repayment of any kind will be

accepted. The funds have been / will be given to _____
(name of recipient)

on _____.
(date)

_____   _____
(Signature of Donor)   (Signature of Donor)

_____   _____
(Address)   (Address)

_____   _____
(City)   (State)   (Zip)   (City)   (State)   (Zip)

_____   _____
(Phone Number)   (Phone Number)

RECEIPT OF GIFT FUNDS

We hereby state that we received a gift of $_____ from _____
(Name of Donor)

_____ and have deposited this amount in account number

_____ at _____
(Name of depository)

_____   _____
(Recipient)   (Recipient)

_____   _____
(Date)   (Date)

Section 1010 of Title 18, U.S.C., "Department of Housing and Urban Development and Federal Housing Administration transactions," provides: "Whoever, for the purpose of influencing in any way the action of such Department—makes, passes, utters, or publishes any statement, knowing that same to be false—shall be fined not more than $5,000 or imprisoned not more than two years, or both." Other Federal Statutes provide severe penalties for any fraud as intentional misrepresentation made for the purpose of influencing the insurance of any guaranty or insurance of the making of any loan by the Administrator of Veterans Affairs.

GENERAL DISCLOSURE
NOTICE TO APPLICANTS

This is notice to you as required by the Right to Financial Privacy Act of 1978 that the Veterans Administration Loan Guaranty Division (VA), Federal Housing Administration (FHA), Federal National Mortgage Association (FNMA), and/or private investor has a right of access to financial records held by a financial institution in connection with the consideration or administration of assistance to you. Financial records involving your transaction will be available to the above listed agencies without further notice or authorization, but will not be disclosed or released to another government agency or department without your consent except as required or permitted by law.

EQUAL CREDIT OPPORTUNITY ACT NOTICE

The Federal Equal Credit Opportunity Act prohibits creditors from discriminating against credit applicants on the basis of race, color, religion, national origin, sex, marital status, age (provided that the applicant has the capacity to enter into a binding contract), because all or part of the applicant's income is derived from any public assistance program, or because the applicant has in good faith exercised any right under the Consumer Credit Protection Act. The federal Agency that administers compliance under this law concerning this creditor is: Federal Trade Commission Equal Credit Opportunity, Washington, D.C. 20580.

RESPA RECEIPT

The undersigned hereby acknowledges receipt of the following or has been advised the following will be mailed to me within 3 days: 1) A completed copy of the "Good Faith Estimate" required to be provided to the borrower(s) under the provisions of the Real Estate Settlement Procedures Act of 1974 (Pub.L. 94-533), 12 U.S.C. 2601, et seq, as amended by the Real Estate Settlement Procedures Act Amendments of 1975 (Pub.L. 95-205) ("Respa") and 3500.7 of Regulation X issued by the Secretary of Housing and Urban Development pursuant to the above mentioned Acts. 2) A copy of the Special Information Booklet prescribed by the Secretary of Housing and Urban Development issued pursuant to the above mentioned Acts and 3500.6 Regulation X issued by the Secretary of Housing and Urban Development pursuant to the above mentioned Acts. 3) A copy of the Equal Credit Opportunity Act Notice as provided for in 202.4(d) of Regulations B (CFR 202) issued by the Board of Governors of the Federal Reserve System pursuant to the Equal Credit Opportunity Act(Pub.L.93-495;88 Stat 1521 et seq., as amended by the Equal Credit Opportunity Act Amendment of 1976).

QUALITY CONTROL AUTHORIZATION

In the event my/our loan is selected by Summit Mortgage Corporation or any other entity for a quality control audit, I/we authorize and permit either of the above parties to verify the current, previous, and future income and employment information in my/our application of even date therewith. I/we are aware that under the Privacy Act of 1974, I/we may decline to make this authorization without prejudice and that a determination would then be made based on information, or lack of information, available to Summit Mortgage Corporation or any of its investors.

AUTHORIZATION FOR CREDIT, COURIER, AND APPRAISAL SERVICES

I/We have applied to Summit Mortgage Corporation for a home mortgage loan. This will authorize you to order a credit report on me/us from any credit reporting agency of your choice for which I/we will pay fees; verify and reverify, where necessary, my/our employment and income with my/our employer(s), and any bank accounts which I/we list with you; and obtain any information from any source you think necessary in underwriting this application. Most of the time, in order to expedite all of the proper documents, couriers must be sent to pick up verifications. I/We authorize Summit Mortgage Corporation to use couriers to process our applications and these fees will be charged to me/us at closing. You are also authorized to forward any and all credit information obtained by you to Federal Housing Administration, Veterans Administration, or any other investor if this loan is to be insured or guaranteed by either of these agencies. (You have the right to a copy of the appraisal report used in connection with your application for credit. If you wish a copy, please write to us at Customer Service Department, Summit Mortgage Corp., 11999 Katy Freeway, Ste 650, Houston, Texas 77079. We must hear from you no later than 90 days after we notify you about the action taken on your credit application or the date you withdrew our application).

ARBITRATION AGREEMENT

Any controversy or claim arising out of or relating to your loan application (including the processing thereof), subsequent loan, or any other contract, or business relationship of any type with Summit Mortgage Corporation, its affiliates, employees, officers, directors, representatives, attorneys and other agents (collectively, Summit for the purposes of this paragraph) shall be settled by arbitration before either Judicial Arbitration & Mediation Service/Endiispute of the American Arbitration Association (the choice of organization to be at the option of Summit or the respondent) in accordance with its customary, expedited rules and procedures of such organization. Provided, however, the arbitrators shall be obligated to comply with all procedural due process as would be afforded the parties under Texas law generally. At the option of either party, the panel may consist of three persons. The decision of the arbitrators shall be final, conclusive and non-appealable and shall be binding upon the parties. Any court of competent jurisdiction is authorized to enter a final judgement incorporating the terms of the decision and award of the arbitrators.

NON-REPAYMENT OF APPLICATION FEE

The undersigned hereby acknowledges that the Application Fee paid to Summit Mortgage Corporation at the time your application is taken as payment for initializing the processing of your loan, and as of the time of payment, is a non-refundable fee. This fee (including but not limited to application fee, credit report fee, bond program fee, commitment fee, long lock fee, and any fee paid before closing) is fully earned by Summit Mortgage Corporation as of the time loan of application, even without showing any specific work or services that have been started or completed. Normally, 100% of the fee is used to cover credit reports, appraisal fees, and courier fees. THERE IS NO PARTIAL OR FULL REFUND OF THIS APPLICATION FEE OR ANY PRE-CLOSING FEE UNLESS THERE IS BOTH A LOAN CLOSING AND A LOAN FUNDING. (Some fees are credited to buyer upon closing)

GENERAL

The undersigned applied for the loan indicated in an application made with Summit Mortgage Corporation to be secured by first mortgage or deed of trust on the property described in same, and represents that the property will not be used for any illegal or restricted purpose, and that all statements made in aforementioned application are true and are made for the purpose of obtaining this loan. Verification may be obtained from any source named in the aforementioned application. The original copy of aforementioned application will be retained by the Lender, even if the loan is not granted.

No amendments to the General Disclosure shall be permitted unless such are in writing and signed by the President or any Vice President of Summit Mortgage Corporation. The costs and expenses provided to loan applicant by same or all of the preferred providers may not be separately tracked or identified by Summit Mortgage Corporation for the benefit of any particular loan application.

Applicants may be required to provide additional documentation, and/or re-execute documentation well after loan closing. This process could continue for up to one year after loan closing and funding. This could be requested by Summit Mortgage or our business associates, investors, FHA, VA, FNMA, FHLMC, mortgage insurance companies, outside quality control companies, or other entities who are securitizing the loan or meeting pool requirements for sale in the open market. At your loan closing, there will be forms that you will sign giving Summit Mortgage the authorization to acquire this documentation.

I acknowledge that I have read, understand, agree, and accept the terms and conditions of this agreement, which a Loan Officer can not alter. They may only be altered by a Corporate Officer of Summit Mortgage Corporation.

_____   _____
Signature   Signature

U.S. Department of Housing and Urban Development

NOTICE TO PURCHASERS OF HOUSING CONSTRUCTED BEFORE 1978.

WATCH OUT FOR LEAD-BASED PAINT POISONING!

If the home you intend to purchase was built before 1978, it may contain lead-based paint. About three out of every four pre-1978 buildings have lead-based paint.

> # YOU NEED TO READ THIS
> # NOTICE ABOUT LEAD

WHAT IT LEAD POISONING?

Lead poisoning means having high concentrations of lead in the body.
LEAD CAN:

* Cause major health problems, especially in children under 7 years old.
* Damage a child's brain, nervous system, kidneys, hearing, or coordination.
* Affect learning.
* Cause behavior problems, blindness, and even death.
* Cause problems in pregnancy and affect a baby's normal development.

WHO GETS LEAD POISONING?

Anyone can get it, but children under 7 are at the greatest risk, because their bodies are not fully grown and are easily damaged. The risk is worse if the child:

* Lives in an older home (built/constructed before 1978, and even more so before 1960).
* Does not eat regular meals (an empty stomach accepts lead more easily).
* Does not eat enough foods with iron or calcium.
* Has parents who work in lead-related jobs.
* Has played in the same places as brothers, sisters, and friends who have been lead poisoned. (Lead poison cannot be spread from person to person. It comes from contact with lead).

Women of childbearing age are also at risk, because lead poisoning can cause miscarriages, premature births, and the poison can be passed onto their unborn babies.

WHERE DOES IT COME FROM?

The lead hazards that children most often touch are lead dust, leaded soil, loose chips and chewable surfaces painted with lead-based paint. A child may be harmed when it puts into its mouth; toys, pacifiers, or hands that have leaded soil or lead dust on them. Lead also comes from:

* Moving parts of windows and doors that can make lead dust and chips.
* Lead-based paint on windows, doors, wood trim, walls and cabinets in kitchens and bathrooms, on porches, stairs, railings, fire escapes and lamp posts.
* Soil next to exterior of buildings that have been painted with lead-based paint and leaded gasoline dust in soil near busy streets.
* Drinking water (pipes and solder).
* Parents who may bring lead dust home from work on skin, clothes, and hair.
* Colored newsprint and car batteries.
* Highly glazed pottery and cookware from other countries.
* Removing old paint when refinishing furniture.

In recent years some uses of lead in products that could cause lead poisoning have been reduced or banned. This is true for lead in gasoline, lead in solder used in water pipes, and lead in paint. Still, a great deal of lead remains in and around older homes, and lead-based paint and accompanying lead dust are seen as the major sources.

HOW DO I KNOW IF MY CHILD IS AFFECTED?

Is your child:

* cranky?
* vomiting?
* tired?
* unwilling to eat or play?
* complaining of stomach aches or headaches?

* unable to concentrate?
* hyperactive?
* playing with children who have these symptoms?

These can be signs of lead poisoning. However, your children might not show these signs and yet be poisoned; only your clinic or Doctor can test for sure.

WHAT CAN I DO ABOUT IT?

Your child should first be tested for lead in the blood between six months and one year old. Ask the clinic or your doctor to do it during a regular checkup. Your doctor will tell you how often you should have your child tested after that. A small amount of lead in the blood may not make your child seem very sick, but it can affect how well he or she can learn. If your child does have high amounts of lead in the blood, you should seek treatment and have your home tested for lead-based paint and lead dust.

HOW DO I KNOW IF MY HOME HAS LEAD-BASED PAINT?

The HUD inspection does not determine whether a home actually has lead-based paint. It only identifies whether there is defective paint in a home that might have lead-based paint. Therefore, the only way you can know for sure is to have the home tested by a qualified firm or laboratory. Both the interior and exterior should be tested. You should contact your local health or environmental office for help.

WHAT DO I DO IF MY HOME DOES HAVE LEAD?

Do not try to get rid of lead-based paint yourself, you could make things worse for you and your family. If your home contains lead-based paint, contact a company that specializes in lead-based paint abatement. Have professionals do the job correctly and safely. This may cost thousands of dollars, depending on the amount of lead-based paint and lead dust found in your home, but it will also protect you and your children from the effects of lead poisoning. In the meantime, there are things you can do immediately to protect your child:

* Keep your child away from paint chips and dust.
* Wet-mop floors and wipe down surfaces often, especially where floors and walls meet.
* Be sure to clean the space where the window sash rests on the sill. Keeping the floor clear of paint chips, dust and dirt is easy and very important. Do not sweep or vacuum lead-based paint chips or lead dust with an ordinary vacuum cleaner. Lead dust is so fine it will pass through a vacuum cleaner bag and spread into the air you breathe.
* Make sure your children wash their hands frequently and always before eating.
* Wash toys, teething rings, and pacifiers frequently.

WILL HUD INSURE A MORTGAGE LOAN ON A HOME WITH LEAD-BASED PAINT?

HUD will insure a mortgage on a house even if it has lead-based paint. If you purchase a property with lead-based paint, HUD will not remove it. You will have to pay for the cost of removal yourself.

ACKNOWLEDGEMENT

I acknowledge that I have received and read a copy of this Notice before signing the sales contract to purchase my property.

Signature	Date	Signature	Date

Signature	Date	Signature	Date

Page 2 of 2

☐☐
Property Description

UNIFORM RESIDENTIAL APPRAISAL REPORT File No.

UNIFORM RESIDENTIAL APPRAISAL REPORT   File No.

COST APPROACH

ESTIMATED SITE VALUE . . . . = $ _____

ESTIMATED REPRODUCTION COST-NEW-OF IMPROVEMENTS:

Dwelling _____ Sq. Ft @ $ _____ = $ _____

_____ Sq. Ft @ $ _____ = $ _____

= _____

Garage/Carport _____ Sq. Ft @ $ _____ = _____

Total Estimated Cost New . . . . = $ _____

Less   Physical   Functional   External

Depreciation _____   = $ _____

Depreciated Value of Improvements . . . . = $ _____

"As-is" Value of Site Improvements . . . . = $ _____

INDICATED VALUE BY COST APPROACH . . . . = $ _____

Comments on Cost Approach (such as, source of cost estimate, site value, square foot calculation and for HUD, VA and FmHA, the estimated remaining economic life of the property): _____

SALES COMPARISON ANALYSIS

ITEM	SUBJECT	COMPARABLE NO. 1		COMPARABLE NO. 2		COMPARABLE NO. 3	
Address							
Proximity to Subject							
Sales Price	$	$		$		$	
Price/Gross Liv. Area	$	$		$		$	
Data and/or							
Verification Source							
VALUE ADJUSTMENTS	DESCRIPTION	DESCRIPTION	+ (-) $ Adjustment	DESCRIPTION	+ (-) $ Adjustment	DESCRIPTION	+ (-) $ Adjustment
Sales or Financing Concessions							
Date of Sale/Time							
Location							
Leasehold/Fee Simple							
Site							
View							
Design and Appeal							
Quality of Construction							
Age							
Condition							
Above Grade	Total : Bdrms : Baths	Total : Bdrms : Baths		Total : Bdrms : Baths		Total : Bdrms : Baths	
Room Count							
Gross Living Area	Sq. Ft.	Sq. Ft.		Sq. Ft.		Sq. Ft.	
Basement & Finished Rooms Below Grade							
Functional Utility							
Heating/Cooling							
Energy Efficient Items							
Garage/Carport							
Porch, Patio, Deck,							
Fireplace(s), etc.							
Fence, Pool, etc.							
Net Adj. (total)		☐ + ☐ -	$	☐ + ☐ -	$	☐ + ☐ -	$
Adjusted Sales Price of Comparable			$		$		$

Comments on Sales Comparison (including the subject property's compatibility to the neighborhood, etc.): _____

ITEM	SUBJECT	COMPARABLE NO. 1	COMPARABLE NO. 2	COMPARABLE NO 3
Date, Price and Data Source, for prior sales within year of appraisal				

Analysis of any current agreement of sale, option, or listing of the subject property and analysis of any prior sales of subject and comparables within one year of the date of appraisal:

INDICATED VALUE BY SALES COMPARISON APPROACH . . . . $ _____

INDICATED VALUE BY INCOME APPROACH (If Applicable) Estimated Market Rent $ _____ /Mo. x Gross Rent Multiplier _____ = $ _____

This appraisal is made ☐ "as is"   ☐ subject to the repairs, alterations, inspections or conditions listed below ☐ subject to completion per plans and specifications.

Conditions of Appraisal: _____

RECONCILIATION

Final Reconciliation: _____

The purpose of this appraisal is to estimate the market value of the real property that is the subject of this report, based on the above conditions and the certification, contingent and limiting conditions, and market value definition that are stated in the attached Freddie Mac Form 439/Fannie Mae Form 1004B (Revised _____).

I (WE) ESTIMATE THE MARKET VALUE, AS DEFINED, OF THE REAL PROPERTY THAT IS THE SUBJECT OF THIS REPORT, AS OF _____

(WHICH IS THE DATE OF INSPECTION AND THE EFFECTIVE DATE OF THIS REPORT) TO BE $ _____

APPRAISER:	SUPERVISORY APPRAISER (ONLY IF REQUIRED):	
Signature	Signature	☐ Did ☐ Did Not
Name	Name	Inspect Property
Date Report Signed	Date Report Signed	
State Certification # _____ State	State Certification # _____ State	
Or State License # _____ State	Or State License # _____ State	

Freddie Mac Form 70 6-93   12 CH   PAGE 2 OF 2   Fannie Mae Form 1004 6-93
BLAKEWOOD BUSINESS FORMS 1 (800) 443-1004

Appendices   **331**

_____ [Space Above This Line For Recording Data] _____

DEED OF TRUST

THIS DEED OF TRUST ("Security Instrument") is made on ....**JULY 17TH**.......................................,
19.**94**. The grantor is ....**JOHN DOE AND SPOUSE, JANE DOE**...
....("Borrower"). The trustee is ....
GEORGE M. SHANKS, JR...., whose address is
11 GREENWAY PLAZA, 10TH FLOOR, HOUSTON, TEXAS 77046-1102......................................
("Trustee"). The beneficiary is .**HOME LOAN CORPORATION**...,
which is organized and existing under the laws of ....**THE STATE OF TEXAS**............................,
and whose address is ......**1717 ST. JAMES, SUITE 200**...
HOUSTON, TEXAS 77056..("Lender").
Borrower owes Lender the principal sum of ......**ONE HUNDRED THOUSAND AND NO / 100**..........
.... Dollars (U.S. $........**100,000.00**.....................). This debt is evidenced by
Borrower's note dated the same date as this Security Instrument ("Note"), which provides for monthly payments, with the
full debt, if not paid earlier, due and payable on ....**AUGUST 01, 2024**......................... .
This Security Instrument secures to Lender: (a) the repayment of the debt evidenced by the Note, with interest, and all renewals,
extensions and modifications of the Note; (b) the payment of all other sums, with interest, advanced under paragraph 7 to
protect the security of this Security Instrument; and (c) the performance of Borrower's covenants and agreements under this
Security Instrument and the Note. For this purpose, Borrower irrevocably grants and conveys to Trustee, in trust, with power
of sale, the following described property located in ....**HARRIS**... County, Texas:

LOT ONE (1) BLOCK FOUR (4) SECTION FIVE 5, SUGARHILL SUBDIVISION.

which has the address of ....**1333 SUGAR LANE**......................., ...**HOUSTON**.....................,
                                                  [Street]   [City]

Texas ....**77333**...................... ("Property Address");
                  [Zip Code]

TOGETHER WITH all the improvements now or hereafter erected on the property, and all easements, appurtenances,
and fixtures now or hereafter a part of the property. All replacements and additions shall also be covered by this Security
Instrument. All of the foregoing is referred to in this Security Instrument as the "Property."

BORROWER COVENANTS that Borrower is lawfully seised of the estate hereby conveyed and has the right to grant
and convey the Property and that the Property is unencumbered, except for encumbrances of record. Borrower warrants
and will defend generally the title to the Property against all claims and demands, subject to any encumbrances of record.

THIS SECURITY INSTRUMENT combines uniform covenants for national use and non-uniform covenants with limited
variations by jurisdiction to constitute a uniform security instrument covering real property.

TEXAS — Single Family — **Fannie Mae/Freddie Mac UNIFORM INSTRUMENT**   **Form 3044 9/90**   *(page 1 of 7 pages)*
ST&L# TX6.NEW

316

UNIFORM COVENANTS. Borrower and Lender covenant and agree as follows:

1. Payment of Principal and Interest; Prepayment and Late Charges. Borrower shall promptly pay when due the principal of and interest on the debt evidenced by the Note and any prepayment and late charges due under the Note.

2. Funds for Taxes and Insurance. Subject to applicable law or to a written waiver by Lender, Borrower shall pay to Lender on the day monthly payments are due under the Note, until the Note is paid in full, a sum ("Funds") for: (a) yearly taxes and assessments which may attain priority over this Security Instrument as a lien on the Property; (b) yearly leasehold payments or ground rents on the Property, if any; (c) yearly hazard or property insurance premiums; (d) yearly flood insurance premiums, if any; (e) yearly mortgage insurance premiums, if any; and (f) any sums payable by Borrower to Lender, in accordance with the provisions of paragraph 8, in lieu of the payment of mortgage insurance premiums. These items are called "Escrow Items." Lender may, at any time, collect and hold Funds in an amount not to exceed the maximum amount a lender for a federally related mortgage loan may require for Borrower's escrow account under the federal Real Estate Settlement Procedures Act of 1974 as amended from time to time, 12 U.S.C. § 2601 *et seq.* ("RESPA"), unless another law that applies to the Funds sets a lesser amount. If so, Lender may, at any time, collect and hold Funds in an amount not to exceed the lesser amount. Lender may estimate the amount of Funds due on the basis of current data and reasonable estimates of expenditures of future Escrow Items or otherwise in accordance with applicable law.

The Funds shall be held in an institution whose deposits are insured by a federal agency, instrumentality, or entity (including Lender, if Lender is such an institution) or in any Federal Home Loan Bank. Lender shall apply the Funds to pay the Escrow Items. Lender may not charge Borrower for holding and applying the Funds, annually analyzing the escrow account, or verifying the Escrow Items, unless Lender pays Borrower interest on the Funds and applicable law permits Lender to make such a charge. However, Lender may require Borrower to pay a one-time charge for an independent real estate tax reporting service used by Lender in connection with this loan, unless applicable law provides otherwise. Unless an agreement is made or applicable law requires interest to be paid, Lender shall not be required to pay Borrower any interest or earnings on the Funds. Borrower and Lender may agree in writing, however, that interest shall be paid on the Funds. Lender shall give to Borrower, without charge, an annual accounting of the Funds, showing credits and debits to the Funds and the purpose for which each debit to the Funds was made. The Funds are pledged as additional security for all sums secured by this Security Instrument.

If the Funds held by Lender exceed the amounts permitted to be held by applicable law, Lender shall account to Borrower for the excess Funds in accordance with the requirements of applicable law. If the amount of the Funds held by Lender at any time is not sufficient to pay the Escrow Items when due, Lender may so notify Borrower in writing, and, in such case Borrower shall pay to Lender the amount necessary to make up the deficiency. Borrower shall make up the deficiency in no more than twelve monthly payments, at Lender's sole discretion.

Upon payment in full of all sums secured by this Security Instrument, Lender shall promptly refund to Borrower any Funds held by Lender. If under paragraph 21, Lender shall acquire or sell the Property, Lender, prior to the acquisition or sale of the Property, shall apply any Funds held by Lender at the time of acquisition or sale as a credit against the sums secured by this Security Instrument.

3. Application of Payments. Unless applicable law provides otherwise, all payments received by Lender under paragraphs 1 and 2 shall be applied: first, to any prepayment charges due under the Note; second, to amounts payable under paragraph 2; third, to interest due; fourth, to principal due; and last, to any late charges due under the Note.

4. Charges; Liens. Borrower shall pay all taxes, assessments, charges, fines and impositions attributable to the Property which may attain priority over this Security Instrument, and leasehold payments or ground rents, if any. Borrower shall pay these obligations in the manner provided in paragraph 2, or if not paid in that manner, Borrower shall pay them on time directly to the person owed payment. Borrower shall promptly furnish to Lender all notices of amounts to be paid under this paragraph. If Borrower makes these payments directly, Borrower shall promptly furnish to Lender receipts evidencing the payments.

Borrower shall promptly discharge any lien which has priority over this Security Instrument unless Borrower: (a) agrees in writing to the payment of the obligation secured by the lien in a manner acceptable to Lender; (b) contests in good faith the lien by, or defends against enforcement of the lien in, legal proceedings which in the Lender's opinion operate to prevent the enforcement of the lien; or (c) secures from the holder of the lien an agreement satisfactory to Lender subordinating the lien to this Security Instrument. If Lender determines that any part of the Property is subject to a lien which may attain priority over this Security Instrument, Lender may give Borrower a notice identifying the lien. Borrower shall satisfy the lien or take one or more of the actions set forth above within 10 days of the giving of notice.

5. Hazard or Property Insurance. Borrower shall keep the improvements now existing or hereafter erected on the Property insured against loss by fire, hazards included within the term "extended coverage" and any other hazards, including floods or flooding, for which Lender requires insurance. This insurance shall be maintained in the amounts and for the periods that Lender requires. The insurance carrier providing the insurance shall be chosen by Borrower subject to Lender's approval which shall not be unreasonably withheld. If Borrower fails to maintain coverage described above, Lender may, at Lender's option, obtain coverage to protect Lender's rights in the Property in accordance with paragraph 7.

ST&L# TX6-2.NEW   **Form 3044 9/90**   *(page 2 of 7 pages)*

All insurance policies and renewals shall be acceptable to Lender and shall include a standard mortgage clause. Lender shall have the right to hold the policies and renewals. If Lender requires, Borrower shall promptly give to Lender all receipts of paid premiums and renewal notices. In the event of loss, Borrower shall give prompt notice to the insurance carrier and Lender. Lender may make proof of loss if not made promptly by Borrower.

Unless Lender and Borrower otherwise agree in writing, insurance proceeds shall be applied to restoration or repair of the Property damaged, if the restoration or repair is economically feasible and Lender's security is not lessened. If the restoration or repair is not economically feasible or Lender's security would be lessened, the insurance proceeds shall be applied to the sums secured by this Security Instrument, whether or not then due, with any excess paid to Borrower. If Borrower abandons the Property, or does not answer within 30 days, a notice from Lender that the insurance carrier has offered to settle a claim, then Lender may collect the insurance proceeds. Lender may use the proceeds to repair or restore the Property or to pay sums secured by this Security Instrument, whether or not then due. The 30-day period will begin when the notice is given.

Unless Lender and Borrower otherwise agree in writing, any application of proceeds to principal shall not extend or postpone the due date of the monthly payments referred to in paragraphs 1 and 2 or change the amount of the payments. If under paragraph 21 the Property is acquired by Lender, Borrower's right to any insurance policies and proceeds resulting from damage to the Property prior to the acquisition shall pass to Lender to the extent of the sums secured by this Security Instrument immediately prior to the acquisition.

6. Occupancy, Preservation, Maintenance and Protection of the Property; Borrower's Loan Application; Leaseholds. Borrower shall occupy, establish, and use the Property as Borrower's principal residence within sixty days after the execution of this Security Instrument and shall continue to occupy the Property as Borrower's principal residence for at least one year after the date of occupancy, unless Lender otherwise agrees in writing, which consent shall not be unreasonably withheld, or unless extenuating circumstances exist which are beyond Borrower's control. Borrower shall not destroy, damage or impair the Property, allow the Property to deteriorate, or commit waste on the Property. Borrower shall be in default if any forfeiture action or proceeding, whether civil or criminal, is begun that in Lender's good faith judgment could result in forfeiture of the Property or otherwise materially impair the lien created by this Security Instrument or Lender's security interest. Borrower may cure such a default and reinstate, as provided in paragraph 18, by causing the action or proceeding to be dismissed with a ruling that, in Lender's good faith determination, precludes forfeiture of the Borrower's interest in the Property or other material impairment of the lien created by this Security Instrument or Lender's security interest. Borrower shall also be in default if Borrower, during the loan application process, gave materially false or inaccurate information or statements to Lender (or failed to provide Lender with any material information) in connection with the loan evidenced by the Note, including, but not limited to, representations concerning Borrower's occupancy of the Property as a principal residence. If this Security Instrument is on a leasehold, Borrower shall comply with all the provisions of the lease. If Borrower acquires fee title to the Property, the leasehold and the fee title shall not merge unless Lender agrees to the merger in writing.

7. Protection of Lender's Rights in the Property. If Borrower fails to perform the covenants and agreements contained in this Security Instrument, or there is a legal proceeding that may significantly affect Lender's rights in the Property (such as a proceeding in bankruptcy, probate, for condemnation or forfeiture or to enforce laws or regulations), then Lender may do and pay for whatever is necessary to protect the value of the Property and Lender's rights in the Property. Lender's actions may include paying any sums secured by a lien which has priority over this Security Instrument, appearing in court, paying reasonable attorneys' fees and entering on the Property to make repairs. Although Lender may take action under this paragraph 7, Lender does not have to do so.

Any amounts disbursed by Lender under this paragraph 7 shall become additional debt of Borrower secured by this Security Instrument. Unless Borrower and Lender agree to other terms of payment, these amounts shall bear interest from the date of disbursement at the Note rate and shall be payable, with interest, upon notice from Lender to Borrower requesting payment.

8. Mortgage Insurance. If Lender required mortgage insurance as a condition of making the loan secured by this Security Instrument, Borrower shall pay the premiums required to maintain the mortgage insurance in effect. If, for any reason, the mortgage insurance coverage required by Lender lapses or ceases to be in effect, Borrower shall pay the premiums required to obtain coverage substantially equivalent to the mortgage insurance previously in effect, at a cost substantially equivalent to the cost to Borrower of the mortgage insurance previously in effect, from an alternate mortgage insurer approved by Lender. If substantially equivalent mortgage insurance coverage is not available, Borrower shall pay to Lender each month a sum equal to one-twelfth of the yearly mortgage insurance premium being paid by Borrower when the insurance coverage lapsed or ceased to be in effect. Lender will accept, use and retain these payments as a loss reserve in lieu of mortgage insurance. Loss reserve payments may no longer be required, at the option of Lender, if mortgage insurance coverage (in the amount and for the period that Lender requires) provided by an insurer approved by Lender again becomes available and is obtained. Borrower shall pay the premiums required to maintain mortgage insurance in effect, or to provide a loss reserve, until the requirement for mortgage insurance ends in accordance with any written agreement between Borrower and Lender or applicable law.

ST&L# TX6-3.NEW   Form 3044 9/90   *(page 3 of 7 pages)*

9. Inspection. Lender or its agent may make reasonable entries upon and inspections of the Property. Lender shall give Borrower notice at the time of or prior to an inspection specifying reasonable cause for the inspection.

10. Condemnation. The proceeds of any award or claim for damages, direct or consequential, in connection with any condemnation or other taking of any part of the Property, or for conveyance in lieu of condemnation, are hereby assigned and shall be paid to Lender.

In the event of a total taking of the Property, the proceeds shall be applied to the sums secured by this Security Instrument, whether or not then due, with any excess paid to Borrower. In the event of a partial taking of the Property in which the fair market value of the Property immediately before the taking is equal to or greater than the amount of the sums secured by this Security Instrument immediately before the taking, unless Borrower and Lender otherwise agree in writing, the sums secured by this Security Instrument shall be reduced by the amount of the proceeds multiplied by the following fraction: (a) the total amount of the sums secured immediately before the taking, divided by (b) the fair market value of the Property immediately before the taking. Any balance shall be paid to Borrower. In the event of a partial taking of the Property in which the fair market value of the Property immediately before the taking is less than the amount of the sums secured immediately before the taking, unless Borrower and Lender otherwise agree in writing or unless applicable law otherwise provides, the proceeds shall be applied to the sums secured by this Security Instrument whether or not the sums are then due.

If the Property is abandoned by Borrower, or if, after notice by Lender to Borrower that the condemnor offers to make an award or settle a claim for damages, Borrower fails to respond to Lender within 30 days after the date the notice is given, Lender is authorized to collect and apply the proceeds, at its option, either to restoration or repair of the Property or to the sums secured by this Security Instrument, whether or not then due.

Unless Lender and Borrower otherwise agree in writing, any application of proceeds to principal shall not extend or postpone the due date of the monthly payments referred to in paragraphs 1 and 2 or change the amount of such payments.

11. Borrower Not Released; Forbearance By Lender Not a Waiver. Extension of the time for payment or modification of amortization of the sums secured by this Security Instrument granted by Lender to any successor in interest of Borrower shall not operate to release the liability of the original Borrower or Borrower's successors in interest. Lender shall not be required to commence proceedings against any successor in interest or refuse to extend time for payment or otherwise modify amortization of the sums secured by this Security Instrument by reason of any demand made by the original Borrower or Borrower's successors in interest. Any forbearance by Lender in exercising any right or remedy shall not be a waiver of or preclude the exercise of any right or remedy.

12. Successors and Assigns Bound; Joint and Several Liability; Co-signers. The covenants and agreements of this Security Instrument shall bind and benefit the successors and assigns of Lender and Borrower, subject to the provisions of paragraph 17. Borrower's covenants and agreements shall be joint and several. Any Borrower who co-signs this Security Instrument but does not execute the Note: (a) is co-signing this Security Instrument only to mortgage, grant and convey that Borrower's interest in the Property under the terms of this Security Instrument; (b) is not personally obligated to pay the sums secured by this Security Instrument; and (c) agrees that Lender and any other Borrower may agree to extend, modify, forbear or make any accommodations with regard to the terms of this Security Instrument or the Note without that Borrower's consent.

13. Loan Charges. If the loan secured by this Security Instrument is subject to a law which sets maximum loan charges, and that law is finally interpreted so that the interest or other loan charges collected or to be collected in connection with the loan exceed the permitted limits, then: (a) any such loan charge shall be reduced by the amount necessary to reduce the charge to the permitted limit; and (b) any sums already collected from Borrower which exceeded permitted limits will be refunded to Borrower. Lender may choose to make this refund by reducing the principal owed under the Note or by making a direct payment to Borrower. If a refund reduces principal, the reduction will be treated as a partial prepayment without any prepayment charge under the Note.

14. Notices. Any notice to Borrower provided for in this Security Instrument shall be given by delivering it or by mailing it by first class mail unless applicable law requires use of another method. The notice shall be directed to the Property Address or any other address Borrower designates by notice to Lender. Any notice to Lender shall be given by first class mail to Lender's address stated herein or any other address Lender designates by notice to Borrower. Any notice provided for in this Security Instrument shall be deemed to have been given to Borrower or Lender when given as provided in this paragraph.

15. Governing Law; Severability. This Security Instrument shall be governed by federal law and the law of the jurisdiction in which the Property is located. In the event that any provision or clause of this Security Instrument or the Note conflicts with applicable law, such conflict shall not affect other provisions of this Security Instrument or the Note which can be given effect without the conflicting provision. To this end the provisions of this Security Instrument and the Note are declared to be severable.

16. Borrower's Copy. Borrower shall be given one conformed copy of the Note and of this Security Instrument.

17. Transfer of the Property or a Beneficial Interest in Borrower. If all or any part of the Property or any interest in it is sold or transferred (or if a beneficial interest in Borrower is sold or transferred and Borrower is not a natural person) without Lender's prior written consent, Lender may, at its option, require immediate payment in full of all sums secured by this Security Instrument. However, this option shall not be exercised by Lender if exercise is prohibited by federal law as of the date of this Security Instrument.

If Lender exercises this option, Lender shall give Borrower notice of acceleration. The notice shall provide a period of not less than 30 days from the date the notice is delivered or mailed within which Borrower must pay all sums secured by this Security Instrument. If Borrower fails to pay these sums prior to the expiration of this period, Lender may invoke any remedies permitted by this Security Instrument without further notice or demand on Borrower.

18. Borrower's Right to Reinstate. If Borrower meets certain conditions, Borrower shall have the right to have enforcement of this Security Instrument discontinued at any time prior to the earlier of: (a) 5 days (or such other period as applicable law may specify for reinstatement) before sale of the Property pursuant to any power of sale contained in this Security Instrument; or (b) entry of a judgment enforcing this Security Instrument. Those conditions are that Borrower: (a) pays Lender all sums which then would be due under this Security Instrument and the Note as if no acceleration had occurred; (b) cures any default of any other covenants or agreements; (c) pays all expenses incurred in enforcing this Security Instrument, including, but not limited to, reasonable attorneys' fees; and (d) takes such action as Lender may reasonably require to assure that the lien of this Security Instrument, Lender's rights in the Property and Borrower's obligation to pay the sums secured by this Security Instrument shall continue unchanged. Upon reinstatement by Borrower, this Security Instrument and the obligations secured hereby shall remain fully effective as if no acceleration had occurred. However, this right to reinstate shall not apply in the case of acceleration under paragraph 17.

19. Sale of Note; Change of Loan Servicer. The Note or a partial interest in the Note (together with this Security Instrument) may be sold one or more times without prior notice to Borrower. A sale may result in a change in the entity (known as the "Loan Servicer") that collects monthly payments due under the Note and this Security Instrument. There also may be one or more changes of the Loan Servicer unrelated to a sale of the Note. If there is a change of the Loan Servicer, Borrower will be given written notice of the change in accordance with paragraph 14 above and applicable law. The notice will state the name and address of the new Loan Servicer and the address to which payments should be made. The notice will also contain any other information required by applicable law.

20. Hazardous Substances. Borrower shall not cause or permit the presence, use, disposal, storage, or release of any Hazardous Substances on or in the Property. Borrower shall not do, nor allow anyone else to do, anything affecting the Property that is in violation of any Environmental Law. The preceding two sentences shall not apply to the presence, use, or storage on the Property of small quantities of Hazardous Substances that are generally recognized to be appropriate to normal residential uses and to maintenance of the Property.

Borrower shall promptly give Lender written notice of any investigation, claim, demand, lawsuit or other action by any governmental or regulatory agency or private party involving the Property and any Hazardous Substance or Environmental Law of which Borrower has actual knowledge. If Borrower learns, or is notified by any governmental or regulatory authority, that any removal or other remediation of any Hazardous Substance affecting the Property is necessary, Borrower shall promptly take all necessary remedial actions in accordance with Environmental Law.

As used in this paragraph 20, "Hazardous Substances" are those substances defined as toxic or hazardous substances by Environmental Law and the following substances: gasoline, kerosene, other flammable or toxic petroleum products, toxic pesticides and herbicides, volatile solvents, materials containing asbestos or formaldehyde and radioactive materials. As used in this paragraph 20, "Environmental Law" means federal laws and laws of the jurisdiction where the Property is located that relate to health, safety or environmental protection.

NON-UNIFORM COVENANTS. Borrower and Lender further covenant and agree as follows:

21. Acceleration; Remedies. Lender shall give notice to Borrower prior to acceleration following Borrower's breach of any covenant or agreement in this Security Instrument (but not prior to acceleration under paragraph 17 unless applicable law provides otherwise). The notice shall specify: (a) the default; (b) the action required to cure the default; (c) a date, not less than 30 days from the date the notice is given to Borrower, by which the default must be cured; and (d) that failure to cure the default on or before the date specified in the notice will result in acceleration of the sums secured by this Security Instrument and sale of the Property. The notice shall further inform Borrower of the right to reinstate after acceleration and the right to bring a court action to assert the non-existence of a default or any other defense of Borrower to acceleration and sale. If the default is not cured on or before the date specified in the notice, Lender at its option may require immediate payment in full of all sums secured by this Security Instrument without further demand and may invoke the power of sale and any other remedies permitted by applicable law. Lender shall be entitled to collect all expenses incurred in pursuing the remedies provided in this paragraph 21, including, but not limited to, reasonable attorneys' fees and costs of title evidence.

If Lender invokes the power of sale, Lender or Trustee shall give notice of the time, place and terms of sale by posting and recording the notice at least 21 days prior to sale as provided by applicable law. Lender shall mail a copy of the notice of sale to Borrower in the manner prescribed by applicable law. Sale shall be made at public vendue between the hours of 10 a.m. and 4 p.m. on the first Tuesday in the month. Borrower authorizes Trustee

ST&L# TX6-5.NEW   Form 3044 9/90   *(page 5 of 7 pages)*

to sell the Property to the highest bidder for cash in one or more parcels and in any order Trustee determines. Lender or its designee may purchase the Property at any sale.

Trustee shall deliver to the purchaser Trustee's deed conveying indefeasible title to the Property with covenants of general warranty. Borrower covenants and agrees to defend generally the purchaser's title to the Property against all claims and demands. The recitals in the Trustee's deed shall be prima facie evidence of the truth of the statements made therein. Trustee shall apply the proceeds of the sale in the following order: (a) to all expenses of the sale, including, but not limited to, reasonable Trustee's and attorneys' fees; (b) to all sums secured by this Security Instrument; and (c) any excess to the person or persons legally entitled to it.

If the Property is sold pursuant to this paragraph 21, Borrower or any person holding possession of the Property through Borrower shall immediately surrender possession of the Property to the purchaser at that sale. If possession is not surrendered, Borrower or such person shall be a tenant at sufferance and may be removed by writ of possession.

22. Release. Upon payment of all sums secured by this Security Instrument, Lender shall release this Security Instrument without charge to Borrower. Borrower shall pay any recordation costs.

23. Substitute Trustee. Lender, at its option and with or without cause, may from time to time remove Trustee and appoint, by power of attorney or otherwise, a successor trustee to any Trustee appointed hereunder. Without conveyance of the Property, the successor trustee shall succeed to all the title, power and duties conferred upon Trustee herein and by applicable law.

24. Subrogation. Any of the proceeds of the Note used to take up outstanding liens against all or any part of the Property have been advanced by Lender at Borrower's request and upon Borrower's representation that such amounts are due and are secured by valid liens against the Property. Lender shall be subrogated to any and all rights, superior titles, liens and equities owned or claimed by any owner or holder of any outstanding liens and debts, regardless of whether said liens or debts are acquired by Lender by assignment or are released by the holder thereof upon payment.

25. Partial Invalidity. In the event any portion of the sums intended to be secured by this Security Instrument cannot be lawfully secured hereby, payments in reduction of such sums shall be applied first to those portions not secured hereby.

26. Waiver of Notice of Intention to Accelerate. Borrower waives the right to notice of intention to require immediate payment in full of all sums secured by this Security Instrument except as provided in paragraph 21.

27. Riders to this Security Instrument. If one or more riders are executed by Borrower and recorded together with this Security Instrument, the covenants and agreements of each such rider shall be incorporated into and shall amend and supplement the covenants and agreements of this Security Instrument as if the rider(s) were a part of this Security Instrument. [Check applicable box(es)]

☐ Adjustable Rate Rider   ☐ Condominium Rider   ☐ 1-4 Family Rider

☐ Graduated Payment Rider   ☐ Planned Unit Development Rider   ☐ Biweekly Payment Rider

☐ Balloon Rider   ☐ Rate Improvement Rider   ☐ Second Home Rider

☐ Other(s) [specify]

28. Purchase Money; Vendor's Lien; Renewal and Extension. [Complete as appropriate]

The Note secured hereby is primarily secured by the Vendor's Lien retained in the Deed of even date herewith conveying the Property to Borrower, which Vendor's Lien has been assigned to Lender, this Deed of Trust being additional security therefor.

BY SIGNING BELOW, Borrower accepts and agrees to the terms and covenants contained in this Security Instrument and in any rider(s) executed by Borrower and recorded with it.

....(Seal)
JOHN DOE   -Borrower

....(Seal)
JANE DOE   -Borrower

....(Seal)
-Borrower

....(Seal)
-Borrower

—————————————— [Space Below This Line For Acknowledgement] ——————————————

STATE OF TEXAS, ... County ss:

BEFORE ME, the undersigned, a Notary Public in and for said County and State, on this day personally appeared JOHN DOE AND SPOUSE, JANE DOE ....

...., known to me to be the person(s) whose name(s)   is/are   subscribed to the foregoing instrument, and acknowledged to me that   he/she/they   executed the same for the purposes and consideration therein expressed.

GIVEN UNDER MY HAND AND SEAL OF OFFICE, this .... day of ....JULY........................... , 19..94..........

....
Notary Public

MY COMMISSION EXPIRES:

ST&L# TX6-7.NEW   Form 3044 9/90   (page 7 of 7 pages)

NOTE

JULY 17 ...., 19 94 ......   HOUSTON ...., Texas
                                                                                       [City]

1333 SUGAR LANE, HOUSTON, TEXAS 77333 ....
                                    [Property Address]

1. BORROWER'S PROMISE TO PAY

In return for a loan that I have received, I promise to pay U.S. $ **100,000.00** (this amount is called "principal"), plus interest, to the order of the Lender. The Lender is **HOME LOAN CORPORATION** .... I understand that the Lender may transfer this Note. The Lender or anyone who takes this Note by transfer and who is entitled to receive payments under this Note is called the "Note Holder."

2. INTEREST

Interest will be charged on unpaid principal until the full amount of principal has been paid. I will pay interest at a yearly rate of **8.500** %.

The interest rate required by this Section 2 is the rate I will pay both before and after any default described in Section 6(B) of this Note.

3. PAYMENTS

(A) Time and Place of Payments

I will pay principal and interest by making payments every month.

I will make my monthly payments on the **1ST** day of each month beginning on **SEPTEMBER 1** , 19 94 . I will make these payments every month until I have paid all of the principal and interest and any other charges described below that I may owe under this Note. My monthly payments will be applied to interest before principal. If, on **AUGUST 1** , **2024** , I still owe amounts under this Note, I will pay those amounts in full on that date, which is called the "maturity date."

I will make my monthly payments at **1717 ST. JAMES, SUITE 200 HOUSTON, TEXAS 77056** or at a different place if required by the Note Holder.

(B) Amount of Monthly Payments

My monthly payment will be in the amount of U.S. $ **768.91**

4. BORROWER'S RIGHT TO PREPAY

I have the right to make payments of principal at any time before they are due. A payment of principal only is known as a "prepayment." When I make a prepayment, I will tell the Note Holder in writing that I am doing so.

I may make a full prepayment or partial prepayments without paying any prepayment charge. The Note Holder will use all of my prepayments to reduce the amount of principal that I owe under this Note. If I make a partial prepayment, there will be no changes in the due date or in the amount of my monthly payment unless the Note Holder agrees in writing to those changes.

5. LOAN CHARGES

If a law, which applies to this loan and which sets maximum loan charges, is finally interpreted so that the interest or other loan charges collected or to be collected in connection with this loan exceed the permitted limits, then: (i) any such loan charge shall be reduced by the amount necessary to reduce the charge to the permitted limit; and (ii) any sums already collected from me which exceeded permitted limits will be refunded to me. The Note Holder may choose to make this refund by reducing the principal I owe under this Note or by making a direct payment to me. If a refund reduces principal, the reduction will be treated as a partial prepayment.

6. BORROWER'S FAILURE TO PAY AS REQUIRED

(A) Late Charge for Overdue Payments

If the Note Holder has not received the full amount of any monthly payment by the end of **FIFTEEN (15)** calendar days after the date it is due, I will pay a late charge to the Note Holder. The amount of the charge will be **5.00** % of my overdue payment of principal and interest. I will pay this late charge promptly but only once on each late payment.

(B) Default

If I do not pay the full amount of each monthly payment on the date it is due, I will be in default.

(C) Notice of Default

If I am in default, the Note Holder may send me a written notice telling me that if I do not pay the overdue amount by a certain date, the Note Holder may require me to pay immediately the full amount of principal which has not been paid and all the interest that I owe on that amount. That date must be at least 30 days after the date on which the notice is delivered or mailed to me.

(D) No Waiver By Note Holder

Even if, at a time when I am in default, the Note Holder does not require me to pay immediately in full as described above, the Note Holder will still have the right to do so if I am in default at a later time.

(E) Payment of Note Holder's Costs and Expenses

If the Note Holder has required me to pay immediately in full as described above, the Note Holder will have the right to be paid back by me for all of its costs and expenses in enforcing this Note to the extent not prohibited by applicable law. Those expenses include, for example, reasonable attorneys' fees.

7. GIVING OF NOTICES

Unless applicable law requires a different method, any notice that must be given to me under this Note will be given by delivering it or by mailing it by first class mail to me at the Property Address above or at a different address if I give the Note Holder a notice of my different address.

Any notice that must be given to the Note Holder under this Note will be given by mailing it by first class mail to the Note Holder at the address stated in Section 3(A) above or at a different address if I am given a notice of that different address.

TEXAS FIXED RATE NOTE —Single Family —FNMA / FHLMC UNIFORM INSTRUMENT   Form 3244 12 / 83

ST&L# 5   Page 1

8. OBLIGATIONS OF PERSONS UNDER THIS NOTE

If more than one person signs this Note, each person is fully and personally obligated to keep all of the promises made in this Note, including the promise to pay the full amount owed. Any person who is a guarantor, surety or endorser of this Note is also obligated to do these things. Any person who takes over these obligations, including the obligations of a guarantor, surety or endorser of this Note, is also obligated to keep all of the promises made in this Note. The Note Holder may enforce its rights under this Note against each person individually or against all of us together. This means that any one of us may be required to pay all of the amounts owed under this Note.

9. WAIVERS

I and any other person who has obligations under this Note waive notice of intention to accelerate, except as provided in Section 6(C) above, and the rights of presentment and notice of dishonor. "Presentment" means the right to require the Note Holder to demand payment of amounts due. "Notice of dishonor" means the right to require the Note Holder to give notice to other persons that amounts due have not been paid.

10. UNIFORM SECURED NOTE

This Note is a uniform instrument with limited variations in some jurisdictions. In addition to the protections given to the Note Holder under this Note, a Mortgage, Deed of Trust or Security Deed (the "Security Instrument"), dated the same date as this Note, protects the Note Holder from possible losses which might result if I do not keep the promises which I make in this Note. That Security Instrument describes how and under what conditions I may be required to make immediate payment in full of all amounts I owe under this Note. Some of those conditions are described as follows:

Transfer of the Property or a Beneficial Interest in Borrower. If all or any part of the Property or any interest in it is sold or transferred (or if a beneficial interest in Borrower is sold or transferred and Borrower is not a natural person) without Lender's prior written consent, Lender may, at its option, require immediate payment in full of all sums secured by this Security Instrument. However, this option shall not be exercised by Lender if exercise is prohibited by federal law as of the date of this Security Instrument.

If Lender exercises this option, Lender shall give Borrower notice of acceleration. The notice shall provide a period of not less than 30 days from the date the notice is delivered or mailed within which Borrower must pay all sums secured by this Security Instrument. If Borrower fails to pay these sums prior to the expiration of this period, Lender may invoke any remedies permitted by this Security Instrument without further notice or demand on Borrower.

WITNESS THE HAND(S) AND SEAL(S) OF THE UNDERSIGNED.

....(Seal)
JOHN DOE   -Borrower

SOCIAL SECURITY NO. ....555-55-5555...

....(Seal)
JANE DOE   -Borrower

SOCIAL SECURITY NO. ....444-44-4444...

....(Seal)
                                                                                 -Borrower

....(Seal)
                                                                                 -Borrower

[Sign Original Only]

Index

gross rate, 58–59
ground lease, 240
growing equity mortgage, 112
guaranty certificates (Ginnie Mae), 64

H

hazard insurance *see* property, insurance
hazardous materials *see* toxic waste
home builder commitments, 236–237
home builders, 50
Home Equity Conversion Mortgage (HECM), 115
home equity revolving loans, 112–113
Home Keeper for Home Purchase Mortgage (Fannie Mae), 115–116
Home Mortgage Disclosure Act, 34, 36–37
home-buyer education programs, 7
homeowners' associations, 197
housing expenses, defined, 162
HUD *see* Department of Housing and Urban Development (HUD); Federal Housing Administration (HUD/FHA)
HUD-1 settlement statement, 95–96, 295, 296–297
hypothecation, defined, 2–3, 76

I

immediate commitment, defined, 44
income approach to estimating property value, 190
income of borrowers
  stability of, 156–157
  types of, 154–156
income qualifications *see* borrower, qualifications of
income ratio method, 167–168
indemnification clause (PMI), 177–178
indemnity, 253–254
index *see* rate index
indoor air pollution, 274–277
innocent landowner defense, 271–273
institutional lenders *see* regulated lenders
insurance *see* banker's environmental risk insurance; flood insurance; pollution insurance; private mortgage insurance (PMI); property, insurance
interest rate reduction refinancing loans (IRRRLs), 145
interest rates, 16–20
  indicators, 18–20
  limiting, on HUD/FHA loans, 126
  of VA loans, 145
  see also rate index
interest-only note, 110
interim loans/financing, 88, 217

Internet, 50–51
  loan applications on, 262
investment bankers, 50, 61

J

joint and several liability, of toxic cleanup, 270
junior mortgages, 88–89, 95

K

kickbacks, 292

L

land development loans, 212–213
land leases, 240–242
land purchase loans, 211–212
land survey, 200
landownership, 1–2
lead
  handling, 279
  lead-based paint rule, 278
  poisoning, 277
  property values and, 278
  sources of, 277–278
  testing for, 278
Lead-Based Paint Poisoning Prevention Act, 277
leased land *see* land leases
leasehold, 240
lenders *see* mortgage lenders
liability
  of borrowers, 157
  of landowner for toxic waste, 271–273
  for toxic waste cleanup, 270–271
licensing of mortgage loan officers, 42
lien
  defined, 76
  mechanics, 94
  special assessment, 94
  tax, 94
  vendor's, 89, 94
lien theory, 76–77
life insurance companies, 35–36
limited partnerships, 242–243
loan agreement, in commercial loan, 174
loan applications, 152–153
  for commercial loans, 153
loan limits, 238–240
  on HUD/FHA loans, 126–128, 239
loan originator, definition of, 3, 22

nonbank lenders, 50
nonrecourse loans, 79

O

obsolescence of property, 187–188
office buildings, commercial loans for, 229–231
Office of Interstate Land Sales, 213
Office of Thrift Supervision (OTS), 26, 29, 33, 101
office/warehouses, 232
one-year Treasury securities, 101–102
online real estate service, 263
open market operations, 13
open-end mortgage, 87
operating statement, for commercial loan applications,
    206, 207–208
opportunity cost, 112
origination fee, 45–46
owner-occupied property, 194, 228, 229, 230–231

P

package mortgage, 90
partial release clause, 88
participation loan, 239–240
pass-through securities *see* mortgage pass-throughs
pension funds, 51
percentage guideline method of income qualification
    (HUD/FHA), 162–164
percentage leases, 227–228
pest inspections, 304–305
Phase I assessment (ASTM), 272–273
Phase I assessments, 266, 271
Phase II assessments, 271
Phase III assessments, 271
physical characteristics of property, 192–193
physical deterioration of property, 187–188
PITI *see* mortgage payments (PITI)
pledged-account mortgage, 107
points, defined, 3, 59
pollution insurance, 273
pooler, defined, 5
preleasing
    office space, 230
    shopping centers, 228
preliminary title report, 288–289
prepaid items, 120–121, 299–300
prepayment penalty, 81–82
price, and yield, 56–57
primary market, 24–31
    defined, 3, 23, 264

prime rate, 19
    defined, 14
priority, 94
private mortgage conduits, 68
private mortgage insurance (PMI), 6, 55–56, 174–178,
    238, 253–254, 299–300
pro forma statement, 208
production-related income, 154
profit and loss statement, 206–207
promissory note, 78–79
    defined, 3
property
    analysis, 179–202
    appraisals *see* appraisals
    characteristics of, 192–196
    depreciation of, 187–188, 207
    deterioration of, 187–188
    identification of, 80, 185
    insurance, 83–85, 300, 301
        at closing, 120, 301–302
    legal descriptions of, 200–202
    management, 222, 231
    rights, 77
    tax, 85–86, 94
        at HUD/FHA closing, 120
    usage of, 195–196
    value, 187–193
        for HUD/FHA loans, 136–137
Public Law 104–105, 67–68
purchase money mortgage, 89

Q

qualified agricultural real estate loan, 68

R

radon gas, 276–277
ranch loans, 233–234
rate index, 100, 101–105
    application of, 102–104
    caps on, 104–105
    indexes compared 102t
rate of return *see* yield
real estate brokerage firms, 50
real estate investment trusts (REITs), 51–52
real estate mortgage investment conduits (REMICs), 73
Real Estate Settlement Procedures Act (RESPA), 46, 83,
    95–96, 257, 288
    prohibited practices of, 292–293, 295, 301
    requirements of, 289–293